# Internet Law:
# A Practical Guide for Legal and Business Professionals

Alan M. Gahtan
Martin P. J. Kratz
J. Fraser Mann

CARSWELL
Thomson Professional Publishing

This publication is designed to provide accurate and authoritative information. It is sold with the understanding that the publisher is not engaged in rendering legal, accounting or other professional advice. If legal advice or other expert assistance is required, the services of a competent professional should be sought. The analysis contained herein represents the opinions of the author and should in no way be construed as being either official or unofficial policy of any governmental body.

**Canadian Cataloguing in Publication Data**

Gahtan, Alan M.
    Internet law: a practical guide for legal and business professionals

Includes index.
ISBN 0-459-25465-0

1. Computer networks — Law and legislation. 2. Internet (Computer network). I. Kratz, Martin P. J. II. Mann, J. Fraser. III. Title.

KE452.C6G32 1998    343.7109'99   C98-932201-7
KF242.C6G32 1998

**CARSWELL**
Thomson Professional Publishing

One Corporate Plaza
2075 Kennedy Road
Scarborough, Ontario
M1T 3V4

**Customer Service:**
Toronto: 1-416-609-3800
Elsewhere in Canada/U.S.: 1-800-387-5164
Fax: 1-416-298-5082
World Wide Web: http://www.carswell.com
E-mail: orders@carswell.com

# Preface

Many existing laws — both criminal and civil — apply to activities carried out in "Cyberspace." But there is also a growing and fast changing body of Internet-related law which lawyers and businesses must understand to succeed in this new environment. This publication provides a review of legal issues relating to electronic commerce and Internet activities in both Canada and the United States to give a North American perspective. It also includes helpful checklists and tips to assist with the drafting and negotiation of Internet-related contracts.

The development of this publication brought together three of the leading legal practitioners in the field, Alan M. Gahtan, Martin P. J. Kratz and J. Fraser Mann. Each author is a well-known authority in this area, possessing extensive practical experience advising clients on technology transactions and having written and lectured extensively on information technology law and Internet-related issues.

This publication should not be viewed as a substitute for legal advice. A business that requires legal advice should retain a professional who has examined the current state of the applicable law and has acquired an understanding of its particular circumstances. Certain examples and references are provided for illustrative purposes and may not constitute a complete statement of the law. The law, with respect to electronic commerce and Internet issues, is changing rapidly and some of the information contained in this publication may only be applicable in certain jurisdictions.

# About the Authors

**Alan M. Gahtan**'s practice focuses on both traditional IT areas, as well as emerging areas such as the Internet and Electronic Commerce. Mr. Gahtan is the author of "The Year 2000 Computer Crisis Legal Guide" (Carswell, 1998), "Electronic Evidence" (Carswell, 1999), and various print publications. Mr. Gahtan maintains various legal and technology law web sites, including the Cyberlaw Encyclopedia, at <www.gahtan.com>. He is a member of the Ontario and California bars. Mr. Gahtan is the founding Chair of the Information Technology and E-Commerce Section of the Canadian Bar Association (Ontario) and a former Chair of the Toronto Computer Lawyers Group. He has been recognized by LEXPERT as one of the leading IT lawyers in Toronto. He has also been interviewed extensively by various print and television news organizations.

**Martin P.J. Kratz** has developed and leads the Technology Law Practice group for Bennett Jones. Mr. Kratz's practice includes establishment of strategic alliances, mergers, acquisitions and technology transfers among technology companies and has a particular focus on the electronic commerce, internet, electronics, software, computer, telecommunication, biotechnology and related industries including addressing national and international intellectual property law issues.

Mr. Kratz is one of Canada's leading lawyers addressing problems involving the Internet and clients include major ISPs, users, electronic commerce businesses, providers of software, internet technology and infrastructure. Mr. Kratz continues to be identified as one of Canada's 500 leading lawyers and was also ranked among the top information technology law lawyers in Canada by LEXPERT and the American Lawyer Media publications.

Mr. Kratz has published over 160 articles or books on various topics involving advanced technology and law including the following books as sole or co-author:

**Internet Law: A Business and Professional Guide**, 1998,

**Canadian Intellectual Property Law**, 1998,

**Obtaining Patents**, 2nd Edition, 1999, (1st Edition published 1995),

**Protection of Copyright and Industrial Design**, 1999, 2nd Edition, (1st Edition published 1994),

**Information Systems Security: A Practitioner's Guide**, 1994,

**The Computer Virus Crisis**, 1992, 2nd Edition, (1st Edition published 1989 and translated in Russian, Japanese and Dutch versions), and

**Control and Security of Computer Information Systems**, 1988.

Martin Kratz is an associate Professor of Law at the University of Calgary, Faculty of Law where he teaches *Intellectual Property Law*. He also teaches courses in *Internet Law* and *Biotechnology Law* at both of the law schools of the University of Calgary and University of Alberta. Mr. Kratz is chairman of the Intellectual Property Committee for CIPS, and a member of the ABA's Science & Technology, Patent, Copyright & Trademark and International Sections.

**J. Fraser Mann** has over 20 years of experience advising clients on matters relating to technology and intellectual property law. He is the author of *Computer Technology and the Law in Canada* (Carswell); Editor-in-Chief of the quarterly newsletter *Information & Technology Law* (Carswell); and co-author of "Overview of the Legal Framework for Electronic Commerce" in *Law of International On-line Business: A Global Perspective* (Sweet & Maxwell, 1998). He has also written many papers and is a frequent speaker at conferences on technology law. Mr. Mann is a director of the York Technology Association and the Canadian IT/Law Association. He is also Co-Chair of the Technology and E-Commerce Law Committee of the International Bar Association Section on Business Law, and Past-Chairman of the International Law Section of the Canadian Bar Association. Mr. Mann was named as one of the leading 500 lawyers in Canada in LEXPERT and the American Lawyer Media 500 Guide published in January 1999, and was also profiled in the Euromoney Legal Group Guide to the World's Leading Information Technology Advisers.

# Table of Cases

# TABLE OF CASES

# TABLE OF CASES

# TABLE OF CASES

# TABLE OF CASES

# TABLE OF CASES

# Summary of Table of Contents

# Table of Contents

# TABLE OF CONTENTS

# TABLE OF CONTENTS

# TABLE OF CONTENTS

# TABLE OF CONTENTS

# 1

# Introduction to the Internet

## 1.1  WHAT IS THE INTERNET?

The Internet was, for a long time, a world reserved primarily for
academics and the US military. In the early 1990s, a new application
called the World Wide Web and the development of integrated user-
friendly browser programs with graphical user interfaces made it
possible for businesses and the world at large to participate in this
phenomenon.

The Internet is many things to many people. In order to fully
exploit the emerging opportunities, business professionals need to
understand how the law applies to their activities on the Internet.

In 1996, the US enacted the *Communications Decency Act*[1] (the
"CDA"), in an attempt to regulate obscene content on the Internet.
Two lawsuits were filed challenging the constitutionality of the CDA,
*ACLU v. Reno*[2] and *Shea v.* Reno.[3] During the course of these
lawsuits, the two courts had the opportunity to examine the nature of
the Internet. Section 1.1 of this chapter quotes liberally from their
findings.

---

[1]   The *Communications Decency Act of 1996* comprised Title V of *The Telecommunications
Act of 1996*, Pub. L. 104, 110 Stat. 56, of which the primary purpose was to reduce
regulation and encourage the rapid deployment of new telecommunications technology.

[2]   *ACLU v. Reno*, 929 F. Supp. 830-31 (E.D. Pa. June 11, 1996) ("ACLU District Court
Decision"). See <http://zeus.bna.com/e-law/cases/reno0627.html>. The court made 410
findings, including 356 paragraphs of the parties' stipulation and 54 findings based on
evidence received in open court.

[3]   *Shea v. Reno*, 96 Civ. Q976 (DLC) S.D.N.Y., (July 29, 1996) (the "Shea Decision").
Available at <http://zeus.bna.com/e-law/cases/shea.html>.

### (a)  History and Nature of the Internet

The Internet is not a physical or tangible entity, but rather a giant network which interconnects innumerable smaller groups of linked computer networks. It is thus a network of networks.[4]

Some networks are "closed", meaning that computers within the network are not linked to other computers or networks. Many networks, however, are connected to other networks, which are in turn connected to other networks in a manner which permits each computer in any network to communicate with computers on any other network in the system. This global web of linked networks and computers is referred to as the Internet.[5] However, the term "Internet" is also used to refer to the wide range of applications that can be accessed through this network infrastructure.

The nature of the Internet is such that it is very difficult, if not impossible, to determine its size at any given time. It is indisputable, however, that the Internet has experienced extraordinary growth in recent years. In 1981, fewer than 300 computers were linked to the Internet, and by 1989, the number stood at just under 90,000 computers. By 1993, however, over 1,000,000 computers were linked. It was estimated that as of 1996, over 9,400,000 host computers worldwide were linked to the Internet. This count does not include the personal computers used to access the Internet by modem. In all, it was reasonably estimated that by mid-1996, as many as 40 million people around the world would access this enormously flexible communication medium. This figure is expected to grow to 200 million users by 1999.[6]

It is difficult, however, to assess the accuracy of this estimate because there does not exist a reliable method to measure the number of Internet users. There is also an issue concerning who should be counted. For instance, some individuals only have e-mail access to the Internet. Others have full access to Internet resources such as the World Wide Web, Usenet and the many other applications that are available.

---

[4]    ACLU District Court Decision finding #1.

[5]    ACLU District Court Decision finding #2.

[6]    ACLU District Court Decision finding #3.

The computers and computer networks that make up the Internet are owned by individuals, corporations, governmental and public institutions, and non-profit organizations. The resulting whole is a decentralized, global medium of communications — or "cyberspace" — that links individuals, corporations, institutions and governments around the world, allowing tens of millions of people to exchange information. These communications can occur almost instantaneously, and may be directed to specific individuals, to a broader group of people interested in a particular subject, or to any persons having access to the Internet as a whole.[7]

The Internet had its origins in 1969 as an experimental project of the US's Advanced Research Project Agency ("ARPA"), and was called ARPANET. This network linked computers and computer networks owned by the military, defence contractors and university laboratories conducting defence-related research. The network later allowed researchers across the country to access directly the extremely powerful supercomputers located at a few key universities and laboratories. As ARPANET evolved far beyond its research origins in the United States to encompass universities, corporations, and people around the world, it came to be called the "DARPA Internet", and finally, just the "Internet".[8]

From its inception, the network was designed as a decentralized, self-maintaining series of redundant links between computers and computer networks, capable of rapidly transmitting communications without direct human involvement or control, and with the automatic ability to re-route communications if one or more individual links were damaged or otherwise unavailable. Among other goals, this redundant system of linked computers was designed to allow vital research and communications to continue even if portions of the network were damaged or destroyed in a war.[9]

The various components of a message sent between computers on the Internet do not necessarily travel along the same path. The Internet uses "packet switching" communication protocols to allow

---

[7]    ACLU District Court Decision finding #4.

[8]    ACLU District Court Decision finding #5.

[9]    ACLU District Court Decision finding #6.

individual messages to be subdivided into smaller "packets"; the individual packets are sent independently to the destination, and are then automatically re-assembled by the receiving computer. While all packets of a given message often travel along the same path to the destination, any of the packets may be re-routed if any computers along the route become overloaded.[10]

At the same time that ARPANET (which subsequently ceased to exist) was maturing, similar networks were developed to link universities, research facilities, businesses and individuals around the world. Many of these networks overlapped and eventually were themselves linked together, allowing users of any computer connected to any network to communicate with users of any computer on another network. It is this series of linked networks, each linking computers and computer networks, that is commonly known today as the Internet.[11]

A characteristic shared by these interconnected networks is that they all utilize a common communication protocol called Internet Protocol (IP). All applications utilized on the Internet were designed to use IP allowing new applications to be implemented without any changes being required to the underlying network infrastructure.

No single entity — academic, corporate, governmental or non-profit — administers the Internet. It exists and functions because hundreds of thousands of separate operators of computers and computer networks use common data transfer protocols to exchange information with other computers (which in turn exchange information with other computers). There is no centralized storage location, control point, or communications channel for the Internet, and it would not be technically feasible for a single entity to control all of the information conveyed on the Internet.[12]

---

[10]    ACLU District Court Decision finding #9.

[11]    ACLU District Court Decision finding #10.

[12]    ACLU District Court Decision finding #11.

## (b)  How Individual Users Access the Internet

A number of different methods can be used to access the Internet. First, many educational institutions, businesses, libraries, and communities maintain a computer network linked directly to the Internet and issue account numbers and passwords enabling users to gain access to the network directly or by modem. Second, "Internet Service Providers", which are generally commercial entities who charge a monthly fee, offer access to computers or networks linked directly to the Internet. Third, commercial "online services" — such as America Online, CompuServe, Prodigy, and The Microsoft Network — allow subscribers to gain access to the Internet while providing extensive content within their own proprietary networks.[13]

## (c)  Methods to Communicate Over the Internet

Upon obtaining access to the Internet, a number of methods may be used to exchange communications and to retrieve information. Because these methods are constantly evolving, they are difficult to categorize. The most common methods of communication can be grouped as follows: (1) one-to-one messaging (such as "e-mail"), (2) one-to-many messaging (such as "listserv"), (3) distributed message databases (such as "USENET newsgroups"), (4) real time communication (such as "Internet Relay Chat"), (5) real time remote computer utilization (such as "telnet"), and (6) remote information retrieval (such as "ftp," "gopher," and the "World Wide Web"). Most of these methods of communication can be used to transmit text, data, computer programs, sound, visual images (i.e., pictures), and moving video images.[14]

### (i)  E-Mail

One common method of communication on the Internet is electronic mail, or "e-mail," which is comparable to sending a first class letter. A user can address and transmit a message to one or more other users. E-mail on the Internet is not routed through a central control point, and can take many and varying paths to the recipients. Unlike regular mail, simple e-mail is generally not

---

[13]  Shea Decision.

[14]  ACLU District Court Decision finding #22.

"sealed" or secure, and can be accessed or viewed on intermediate computers between the sender and recipient (unless the message is encrypted).[15]

Also, unlike mail sent by the post office, Internet messages can generally not be sent as "registered mail". There is usually no way for a sender to confirm that a message was actually received by the intended recipient. Notwithstanding these limitations, Internet e-mail has become quite a popular method of communication, and e-mail addresses are often found beside fax numbers on many business cards.

### (ii) Listserv

A user can also "subscribe" to an electronic mailing list on a topic of interest; the user receives a copy of messages posted by other subscribers and, in turn, can post messages for forwarding to the full mailing list. Once a mailing list is established, it is typically maintained using a "mail exploder," a program running on the server on which the list resides that automatically (i.e., without human intervention) responds to a user's request to be added to or removed from the list of subscribers, and retransmits messages posted by a subscriber to others on the mailing list. Some mailing lists are "closed", meaning that a user's request to join the list requires the approval of the person maintaining the list. Mailing lists (both open and closed) may also be "moderated": all messages posted to the list are forwarded to a moderator, who approves the messages before retransmitting them to subscribers.[16]

### (iii) Distributed Message Databases — Newsgroups

Internet users may also transmit or receive "articles" posted daily to thousands of discussion groups, known as "newsgroups," which are arranged by subject matter and are available through an electronic bulletin-board system known as "Usenet".[17] Distributed message databases such as "USENET newsgroups" have a similar function to listservs, but operate very differently in how communications are

---

[15]    ACLU District Court Decision finding #23.

[16]    Shea Decision.

[17]    Shea Decision.

transmitted. Like listservs, newsgroups provide for open discussions and exchanges on particular topics. Users, however, need not subscribe to the discussion mailing list in advance, but instead may access the database at any time.

When a user with access to a Usenet server — that is, a computer participating in the Usenet system — posts an article to a particular newsgroup, the server automatically forwards the article to adjacent Usenet servers, which in turn forward it to other servers, until the article is available on all Usenet sites that furnish access to the newsgroup in question. A message that reaches a particular Usenet site is temporarily stored at that site to permit an individual user running client software known as a "newsreader," which is capable of sorting articles according to header information identifying the newsgroup to which the article was posted, to review and respond to the message. Some Usenet newsgroups are moderated: messages to the newsgroup are forwarded to an individual who selects those appropriate for distribution. Because Usenet articles are distributed to and made available on multiple servers, a person who posts an article to a newsgroup has no way of knowing who will choose to retrieve it, or whether or not the newsgroup is moderated. There is no newsgroup equivalent of a "closed" mailing list: access to a particular newsgroup can only be limited by restricting the number of servers participating in the newsgroup.[18]

Newsgroups exist on many thousands of different subjects. In 1994, approximately 70,000 messages were posted to newsgroups each day for distribution to the approximately 190,000 computers or computer networks that participate in the USENET newsgroup system.[19]

### (iv)  Real-Time Text-Based Communications (Talk and IRC)

The Internet also offers opportunities for multiple users to interact in real time. Using a program called "Talk," two users can exchange messages while they are both online; a message typed on one user's computer will appear almost immediately on the other user's screen.

---

[18]  Shea Decision.

[19]  ACLU District Court Decision finding #26.

Servers running so-called "chat" software, such as Internet Relay Chat ("IRC"), permit multiple users to converse by selecting one of many discussion "channels" active at any time. Commercial online services such as America Online, CompuServe, Prodigy, and The Microsoft Network offer their own chat systems for their members. Having joined a channel, a user can see and read messages transmitted by other users, each identified by a name the user selected upon joining the channel. Individual participants in IRC discussions know other participants only by the names they choose upon entering the discussion, allowing users to participate anonymously by using a pseudonym.[20]

These chat facilities have become the CB radio or "party lines" of the 90s. They permit one-to-one or one-to-many discussions among individuals who may be located anywhere in the world. Vendors are increasingly utilizing Internet chat facilities to provide access to their technical support staff.

### (v)  Real-Time Remote Computer Utilization (Telnet)

Another method of using information on the Internet is to access remote computers in "real-time" using "telnet". Telnet is an Internet application that allows a user's PC to function as a terminal to a remote system. For example, telnet permits a researcher at a university to use the computing power of a supercomputer located at a different university, or permits a student to obtain access to a remote library's online card catalogue program.[21]

### (vi)  Remote Retrieval of Information

The final major category of communication may be the most well known use of the Internet: the search for and retrieval of information located on remote computers. There are three primary methods to locate and retrieve information on the Internet.[22] A simple method uses "ftp" (file transfer protocol) to list the names of computer files available on a remote computer, and to transfer copies of one or more

---

[20]  Shea Decision.

[21]  ACLU District Court Decision finding #29.

[22]  ACLU District Court Decision finding #30.

of those files to an individual's local computer.[23] Another approach uses a program and format named "gopher" to guide an individual's search through the resources available on a remote computer.[24]

The third method of retrieving information, which is rapidly becoming the most important function of the Internet, is the "World Wide Web" or the "Web." The Web utilizes a "hypertext" formatting language called hypertext markup language (HTML). Programs that "browse" the Web can display HTML documents containing text, images, sound, animation and moving video. Any HTML document can include links to permit a viewer of the document, upon the "click" of a mouse, to be connected to other related information or resources on the Internet. Such "hyperlinks" allow users to locate and view related information stored on computers located in many parts of the world.[25]

The World Wide Web represents a global, online store of information from a variety of sources accessible to Internet users around the world. Although information on the Web is contained in individual computers, the connection of these computers to the Internet through W3C protocols (the protocols used to support the exchange of information on the Web) allows all of the information to become part of a single body of knowledge. The Web is currently the most advanced information system developed on the Internet, and embraces within its data model most information in previous networked information systems such as ftp, gopher and Usenet.[26]

Information contained on the World Wide Web is stored in a variety of formats, including text, still images, sounds and video. Each document has an address (rather like a telephone number). Most Web documents contain "links," being words or images which refer to other documents. Clicking on any linked text or image, which may

---

[23]   ACLU District Court Decision finding #31.

[24]   ACLU District Court Decision finding #32. A gopher server presents information in a set of menus, enabling a user who gains access to the server to select a series of increasingly narrow menu items before locating a desired file that can be displayed on or copied to the user's computer.

[25]   ACLU District Court Decision finding #33.

[26]   ACLU District Court Decision finding #34. This means that Web browsers can also access information from these other forms of Internet services.

be blue or underlined when displayed, results in the referenced document being automatically displayed, wherever in the world it is actually stored. Links are used to lead from overview documents to more detailed documents, from tables of contents to particular pages, and from one set of documents to other documents which are shown by cross-references, footnotes, and new forms of information structure.[27] Alternatively, a user can type in the "universal resource locator" (URL),[28] an Internet address for the document, and move directly to that source.

Many organizations now have "home pages" on the Web. The home page will typically contain links that guide the user to other sources of information about the organization.[29] The links may lead to a different location in the same document or to a different document on the same Web site. Links may also take the user from the original Web site to a different site located on another computer connected to the Internet. The links from one document to another, whether on the same computer or on another computer on the Internet, unify the Web into a single body of knowledge.[30] It is these millions of links between Web sites that help make the Web such a powerful tool for sharing knowledge.

When information is made available on the World Wide Web, it is said to be "published" on the Web. Publishing on the Web simply requires a user to connect a computer to the Internet and to run W3C server software on the computer. The computer can be as simple as a small personal computer or as complex as a multimillion dollar mainframe computer. Many Web publishers choose to lease disk storage space from another entity which has the necessary computer facilities, eliminating the need for actually owning any equipment.[31]

Information published on the Web must also be formatted according to certain Web standards. The use of these standardized formats permit all Web users to view the material. Web standards are

---

[27]    ACLU District Court Decision finding #36.

[28]    For instance, the URL for Carswell's "home page" is <http://www.carswell.com>.

[29]    ACLU District Court Decision finding #37.

[30]    ACLU District Court Decision finding #39.

[31]    ACLU District Court Decision finding #40.

sophisticated and flexible enough to meet the needs of many large corporations, including banks and brokerage houses, of newspapers and magazines which now publish "online" editions of their material, and of government agencies and even courts, which use the Web to disseminate information to the public. At the same time, Web publishing is simple enough to permit thousands of individual users and small community organizations to publish their own personal "home pages," which are equivalent to personalized newsletters, available to every other user on the Web.[32]

Web publishers may choose to make their Web sites open to the general pool of all Internet users, or to close them by permitting access only to those persons with advance authorization. Many publishers choose to keep their sites open to all users in order to give their information the widest possible audience. If publishers wish to limit access, this may be accomplished by assigning specific user names and passwords as a prerequisite to access to the site. In the case of a Web site maintained for an organization's internal use, access will be allowed only from other computers within that organization's local network.[33]

A number of "search engines" — such as Yahoo, Magellan, Alta Vista, WebCrawler, and Lycos — are available to help users navigate the World Wide Web. For example, Yahoo maintains a directory of documents available on various Web servers. A user can gain access to Yahoo's server and type a string of characters as a search request. Yahoo returns a list of documents whose entries in the Yahoo directory match the search string and organizes the list of documents by category. Search engines make use of software capable of automatically contacting various Web sites and extracting relevant information. Some search engines, such as Alta Vista, store the information in a database and return it in response to a user request. Others, such as Yahoo, employ persons who determine whether and how a site should be categorized in the Yahoo directory.[34] Once a search engine discloses to a user a number of sites that might contain

---

[32]    ACLU District Court Decision finding #42.

[33]    ACLU District Court Decision finding #43.

[34]    Shea Decision.

the desired information, the user would then browse through the information on each site, until the desired material is found.[35]

The World Wide Web permits information to be accessed from an ever-increasing number of Internet-linked computers by setting common information storage formats (HTML) and a common language for the exchange of Web documents (HTTP). While the information itself may be in many different formats, and stored on computers which are not otherwise compatible, the basic Web standards permit communication and the exchange of information.

Because hundreds of thousands of computers are linked to the Internet, the Web represents a "distributed system". Any organization can become part of the Web simply by connecting its computers to the Internet and running the appropriate software. No single organization controls membership in the Web, nor is there any centralized point which can block access to individual Web sites or services. While the Web may appear to be a single, integrated system, there is in fact no centralized control point.[36]

The Web's open, distributed, decentralized nature stands in sharp contrast to earlier information systems. Private information services such as Westlaw, Lexis/Nexis, and Dialog, contain large storehouses of knowledge, and may be accessed from the Internet with the appropriate passwords and access software. However, these various databases are not linked together in a single whole, as is the World Wide Web.[37]

The World Wide Web has become a popular medium because of its open, distributed, and easy-to-use nature. Rather than requiring a user to purchase new software or hardware, and to learn a new kind of system for each database of information to be accessed, the Web environment provides an easy means of access to a wide variety of information sources. The open nature of the Web also makes it easy for disseminators of information to reach their intended audiences

---

[35]  ACLU District Court Decision finding #44.

[36]  ACLU District Court Decision finding #46.

[37]  ACLU District Court Decision finding #47.

without regard to the type of computer or software that may be used by a potential user.[38]

## (d) Content on the Internet

The types of content available on the Internet defy easy classification. The entire card catalogue of the Carnegie Library is online, together with journals, journal abstracts, popular magazines and titles of compact discs. The director of the Carnegie Library, Robert Croneberger, has testified that online services are the emerging trend in library services.[39]

Many commercial entities maintain Web sites to inform potential consumers about their goods and services, or to solicit purchases. Other Web sites exist solely for the dissemination of non-commercial information. The other forms of Internet communication — e-mail, bulletin boards, newsgroups, and chat rooms — frequently have non-commercial goals.[40]

The diversity of content on the Internet is possible because the Internet provides an easy and inexpensive way for any person to reach a large audience, potentially in the millions. The start-up and operating costs required for communication on the Internet are significantly lower than those associated with other forms of mass communication, such as television, radio, newspapers and magazines. This enables not only large companies, such as Microsoft and Time Warner, but also small, not-for-profit groups to operate their own Web sites. Except for large complex sites, the cost of creating a Web site is generally in the range of $1,000 to $15,000, with monthly operating costs varying according to the objective of the site and the amount of traffic. Commercial online services such as America Online allow subscribers to create Web pages free of charge. Any Internet user can post a message to any one of the thousands of newsgroups and bulletin boards or by engaging in an online "chat",

---

[38] ACLU District Court Decision finding #48.

[39] ACLU District Court Decision finding #74.

[40] ACLU District Court Decision finding #75.

thereby reaching a world-wide audience of other users who share an interest in a particular topic.[41]

Because of the different forms of Internet communication, there is a blurring in the distinction between "speakers" and "listeners" on the Internet. Chat rooms, e-mail, and newsgroups are interactive forms of communication, providing the user with the opportunity to both speak and listen.[42]

It follows that, unlike traditional media, there are very few barriers to using the Internet to communicate messages to other people. Any user may engage in the dialogue that occurs on the Internet. The receiver of messages can and does become the content provider.[43]

Users who have more sophisticated equipment and greater technical expertise can make content available on the Internet for retrieval by others by running a server supporting anonymous FTP, a gopher server, or a Web server. However, content providers need not run their own servers or have the programming expertise to construct their own sites; they can lease space on a Web server from another or create a "home page" through an online commercial service.[44]

Another unique attribute of the Internet is that once a user posts any material on a Web site, then, in the absence of any restrictions imposed by the owner of the site, the material is available to all other Internet users worldwide. Similarly, once a user posts a message to a newsgroup or bulletin board, that message becomes available to all subscribers to that newsgroup or bulletin board.[45] Unlike the newspaper, broadcast station, or cable system, Internet technology gives a speaker a potential worldwide audience.

---

[41]   ACLU District Court Decision finding #76.

[42]   ACLU District Court Decision finding #79.

[43]   ACLU District Court Decision finding #80.

[44]   Shea Decision.

[45]   ACLU District Court Decision finding #85.

## 1.2 ELECTRONIC COMMERCE ON THE INTERNET

### (a) How the Web is Being Used to Facilitate Electronic Commerce

Early advertising on the Internet consisted of commercial messages inserted in Usenet newsgroups or mass e-mail mailings. Many users of the Internet saw this as an unwanted encroachment on their non-commercial systems.[46] However, newer methods of marketing products and services on the Internet, especially the use of the World Wide Web, have become quite acceptable and effective.

The Web can be an ideal marketing vehicle for a number of reasons. Documents published on the Web can include embedded images and links to multimedia clips including graphics, audio and even video. The text contained in such documents can be tagged with special attributes to produce an organized and visually friendly publication. The hypertext nature of Web documents allows for easy linking of informational material with marketing information, product data and direct online order-taking facilities.

Web documents can be retrieved and viewed on almost any brand of computer system which supports a Web browser program. Web browsers are available for a variety of computer platforms including Unix, DOS, Windows and Macintosh. The Web browser program retrieves the document from a Web server, interprets the tags and then displays the document including any embedded icons or graphics.

### (b) Online Marketing

One of the most common commercial applications of the Internet is the use of the World Wide Web to display advertising and promotional material about the originating entity. For example, many business entities now include in their Web sites: copies of corporate brochures, press releases, product catalogues, investor relations information[47] and e-mail address directories. Some computer

---

[46] Unsolicited commercial e-mail is discussed further in Chapter 6, section 6.7 *Spam*.

[47] For example, Microsoft provides investors with online access to its annual report, 10-K, earning releases, proxy and other securities filings. In Microsoft's case, this not only provides access to current financial information about the company but also demonstrates the capabilities of some of its products.

companies are also using their Web site to provide access to beta or time-limited demonstration versions of software programs, as well as for product support purposes. Many companies, especially high-tech firms, are also incorporating a recruitment section on their corporate Web site.

### (c)  Online Retailing

The Internet has spawned the creation of new businesses that are run almost exclusively online. These include pioneering sites such as Amazon.com[48], E*Trade and Virtual Vineyards. Selling books through the Internet has become one of the most successful types of Internet retailing. While enjoying success online, these ventures are still relatively small when compared to their established competitors. These Web pioneers may encounter difficulty when their larger competitors launch their own online initiatives. However, the ability to move quickly and with innovative ideas is essential for success on the Web. These attributes are not always shared by larger enterprises.

### (i)  Online Ordering

Some business entities are making use of the Internet to provide order processing services, providing a potential customer with an interactive product demonstration. The potential customer may then request additional information or in some cases make an online purchase.

Where the product consists of information or software that can be delivered electronically, the entire transaction can then be initiated and completed across the Internet (for example, a person may subscribe to an electronic edition of a newspaper such as the *Wall Street Journal*).[49] In some cases, the Internet may make it feasible to offer new products and services that would not be economical using another medium. In other cases, the Internet is used to complete

---

[48]    Amazon.com, an online bookstore, has become the industry pacesetter and has enjoyed exponential growth since its launch in July, 1995.  However, Amazon.com's success prompted Barnes & Noble, North America's biggest bookstore chain, to launch its own online bookselling site in February, 1997.

[49]    East West, the world's largest provider of CD's containing sampled sounds, operates a Web site where musicians or multimedia producers can electronically purchase and download sampled sounds from a collection that numbers in the tens of thousands.

the sale transaction but physical delivery of the product is made by mail or courier service.

The Internet is also being used to facilitate order processing for services, including travel-related services such as hotel accommodations, car rentals and airline reservations. These services can be offered to end users directly by suppliers, potentially eliminating the need for intermediaries such as travel agents.

### (ii) Online Publishing

One of the most significant uses of the Internet is for electronic publishing. Many publishers of print publications such as newsletters, magazines and newspapers now provide Web sites which include varying amounts of information from the print editions. These online publishing initiatives may be either supported by advertising,[50] or in limited cases made available only to paid subscribers.[51] Anyone can now self-publish at a relatively low cost.

The advertising-supported sites can be directed to a target audience with common characteristics. Online advertising provides the opportunity for immediate interaction with consumers, an advantage not offered by traditional media. In some cases the advertisers can leverage off the brand name of the sponsor's site.

### (d) Alternative to Private Networks

The Internet is increasingly being utilized for the exchange of electronic messages, documents and other communications that in the past required the use of a private network. These communications include EDI,[52] remote employee access, electronic filings and wide area corporate networks to connect branches and subsidiaries within

---

[50] Banner ads, small rectangular images, are displayed along with the relevant content. Advertisers pay a fee based on either the number of "impressions" (people who see the ad) or on the number of "click-throughs" (people who actually click on the ad and go on to visit the advertiser's site). An example is Time Warner's Pathfinder site which provides access to many leading print publications including *Time, Fortune, Life, Money Magazine,* and *Sports Illustrated.*

[51] For example, the *Wall Street Journal* charges a subscription fee for access to its electronic edition.

[52] Electronic Data Interchange or EDI, is the exchange of business data in a structured format from one computer to another.

a corporate group. The Internet is also used to create industry networks, which connect manufacturers to their suppliers, to exchange order information and other communications which would not have been feasible using traditional EDI. These applications are made possible due to the growing number of resources connected to the Internet as well as the use of sophisticated encryption and authentication systems that can create a secure virtual private network across the Internet.

### (e)  Other Applications

A number of innovative uses for the Internet are also emerging. For instance, Axis Communications and ParentNet have introduced technology to allow a camera mounted in daycare centres to be linked to the Internet. This facility permits parents to obtain a live video feed of their child's daycare room from any location. The cost of the service is approximately $20 a month together with the cost of obtaining Internet access.[53] While this application may be of benefit to parents, it also raises privacy concerns.

Multi-user computer games are another popular application for the Internet. Revenues from online games could reach $1 billion by the year 2000. In some cases, the online game sites are used to boost retail sales of CD-ROM games made by the same vendor. In other cases, the sites are run by vendors on a subscription basis.

The Internet is also being used to provide electronic access to different types of financial services such as banking and trading in securities. A number of major banks now provide various levels of access for their account holders using the Internet as the communication vehicle. Many banks also offer a wider range of services (such as approval of loan transactions) through so-called "virtual branches" which are meant to replace the traditional and more expensive brick and mortar equivalents.

Brokerage firms were early users of Internet technology and are now increasingly providing online trading facilities. The advantages to the customer of using the Internet for trades in securities include lower commission rates and round-the-clock access (although trades

---

[53]    <http://www5.zdnet.com/anchordesk/story/story_812.html>.

can only be executed while exchanges are open for business). In most cases, transactions submitted electronically must still be confirmed by a representative of the broker before being released to the exchange. Subject to regulatory controls, expert systems in the future may allow many transactions to be completed without any human intervention.

Securities regulators are also exploring the use of the Internet to provide electronic delivery of disclosure documents. In the US, the Securities and Exchange Commission (SEC) permits documents to be delivered electronically provided that the intended recipients receive information equivalent to that required to be delivered in printed form. The SEC has also permitted secondary trading of securities (on electronic bulletin boards where each investor negotiates his/her own trade) on an experimental basis. In both Canada and the US, securities regulators have created systems to support electronic filings of securities documents (SEDAR and EDGAR, respectively).

While the Internet has provided a number of opportunities to the securities industry, it also created new problems. Securities-related fraud, where the Internet is used as a tool to disseminate misleading information or otherwise influence or manipulate share prices, is a growing problem. The SEC has assigned over 50 investigators to monitor the Internet. Canadian regulators are likely to experience greater difficulty in monitoring usage of the Internet and in enforcing applicable laws due to the patchwork of provincial securities regulation in Canada and the absence of a national securities regulatory body.

# 2

# Regulation of the Internet

## 2.1 AN OVERVIEW OF REGULATION

Many users of the Internet oppose any kind of government regulation, and describe the Internet as unregulated. However, many existing laws apply both to the deployment and use of the infrastructure of the Internet, and to the transmission of content on the Internet. In fact, communications sent by means of the Internet may pass through many jurisdictions, and accordingly may be subject to a greater number of laws than would apply to other forms of communication. The real difficulty, however, typically lies in the enforcement of the applicable laws.

A number of jurisdictions have reviewed the application of existing laws to the Internet and the changes that may be required. In the US, the Intellectual Property Rights Working Group (Task Force) issued a report entitled "Intellectual Property and the National Information Infrastructure" (the "White Paper") in September 1995. The White Paper explained the application of laws in cyberspace and recommended certain changes in the intellectual property laws to accommodate the digital age.

The applicability of existing laws to the Internet was also addressed in an Internet Liability Study commissioned by Industry Canada and released in the spring of 1997.[1] The Internet Liability Study followed earlier work by the Information Highway Advisory Council (IHAC), which was commissioned by Industry Canada to make recommendations in respect to policy issues relating to the

---

[1]    The contents of the Internet Liability Study are discussed in Chapter 8.

Internet. IHAC's recommendations are contained in a series of reports commencing with the "Challenge of the Information Highway".[2]

The Canadian Government has indicated that it favours a regulatory approach to the Internet that blends framework laws with sectoral codes, consumer awareness and privacy-enhancing technologies. In January, 1998, an Industry Canada Task Force on Electronic Commerce issued a report which included recommendations for new legislation for the protection of personal information.[3]

## 2.2 REGULATION THROUGH INTERNATIONAL TREATIES

While no international treaties deal specifically with the Internet, some treaties contain provisions which may apply to activities carried out on the Internet. Two such treaties are the WIPO Copyright Treaty and the WIPO Performances and Phonograms Treaty which were adopted by the WIPO (World Intellectual Property Organization) Diplomatic Conference on Certain Copyright and Neighbouring Rights Questions (the "WIPO Conference") on December 20, 1996.[4]

These Treaties represent the first significant step in international law to update protection for intellectual property to facilitate entry into the digital world of the 21st century. In many countries, implementation of the Treaties will require the enactment of legislation to amend existing intellectual property statutes.

Among the provisions in the treaties which address some of the challenges arising from digital technology, particularly the Internet, is an exclusive "making available" right, which would appear to cover on-demand, interactive transmissions on the Internet. The

---

[2]    Final Report of the Information Highway Advisory Council, September 1995.

[3]    Industry Canada Task Force on Electronic Commerce, *The Protection of Personal Information-Building Canada's Information Economy and Society*, January 1998.

[4]    For an overview, see Gahtan, Alan M., "WIPO Diplomatic Conference:  Updated Intellectual Property Rights for a Digital World", *Information & Technology Law* 1:4 (May 1997). Also, in the US, see  "The Digital Era Copyright Enhancement Act" (H.R. 3048). See also the "Digital Millenium Copyright Act of 1998" (s. 2037, 105th Congress, 2d session) which was introduced to implement the WIPO treaties. For an introduction to these rights see Kratz, *Canadian Intellectual Property Law* (Carswell, 1998).

Treaties also oblige Contracting Parties to provide legal protection against tampering with technological protection measures and rights management information. However, these Treaties are unlikely to put an end to ongoing uncertainty regarding many legal issues related to the conduct of business over the Internet.

The Diplomatic Conference considered but rejected certain provisions concerning the application of the right to reproduction of temporary, transient, or incidental copies. The provisions which were contained in a draft version of the Treaties would have required Contracting Parties to recognize any direct or indirect reproduction, whether permanent or temporary, in any manner or form, as coming within the exclusive rights of copyright owners. Various parties who opposed these provisions believed that such language would have expanded the reproduction right to cover copies made in the temporary storage facilities (i.e., read-write, random access memory or RAM) of a computer and would likely have inhibited "browsing" on the Internet. Other parties took the position, however, that the reproduction right in national copyright legislation already covers any form of temporary copies.

The Copyright Treaty also grants to the owners of copyright in literary and artistic works the exclusive right of communicating their works to the public in such a way that members of the public may access these works from a place and time individually chosen by them (i.e., "on-demand" access). This right would cover making a work available even if it is not actually accessed. The determination of who is a member of the public may vary from one country to another.

The Agreed Statement accompanying the Copyright Treaty notes that the mere provision of physical facilities for enabling or making a communication does not in itself amount to communication within the meaning of the Treaty.

The Agreed Statement concerning the WIPO Performances and Phonograms Treaty states that the reproduction right, and the exceptions to such right which are permitted by the Treaty, fully apply in the digital environment, and in particular to the use of performances and phonograms in digital form. They also clarify that the storage of a protected performance or phonogram in digital form in an electronic medium constitutes a reproduction.

Another treaty that was on the agenda but was not dealt with at the WIPO Conference of December, 1996 was a treaty on Intellectual Property Rights in Databases (the Database Treaty). The Database Treaty would have created a *sui generis* right in favor of the makers of databases which embody a "substantial investment" whether or not such databases constitute original works for purposes of copyright law. The treaty would have extended the level of protection currently granted to databases in countries such as the United States, where copyright protection is limited to databases which embody creativity in the selection or arrangement of the underlying material.[5] In contrast, the European Union adopted a Database Directive on March 11, 1996 which requires member states to grant owners of databases which embody any substantial investment a *sui generis* right to prohibit unauthorized extraction from and re-utilization of all or a substantial portion of such databases.[6] This protection is in addition to copyright protection for databases which constitute original intellectual creations.

While the various international agreements referred to above may apply to activities on the Internet, they are not directed specifically at Internet activity. A strong argument may be made that because the Internet transcends physical and political space, it should be recognized as a separate community with its own rules. If the Internet represents a new form of community, the interests of its users would not be well-served by inconsistent actions of law-makers in different countries. Actions taken, or not taken, in one jurisdiction can have a dramatic effect on activities and users located in another jurisdiction.

If one country introduces legislative changes regulating the Internet that are poorly considered or fail to balance the interests of all constituents, then certain users may simply move their Internet-related activities to countries they consider more advantageous to their interests. Several international bodies are seeking to avoid this result by harmonizing efforts aimed at the regulation of the Internet.

---

[5]    See Chapter 5 for a discussion of the availability of copyright protection for databases.

[6]    Most members of the European Union adopted implementation legislation by January 1, 1998.

The United Nations adopted a Model Law on Electronic Commerce[7] in 1996, and has created various working groups who continue to study the issues. The OECD (Organization for Economic Cooperation and Development) has issued reports on the use of cryptography and electronic signatures. The Hague Conference on Private International Law has established a project with the objective of adopting a convention by the year 2000 in respect to the enforcement of foreign judgments. Within Canada, the Uniform Law Conference of Canada has formed a working group to consider the development of model laws that would remove legal impediments to electronic commerce. Industry Canada is also continuing to study various issues relating to electronic commerce and has issued a number of reports on these issues.

## 2.3 INDUSTRY SECTOR REGULATION

Many business entities already operate in highly regulated sectors. Their activities on the Internet would generally come within the scope of any legislation that already governs their conduct. For instance, any offering of, or solicitation regarding securities using the Internet is subject to the same regulatory regime as may be applicable to offerings or solicitations made through other forms of communications. As well, any form of stock manipulation, whether conducted on the Internet or more traditional forms of communications, will be subject to prosecutions and regulatory actions. US regulators have started to take action against Internet fraud involving securities. Some Canadian securities regulators are also beginning to tackle the problem.[8]

---

[7]    UNCITRAL (United Nations Commission on International Trade Law) Model Law on Electronic Commerce (1997). See <http://ananse.irv.uit.no/trade_law/doc/UN.Electronic. Commerce.Model.Law.1996.html>.

[8]    See Janet McFarland and Paul Waldib, "Hype artists spin stocks on the Web", *The Globe and Mail*, Report on Business, B1 (Aug. 9, 1997).

## 2.4  NETIQUETTE

The activities of Internet users may also be restricted by customary rules and self-regulation. For example, the Usenet service on the Internet has a type of self-regulation called netiquette.[9] Examples of behaviour generally accepted as undesirable include posting the same message to numerous Usenet discussion groups or posting commercial messages to other than specially designated Usenet discussion groups. A breach of these rules can result in sanctions by other users and other detrimental consequences.

## 2.5  REGULATION OF CONTENT

Many users of the Internet view any attempts to control access a futile exercise. This view is reflected in the following statement:

> "Today, the Internet is a great borderless country. Packets of data travel unfettered from any computer to any other computer in the world, hindered only by slow connections and a few corporate firewalls. Netizens laugh at attempts by countries like China and Singapore to limit their citizens' access to the Internet. In the immortal words of John Gilmore, "The Net treats censorship as a form of damage and routes around it."[10]

The growth of the Internet has been accompanied by the proliferation of undesirable content. Many adult-oriented sites sell access to pornography and numerous Usenet newsgroups distribute pornographic images and advertise the adult-oriented Web sites. While many of the adult-oriented Web sites limit access by requiring subscribers to pay for the content, anyone with access to newsgroup readers (now integrated into popular Web browsers) can easily access pornographic images by subscribing to the appropriate newsgroups.

Authorities in Germany have been among the toughest in trying to curb misuse of the Internet and have passed legislation setting the framework for government regulation. Germany's *Information and Communication Services Bill*, which went into effect on August 1, 1997, represents one of the first attempts to provide a comprehensive

---

9    These are informal rules of behavior which include a tolerance for free speech and an intolerance for commercial advertising. See Chapter 6 for more details.

10   "Electronic Border Control", Simson L. Garfunkel, *Hot Wired* (July 14, 1997).

legal framework for the Internet and other interactive information services. The new law is intended to support electronic commerce by establishing a certification scheme for digital signatures. It also aims to protect children, tighten rules for the collection of personal data and address liability for illegal content. The provisions dealing with responsibility for illegal content have been particularly controversial. Under the law, Internet service providers would be liable for providing access to illegal material if they had been alerted to the existence of such material, and if they had the technical ability to delete the offending material but failed to do so.

Canada does not specifically ban pornography on the Internet. However, the Internet Liability Study sponsored by Industry Canada states that existing laws on obscenity, child pornography and hate literature are applicable to such activities conducted in cyberspace. The results of this study are discussed in greater detail in section 8.4 on Service Provider Liability.

In the United States, a federal law known as the *Communications Decency Act*[11] was enacted in 1996 to impose restrictions on material placed on the Internet. In *Reno v. ACLU,*[12] the US Supreme Court struck down two key provisions of that Act.

At issue in that case was the constitutionality of provisions enacted to protect minors from "indecent"[13] and "patently offensive"[14] communications on the Internet. Violators risked a sentence of up to two years in jail and a $250,000 fine. The Supreme Court found that, notwithstanding the legitimacy and importance of the congressional goal of protecting children from harmful materials, the statute abridged "freedom of speech," as protected by the First Amendment.

In its decision, the Supreme Court acknowledged that sexually explicit material is available on the Internet and that such material

---

[11]   The *Communications Decency Act of 1996* comprised Title V of *The Telecommunications Act of 1996*, Pub. L. 104, 110 Stat. 56, of which the primary purpose was to reduce regulation and encourage the rapid deployment of new telecommunications technology.

[12]   No. 96-511 (U.S.S.C. June 26, 1997).

[13]   47 U.S.C.A. 223(a) (Supp. 1997) prohibits the knowing transmission of obscene or indecent messages to any recipient under 18 years of age.

[14]   47 U.S.C.A. 223(d) prohibits the knowing sending or display of patently offensive messages in a manner that is available to a person under 18 years of age.

"extends from the modestly titillating to the hardest core." Although such material is widely available, the court found that it is seldom encountered accidentally. The title or a description of the document will usually appear before the document itself and, in many cases, the user will receive detailed information about the contents of an Internet site before taking the required steps to access the document.

The court distinguished prior cases which recognized special factors justifying regulation of broadcast media. In comparison with broadcasting, the receipt of information on the Internet requires the user to take a series of affirmative steps which are more deliberate and direct than merely turning a dial. Therefore, the Internet was found not to be as invasive as radio or television transmissions. Another justification for regulation of the broadcast spectrum, the scarcity of frequencies, was not applicable to the Internet. These factors served to distinguish Internet communications from those received by radio or television and could justify different treatment.

The court also acknowledged the availability of systems to help parents control material that may be accessed from a home computer connected to the Internet.[15] Such filtering software may be used to limit access to an approved list of sources that have been identified as containing no adult material or may be configured to block designated inappropriate sites. It may also be set up to block messages containing identifiable objectionable features. However, the court recognized that such software cannot currently screen for sexually explicit images.

The court considered the various alternatives that were available to deal with the problem of age verification (i.e., restricting access based on verification of requested information such as a credit card number[16] or an adult password). However, it appeared to adopt the District Court's finding that there "is no effective way to determine the identity or age of a user."

The Supreme Court held that the CDA lacks the precision that the First Amendment requires when a statute regulates the content of

---

[15]    Examples include Net Nanny, SurfWatch and Cyber Patrol.

[16]    However, the imposition of such a requirement would completely bar adults who do not have a credit card and lack the resources to obtain one from accessing any blocked content.

speech. By denying minors access to potentially harmful speech, the CDA effectively suppresses a large amount of speech that adults have a constitutional right to receive and to address to one another.

The court also held that the breadth of the CDA's restriction of speech is wholly unprecedented and a violation of the First Amendment.[17] The CDA's restrictions on adult speech would be a violation of the First Amendment if less restrictive alternatives would be at least as effective in achieving the Act's legitimate purposes. The Government was unable to persuade the court that there were no other such alternatives.

The ruling in this case only affects the provisions relating to indecent or "patently offensive" content on the Internet. Banning of obscene material, including child pornography, is not affected by the decision.

Also unaffected by the decision are the so-called "Good Samaritan" provisions[18] of the CDA which were applied in *Zehran v. America Online, Inc.*[19] These provisions provide a defence against civil liability for a service provider who takes action in respect of inappropriate materials provided by a third party.[20]

Following the Supreme Court's decision, the Clinton Administration dropped its strong support for the impugned provisions of the CDA in favour of an approach based on self-regulation to address the problem of pornography and other content deemed unsuitable for children browsing on the Internet. This approach might include a requirement that Internet access providers provide all subscribers with filtering software. This would place the

---

[17] For instance, sexually explicit words and pictures are protected by the First Amendment if they are deemed indecent but not obscene.

[18] 47 U.S.C. s.230(c)(1)-(2).

[19] Civil Action 96-952-A. (E.D. Virginia, March 21, 1997).

[20] A defence is provided against civil liability for a service provider or user of an interactive service in respect to any action taken in good faith to restrict access to or availability of material that the service provider or user considers to be obscene, lewd, lascivious, filthy, excessively violent, harassing or otherwise objectionable. These provisions also provide that "no provider or user of an interactive service shall be treated as the publisher or speaker of any information provided by another information content provider." *Zehran* is discussed in more detail in section 8.4 dealing with Service Provider Liability Issues.

burden of censorship on parents rather than the government and may satisfy the concerns of civil libertarians while providing a potentially effective solution to the problem of minors gaining access to pornography. The White House has encouraged the development of an Internet "V-chip" proposal.

Another attempt at legislative control may be made at a future date. Justice O'Connor, who wrote a separate opinion that partly dissents from the majority, indicated that technology could be used to restrict certain areas in cyberspace to adults. Justice O'Connor also indicated that a law that more narrowly targets indecent transmissions between an adult and a minor might be upheld.

A number of states have also attempted to regulate content placed on the Internet. In *American Library Association v. Pataki*,[21] the plaintiffs challenged the constitutionality of New York State's ban on online indecency.[22] That statute was ruled unconstitutional on the grounds that it violated the provision of the US Constitution which forbids one state from regulating another state's commercial activity (commonly referred to as the "Interstate Commerce Clause").[23]

Georgia legislation[24] prohibiting anonymous and pseudonymous online speech, as well as the use of trademarked logos without permission, has also been ruled unconstitutional as being overly broad and vague in violation of the First Amendment.[25] Georgia had alleged that the purpose of the statute was the prevention of misrepresentation and fraud in cyberspace, which the court agreed represented a compelling state interest. However, the court held that the statute was not narrowly tailored to achieve that end and instead would sweep innocent, protected speech within its scope.

---

[21]  97 Civ. 0222 (S.D.N.Y., June 20, 1997).

[22]  New York Penal Law 235-21 prohibits the dissemination of indecent or obscene material which is "harmful to minors" on computer networks.

[23]  District Judge Loretta A. Preska found that because of the nature of the Internet, it was impossible to restrict the effects of the *New York Act* to conduct occurring within New York and that the Internet "requires a cohesive national scheme of regulation so that users are reasonably able to determine their obligations." As the violation of the Interstate Commerce Clause provided an adequate support for the decision, Judge Preska declined to rule on the plaintiffs' First Amendment challenge.

[24]  No. 1029, Ga. Laws 1996, p. 1505 codified at O.C.G.A. 16-9-93-1.

[25]  *ACLU v. Miller*, No. 1:96-CV-2475-MHS (N.D. Ga., June 20, 1997).

The regulation of content on the Internet is made difficult by the fact that an Internet server can be located in a foreign jurisdiction where its operator is not subject to domestic laws. Barring a coordinated multilateral or international approach, prohibitions imposed in one country can easily be circumvented by relocating the content to a server located elsewhere. This approach has already been adopted by online gambling facilities that have simply set up shop in jurisdictions that do not prohibit such activities. Differences in national laws may serve as an incentive for certain countries to set up high-speed connections to the Internet for purposes of hosting material that may be illegal to disseminate in other countries.

## 2.6  THE INTERNET AS BROADCASTING

### (a)  Audio/Video Services Available Over the Internet

There is a growing trend toward convergence of cable television and telephone services. Cable operators are seeking to upgrade their facilities to provide two-way communications that may include the provision of telephone services. Telephone carriers are also increasing the bandwidth of their system, using technology such as Asymmetrical Digital Subscriber Line (ADSL) in order to provide the capacity for delivery of video and multimedia services. Each industry group has sought regulatory approval to enter into the business of the other industry group. On August 6, 1996, Industry Canada and Heritage Canada released the federal government's Convergence Policy Statement setting out the policy framework for the convergence of broadcasting and telecommunications.[26] However, each industry's initiatives will require substantial investments and are not likely to occur for some time.

Substantial technological progress is being made to allow the delivery of real-time video programming through the Internet. Until recently, computer networks were used primarily for the transmission of textual and/or graphical information. However, the availability of high speed connections now permits the transmission of limited screen size, low frame rate audio and video programming through the Internet. Audio-only and combined audio-visual content can be used

---

[26]  For an overview, see Martin, Stanley W. and Dalik, Donald M., "Canadian Government's Convergence Policy Statement", *Information & Technology Law* 1:3 (December 1996).

to enhance an existing Web site or to deliver a program that previously required a broadcast channel.

It has been possible to transmit digitized audio signals or combined audio/video content across the Internet for some time. However, traditional file-transfer technology requires users to download the entire file before it can be "played". Depending on the compression algorithm utilized, downloading audio-only content typically requires 5 minutes of download time for every one minute of playback time. Download time for combined audio-visual content is substantially longer.

Recently developed "streaming" technology permits users to begin playing an audio or combined audio/video program in real time within a few seconds after the material is requested. These products compress the content and optimize the transmission to the available bandwidth. The technology is simple to use and permits the integration of players with a variety of Web browsers and platforms. Some products require the installation of special audio or video servers,[27] while others can use ordinary Web servers to broadcast content.[28]

While the quality of transmission of audio-video content sent by means of the Internet is still lower than traditional broadcasting transmissions (i.e., because of smaller size video viewing windows and "choppy" images), the quality should improve as greater use is made of faster communication links such as ISDN, cable modems and direct broadcast satellites.

Streaming media technology is being used by hundreds of Web sites to provide video-on-demand programs consisting of advertising,

---

[27]  For instance, VDOnet Corp.'s VDOLive 2.0 requires use of a VDOLive Video Server.

[28]  Vivo Software's VivoActive requires no server component and uses international video and audio compression standards from the world of videoconferencing, namely H.263 video compression and G.723 audio compression (Vivo's compression technology is also licensed to PictureTel Corp., which uses it as the basis for its PC-based video conferencing products).  The files created by VivoActive can be loaded on any Web server and additional fees "by the stream" need not be paid as is the case with some competitive products.

promotion and corporate communications[29] including product information, training, product support and entertainment.

Traditional radio and television broadcasters are also using their Web sites to transmit reports from their programs, and in some cases, full-length programs. In addition to providing playback of pre-recorded content, many streaming media products allow live broadcasts to be sent through the Internet. Real-time audio-visual broadcasts of live events have included the 1996 US Republican and Democratic National Conventions, Japanese baseball games and Microsoft developers' conferences.

## (b) Regulation of Internet Transmissions Under Broadcasting Legislation

As the quality of Internet transmissions continues to improve, and as traditional broadcasters increase their use of the Internet for retransmitting or simulcasting their off-the-air broadcasts, broadcast regulators will likely turn their attention to this new communications channel. Most countries provide for the regulation of broadcasting and communications activities by public authorities which may be a combination of an administrative tribunal and government departments and agencies. Broadcasting legislation tends to focus on content and may include, as a policy objective, the protection and enhancement of the country's cultural identity and sovereignty.

A government commission or agency responsible for the enforcement of broadcasting regulations may view the unregulated distribution of Internet-based broadcasting as a threat to its mandate. Indeed, the widespread distribution of programming from video servers located in foreign jurisdictions could compete with domestically regulated entities and thereby undermine the country's regulatory framework for broadcasting.

Broadcasting legislation may be interpreted broadly enough to encompass multimedia programming sent through the Internet. Such legislation may even apply to pre-recorded video files accessible from

---

[29]    Companies who are providing such materials on their Web sites include Hewlett Packard, NCR Corporation, Nokia, PictureTel, Shell Oil Company and others.

Web pages or downloadable from FTP sites.[30] Providers of video and multimedia services which utilize the Internet may therefore be subject to the licensing and regulatory requirements of broadcasting legislation. However, several possible exemptions may be applicable to Internet-based broadcasting services.

For example, an exemption may be available for programming that consists predominantly of alphanumeric text or still images. The latter exemption may apply to Internet-based broadcasting because the limits on the available bandwidth mean that such broadcasting is often displayed on a viewing screen that is only a fraction of the size of the PC screen, or on a split screen which also includes text-based information. It is arguable that as long as at least 51% of the screen display of a service is devoted to alphanumeric text, the service falls outside the type of programming regulated by broadcasting legislation.[31]

Due to the bandwidth restrictions, most Internet-based broadcasting technologies provide continuous audio but break up the video into very slow frame rate transmission. If the frame rate is low enough, such broadcasts may fall within an exemption from broadcasting regulation for still images.

If the provision of programming via the Internet is held to constitute broadcasting, and an exemption is not otherwise available, then the provider of Internet content may be required to obtain a broadcasting licence and to comply with other requirements which may include ownership restrictions and requirements for carrying domestic content.

Where a business entity located in one jurisdiction is engaged in the provision of Internet-based broadcasting and advertises its services or collects fees from subscribers in another jurisdiction, a regulatory authority in that other jurisdiction may bring enforcement action under broadcasting legislation.

---

[30]   For example, many motion picture studios now commonly provide short previews of new movies that can be downloaded through the Internet.

[31]   However, the exemption may not be available if the visual image or combined media portion predominates notwithstanding that a larger portion of the screen is allocated to text-based information.

The regulator may also have the power to direct common carriers which may include Internet Access Providers within the jurisdiction to block access to the unlicensed broadcasting services. However, any attempt at regulation will likely face a difficult technical challenge in developing a mechanism to distinguish packets carrying different types of digital data. Any such blocking may need to be effected through filtering all traffic originating at a specified Internet address or domain name.

### (c) Application of Canadian Broadcasting Legislation to the Internet

In Canada, the federal Parliament has the authority to regulate both broadcasting undertakings and the content transmitted by such undertakings. In *Capital Cities Communications Inc. v. Canada (Radio-Television & Telecommunications Commission)*[32] federal jurisdiction was found to extend over the entire field of radio broadcasting. Similarly, in the case of *C.F.R.B. v. Canada (Attorney General) (No.2)*,[33] federal jurisdiction was held to extend over "the whole of the undertaking of broadcasting."[34] The authority of the federal Parliament extends not only to the technical aspects of transmitting and receiving radio signals but also the intellectual content of such communication.[35]

Federal jurisdiction over broadcasting has also been found to extend to the activities of cable operators that receive and re-transmit off-air signals.[36] Thus a cable distribution system which receives broadcast signals and transmits them to the homes of cable subscribers was found to be part of a communications undertaking within the competence of the federal Parliament. The court noted that

---

[32]   [1978] 2 S.C.R. 141, 18 N.R. 181, 81 D.L.R. (3d) 609, 36 C.P.R. (2d) 1 (S.C.C.) aff'g [1975] F.C. 18, 7 N.R. 18, 52 D.L.R. (3d) 415, 19 C.P.R. (2d) 51 (Fed C.A.).

[33]   [1973] 3 O.R. 819, 38 D.L.R. (3d) 335, 14 C.C.C. (2d) 345 (Ont. C.A.), aff'g [1973] 1 O.R. 79, 30 D.L.R. (3d) 279, 9 C.C.C. (2d) 323 (Ont. H.C.), leave to appeal to S.C.C. refused November 13, 1973.

[34]   *Ibid.*, at O.R. 822.

[35]   *Ibid.*, at O.R. 824.

[36]   *Capital Cities Communications v. C.R.T.C.*, [1978] 2 S.C.R. 141, 18 N.R. 181, 81 D.L.R. (3d) 609, 36 C.P.R. (2d) 1 (S.C.C.) aff'g [1975] F.C. 18, 7 N.R. 18, 2 D.L.R. (3d) 415, 19 C.P.R. (2d) 51 (Fed. C.A.).

it would be incongruous "to deny the continuation of regulatory authority because the signals are intercepted and sent on to ultimate viewers through a different technology."[37]

The question of whether the Canadian Parliament has jurisdiction to regulate the Internet when it is used for the transmission of video programming and various multimedia services depends on whether the use of the Internet for these purposes constitutes the undertaking of "broadcasting" for purposes of the *Broadcasting Act*.[38]

Section 2(1) of that Act defines "broadcasting" as:

"any transmission of ***programs***, whether or not encrypted, by radio waves or other means of telecommunication *for reception by the public* by means of broadcasting receiving apparatus, but does not include any such transmission of programs that is made solely for performance or display in a public place." [*Emphasis added.*]

The term "program" is also defined in subsection 2(1) as:

"sounds or visual images, or a combination of sounds and visual images, that are intended to inform, enlighten or entertain, but does not include visual images, whether or not combined with sounds, that consist predominantly of alphanumeric text."

This definition of "program" is broad enough to encompass many of the multimedia and interactive video and game services which are being transmitted across the Internet. In light of the legislative history of the Act, in conjunction with relevant definitions contained in the *North American Free Trade Agreement* concerning transmission of programs to the public, it is quite possible that broadcasting "for the reception by the public" would include programs broadcast on demand for individual users such as pay-per-view television or

---

[37]   *Ibid.*, at S.C.R. 162. See also *Dionne* v. *Quebec (Public Service Board)* [1978] 2 S.C.R. 191, 18 N.R. 271, 83 D.L.R. (3d) 178, (*sub nom. Québec (Régie des services publics) c. Dionne)* 38 C.P.R. (2d) 1 (S.C.C.), in which the court found that the authority of Parliament extended to a cable distribution system which made use of television signals received at its antennas from both within and outside the province.

[38]   S.C. 1991, c.11.

interactive video games.[39] In April 1994 the director of public affairs for the Canadian Radio-television and Telecommunications Commission (the "CRTC") stated that the CRTC was not planning to devise a system of licensing for bulletin board systems ("BBSs") but noted "that advancements in the online market which allow users to "broadcast" sound and video over the BBSs, push the activities closer and closer into CRTC jurisdiction."[40]

As noted above, the definition of "program" explicitly excludes "visual images ... that consist predominantly of alphanumeric text" and accordingly, such images are exempt from regulation under the Act. A "visual image" should be "predominantly" alphanumeric so long as 51% of the display comes within that description.[41] Thus, multimedia and other computer services that are delivered through the Internet that consist of *combined* text and other images, moving or static, should be exempt from such regulation, provided that such images contain 51% or more of alphanumeric text. However, there is no guarantee that the numeric proportion of text to images will be a determining factor as to which predominates.

In light of the decisions in *Capital Cities* and *Dionne*, as noted above, multimedia services transmitted through computer networks which are both produced and transmitted only within the province should come within provincial regulatory authority.

### (d)  Application of Provincial Legislation

Notwithstanding the authority of the federal Parliament over broadcasting and cable companies, the program content of such

---

[39]  Bill C-40, which became the *Broadcasting Act*, dropped from the definition of "broadcasting", "any such transmission ... made on the demand of a particular person for reception only by that person" which had been contained in the predecessor Bill C-136. Article 1721(2) of the NAFTA states, in part, that "[f]or the purposes of this Agreement ... **public** includes ... any aggregation of individuals intended to be the object of, and capable of perceiving, communications or performances of works, regardless of whether they can do so at the same or different times or in the same or different places ...."    See also H. Intven, "Traffic Rules on Canada's Information Highway: The Regulatory Framework for new Cable and Telephone Services" (*Insight*, April 28-29 1994) at 11-14.

[40]  See T. Pobuda, "CRTC will look, not act on BBSs" *Computer Dealer News* (04 May 1994) 2.

[41]  *Ibid.*, at 10.

undertakings may also be subject to provincial legislation. In *Kellogg Co. of Canada v. Québec (Procureur Général)*,[42] the Supreme Court of Canada upheld the validity of certain provisions of the Quebec *Consumer Protection Act* L.R.Q., ch. P-40.1 that prohibited the use of cartoons in advertising intended for children. The court held that since the challenged provisions were part of the general regulation of advertising for children, and since the main purpose of the law was to control commercial activity in the province, there was no objection that it incidentally affected what could be shown on television.

The validity of the provisions of the Quebec *Consumer Protection Act* prohibiting commercial advertising directed at persons under thirteen years of age, was also considered by the Supreme Court of Canada in *Irwin Toy Ltd. c. Québec (Procureur Général)*.[43] Such provisions were found to be legislation of general application enacted in relation to consumer protection rather than a colourable attempt to legislate in relation to television advertising. The court held that the dominant aspect of the law was the regulation of all forms of advertising directed at persons under thirteen years of age, rather than the prohibition of television advertising.

Accordingly, the court found that such provisions did not trench on exclusive federal jurisdiction by purporting to apply to a federal undertaking, and in so doing, affecting a vital part of its operations. Moreover, such provisions did not have the effect of impairing or paralysing the operations of any such undertaking in the sense of sterilizing the undertaking "in all its functions and activities."

The fact that an interprovincial communications system is used to effect trades in securities does not invalidate provincial legislation regulating the conduct of such trades. In *Bennett v. British Columbia*

---

[42]   (*sub nom. Quebec (Attorney General) v. Kellogg's Co.*) [1978] 2 S.C.R. 211, 19 N.R. 271, 83 D.L.R. (3d) 314 (S.C.C.).

[43]   94 N.R. 167, (*sub nom. Irwin Toy Ltd. v. Quebec (Attorney General)*) [1989] 1 S.C.R. 927, 58 D.L.R. (4th) 577, 24 Q.A.C. 2, 25 C.P.R. (3d) 417, 39 C.R.R. 193 (S.C.C.), rev'g [1986] R.J.Q. 2441, 3 Q.A.C. 285, 32 D.L.R. (4th) 641, 14 C.P.R. (3d) 60, 26 C.R.R. 193 (Que C.A.), rev'g [1982] C.S. 96 (Que S.C.).

*(Securities Commission)*,[44] the appellant claimed that section 68 of the British Columbia *Securities Act*, which regulated insider trading, was invalid on the grounds that the trades in question were carried out through the facilities of the Computer Assisted Trading System ("CATS"), being a national communications system to facilitate trading in securities listed on The Toronto Stock Exchange. The court held that the substance of the legislation in question, namely to lay down ethical standards for persons engaged in the trading of securities, related to matters within the competence of the provincial legislature. The fact that the conduct in question was carried to fruition via a national "mechanical" system did not render the legislation *ultra vires* since the legislation had only an incidental or consequential effect on extra-provincial rights.

The foregoing authorities indicate that a province may enact legislation of general application to regulate commercial activity within the province, notwithstanding that the activity is carried out by means of the Internet. Such legislation may regulate matters such as the protection of consumers or trades in securities, even if the acts in question are carried out in whole or in part on the Internet. However, such legislation may be invalid as coming within the jurisdiction of the federal Parliament if it affects a vital part of the operation of the provider of inter-provincial communication services so as to impair or paralyze the operations of such an entity. It must also be determined whether the activity in question occurs wholly within the province or otherwise has a sufficient connection to the province for it to come within the legislative authority of the province.

## 2.7 REGULATION OF THE INTERNET UNDER TELECOMMUNICATIONS LEGISLATION

### (a) Recent Developments in Internet Telephony

Another challenge for regulators has been the recent growth of Internet telephony. A number of vendors are currently marketing

---

[44] (1992), 69 B.C.L.R. (2d) 171, 94 D.L.R. (4th) 339, [1992] 5 W.W.R. 481, 18 B.C. A.C. 191, 31 W.A.C. 191 (B.C. C.A.), aff'd. (1991), 82 D.L.R. (4th) 129 (B.C. S.C.), leave to appeal refused [1992] 6 W.W.R. 1 vii, 70 B.C. C.R. (2d) xxxii, 143 N.R. 396 (note), 20 B.C. A.C. 80 (note), 35 W.A.C. 80 (note), 97 D.L.R. (4th) vii (S.C.C.).

software products that allow the Internet to be used to place long-distance or local voice telephone calls. Such calls may be made for the cost of the Internet service providers' connect-time charges rather than the cost of a traditional phone call. As a growing number of Internet Service Providers offer flat-rate Internet access, there may be virtually no incremental cost of placing phone calls through the Internet.

A research report from International Data Corporation reveals that new technological advances will permit Internet telephony to expand from a specialty market to a large-scale business activity.[45] The study predicts that the number of active Internet telephony users will expand from 500,000 as at the end of 1995 to 16 million by the end of 1999, driven primarily by business users.

In the spring of 1994, Vocaltec introduced the first widely-available, commercial Internet telephony product. The first version provided choppy, but useable, real-time transmission of voice communications. Versions that followed from Vocaltec, as well as comparable technology developed by its competitors,[46] now offer improved quality duplex communications and a wealth of new features.[47] These products allow users to carry on, through the Internet, voice conversations across the country or even around the world for the cost of the Internet connection. The per minute cost of carrying on long-distance telephone calls between users of these products can therefore amount to pennies instead of dollars.

At present, Internet telephone products still have various limitations, including poor sound quality and the need for the user at each end of the communications link to have a PC equipped with a

---

[45] *The World Wide Web Phones Home: Internet Telephony Market Assessment, 1996-1999* (IDC#11407).

[46] Other Internet telephony products include Netspeak's *Webphone*, Quarterdeck's *WebTalk*, Third-Planet Publishing/Camelot Distributing's *Digiphone*, Microsoft's *NetMeeting*, Netscape's *CoolTalk* and products from IBM, Cisco Systems, Intel and others. Another interesting contender is *PGPfone* which uses speech compression and cryptography to allow users to hold a real-time secure telephone conversation modem-to-modem or across the Internet.

[47] These include voice-mail, whiteboarding and document sharing, cross-platform capabilities, call waiting, muting, blocking, caller I.D., call screening, directory assistance, file transfer, text chat and automatic voice activation.

microphone, speakers and sound card. However, these limitations are likely to disappear as Internet telephony products are enhanced to provide improved sound quality with higher speed links to the Internet[48] and as more users acquire PCs with multimedia capabilities.

The fact that each Internet telephony product utilizes its own proprietary protocols means that users at each end must also use the same brand of software. However, the inclusion of Internet telephony products bundled with popular Web browsers from Netscape and Microsoft increases the likelihood that any two users on the Internet will have access to at least one common telephony application. Also, as this market segment matures, common standards will develop to facilitate interoperability.[49]

A more significant limitation on the use of Internet telephony is that a caller can communicate only with another user whose computer is turned on and who is connected to the Internet at the time the call is placed. However, even this limitation is being overcome.

A number of vendors of Internet telephony products, such as VocalTec, and even major switch vendors, such as Northern Telecom and Siemens, are developing gateways that will let PC users on the Internet call people with standard analog telephones attached to traditional voice networks. Initial versions of these products allowed international subscribers located outside the US to utilize a telephone application on their PC to connect through the Internet with a gateway located in the US, through which they could place the call to a US or international destination. A suitably-equipped PC and Internet connection were required by the party placing the call, but the recipient of the call only required a normal telephone set.

---

[48]   Internet telephony products are limited by the amount of data that can be transmitted across the Internet. To achieve telephone-quality sound, it is necessary to send approximately 8,000 bytes of data per second. A typical 28,800 bit-per-second modem can transmit less than 3,000 bytes per second. Another important factor limiting sound quality is the need to send the packets isochronously (at a guaranteed interval between packets). The TCP/IP protocol used on the Internet can guarantee delivery but not the delivery interval.

[49]   The "Voice Over IP Forum", a vendor group within the International Multimedia Teleconferencing Consortium, has been established to specify technical guidelines for enabling interoperability between Internet voice communications products.

More advanced applications of Internet telephony now incorporate gateways to serve both ends of a conversation. These products can bridge the gap between the Public Switched Telephone Network (PSTN) and the Internet to enable phone-to-phone calling over the Internet. For example, a user in London, England can use an ordinary telephone to make a call which will be connected to a PSTN-to-Internet telephony gateway and transmitted through the Internet to a compatible gateway located near the destination. These gateways can be especially attractive to corporations who use existing private networks or other means of communications, including the Internet, to communicate between multiple offices located in different countries.

### (b)  Calls for Regulatory Control of Internet Telephony

The opportunities provided by Internet telephony may be regarded by some entities as a threat to their business. In March 1996, the America's Carriers' Telecommunications Association (ACTA), a group representing approximately 130 small long-distance telephone carrier resellers, petitioned the US Federal Communications Commission ("FCC") to issue a declaratory ruling confirming its authority to regulate interstate and international telecommunications services over the Internet. ACTA further requested the FCC to restrict the sale of Internet telephony software on the grounds that providers of such software do not comply with the rules that apply to conventional circuit-switched voice telecommunications carriers.

ACTA also complained that Internet access service providers do not pay interstate access charges, which long-distance carriers must pay to local phone companies for originating and terminating calls. As a result of an FCC decision in the early 1980s, such charges need not be paid by enhanced service providers. ACTA argues that these ISPs do not provide the revenue to cover the additional costs that they impose on the network.

ACTA's submission to the FCC failed to recognize that software providers only provide products and do not provide any form of transmission services and accordingly cannot be treated as telecommunications carriers. ACTA would have been better advised to target the Internet Service Providers who provide the communications infrastructure that supports the use of Internet telephony.

Hundreds of submissions were made in response to the ACTA petition, including submissions by regional Bell operating companies, interexchange carriers, computer software developers, and Internet Service Providers. With one exception, these submissions opposed the relief sought by ACTA.[50] Interestingly, the opponents of ACTA's position included a large number of telecommunications carriers. In this regard, AT&T indicated that it had no objections to Internet telephony and, in fact, would try to play a leading role.[51]

On March 27, 1997, the FCC's Office of Plans and Policy released a staff working paper, "Digital Tornado: The Internet and Telecommunication Policy", setting out telecommunications policy as it relates to the Internet.[52] The working paper reviewed some of the major Internet-related issues that had come before the Commission, as well as those that may come before the FCC in the near future. It examined the applicability of existing FCC regulatory and statutory requirements to services provided over the Internet. The working paper acknowledged that, in the area of telecommunications policy, the FCC had explicitly refused to regulate most online information services under the rules that apply to telephone companies. The paper recommended that the government exercise caution in imposing pre-existing statutory and regulatory classifications on Internet-based services.

### (c) Authority of Canadian Parliament Over Internet Telephony

In Canada, it has been clearly established that the federal Parliament has the exclusive authority to regulate undertakings which are engaged in the provision of telecommunications services where they are provided across national or provincial boundaries. This was confirmed by the Supreme Court of Canada in *Alberta Government Telephones v. Canada (Canadian Radio-Television &*

---

[50]  Joint Opposition of VocalTec Ltd. and Quarterdeck Corporation, RM No. 8775, June 10, 1996.

[51]  *Inter@ctive Week*, May 6, page 1.

[52]  OPP Working Paper No. 29 at <http://www.fcc.gov/>.

*Telecommunications Commission)*,[53] where the Supreme Court found that Alberta Government Telephones ("AGT"), created by an Alberta statute to provide telephone and telecommunications service within the province, was a federal undertaking. The Supreme Court held that the primary concern in determining whether an undertaking comes within federal jurisdiction is the service which is provided through the use of the physical equipment rather than the location of the equipment. The court found that, through the various bilateral and multilateral arrangements with other telephone companies, AGT was organized as a critical part of the national telecommunications systems so as to provide its subscribers with interprovincial and international services. The fact that the separate members of Telecom Canada owned their respective works did not take away from the degree of integration existing among the members of the system.

Subsequent to the Supreme Court's decision, the federal *Railway Act*,[54] which had regulated telecommunications in Canada for over 80 years, was replaced by the *Telecommunications Act*.[55] Section 3 of the *Telecommunications Act* provides that the Act "is binding on Her Majesty in right of Canada or a province". Hence, the *Telecommunications Act* applies to provincial telephone companies engaged in interprovincial undertakings.

In *Téléphone Guèvrement Inc. c. Québec (Régie des télécommunications)*,[56] the Quebec Court of Appeal found that Parliament had authority to legislate in relation to the operations of a Quebec company known as Téléphone Guèvremont Inc. ("TG"), which offered its customers local, interprovincial and international telephone and data transmission services. There was a sufficient

---

[53]  [1989] 2 S.C.R. 225, 68 Alta. L.R. (2d) 1, 61 D.L.R. (4th) 193, [1989] 5 W.W.R. 385, 26 C.P.R. (3d) 289, *(sub nom. Canadian National/Canadian Pacific Telecommunications v. Alberta Government Telephones)* 98 N.R. 161, (S.C.C.) rev'g (1985), [1986] 2 F.C. 179, 63 N.R. 374, 24 D.L.R. (4th) 608, 9 C.P.R. (3d) 356, 17 Admin. L.R. 190 (Fed. C.A.).

[54]  The relevant section in AGT, R.S.C. 1970, c. R-2, s. 320, became ss. 334-339 in R.S.C. 1985, c. R-3, which were repealed by s. 105 of the *Telecommunications Act*, S.C. 1993, c. 38.

[55]  S.C. 1993, c. 38.

[56]  (1992), *(sub nom. Québec (Procureur Général) c. Téléphone Guèvrement Inc.)* [1993] R.J.Q. 77, 99 D.L.R. (4th) 241, (Que. C.A.); aff'd [1994] 1 S.C.R. 878, 112 D.L.R. (4th) 127, 54 C.P.R. (3d) 401, 168 N.C. 7, 61 Q.A.C. 175 (S.C.C.).

operational link between TG and the national telecommunications system for the company to come within federal jurisdiction.

The *Telecommunications Act* grants the CRTC the authority to, *inter alia*, determine technical standards, approve the establishment of classes of services and approve rates, order accounting and periodic reports from carriers, prohibit or regulate unsolicited telecommunications "telemarketing", refrain from exercising its power when it finds that there is sufficient competition, order carriers to provide services where there is insufficient competition, order the construction, alteration or removal of facilities including consequential expropriation of lands, and order the interconnection of any carrier's telecommunications facilities with another carrier's facilities.

# 3

# Obtaining and Protecting Domain Names

## 3.1 INTRODUCTION

A domain name is the unique address of a Web site on the Internet for an individual, business or other entity. Often this address will contain a trademark or unique identifier of a business. For example, a generic Internet address (or URL)[1] may be in the form: <http://www.name.com>[2] where the "name" element may be the business' name, trademark or other identifier. This means that the particular address of the Web site is unique. No two sites can have the same address on the Internet.

The element "name" in our example is referred to as the second level domain. The ".com" element is referred to as the top level domain.[3] Some domain names have subdomains, such as

---

[1]   The URL, or Uniform Resource Locator, is the address for a specific location on the Internet. It consists of: (i) a transfer protocol, such as "http://" in this example, for hypertext transfer protocol (however, this portion of the URL is often omitted); (ii) the "www" refers to the world wide web, a portion of the systems which make up the Internet; (iii) a specific and unique domain or address ("name" in the example); and (iv) a top level domain (".com" in the example). The domain name system was developed to make it easier to remember Internet addresses in contrast to using the numerical IP (Internet protocol) address system, where each Internet address is typically composed of four groups of numbers separated by decimals. It also facilitates the ability to move a web site to a different ISP.

[2]   Throughout this text an Internet address or URL is shown within two brackets, as follows: <http://www.name.com>. Note that the brackets, < and >, are not part of the address.

[3]   Top level domains are generally of two types. The first type of top level domain is geographic and describes or represents a particular jurisdiction, such as ".ca" the Canadian top level domain. The second type of top level domain is generic and, while having no reference to a geographic location, suggests a common type of use. Examples of this type of top level domain are ".edu" for educational uses, ".gov" for government uses and the

<http://www.name.edm.ab.ca>. Top level domains ("TLD") are either characterized as generic (as in the case of the ".com" domain) ("gTLD") or geographic (as in the case of the Canadian ".ca" domain). The geographic abbreviations are the two letter country codes derived from international ISO standards.[4] Aspects of each of these types of domain names are described in section 3.3.

The domain name system was developed by the Internet Assigned Numbers Authority (IANA) which acts as the central coordinator for the assignment of unique parameter values for Internet protocols. The IANA is chartered by the Internet Society and the Federal Network Council.

## 3.2  RELATIONSHIP OF DOMAIN NAMES TO TRADEMARKS

Often a URL or Internet site address will contain a trademark as the second level domain and as a unique identifier of a business. For example, a generic Internet URL may be in the form: <http://www. trademark.com> where the "trademark" element may be the business' trademark.

A basic problem arises from basic principles of trademark law and the nature of the domain name system: each domain name must be unique. In addition, a specific domain name can only be associated with one entity.[5] Since most elements of the URL are generic, the distinguishing element in a domain will typically be the second level domain name or "trademark" in our example. This should be contrasted with trademark law where more than one person can legitimately use the same names as trademarks so long as the

---

popular ".com" for commercial uses. The ".com" domain has become the most desirable top level domain and has a high level of recognition among users.

[4]  See the International Organization for Standardization (ISO) 3166 standard which provides a two character country code for each country. Canada's country code is "ca" and the United States' country code is "us".

[5]  For example, <http://www.abc.com>, <http://www.abcinc.com>, <http://www.abc_inc.com> and <http://www.abc_us.com> are all unique addresses but all include the same common distinctive element "abc". Technically all such domains can co-exist. However, there may be a legal issue if use of an address results in dilution or confusion with another person's trademark due to the manner of use of an address which is similar to another person's mark particularly where that element is also used as a trademark.

trademarks are used for different products or services, and create no likelihood of confusion.[6] Since two or more entities may both have legitimate rights to use the same name as a trademark, a dispute may arise as to which entity should have the exclusive right to use the trademark as part of their Internet address. This problem is compounded by the global nature of the Internet since the registration of a domain name containing a trademark may preclude many legitimate uses of the trademark in jurisdictions other than those in which the registrant is carrying on business.

Disputes that arise due to this incompatibility between the Internet domain name system and traditional trademark doctrine must be resolved by the general law on the adoption and use of trademarks in each jurisdiction and, where applicable, by the application of the relevant domain name dispute policy implemented by the applicable domain name registrar.

The various types of domain name disputes may be categorized[7] as follows:

- **Name Napping** — An entity has sought to appropriate the unique name or trademark of a business as a domain name and is using it for a confusing commercial use or seeks to sell it "back" to the business. If the business has a unique name (i.e., there are no other legitimate users of the same name) and has secured registration of that name as a trademark in applicable jurisdictions then the business should be entitled to rely on rights under trademark law to prevent use of that mark as a domain name in those jurisdictions.

---

[6]   For example, <http://www.xyz.com>, used by a grocery retailer who carries on business under the tradename or trademark "xyz" may not be confused with <http://www.xyzinc.com> used by an automobile manufacturer selling a sport utility vehicle under the trademark "xyz". The channels of trade, nature of the products, type of customers and other factors are sufficiently different that there is little likelihood of confusion. The issue of whether or not there is confusion is guided by s. 6(5) *Trade-Marks Act*. R.S.C. 1985, c. T-13. See also *Forum Corp. of North America v. Forum Ltd.* 14 U.S.P.Q. 2d 1950 (7th Cir. 1990) which sets out seven factors which should be considered in determining the likelihood of confusion under US trademark law. More information on this issue is provided in Chapter 5.

[7]   A review of legal issues relating to domain name disputes under US trademark law may be found in Oppendahl, "Remedies in Domain Name Lawsuits: How is a domain name like a cow?", 15 *John Marshall J. Of Computer & Information Law* 437 (1997).

- **Reverse Name Napping** — An entity has adopted a name as a domain name and has used the name legitimately for some time. Another business holds a registered trademark that is identical or similar to the domain name (which is used in association with different products or services). Often there are other businesses who also use the same mark and there is no likelihood of confusion. Typically, the registered trademark owner merely wants to use what he or she was not diligent enough to obtain first—the particular domain name. Assuming that there is no issue of confusion, the entity who first secured the domain name should be entitled to keep it.[8] It would appear that "first come, first served" is the fairest approach to all parties.[9]

However, if the domain name was registered with NSI, the trademark registrant may obtain recourse under NSI's domain name dispute rules, which do not recognize the basic principle that different parties may own rights to an identical trademark.[10] In addition, a trademark registrant in the US may also seek recourse under the *Federal Trademark Dilution Act*[11] and claim its mark is famous.[12] This Act is discussed in Chapter 5. It has been

---

[8]    Care must be taken when relying on cases in this area. Many courts have looked to *Actmedia Inc. v. Active Media International Inc.*, 1996 WL 466527 (N.D. Ill. Jul. 17, 1996), No. 96C3448, as authority for the proposition that the act of securing a domain name precludes the trademark registrant from use of the trademark on the Internet. However, this finding appears incorrect as the trademark registrant is unrestricted in its use of the identical trademark as a second level domain name on any one (or more) of countless other top level domains and can use variations of the trademark on the disputed top level domain.

[9]    See, for example, the success in retaining the prior domain registration in the face of conflicting claims based on narrow prior trademark registrations in *Roadrunner Computer Systems, Inc. v. Network Solutions, Inc.* E.D. Va. 96-Civ-413-A; *Network Solutions, Inc. v. Clue Computing, Inc.* 41 U.S. P.Q. 2D 1062 (D. Col. 1996); *Data Concepts Inc. v. Network Solutions, Inc.* M.D. Tenn 96-civ-429; *Giacalone v. Network Solutions, Inc.* N.D. 96-Civ-20434; and *Dynamic Information Systems Corp. v. Network Solutions, Inc.*, D. Col. 96-Civ-1551. In each of the above examples, Network Solutions, Inc. was the defendant.

[10]   NSI's domain name dispute policy gives precedence to holders of registered federal trademarks over users of unregistered marks even if they are used in respect of different goods and services.

[11]   Signed into law January 16, 1996, Pub. Law 104-98. This Act created a new Section 43(c) of the *Lanham Act*, 15 U.S.C. 1125.

[12]   However, this claim should fail where other legitimate users of the same trademark coexist in the applicable marketplace. Otherwise how should a court choose among several trademark owners (and possibly several trademark registrations).

suggested that if a prior trademark registrant seeks relief under the NSI's domain name dispute policy, in cases where there is no likelihood of confusion nor any unlawful dilution, then a case of trademark misuse[13] may be made out justifying, among other possible remedies, cancellation of the registered trademark[14] or awarding of legal fees or costs.[15]

Of course, the applicability of US trademark law is only effective in the US or for businesses under US jurisdiction. However, non-US businesses who register their domain names on the ".com" or other InterNIC managed domains should note that NSI would appear to be subject to the jurisdiction of US courts and US trademark law. Non-US businesses who do not wish to be at a disadvantage in relation to US businesses under US trademark law may therefore wish to secure a domain name based on a geographic top level domain, such as ".ca" or take steps to secure a US trademark.

- **Non-Commercial Uses Cases** — Trademark law remedies deal with the use of a trademark in commerce.[16] Use of a trademark

---

[13]   A plaintiff may be denied relief in a trademark case where the plaintiff violated antitrust laws. See, for example, *Carl Zeiss Stiftung v. V.E.B. Carl Zeiss*, Jena 298 F. Supp. 1309 (S.D. N.Y. 1969). An equitable form of trademark misuse also exists. See, for example, *United States Jaycees* v. *Cedar Rapid Jaycees*, 614 F. Supp. 515 (N.D. Iowa 1985) where a court found that a trademark owner who deals in an unjust manner with the defendant in the very transaction upon which the cause of action is based may be denied relief. It has been suggested this doctrine has applicability to cases of reverse name napping. Stephen J. Davidson, Nicole A. English, "Trademark Misuse: Applying the Trademark Misuse Doctrine to Domain Name Disputes". See <http://www.leonard.com>.

[14]   See, for example, the Canadian *Trade-Marks Act* and the *Lanham Act*, Section 37, providing for the ability of a court to cancel a trademark registration. In *Phi Delta Theta Fraternity v. J.A. Buchroeder & Co.*, 251 F. Supp. 968 (W.D. Mo. 1966) a court held that trademark misuse justified cancellation of a trademark registration.

[15]   In exceptional cases a court of superior jurisdiction can award legal fees to the prevailing party. See also Section 35, *Lanham Act*, 15 U.S.C. S. 167; 1117(a) and *General Motors Corp. v. Cadillac Marine & Boat Co.*, 226 F. Supp. 716 (W.D. Mich. 1964).

[16]   See, for example, the definition of use of a trademark in Section 4, *Trade-Marks Act*, R.S.C. 1985, c. T-13, as amended. Use in relation to products is placement of the mark on the products or their packaging. Use in relation to services means placement of the mark in performance or advertising for the services. Other uses of the mark may be outside the concept of use for purposes of the Act. See, for example, *Clairol International Corp. v. Thomas Supply & Equipment Ltd.* [1968] 2 Ex. C.R. 552, 55 C.P.R. 176, 38 Fox Pat. c. 176 (Can. Ex. Ct.) and the cases following it, interpreting Section 22.

in a domain name for a non-commercial use which does not create a likelihood of confusion may not infringe a trademark registration in Canada. However, some US courts have broadened the scope of a commercial activity, particularly in name napping cases.[17]

These issues and their interaction with the domain name dispute policy of NSI are discussed in detail in the section 3.5 (protection of domain names), below. Issues regarding use of trademarks on Web sites are discussed in Chapter 6. Basic trademark law issues and the doctrine of confusion under US and Canadian trademark law are discussed in Chapter 5.

## 3.3  How to Obtain a Domain Name

In order to obtain a domain name an applicant will typically approach the registrar of the applicable top level domain and request assignment of the desired domain name in accordance with the applicable domain name allocation policies of that registrar[18]. An applicant for a domain name should consider the top level domain for which he or she wishes to obtain a registration. The following discussion focuses on the Canadian geographic top level domain (.ca) and the generic top level domains administered by the InterNIC (i.e., .com, .edu, .org). An applicant can also consider registration under many other geographic (i.e., country-specific) top level domains.[19]

---

[17]  See, for example, *Intermatic Inc. v. Toeppen*, 40 U.S. P.Q. 2D 1412 (ND Ill. D.C. 1996) where the site showed a map and the court noted there was no likelihood of confusion (and accordingly no traditional trademark law remedy was available); however, the court relied on the *Federal Trademark Dilution Act* and found that Toeppen had intended to sell the domain name which was sufficient to establish commercial activity.

[18]  The IANA has delegated the domain name registration activity to a number of registrars in a franchise type approach. Most readers will be familiar with the InterNIC operated by Network Solutions, Inc. (NSI). The domain name polices of NSI have created some controversy and litigation.

[19]  See, for example, Island Networks, at <http://www.isles.net> who register domain names for the Channel Islands, i.e, .gg (Guernsey, Alderney and Sark) or .je (Jersey). These registrations are not subject to UK Value Added Tax. Another example of a geographic top level domain is Israel. See <http://www.isoc.org.il>.

Many applicants secure their domain name through their Internet access provider.[20] Most Internet access providers offer this service. Where an applicant uses an Internet access provider to register a domain name, the applicant should ensure that it can control the domain name and move it to another host or service provider if desired.

An entity seeking a domain name may also consider acquiring a pre-existing domain name. Services such as MailBank[21] or DomainSale[22] secure a large number of names which they then attempt to sell or rent to prospective customers. A variation of this approach is to purchase a pre-existing domain name directly from another person who has acquired the name for its own use. In all such cases it is important to review compliance with the domain name transfer policies of the applicable top level domain registrar.

The registrar of the applicable top level domain typically requires an applicant to assert the legal right to adopt and use the applicable second level domain name. The applicant should conduct searches of the domain names it intends to register in all applicable jurisdictions to see if the applicable second level domain name is available. In addition, searches should be performed on all applicable trademark registries of the jurisdictions where it intends to conduct business activity using the Web site. It is desirable that the applicant's trademark lawyers provide an opinion on whether or not the second level domain name may be adopted and used by the applicant as a trademark in each such jurisdiction. The applicant should also review compliance with the applicable top level domain registrar's policies. For example, the applicant may be prohibited from using objectionable or obscene words as second level domain names.[23] In

---

[20]  For example, see the domain name registry services on Yahoo! Canada's Domain Registration site. See also My Domain, at <http://www.mydomain.co.uk>, who will register domain names on the .uk top level domain and offer similar services throughout Europe.

[21]  See <http://www.mailbank.com> for the procedures offered by this company. Note that they also offer a Web site or domain hosting service as well.

[22]  See <http://www.domainsale.com> for a list of domain names for sale and the asking prices.

[23]  While a few might object to Proctor and Gamble's domain name <http://www.diarrhea.com>, sites which include profanities or obscene names are likely to offend a larger group and may be the subject of censorship efforts.

some cases certain words (such as geographic identifiers) may be reserved and not available for use as the organizational name or unique identifier portion of a domain name.

Registration of a domain name will not prevent a third party from disputing the validity of the registration. An applicant would be well advised to seek trademark protection for any distinctive second level domain name in relation to the services and transactions provided through use of the Web site and otherwise as may relate to the applicant's products or services. If the applicant's present or future business activities may occur in part in the US it would be prudent to register a US federal trademark.

A basic requirement in applying to register a domain name is that the person submitting the application should have authority to act on behalf of the entity whose name appears on the application. Where an employee registers a domain name corresponding to the name of his or her employer, the employer will be entitled to secure ownership of the name, especially where the name corresponds to the employer's trademark.[24]

Domain names are generally issued on a "first-come, first-served" basis by the registrar for each top level domain. Section 3.4 below, discusses differences between the ".ca" domain and the NSI managed generic domains and describes the different approaches that may be taken with respect to the entitlement and use of the elements of the particular domain name address.

## (a)  Registration on the Canadian Top Level Domain

The Canadian top level domain (.ca) is managed by the CA Domain Committee (CADC) and is administered by a University volunteer. An applicant who seeks to obtain a Canadian top level domain must provide the registrar with the following information:

(1) Designation of the applicable top level domain and any applicable sub-domains on which registration is sought.

---

[24]  See, for example, *MTV Networks v. Curry* 867 F. Supp. 202 (S.D. N.Y. 1994) where a former employee continued to use the domain name, which he had obtained while he was an employee, at a time when the employer did not wish to secure a domain name. The employer, MTV, was successful in using trademark law to secure control over the domain name.

The Canadian domain, ".ca", uses a hierarchical domain name system.[25] The general format of the top level of a Canadian domain name is "locality.province-or-territory.ca" (eg., www.name.toronto.on.ca). An applicant will generally not be permitted to secure a "national" domain name which contains only the ".ca" portion (i.e., www.name.ca) unless the applicant satisfies one of the following conditions: (i) it carries on business in more than one province (i.e., the applicant has offices or a substantial business presence in more than one province); (ii) it is a federally incorporated company; or (iii) it owns a registered Canadian trademark which will be used as the "name" portion of the domain name.[26]

For example, a Calgary incorporated business registering a ".ca" domain name may be assigned the domain name ending with ".ab.ca" where the Calgary business does not have offices in another province and does not own a registered Canadian trademark. The sub-domains assigned in Canada indicate provincial sub-domains and may also indicate municipal or other sub-sub-domains. For example, a Vancouver based company may be registered on the sub-sub-domain ".vcn.bc.ca".

Once an organization has secured a domain name it can create and administer further sub-domain names.[27]

(2) The name that the applicant is seeking to register as the second level domain, i.e., "name.ca". This, together with the top level domain, must contain no more than 24 characters. The applicant may use numbers, letters and a hyphen in the name.

---

[25]  Based on the CCITT X.500 directory naming system, involving a multilevel tree structure.

[26]  Provincial and Territorial names are subordinate to the national domain. Municipal and other locality names are subordinate to the Provincial and Territorial names. Further local organization names and individual names are subordinate to the Municipal and other locality names.

[27]  In Gahtan, "A Site By Any Other Name: Domain Name Issues for Canadian Organizations", Jan. 1997 at <http://www.gahtan.com/alan/articles/> the author provides an example of such use through the designation of a local Toronto news operation of CBC under its national (.ca) top level domain <cbc.ca> at the address <news.toronto.cbc.ca>.

(3) The name and a physical address of the organization for which the domain is being established.

(4) The date that the domain will be operational.

(5) An administrative contact including the e-mail address, organization and name of the individual who can address policy issues regarding the domain. This is the person who approves and is responsible for the application.

(6) A technical contact including the e-mail address, organization and name of the individual who can address technical problems and issues regarding the domain.

(7) The addresses of two independent servers for translating names to addresses for hosts in the domain.[28] These servers must respond to DNS queries before an application is submitted to the CADC.

(8) A description of the organization for whom the domain is registered. The trademark position of the organization should be considered in completing this information.

The Canadian top level domain policy requires the applicant to complete an electronic form requesting the domain name.[29] Priority to adoption and use of a domain name on the ".ca" top level domain is based on the "first come, first served" principle.

Canadian businesses need not secure an address on the Canadian domain. Since the Internet is worldwide, many Canadian businesses secure addresses on the generic top level domains such as the ".com", ".net", or other such generic top level domains. Similarly, a Canadian business could acquire a domain name on one of the other geographic top level domains. See section 3.7 for a discussion of new developments concerning domain names.

---

[28]  Many Internet Service or Internet Access Providers provide this service. A domain name owner should consider the solvency of any service provider so as to avoid loss of the domain name as a result of loss of the DNS servers of the service provider. See also the services provided by MailBank at <http://www.mailbank.com>.

[29]  The form may be found at <ftp://ftp.cdnnet.ca/ca-domain/application-form>.

## (b) Registration on the InterNIC/NSI Managed Top Level Domains

The most popular top level domain for business Web sites in recent years is the generic ".com" domain.[30] The present registrar of the ".com" domain is the InterNIC operated by Network Solutions, Inc. (NSI). Other top level domains managed by NSI include ".net", ".gov", ".edu" and ".org".

The NSI requires the applicant to complete an electronic form to request a domain name. Registration of a domain name on the top level domains managed by NSI is based on the "first come, first served" principle. A search facility is available to review existing domain names registered on top level domains managed by NSI.[31]

An application for use of a domain name on the ".com" or other NSI managed top level domain must provide information similar to that requested for CADC administered domain names.[32]

The applicant must state the applicable top level domain on which registration is sought, eg., .com, .net, etc. NSI will register almost any domain name provided the exact domain name has not already been registered on the applicable top level domain (i.e., X42.com can be registered even if X42.net has already been registered).

Unlike the ".ca" domain there are no sub-domains in the generic top level domains (although once a domain name is registered, the registrant is free to create its own sub-domains). Many businesses prefer the NSI domain names over geographical domain names since NSI domain names have a more global look and feel.

The cost of obtaining a domain name from NSI is currently US$100 which covers the first two years of use.[33] Maintenance of

---

[30]   It is not clear if the ".com" address will continue to be so popular in the future. Also the proposed creation of new generic top level domains and the authorization of many new top level domain registries may diminish the appeal of the ".com" top level domain. See section 3.7 for more details on these proposed developments.

[31]   See <http://rs.internic.net> and the WHOIS service for this search capability.

[32]   The various forms used by the InterNIC/NSI are found at <http://rs.internic.net>.

[33]   A class action suit has been filed against NSI alleging that charging the new fees and essentially making a profit was performed without statutory authority. See *Thomas, MyHouse Communications, et al v. Network Solutions, Inc. and the National Science*

the registration each subsequent year will cost the applicant US$50.[34] As stated previously, most businesses will look to their Internet access provider to secure their domain names and an additional administrative fee may be payable for such service.

## 3.4 DIFFERENCES BETWEEN NSI AND CADC REGISTRATIONS

Unlike the ".ca" domain, the generic top level domains managed by NSI do not contain geographical identifiers. Many businesses like the appearance of a top level domain without any geographic connection or association.

An advantage of the hierarchical domain names used in the CADC system is that there is less likelihood of confusion between different registered domain name users. A disadvantage of this system arises when a business who has registered on one domain expands its business, moves to another region or changes the place of its incorporation. This may necessitate the desire or need to change its domain name which will likely result in disruption for the business' customers.

It should be noted that unlike NSI, CADC does not presently charge a fee to register domain names in the .ca domain.

An applicant on the CADC top level domain is only entitled to register one domain name per organization.[35] NSI will permit multiple registrations by each applicant.

A key distinction between CADC and NSI registrations is the manner in which the two registrars manage domain name disputes. In both cases the registrars require the applicant to assume responsibility for its entitlement to use the domain name. The domain name dispute policies of the two registrars are otherwise quite different. CADC will not interfere with an existing domain name unless ordered to do so

---

*Foundation* DC 97-Civ.-2412, Complaint filed Nov. 1997.

[34]   NSI's policy suggests that failure to pay the renewal fee within the applicable time frame and in the form required by NSI will result in loss of the domain name.

[35]   There are exceptions for two domain names in the case of bilingual names (French and English) and also in the case where a domain name user is making a transition to the use of another domain name.

by a court. NSI has a controversial domain name dispute policy which may include an interim "on hold" remedy. This remedy may be obtained by a prior trademark registrant without any requirement to show any legal wrongdoing by the existing domain name owner. The CADC and NSI domain name dispute policies are discussed further in section 3.5 below.

Selection of an NSI top level domain means that the domain name will be subject to US legal principles, even if the Canadian business does not carry on business in the US, because NSI, at least, will be subject to US trademark law. A Canadian business that is concerned about becoming subject to the anti-dilution provisions of US trademark law may wish to obtain a geographic top level domain, such as ".ca".

## 3.5  NSI AND CADC DISPUTE POLICIES

### (a)  Canadian Top Level Domain Name Dispute Policy

CADC's policy regarding rights to domain names provides that:

> "It is your responsibility to ensure that you have the right to use the name you have chosen. Registering a domain name does not confer any legal rights to that name; you should consider registering your trademark if you have not already done so. Any disputes between the parties over the rights to use a particular name are to be settled between the contending parties using normal legal methods."[36]

The Canadian domain name information encourages all domain name applicants to secure trademark registration for the unique second level domain. Unlike NSI, the CADC policy recognizes only those trademarks that are registered in Canada for the purposes of securing registration on the top level domain.

The CADC will not typically intervene in any dispute concerning a domain name and will respect any Canadian court order in relation to such a dispute. The ".ca" top level domain has operated well and without the controversy and litigation that has accompanied the

---

[36]    See the ".ca" domain application policy at <ftp://ftp.cdnnet.ca/ca-domain>.

generic top level domains managed by NSI.[37] This is due in part to the geographic hierarchical nature of the CADC system which tends to decrease the likelihood of confusion, the lower demand for the ".ca" top level domain addresses and the stricter registration requirements.

### (b)  InterNIC/NSI Top Level Domain Name Dispute Policy

The NSI has attempted to provide a quick and inexpensive remedy to resolve domain name disputes by placing the disputed domain name "on hold" in certain circumstances, thereby effectively denying anyone the use of the disputed domain name. This aspect of NSI's policy has been very contentious. In other respects the NSI policy seeks to have the parties resolve their dispute and then advise NSI on the resolution. In many cases, however, a party to a domain name dispute will sue NSI itself due to NSI's "on hold" remedy or the fact that NSI had allocated a domain name to a party other than the complainant.

The greatest number of domain name problems seem to have arisen in respect of the ".com" domain. This appears to be because of the popularity of the ".com" top level domain for registration by many businesses. The various domain name policies of NSI have also contributed to the disputes.

NSI's domain dispute policy has undergone several revisions. The first policy reflected a "first come, first served" principle, with NSI disclaiming any responsibility for policing trademarks. That policy required applicants to represent that their domain name did not infringe on a registered federal trademark.

Many businesses did not initially appreciate the increasing importance of the Internet and were dismayed, in many instances, that

---

[37]    In a Canadian case involving a domain name, *Peinet Inc. v. O'Brien* (1995) 61 C.P.R. (3d) 334, 40 C.P.C. (3d) 58, 130 Nfld. & P.E.I.R. 313, 405 A.P.R. 313, (P.E.I. T.D.). [In Chambers], a passing off action was brought to preclude use of "pei.net" as a domain name as the plaintiff alleged the domain name was confusing with its corporate name. The court found the plaintiff did not meet the requirements for injunctive relief. One of the factors was the defendant's evidence showing lack of confusion and the fact that the domain name was all lower case and separated by a period (i.e., pei.net) where the corporate name was "Peinet". Canadian and US law on trademark confusion is discussed in more detail in Chapter 5.

another company had already registered a ".com" domain name using the businesses' registered trademarks. The businesses who were late in seeking domain name registrations included larger companies that were not active in the computer industry or otherwise did not appreciate the importance of the Internet. In some cases, "name nappers" registered domain names containing elements that were identical or substantially similar to the trademarks or business names of major businesses.[38] NSI came under pressure by trademark owners to change its domain name policy to favour applicants who owned registered trademarks. Many trademark registrants asserted that NSI was liable for registering domain names that allegedly infringed the registered marks.[39]

On November 23, 1995 NSI changed its domain name policy. The revised policy provided that if a trademark owner wrote a letter alleging infringement of its registered trademark, NSI would send the letter to the domain registrant stating that NSI would suspend the domain name in thirty days unless the domain name registrant was able to supply a copy of a trademark registration.[40] Under the revised policy NSI suspended hundreds of domain names. However, this did not solve the problem and new disputes continued to arise.

In a high profile case, a New Mexico computer company, Roadrunner Computer Systems, Inc.,[41] had registered <http://www.roadrunner.com> as its domain name in 1994 under the original "first come, first served" domain name policy. The

---

[38]  See, for example, *Intermatic Inc. v. Toeppen*, (1996) 40 U.S.P.Q. 1412 (Illinois D.C.).

[39]  See, for example, the complaint filed in *Academy of Motion Picture Arts and Sciences v. Network Solutions, Inc.* (Central District of California, complaint filed August 26, 1997). In that case it was alleged that NSI knowingly assisted a number of John Doe defendants to either dilute or infringe the plaintiff's rights under its "Oscar" and "Academy Award" trademarks by permitting the defendants to acquire domain names including the plaintiff's trademarks or variations of them as second level domain names.

[40]  The policy ignored the fact that the prior domain name registrant might have existing trademark rights, including rights of common law, and focused exclusively on whether there was a registration for a trademark. Some domain name registrants who might wish to secure such a registration quickly would obtain a registration in a jurisdiction, such as Tunisia, where no substantial internal or external review is carried out. For more details on this tactic see the comments on the Roadrunner case at the Oppendahl site <http://www.patents.com>.

[41]  The suit filed is E.D. Va. 96-Civ-413-A.

roadrunner is the state bird of New Mexico. Much later, Warner Bros. sought to stop use of that domain name based on its ownership of a federally registered trademark for "Roadrunner" for "toys, namely, plush dolls, and halloween costumes and masks." Observers of the dispute had difficulty seeing any likelihood of confusion between the provision of communication services and the toys. Apparently, Warner Bros. sought to take advantage of the NSI domain name policy since it was unlikely that Warner Bros. would succeed in a trademark based action. As a result of Warner Bros.'s objection, Roadrunner Computer Systems was required to provide to NSI a certified copy of a registered trademark in order to maintain its right to use the domain name. In response to NSI's request, Roadrunner Computer Systems registered a Tunisian trademark and provided proof of the trademark registration to NSI. NSI refused to accept the Tunisian trademark on the basis that Roadrunner Computer Systems did not respond within the 30 day grace period. Roadrunner sued, alleging, among other things, that:

- NSI had a public duty to implement its policies in an even-handed manner since NSI is a contractor of a public institution;

- It is an implied term of the contract between NSI and a domain name registrant that NSI will not arbitrarily interfere with the registrant's right to make continued use of the domain name; and

- NSI would be liable for any damages resulting to Roadrunner if its access to its domain name was suspended.

The case was finally settled and Roadrunner was permitted to continue using its domain name. Numerous similar lawsuits were filed in cases of such alleged reverse name napping.[42]

---

[42] See, for example, *Network Solutions, Inc. v. Clue Computing, Inc.* 41 U.S. P.Q. 2D 1062 (D. Col. 1996) where Hasbro had used NSI's domain name policy to assert a right to prevent a computer company from using a domain name that was the same as the name of a game covered by its registered trademark; *Data Concepts Inc. v. Network Solutions, Inc.* M.D. Tenn 96-civ-429 where Digital Consulting Inc. used NSI's domain name policy to assert rights to Data Concepts Inc.'s dci.com domain name based on its trademark registration of DCI for one class of products; *Giacalone v. Network Solutions, Inc.* N.D. 96-Civ-20434 where TY, Inc. used NSI's domain name policy to assert rights to Giacalone's ty.com domain name based on its trademark registration of TY for one class of products; and *Dynamic Information Systems Corp. v. Network Solutions, Inc.*, D. Col. 96-Civ-1551, where Distributor Information Systems Corp. used NSI's domain name policy to assert

The main complaint made about NSI's domain name dispute policy was that it could be used by a trademark registrant to require that a domain name be put on hold which would have a similar effect as obtaining an interlocutory injunction. Such a remedy could be obtained merely by claiming trademark rights without the need for legal process to substantiate the claim alleged by the trademark owner. Since a domain name registrant could very well have legitimate interests in the domain name, some of the parties affected by NSI's policy sued NSI seeking injunctive relief. The issue was stated by Judge Dean Pregerson as follows:

"The Court begins with the observation that, unlike a patent or copyright, a trademark does not confer on its owner any rights in gross or at large... Therefore, the law does not *per se* prohibit the use of trademarks or service marks as domain names. Rather, the law prohibits only uses that infringe or dilute a trademark, service mark or owner's mark."[43]

NSI changed its domain name policy again in September 1996.[44] Under that version, the owner of a registered trademark is entitled to prevent the use of an identical domain name unless the domain name owner has used the domain name before the date of first use or effective date of the conflicting trademark; the domain name owner can provide evidence of its ownership of an identical federally registered trademark; or the domain name owner commences a lawsuit to resolve rights to the disputed domain name.

If a complaint is filed with NSI,[45] NSI will send out an "on hold" letter.[46] That letter advises the domain name owner of the complaint

---

rights to Dynamic Information Systems Corp.'s disc.com domain name based on its trademark registration of DISC for one class of product.

[43]  See *Lockheed Martin Corporation v. Network Solutions Inc.*, (1997) Decision N. CV 96-7438 D.D.P., March 19, 1997, California Central District Court. The dispute was over a domain name involving the word "Skunk Works" for which Lockheed had a registered trademark. The full decision is found at <http://www.patents.com/skunk/mar19.sht>.

[44]  See NSI's domain name policy, Revision 02, effective as of September 9, 1996 at <http://rs.internic.net/domain-info/internic-domain-6.html>.

[45]  The complainant must provide NSI with a copy of the demand letter sent to the domain name owner and a certified copy of a federally registered trademark or service mark for a name that is virtually identical to the second level domain name.

[46]  Although NSI's policy is permissive and does not require action by NSI, NSI usually does respond to a complaint by sending out the "on hold" letter.

and provides a copy of the NSI domain name policy, the complaint letter and a copy of the registered trademark.

The domain name owner is given a number of choices on how to respond to the complaint. To continue using the domain name, within 30 days of receipt of the "on hold" letter from NSI, the owner must: (i) provide NSI with a certified copy of a federally registered trademark, identical to the second level domain being used, owned by the domain name owner, for which registration was made before first notification of any dispute over the domain name; or (ii) commence an action in any court of competent jurisdiction[47] and provide a file-stamped copy of the Complaint to NSI before the name goes "on hold". In the latter case NSI will not place the domain name "on hold" but will abide by any subsequent court order provided that in the interim the domain name is placed into the registry of the court.

NSI's domain name dispute policy also provides such options as withdrawing the domain name or transferring it to the complainant. A further option is that the domain name owner can select a new domain name and maintain the new and old names simultaneously for 90 days. After that period the old domain name is put "on hold" and will not be usable by anyone until the parties resolve the dispute. If the domain name owner does not respond setting out what option it wishes to select within 30 days of receipt of the NSI "on hold" letter, or if the owner is unable to comply with any requirements set out by NSI, then its domain name is suspended.

The "on hold" remedy still lacks legal process or legal review to establish the rights of the trademark registrant. NSI's current policy continues to ignore legitimate trademark rights that a domain name registrant may have, even if that party failed to secure a trademark registration, and forces the domain name owner to bring legal action against the complainant. On the other hand, the policy is more helpful

---

[47]    NSI has recognized actions filed in the US and the English courts. It appears that a case properly brought in the Canadian courts may be recognized by NSI provided a contrary decision is not made by a US court.

in addressing situations where a party intentionally uses another's trademark as part of its domain name.[48]

NSI's policy has created the situation of "reverse hijacking" where a trademark registrant can use the NSI policy to "expropriate" what may be the legitimate use of a domain name by a prior domain name registrant. NSI's policy also ignores the basic principle of trademark law that more than one entity may properly and lawfully use the same trademark so long as the trademarks are used for different products or services and do not create a likelihood of confusion.

NSI has suspended a large number of domain names under this policy. The existing domain name owner is limited in its options upon receiving such a notice from NSI, since an owner that lacks a trademark registration only has the choice of suing the complainant or losing its use of the domain name.[49] Not satisfied with either of these choices, many prior domain name owners have chosen to sue NSI and have sought injunctive relief to prevent loss of the domain name. Where a domain name owner had secured a trademark registration prior to the dispute arising, the owner has often been able to retain the use of its domain name.[50] In some cases, settlement agreements have preserved the rights of the prior domain name owners to use the domain name.[51]

NSI updated its domain name dispute policy on February 25, 1998. The new policy clarifies that NSI neither arbitrates nor resolves domain name disputes but it will follow its administrative policies when it receives notification that a trademark owner's rights are being violated by an existing domain name registration. The revised policy is more specific as to what NSI will do when it encounters a dispute.

---

[48]   See, for example, the site describing Microsoft Corporation's efforts to prevent use of "micr0soft" as a second level domain name by zero micro software at <http://www.micr0soft.paranoia.com>.

[49]   See the discussion on remedies for domain name cases in Oppendahl, "Remedies in Domain Name Lawsuits: How is a domain name like a cow?", 15 John Marshall J. of *Computer & Information Law* 437 (1997).

[50]   See, for example, the description of the dispute between Esquire magazine and the Esqwire legal information service at <http:www.esqwire.com>. A settlement ultimately provides for continued use of Esqwire.com as a domain name.

[51]   See the Roadrunner Computer Systems case for an example of this approach. <http:www.patents.com>.

Depending on the circumstances, NSI may suspend, transfer, revoke or modify a disputed domain name registration.[52]

## 3.6   PROTECTING A DOMAIN NAME

A business seeking to establish itself on the Internet should ensure compliance with the applicable registrar's domain name policy. Being required to change a domain name (and therefore the address of one's Web site and all associated e-mail addresses) is very disruptive. As a result the business should seek to secure a registered trademark in the applicable jurisdictions for the unique elements used in its second level domain.

Businesses wishing to use (or continue to use) the ".com" top level domain should secure a US or other registered trademark. The importance of ensuring the continued right to use the domain name should make this an easy business decision.[53] The United States Patent and Trademark Office has reported a substantial increase in the number of applications for trademarks as domain names as a result of NSI's domain name dispute policy.

Where the continued use of a domain name is challenged by another party, the domain name owner should review its right in the context of trademark and intellectual property law and the domain name policies of the applicable registrar. In some cases the domain name holder should use the domain name registrar's policy to resolve the dispute.

In some circumstances, the best response to such a challenge may be to bring an action in the applicable court for infringement of the domain name owner's trademark rights. In such a case, the owner may seek an order to expunge or limit the complainant's trademark

---

[52]   See <ftp://rs.internic.net/policy/nic-rev03.txt>.

[53]   NSI had released public statements suggesting that no trademark registrations were necessary to obtain and use a domain name. However, while such advice may have been technically correct, reliance on such statements could result in loss of the domain name under NSI's domain name dispute policy. These statements by NSI only further angered early domain name registrants when later faced by narrow trademark registration claims used by owners of such trademarks.

registration.[54] Obviously such a suit must be based on sound trademark rights. In certain cases where the current domain name holder does not own a registered trademark, the business could consider using the so-called "Tunisian gambit" if it acts quickly enough.[55]

In other cases and particularly in cases of "reverse name napping," the appropriate course of action, given the NSI domain name dispute policy, may be to sue NSI over the alleged discriminatory basis[56] of its domain name policies.[57] Another alternative may be to assert that the conduct of the plaintiff amounts to trademark misuse, thereby denying the trademark owner relief.[58] In an extreme case of misuse

---

[54] See Chapter 5 for more information on the trademark law aspects of use of a domain name. Note also that NSI's policy requires legal action to be brought in a court of competent jurisdiction. A proper case brought in a Canadian court may satisfy this requirement (e.g., if the action were brought based on a claim of infringement of a Canadian trademark).

[55] Since the NSI policy acknowledges prior trademark registrations, if the domain name owner receives early informal notice of the likely challenge then the domain name owner might consider quickly securing a trademark registration in a jurisdiction, such as Tunisia, where no substantial internal or external review is carried out. For more details on this tactic see the comments on the Roadrunner case at the Oppendahl site <http:// www.patents.com>.

[56] In *Network Solutions, Inc. v. Clue Computing, Inc.* 41 U.S. P.Q. 2D 1062 (D. Col. 1996) the judge found NSI "was not free from blame in causing the controversy" and saw its position akin to "a wrongdoer with respect to the subject matter of the suit." This was the case where Hasbro had used NSI's domain name policy to assert a right to prevent a computer company from using a domain name that was the same as a game covered by Hasbro's registered trademark.

[57] See, for example, this tactic used in *Roadrunner Computer Systems, Inc. v. Network Solutions, Inc.* E.D. Va. 96-Civ-413-A; *Network Solutions, Inc. v. Clue Computing, Inc.* 41 U.S. P.Q. 2D 1062 (D. Col. 1996); *Data Concepts Inc. v. Network Solutions, Inc.* M.D. Tenn 96-Civ-429; *Giacalone v. Network Solutions, Inc.* N.D. 96-Civ-20434; and *Dynamic Information Systems Corp. v. Network Solutions, Inc.*, D. Col. 96-Civ-1551. In each of these cases, a party with a narrow federal trademark registration sought to use the NSI domain name dispute policy to acquire the prior domain name owner's domain name. In the above cases, it is questionable whether or not there was any real trademark basis for the attack on the use of the domain name.

[58] A plaintiff may be denied relief in a trademark action if the plaintiff's conduct results in a violation of antitrust laws: see for example, *Carl Zeiss Stiftung v. V.E.B. Carl Zeiss*, Jena 298 F. Supp. 1309 (S.D. N.Y. 1969). A plaintiff may also be denied relief based on an equitable form of trademark misuse: see for example, *United States Jaycees v. Cedar Rapid Jaycees*, 614 F. Supp. 515 (N.D. Iowa 1985) where the Court found that a trademark owner dealing in an unjust manner with the defendant in the very transaction upon which the cause of action was based may be denied relief. It has been suggested this doctrine has applicability to cases of reverse name napping: Stephen J. Davidson, Nicole A. English, "Trademark Misuse: Applying the Trademark Misuse Doctrine to Domain Name Disputes".

the trademark owner may risk cancellation of its registered trademark.[59] If successful the domain name owner might also seek costs of the action and/or legal fees.[60]

When a claim is made by a prior trademark registrant, the domain name owner might also challenge the basis for transferring the domain name to the trademark owner. Nothing in NSI's policy permits the trademark owner to acquire the domain name. There does not appear to be provision for this type of relief under the *Lanham Act* or the *Federal Trademark Dilution Act*[61] nor, in Canada, under the *TradeMarks Act*.[62] Nonetheless courts have routinely awarded this form of relief to a successful trademark registrant without addressing the issue of the authority for granting such a remedy. Perhaps this matter will be examined more critically if a domain name owner takes issue with such a remedy.

The best approach for a business that wishes to protect its continued use of its domain name is to secure registration of trademarks in applicable jurisdictions where substantial activity concerning the Web site is likely to occur, and most importantly, in the jurisdictions applicable to the relevant registrar under which the top level domain was issued.

---

See <http://www.leonard.com>.

[59] See *Lanham Act* , Section 37, providing for the ability of a court to cancel a trademark registration. In *Phi Delta Theta Fraternity v. J.A. Buchroeder & Co.*, 251 F. Supp. 968 (W.D. Mo. 1966) the Court held that trademark misuse justified cancellation of a trademark registration.

[60] In exceptional cases a court can award costs and legal fees to the prevailing party. See also Section 35, *Lanham Act*, 15 U.S.C. S. 167; 1117(a) and *General Motors Corp. v. Cadillac Marine & Boat Co.*, 226 F. Supp. 716 (W.D. Mich. 1964).

[61] For a critical analysis of the US statutory provisions and cases awarding this type of relief see Oppendahl, "Remedies in Domain Name Lawsuits: How is a domain name like a cow?" 15 John Marshall J. of *Computer & Information Law* 437 (1997).

[62] Section 53.2, *Trade-Marks Act*, does provide for an order of delivery involving "other dispositions of any offending wares, packages, labels and advertising material and of any dies used in connection therewith." All of the references are to tangible goods. At best, a domain name, merely an address, may facilitate advertising if used as the address of a Web site, but it is questionable whether a domain name would constitute "advertising materials."

## 3.7  NEW DEVELOPMENTS

### (a)  The Ad Hoc Committee

A number of parties have called for an end to NSI's monopoly over registration of generic top level domains and the establishment of a more competitive system of new registries for generic top level domains.[63] The Ad Hoc Committee proposed that there will be new generic top level domains such as: ".arts" for cultural and similar sites; ".firm" for businesses; ".info" for information services; ".nom" for individuals; ".rec" for recreational and similar activities; ".shop" (or ".store") for sites which sell products; and ".web" for sites involved with organization of the world wide web.

The Ad Hoc Committee also proposed a new domain name dispute policy which would provide for either an administrative, mediation or arbitration process for resolving domain name challenge process. It is proposed that a domain name applicant can choose to agree to the mediation approach at the time of application for the domain name. If the mediation does not resolve the issue within thirty days then the complainant has the option (but not the obligation) to request the dispute move to arbitration.[64] Domain name applicants will need to decide in advance whether or not to commit to arbitration as it would be bound to the arbitration if, upon registration, it chose to participate in this process, where the complainant is not so bound.

Another dispute resolution approach provides for an administrative domain name challenge process. Administrative Domain Name Challenge Panels would hear complaints instituted by any interested party. This formal process would be conducted online and would not preclude recourse to any court of competent jurisdiction. The procedural rules that would have to be followed by these

---

[63]  See the report of the Ad Hoc Committee formed by the Internet Society, the IANA and others (the "Ad Hoc Committee") at <http://www.iahc.org/>.

[64]  The arbitration would be a binding process. The WIPO Centre would provide assistance with the choice of mediation or arbitration. It appears that the national or regional law applicable to the parties will be used for the arbitration process.

Administrative Domain Name Challenge Panels seek to resolve many of the problems with NSI's domain name policies.[65]

Assuming that these new policies become effective, it is unclear what impact they will have on existing domain names registered on the NSI top level domains. In addition, there are likely to be additional issues during the transition to new generic top level domain names.

Other issues for businesses to consider include securing multiple registrations under all applicable top level domains in order to avoid the prospect of a confusing use by a third party. For example, a software company selling entertainment or game software from its Web site might seek registrations in each of the following new top level domains: ".arts" for the cultural or entertainment aspects of the site or products; ".firm" because the software company is a business; ".info" for information services provided by the software company; ".rec" for the recreational and entertainment aspects of the site; and ".shop" because the site sells products. As a result, it remains to be seen whether or not the establishment of additional generic top level domains will solve any of the existing problems or merely create new ones.

While it is reported that the National Science Foundation will not renew its contract with NSI to provide generic top level domain name registry services, NSI has advised it will continue to register domain names after expiry of its exclusive arrangement. As a result, businesses with domain names registered on top level domains managed by NSI will need to watch developments closely and decide whether or not any change might be desired.

## (b)  US Government

On January 30, 1998, the US Department of Commerce released a discussion paper called *A Proposal to Improve Technical Management of Internet Names and Addresses* (the "Green

---

[65]    For example, the new policy would recognize that a challenger and prior domain name registrant may have the same or similar alphanumeric text (distinctive element) as a portion of the domain name.

Paper").[66] The Green Paper proposes to reform the current operation of the domain name system on the Internet.

As NSI's five-year agreement for management of the gTLDs comes to an end, the Department of Commerce has proposed the creation of a new not-for-profit corporation to oversee and coordinate the domain name system. The Green Paper proposes that the system for registering second-level domain names (the registrar function) and the management of the TLD registries (the management function) would be split up and made competitive.

The Department of Commerce recognizes that there is disagreement about who should decide when a new-level domain can be added and how the decision should be made. Some Internet stakeholders believe that anyone should be able to create a new TLD. Others believe that rapid growth in the number of TLDs would increase confusion and the complexity of the system, and would make it much more difficult for trademark holders to protect their trademarks if they had to police a large number of TLDs. The Green Paper proposes the addition of up to five new TLDs, which should be large enough to create competition among registries (with each TLD being administered by a separate competing registry) but not so large as to destabilize the system.

Any entity would be permitted to provide registrar services so long as it meets basic technical, managerial and site requirements. Registrars would be allowed to register clients into any TLD for which the client satisfies the eligibility rules, if any.

The Department of Commerce recognizes the potential for conflict between domain name holders and trademark holders. The Green Paper proposes the implementation of better tools for searching domain name databases and the possible use of online dispute resolution mechanisms. However, it does not propose to establish a trademark dispute resolution process at this time. Instead, a study would be undertaken on the effects of adding new TLDs and related dispute resolution procedures on trademark and intellectual property right holders.

---

[66]    The offical version was published in the Federal Register on February 18, 1998 <http://www.ntia.doc.gov>.

Soon after their publication, the US proposals came under criticism from the European Union and the government of Australia who were concerned that, according to the plan, too much control of the Internet was concentrated in the United States.

More than 650 comments were received in respect to the Green Paper and as such, meetings were held with representatives of key players in the domain name debate. On June 5, 1998, the US Department of Commerce released a policy statement known as the White Paper.[67] The White Paper builds on the proposals set in the Green Paper and reiterates the Green Paper's goal of creating a new, private, non-profit US-based corporation to assume responsibility for coordinating specific domain-name system functions. It is intended that the new corporation would assume operational responsibility by October 1998.

The White Paper departs from the Green Paper's proposal for the establishment, in the short term, of five new gTLDs and defers that decision to the new corporation. The White Paper also calls for greater involvement from the World Intellectual Property Organization in the development of the domain name dispute resolution processes.

## (c) CADC

Reforms of the Canadian domain name system may also be on the horizon. The Canadian Domain Name Consultative Committee (CDNCC) has issued a proposal to initiate changes to registrations under the ".ca" TLD (the "proposal").[68] Proposed changes from the current system include:

- removal of limits on the number of names that may be registered

- imposition of registration fees

- registration of names on a "first come, first served" basis (i.e., the domain name would no longer need to correspond to a company's name or trademark).

---

[67] See <http://www.ntia.doc.gov/>.

[68] "Public Consultation on the Administration of the Canadian Internet Domain Name .ca by The Canadian Domain Name Consultative Committee," January 25, 1998.

These proposed changes may have a significant impact on Canadian businesses. Under the revised system it will be possible for an entity to register a domain name corresponding to the business name of another entity if that entity has not already registered such name. This may lead to the same widespread pirating of domain names that has occurred under the gTLDs. Disputes would then be settled according to established trademark principles rather than giving a preference to holders of registered trademarks as is done under NSI's domain name dispute policy.

Finally, the proposal reminds Canadian entities that registration in a foreign registry (of domain names such as ".com") will probably be governed by that foreign country's legal system in the event a dispute arises concerning the use of the domain name. An owner of a US trademark in respect of a particular domain name may therefore be able to assert priority over a Canadian user who lacks trademark rights in the US.

To avoid this situation and to ensure Canadians that the domain names they register are subject to Canadian law, the CDNCC recommends that Canadian Internet users register their domain names under the ".ca" TLD.

# 4

# Developing a Web Site

## 4.1 ACQUIRING RIGHTS TO WEB SITE CONTENT

A Web site may contain a wide variety of creative content. This can include textual material, graphics, pictures, audio clips, Java and Active-X programs[1] and multimedia files. A Web site can also act as the front-end to a database of other information (for instance, a directory or company catalogue). Before placing any such content on a Web site, an organization must ensure that it owns the intellectual property rights to such material or that it has obtained all necessary rights and releases from the holders.

For certain types of work (i.e., musical works), the necessary rights may be obtained through a licence from the appropriate collective society. For example, SOCAN is the Canadian collective society for performing rights in dramatico-musical or musical works. For other works, information as to ownership, authorship and any applicable assignment or licensing may be difficult to obtain because registration is not mandatory for such works to qualify for copyright protection. Nevertheless, since copyright legislation in Canada and the US permits the registration of copyright in works and of assignments of copyrights, it is advisable to conduct searches in the Copyright Offices in both countries.

In some cases, rights to copyrighted material may have been granted for a limited purpose or for use only in a particular jurisdiction. Placing such material on a Web site with global access may result in infringement.

---

[1] Java and Active-X programs are software programs which can be embedded into a Web page and are executed on the computer which retrieves the particular Web page.

Obtaining copyright permissions, and where appropriate, publicity releases, is a commonly accepted requirement in the entertainment industry. It has also become an accepted practice in the production of CD-ROMs and multimedia titles. However, the requirements are still in the process of gaining acceptance in the Web publishing industry.

In some cases, a single creative element may require clearance of different rights from different parties. For instance, use on a commercial Web site of a photograph of a well-known skating professional may require copyright permission from the photographer and a separate publicity release from the individual who is photographed.

Use of a musical work on a Web site also often requires obtaining multiple permissions from the composer and author of the lyrics (although in most cases, both parties would have assigned their rights to a publishing company which, in turn, may have assigned the rights to one or more copyright collective). A consent for reproduction may also have to be obtained from the owner of the master copy of the song's recording (usually the record company). As well, where a sound recording is performed in public or is communicated to the public by telecommunication, the maker and performer of such sound recording are entitled to remuneration.

If the musical clip is to be synchronized with a visual display to produce a multimedia work then separate "synchronization rights" must also be obtained. In the case of a film clip or multimedia work, additional consents may be required from the individuals who appear in the work. Although consents may have been obtained by the film producer, such consents may be restricted to use of the actor's persona in the film but not necessarily in other types of works.

Multiple clearances may be required even for textual works. For instance, the author of an original literary work may have used characters that may be protected under trademark law. Many jurisdictions also provide different types of protection for privacy rights. An article about a well-known person could be subject to a claim for invasion of privacy.

In Canada, if the work is to be modified or combined with other types of content, or if the author of any part of the work is not to be identified, then a waiver of "moral rights" in the work should also be obtained from the author or creator.

The foregoing issues are discussed in more detail in Chapter 5.

## 4.2 NEGOTIATING A LICENCE AGREEMENT FOR WEB SITE CONTENT

The use of creative elements owned by a third party will typically involve the grant of a licence to cover the intended use of the material on the Web site. The licence grant should be broad enough to include the various types of rights that will be required for online use of the material. These may include the right to reproduce the work, to create derivative works, to perform the work in public and/or to communicate the work to the public by telecommunication, and where the work is to be distributed in the US or another country which recognizes a separate right of distribution, to distribute the work.

The licence agreement should include the following provisions:

(1)  A full description of the work being licensed;

(2)  An outline of the intended uses of the work: these uses should cover all activities required to utilize the work on a Web site that may involve the exercise of rights granted under copyright or other law. These activities may include: digitization of the work, conversion or translation of the work from one format to another or from one language to another, reproduction or modification of the work and combination or synchronization of the work with other works. The licence grant should also cover other activities that may be involved in the creation and maintenance of the Web site (such as the creation of archival or backup copies of the work on the Web server), and any planned promotional activities, such as use of portions of the works in advertisements in various media and in demonstration copies of the Web site (which may be distributed on a diskette or in a CD-ROM collection of Web sites).

The licence should also set out the intended uses of the work arising from access to the Web site by visitors. These activities would include reproduction of the work so that it may be viewed by visitors on their Web browser. They may also include the making of copies of the work in internal memory and/or hard disk memory of users' computers, and the making of intermediate copies in routers and gateways utilized in the Internet connection between the Web site and each individual visitor's computer. The licence grant should also set out whether Web visitors are permitted to print copies of the work and if so, what restrictions may be applicable;

(3) Geographical scope of licence: In the case of material to be used on the Web, the geographical scope of the licence must be worldwide unless technical measures are to be implemented to restrict access to persons located in certain jurisdictions;

(4) Term of the licence: in many cases, the licensee will wish to obtain a licence either in perpetuity or so long as the underlying intellectual property rights might subsist.

(5) Representations and warranties to be provided by the licensor, including representations and warranties that:

- the licensor is the owner of all rights to the work or such rights as are necessary to grant the licence;

- the licensor has secured all necessary licences, consents, permissions and releases for use of all components or elements of the work, including all copyrights, trademarks, names, logos and likenesses contained in the work;

- there are no claims outstanding or threatened that would restrict or interfere with the exercise by the licensee of the above-mentioned rights in the work;

- the use of the works as permitted under the licence does not infringe any rights of another party, and specifically does not:

— constitute an infringement of any copyright, trademark or other intellectual property or proprietary right of any person;

— constitute a defamation, or a violation of any right of privacy or publicity of any person;

— result in a breach of any moral right of any person including the right of integrity or the right to be identified as the author or creator of the work, or any similar right;

- the licensor has complied with all legislation, regulations and rules regarding the creation, ownership and licensing of the work;

- the work is not obscene or otherwise in violation of any law of any jurisdiction;[2]

- the work is and will remain accurate;

(6) an indemnity from the licensor for any payments to be made to any third parties or for any damages and expenses incurred by the licensee due to breach of the warranties set forth above or due to any default under the agreement including the failure of the licensor to obtain the necessary consents; and

(7) a clause setting out the law which is to govern the interpretation of the agreement and the competent courts in which any action, claim or dispute arising out of the agreement is to be tried. This is particularly important when dealing with works of authors from foreign jurisdictions which may have a different legal regime in certain matters, such as moral rights. In most civil law countries, moral rights are broader in scope and may be inalienable.[3] In cases where moral rights may be an issue, the agreement should be governed by Canadian or US law and made subject to the jurisdiction of the courts of the appropriate province or state.

---

[2]  A licensor may be very reluctant to provide this warranty, especially in respect to any jurisdiction other than that in which the licensor is carrying on business.

[3]  In some civil law countries like France, the author's moral rights include the right of paternity (droit de paternité), the right to control the publication of the work (droit de divulgation), and the right to withdraw the work after publication (included in the "droit de divulgation"). As well, moral rights in France (and other civil law countries) have three essential characteristics: they are inalienable, they cannot be waived, and they are perpetual.

## 4.3    NEGOTIATING A WEB SITE DEVELOPMENT AGREEMENT

The development of a professional quality Web site or an Internet-based electronic commerce service can be an expensive undertaking. The development of such a Web site will usually require the services of Web site and software developers. A corporation should protect itself by entering a Web Site development agreement to address issues such as the ownership and confidentiality of Web site content and limits on costs.

A Web site should be developed according to pre-defined specifications. Where these are not available upon the commencement of a project, the agreement should provide for the work to be carried out in phases, with the specifications to be deliverable during the first phase. Because new ideas are likely to emerge once the project gets underway, it is important to incorporate procedures for dealing with changes in the scope of the project or the specifications.

Many of the issues in a Web development agreement are similar to those which arise in contracting for consulting or software development services. These issues include the following:

(1)  The services to be provided and the work product to be developed should be adequately described and documented. The description should be comprehensive enough to avoid uncertainty as to the work to be performed by the developer. If the description of the deliverables is set out in any supplementary documentation such as proposals, requests for proposals, project descriptions or timetables, these should be incorporated into the agreement by reference. The description of services should address the following issues:

  • Hypertext Markup Language ("HTML") coding of text documents provided by the client, including encoding of images and the creation of hyperlinks;[4]

---

[4]    The developer will likely be required to translate existing content (i.e., text documents) to the HTML format used on the Web. The agreement should indicate if the original text documents are to be supplied by the client in electronic form. The agreement should require the HTML coding to be compliant with the then current version of HTML. It should also set out any special "extensions" to standard HTML, such as those recognized by Netscape, Microsoft or another browser vendor.

- Design or development of graphics or icons and scanning, retouching and colour reduction of images provided by the client;

- Integration of a search engine or other search technology to permit searching of the site;

- Graphic design and layout for the Web site, including:

    — Alternative pages for high and low graphics;

    — Scheme for navigation including development of menus and button bars;

- Development of any secure forms or password-protected areas;

- Programming of scripts or database interfaces;

- Development of any special tools for access log analysis and reporting;

- Development of any interfaces with any third party resources such as online credit verification;

- Registration of new domain names (certain domain name registrars, such as InterNIC, invoice the domain owner directly for the registration fee);

- Registration of the site with Internet indexes and search engines (for example, Yahoo! and Alta Vista);

- Solicitation of other related sites to be directly linked to the site under development;

- Art work for icons, graphics and "image maps;"

- Enhancement of the Web site through the use of additional technologies such as search engines or discussion databases; and

- Ongoing maintenance of the Web site.

(2) The agreement should indicate the method of calculating the price for the work to be performed, and in particular whether the work is to be based on a fixed price or agreed hourly rates. It is particularly important that the agreement include a proper description of the work, state if the work

is to be performed for a fixed price and indicate whether the developer is to be responsible for cost over-runs.

(3)   The agreement should deal with the parties' ownership rights to the content being developed. In general, the client will want all component elements which are contributed by the client or which are developed specifically for the client at its expense to belong to the client. Any elements for which ownership is to remain with the developer (i.e., to permit the developer to use such components in performing work for other clients) should be clearly identified.

(4)   The agreement should require the developer to provide a copy of the completed Web content on computer-readable media for backup purposes even if the developer agrees to mount or host the original material on a Web site on behalf of the client. If the developer will be performing ongoing updates to the content of the Web site, the agreement should set out a process to be followed by the developer to provide copies of the updates on an on-going basis.

(5)   The client will want the developer to warrant that, subject to any exceptions agreed to by the client, any content contributed by the developer will be an original work. In the absence of such a warranty, a client may find that other sites created by the developer incorporate many of the same elements as the client's site. If any elements used for the client's site are taken from the public domain or are to be used in other sites, these should be clearly identified.[5] The client should ensure that the Web site to be developed will not rely on scripts or other proprietary components which are available only on the developer's site.

(6)   If the content being developed is to include audio, video or images of real people, the client will want the developer to obtain waivers or releases from all persons who appear. Similarly, if the content to be developed includes musical works, then as noted above, appropriate licences or assignments may be required from one or more of the

---

[5]   Such elements may include icons or graphical elements that are obtained from the Internet or included in Web site development software.

recording company, the writer and the composer, the performers and the applicable copyright collective.

(7) The client will want the agreement to provide for an appropriate indemnification from the developer in case any part of the work is found to be infringing on the rights of another party.

(8) The client will want the agreement to include confidentiality covenants by the developer; such covenants should be provided before work begins on the project and in some cases will be set out in a separate confidentiality agreement. The parties should also consider whether the developer may use the client's name in its promotional materials, or whether the client's Web site will include a reference or link to the developer.

(9) The client will want the developer to completely test the Web site, and to provide the client with the right to carry out its own testing to confirm that the work complies fully with the agreed specifications.

(10) The successful and timely completion of a Web development project may be significantly affected by the removal or substitution of personnel. A client may also select a particular developer based on the client's confidence in particular personnel. Therefore, the client may wish to state in the agreement that the developer will not remove or substitute personnel without the client's approval. If any such personnel leave the developer's employment, the developer should undertake to replace them with persons of equivalent skill and experience.

(11) The client will want the agreement to include a representation and warranty by the Web developer that it has the necessary skill and experience in producing Web content, and that the services will be performed in accordance with the professional standards of the industry and that the Web site (including all content and any software) is Year 2000 compliant.[6]

---

[6]   For more information on Year 2000 issues, see Gahtan, *The Year 2000 Computer Crisis Legal Guide* (Carswell, 1998).

(12) The agreement should provide for a completion date, stating when the Web site shall be available for testing by the client and for public access.

(13) The agreement should list all technical specifications. Some sample specifications which are unique to a Web site development project include the following:

- All components and pages shall not exceed 640 pixels in width; and

- All graphics and icons are to be in interlaced GIF format and optimized for quick loading.

(14) The client will want the developer to warrant that the Web site will be developed with appropriate means to detect and prevent tampering or unauthorized modification.

## 4.4  NEGOTIATING A WEB SITE HOSTING AGREEMENT

Once developed, a Web site must be installed and operated on a Web server. The Web server may be located at the client's premises or may be operated on behalf of the client by an Internet Service Provider or Web Presence Provider.[7]

The internal hosting of a Web site is most appropriate when an organization requires a full-time connection to the Internet for other purposes (such as to provide Internet access to employees), when the organization requires a high level of security, and where the Web server must be linked to internal databases or systems in order to support real-time transactions.

External hosting, on the other hand, may be less expensive. In addition, some service providers can provide redundant links to reduce the impact of a failure or heavy traffic in one segment of the Internet. The terms governing the hosting of a Web site by a Web Service Provider should be set out in a Web site hosting agreement.

One of the issues to be addressed in such an agreement is whether the client's Web site is to be hosted on a dedicated server or

---

[7]    Web Presence Provider is a common industry term for an ISP that specializes in providing Web hosting services.

a shared Web server. In the latter case, the client will wish to obtain service level guarantees. In the case of a shared server, the client will also want to have the right to utilize CGI scripts and install other server extensions such as Microsoft FrontPage and Microsoft Active Server pages.[8] In the case of a dedicated server, the agreement should specify the minimum specifications applicable to the system (e.g., CPU class, speed, memory).

The Web site hosting agreement should indicate the amount of bandwidth between the service provider's server and the primary Internet backbone, and the extent to which such bandwidth is shared with other parties. The amount of bandwidth to a number of key Internet segments is an important factor in the overall performance of a Web site. Connections to more than one primary Internet segment can also be important for redundancy and performance.

A Web site hosting agreement should also set out the types of reports to be provided. An analysis of the identity of visitors can provide useful marketing data.

If the operator of a Web site intends to conduct electronic commerce, then the operator will wish to obtain support for secure transactions. Such support will allow certain designated pages or forms to be transferred in an encrypted manner to prevent interception by third parties.

The agreement should set out the basis for calculating applicable charges. The typical charges for an Internet hosting agreement include a set-up fee, monthly service fees and charges based on the amount of data downloaded from the Web server or the number of pages or other elements accessed.

A Web site hosting agreement should also describe the services to be provided upon termination of the agreement to assist the client in moving the hosting in-house or to another service provider. The service provider should also have a general obligation to provide such cooperation and assistance as the client may reasonably request in connection with such a move.

---

[8]    These are special programs or processes that run on the Web server and provide special functionality.

Some Web Presence Providers will seek to obtain an indemnity for any claims that may be made as a result of the content provided by the client. In many cases, a client will be provided with direct access to the services for purposes of adding or modifying the materials hosted at a Web site (for instance, through the use of an "FTP" account). In such cases, the operator will wish to impose guidelines as to the type of content that may be placed at the Web site. For instance, the client may be asked to warrant that all materials placed on the Web site will not infringe the proprietary rights of another party and will not include libellous or defamatory statements. The client will also be expected to provide appropriate indemnities to the Web Presence Provider for any breach of such warranties.

The customer will typically want to insert a provision acknowledging its ownership of the Web site and domain name and specifying that the Web Presence Provider will assist in transferring the Web site to another provider (or to the customer) upon termination of the hosting arrangement.

## 4.5  NEGOTIATING AN INTERNET ACCESS AGREEMENT

An Internet Access Agreement is intended to govern the provision of a communications link between a subscriber and an Internet Access Provider ("IAP").[9] An organization may obtain such a communications link in order to connect its own Web server to the Internet or to provide Internet access to its employees. Dedicated links to the Internet (in contrast to dial-up connections) commonly utilize ISDN circuits to provide a bandwidth of up to 128K bps or a T1 circuit to provide a link of up to 1.544 Mbps.[10]

Some of the issues which should be documented in an Internet Access Agreement include the following:

---

[9]    In this book, references to an IAP refer to an ISP that simply provides a network connection to the Internet without ancillary services such as Web site hosting.

[10]    These are special high speed data circuits that are available from the telephone company.

(1) Periodic fees for the connection (these fees are typically fixed amounts without any surcharges based on traffic);

(2) Provisions for upgrading the connection to higher speeds and the costs of such upgrades;

(3) Provisions concerning access to any supplementary facilities operated by the IAP, such as UseNet servers;

(4) Provisions governing the right to use e-mail facilities such as SMTP for outgoing e-mail and POP3 for incoming e-mail; these may be necessary if the subscriber is not intending to operate its own e-mail servers;

(5) Agreement by the IAP to provide Web and e-mail forwarding/redirection following termination;

(6) Service level guarantees to ensure that the IAP does not provide access to more subscribers than the number that may properly be handled by the IAP's limited connection to the Internet;

(7) Provisions indicating whether the IAP or the subscriber is responsible for providing a router to connect the subscriber's equipment to the Internet connection; and

(8) Responsibilities of the IAP to provide firewall or other security services.

## 4.6  TERMS AND CONDITIONS GOVERNING USE OF A WEB SITE

New visitors to a Web site should be presented with a list of terms and conditions (including notices and disclaimers) when they first arrive at the Web site. It is advisable to require visitors to acknowledge their agreement to such conditions before being granted access to the Web site. However, this procedure is often not followed for marketing reasons. Another option is to provide a prominent notice that use of the site is subject to certain terms, along with a descriptive hypertext link that can be followed to access the text of such terms. In order to enhance the probability that such terms will be enforceable, their existence must be brought to the attention of the user.

One of the more prominent forms of notices appears on the "www.movies.com" Web site operated by Buena Vista. The notice at the bottom of the home page provides:

"Please click here for legal restrictions and terms of use applicable to this site" and "Use of this site signifies your agreement to the terms of use."

This "Legal Web Wrap" page provides that any software available from the site is subject to United States export controls. "No software from this site may be downloaded or otherwise exported or re-exported into (or to a national or resident of) Cuba, Iraq, Libya, North Korea, Iran, Syria or any other country to which the US has embargoed goods or to anyone on the US Treasury Department's list of Specially Designated Nationals or the US Commerce Department's Table of Deny Orders."

Links to the terms governing the use of a site should be provided from each page and not just the home page of a Web site. This is important because new visitors may obtain access directly to the other pages through an external link so that visitors will not see a notice placed only on the home page.[11]

A more formal procedure requiring a user to read through and to signify their acceptance of the legal notices page should be used in any case where a visitor is to be granted access to a non-public portion of the site or is to be given the right to initiate a transaction to purchase a product or service.

To obtain full protection under certain international copyright conventions, a work should be marked in a particular way.[12] Such notice should apply to the contents of the Web site as a whole (which may be protected as a compilation), as well as each significant work

---

[11]    Due to the "hypertext" nature of the Web, a visitor may go directly to a specific page on a Web site without having gone through the "home page." This can occur due to a link from another Web site or as a result of a search conducted on an Internet search engine. It is, therefore, advisable that links to the legal notice page be placed from all pages on the Web site or at least all significant pages.

[12]    A work should be marked with the word "copyright" or a "c" in a circle, the year of publication, and the name of the copyright owner, and be accompanied by the words "All Rights Reserved." For more details, see Chapter 5.

placed on the Web site (which may be entitled to its own copyright protection).

Certain types of content placed on a Web site should be accompanied by additional and more prominent notices or disclaimers. Examples include downloadable software programs, data that may be relied upon for purposes of financial or other transactions (e.g., stock market or interest rate information) or tools (for instance, financial calculators).

## 4.7  SAMPLE LEGAL NOTICE AND DISCLAIMER PAGE

The following is a sample legal notice and disclaimer page that may be found on an Internet Web site:

> Your access to and continued use of [name of Web site] at [Web address] (the "Site") constitutes your acceptance of and compliance with the following provisions. If you have not already done so, please take some time to familiarize yourself with these provisions. If you do not agree to these terms and conditions, you should immediately discontinue any use of the Site. Also note that these terms and conditions may change from time to time and it is your responsibility to check for such updates. The last revision date for these terms and conditions is set forth below.

Last revised: [Insert date]

### (a)  Reserved Rights and Grant of Limited Licence

- Copyright © 1998 Owner. All rights reserved. Owner either owns the intellectual property rights, including copyright, or has acquired the necessary licences, in the information, including all text, HTML code, multimedia clips, images, graphics, icons, Java code, and the selection and arrangement of the contents of the Site (collectively the "Information"). Portions of the Information have been licensed to the Owner by..... [to be completed with name(s) of licensors].

- As a user of the Site, you are granted a limited licence to use (display or print) short extracts of the Information for your own personal non-commercial use only, provided the Information is not modified and you shall be fully responsible for any consequences resulting from such use. Any other use of the Information is prohibited. None of the Information may be otherwise reproduced, republished or re-disseminated in any manner or form without the prior written consent of Owner.

- Owner will take appropriate legal action to enforce its rights.

**(b)  No Solicitation**

- No part of the Site should be taken to constitute an offer or solicitation to buy or sell products or services. Some products or services mentioned on the Site may only be available in certain areas or jurisdictions.

- Any products or services mentioned on the Site are made available in accordance with local law and only where they may be lawfully offered for sale.

**(c)  No Endorsement**

- The Site may contain links to other sites. These links are provided as references to help you identify and locate other Internet resources that may be of interest. These other sites were independently developed by parties other than Owner, and Owner does not assume responsibility for the accuracy or appropriateness of the information contained at such sites. In providing links to other sites, Owner is in no way acting as a publisher or disseminator of the material contained on those other sites and does not seek to control the content of, or maintain any type of editorial control over, such sites.

- A link to another site should not be construed to mean that Owner is affiliated or associated with, or is legally authorized to use any trademark, trade name, logo or copyrighted symbol that may be reflected in the link or the description of the link to such other sites.

- The mention of another party or its product or service on the Site should not be construed as an endorsement of that party or its product or service.

**(d)  No Advice or Warranties**

- The Information on the Site including, but not limited to, newsletters, articles, opinions and views, is provided for educational or information purposes only. It is not intended to provide legal, accounting or tax advice and should not be relied upon in that respect. You should not act or rely on any information at the Site without seeking the advice of a professional.

- Information provided on the Site is believed to be reliable when posted. However, Owner does not guarantee the quality, accuracy, completeness or timeliness of the information provided. Owner assumes no obligation to update the Information or advise on further developments concerning topics mentioned. Information contained on the Site may contain typographical errors. Information provided may be changed without notice.

- Access to this Site is provided on an "as is" basis. You should not assume that the Site will be error-free or that the Site will operate without interruption.

- Owner disclaims all warranties, representations and conditions regarding use of the Site or the information provided, including all implied warranties or conditions of merchantability, fitness for a particular purpose, non-infringement, whether express or implied, or arising from a course of dealing, usage or trade practice.

- Owner is not responsible for any content or information that you may find undesirable or objectionable.

**(e)  No Liability**

- Owner is not responsible for any direct, indirect, special, incidental or consequential damage or any other damages whatsoever and howsoever caused, arising out of or in connection with the use of the Site or in reliance on the information available on the Site, including any loss of use, lost data, lost business profits, business interruption, personal injury, or any other pecuniary loss, whether the action is in contract, tort (including negligence) or other tortious action.

- Owner disclaims any liability for unauthorized use or reproduction of any portion of the Site.

## (f)  Trademarks

- Certain words, phrases, names, designs or logos used on the Site may constitute trademarks, service marks or trade names of Owner or other entities. The display of any such marks or names on the Site does not imply that a licence has been granted by Owner or other entities.

## (g)  Confidentiality Warning

- Absent the use of encryption, the Internet is not a secure medium and privacy cannot be ensured. Internet e-mail is vulnerable to interception and forging. The Owner will not be responsible for any damages you or any third party may suffer as a result of the transmission of confidential information that you make to Owner through the Internet, or that you expressly or implicitly authorize the Owner to make, or for any errors or any changes made to any transmitted information.

## (h)  Computer Viruses

- While every effort is made to ensure that all information provided at the Site does not contain computer viruses, you should take reasonable and appropriate precautions to scan for computer viruses and should ensure that you have a complete and current backup of the applicable items of information contained on your computer system. You should pay specific attention to some of the newer viruses that have been written to automatically execute when an infected word processing document is loaded into certain word processing programs.

## (i)  Conformance with Law

- You agree that your use of the Site shall not violate any applicable local, national or international law, including but not limited to any regulations having the force of law. Some jurisdictions may have restrictions on the use of the Internet by their residents.

- You agree not to impersonate another person in your use of the Site or the sending of any e-mail to an address listed on the Site.

### (j)  Choice of Law

The laws of the [Province of Ontario] and the laws of [Canada] applicable therein shall govern as to the interpretation, validity and effect of this greement notwithstanding any conflict of laws provisions or your domicile, residence or physical location. You hereby consent and submit to the non-exclusive jurisdiction of the courts of the [Province of Ontario] in any action or proceeding instituted under or related to this agreement.

### (k)  Submissions

All information submitted to the Owner via the Site shall be deemed and remain the property of the Owner and the Owner shall be free to use, for any purpose, any ideas, concepts, know-how or other techniques contained in information provided to the Owner through the Site or sent through e-mail. Owner shall not be subject to any obligations of confidentiality regarding any such information submitted to it unless specifically agreed by the Owner or required by law.

You agree that any information submitted for inclusion at the Site does not infringe on the intellectual property or other rights of any third parties and you grant the Owner a right to provide access to the information from the Site. You warrant that any software submitted to the Owner shall be free of computer viruses.

# 5

# Protection of Intellectual Property on the Internet

## 5.1 INTRODUCTION

Access to the Internet is particularly attractive in countries such as Canada which has a small population spread over a large geographical area and an advanced telecommunications system to permit Internet access at a relatively low cost.[1] Broad and increasing access to the Internet, in Canada and elsewhere, means even more and disparate uses of content on the Internet. As a result it is increasingly important to understand the intellectual property laws that may apply to materials that are disseminated and used by means of the Internet.

The Internet brings together the problems of protecting intangible works such as computer programs and databases in digital form and the problems arising from the very nature of the Internet and the many uses that it supports. Some of these issues arise from the nature of the digital media which embody the works made on the Internet. The digital form of audiovisual works, text, sound recordings and art works means that all of these types of works may be dealt with in the same manner and may easily be copied and distributed. Another aspect of the Internet which creates legal issues is the ease with which any visitor to a Web site may download any work and modify it. All of these factors are compounded by the global reach of the Internet which permits materials to be viewed and used at any time and from any location.

---

[1]   *Communications Outlook*, OECD, Paris, 1997 suggests that Canada has the lowest Internet access charges for users among OECD (Organization for Economic Cooperation and Development) countries.

The main forms of intellectual property protection for works which are available on the Internet are copyright law (which includes issues in relation to moral rights and performers' rights), trade secrecy law and trademark law. Each of these areas will be discussed in this Chapter. For further information, Chapter 3 contains a discussion of specific trademark issues related to domain name problems and Chapter 6 deals with trademark issues relating to advertising and marketing activities on Web sites.

## 5.2 COPYRIGHT

As the Internet has evolved from a network providing a means of information exchange to a major new marketplace, it becomes more important to review the legal framework for the posting, use and dissemination of materials exchanged on the Internet. That legal framework is largely provided by copyright law.

The *Copyright Act*[2] has been interpreted in a broad manner with respect to its application to new forms of creative expression.[3] This broad approach is also supported by the language of the statute which grants protection and permits the enforcement of rights regardless of the material form in which any work is embodied.[4] A similar result arises under the United States copyright law.[5]

The Government of Canada established an Information Highway Advisory Council which reviewed a number of aspects of government policy in relation to the Internet. The Council considered that the act of digitization of a work (regardless of the nature of the work[6] or the form in which it is originally expressed) does not result in the

---

[2]   R.S.C. 1985, c. C-42, as amended. For an electronic version of the Act see <http://www.info.ic.gc.ca/>. For the United States *Copyright Act* see 17 U.S.C. s. 101-810.

[3]   See, for example, *Apple Computer Inc. v. MacIntosh Computers Ltd.*, (1986) 8 C.I.P.R. 153, 10 C.P.R. (3d) 1, 3 F.T.R. 118, [1987] 1 F.C. 173, 28 D.L.R. (4th) 178 (Fed. T.D.), varied (1987) 16 C.I.P.R. 15, [1988] 1 F.C. 673, 44 D.L.R. (4th) 74, 81 N.R. 3, 18 C.P.R. (3d) 129 (Fed. C.A.), affirmed 110 N.R. 66, [1990] 2 S.C.R. 209, 71 D.L.R. (4th) 95, 30 C.P.R. (3D) 257, [1990] 2 R.C.S. 209, 36 F.T.R. 159 (note) (S.C.C.). (4th) (S.C.C.)

[4]   See section 3 (1), *Copyright Act* (Canada).

[5]   Section 102(a) of 17 U.S.C. provides that "copyright exists in original works of authorship fixed in any tangible medium of expression, now known or later developed, ...".

[6]   Whether a sound recording, text, photograph, film, computer program, dramatic work or otherwise.

creation of a new work. This is consistent with the approach taken by the Canadian courts.[7] As a result, any analysis of copyright law in relation to the Internet must focus on the nature of the original work as well as any unique issues arising from the embodiment of the work in a digital form.

Copyright law provides a bundle of rights which include the protection of the work regardless of the *form* in which concepts or ideas may be expressed. The specific rights which make up this bundle of rights are discussed in section 5.2 (b), below.

An important aspect of copyright law is that the rights arise automatically upon the creation of an original work. The limited formal requirements which must be met for copyright protection to apply, as well as issues relating to ownership of copyright and the term of protection, are discussed in section 5.2 (a), below.

As a general principle, copyright does not extend to ideas, facts, processes, methods or useful features of works. For example, in the case of computer programs, copyright law protects the form in which the instructions are set out. In the case of a book, copyright protects the phrases used to express the plot but not the concepts underlying that plot. As a result, the copyright in an e-mail message, document, musical work or graphic image extends to the form or expression of the various components of the message, document or other work but not the ideas contained in it. In some cases, copyright law may be invoked to provide limited protection for the structure, sequence and organization of some works, such as databases. These special issues are discussed in section 5.2(e)(iv), below.

Copyright is an intangible right and must be distinguished from other rights which may attach to a tangible object which embodies copyright protection, such as a right of possession. Possession of a work protected by copyright (i.e., this book) may allow the possessor to use the work in many ways but the possessor is not permitted to make copies of the work (or otherwise carry out any of the conduct

---

[7]    In *Apple Computer Inc. v. MacIntosh Computers Ltd.*, [1986] C.I.P.R. 153; 28 D.L.R. (4th) 178, varied (1988) 16 C.I.P.R. 15 (Fed. C.A.), Appeal dismissed (1990), 71 D.L.R. (4th) (S.C.C.) the court found that a machine-readable version of a computer program which had been stored on a ROM chip was not a new work but the embodiment in another form of the original human-readable version of the computer program.

reserved to the copyright owner). As a result the recipient of an e-mail message or document will generally not have any copyright in the document.

The works available on the Internet include computer programs, textual materials (e.g., notes, messages, documents, poems, plays, dialogue), graphic images (e.g., logos, drawings), maps, charts, plans, databases, sound recordings, musical recordings, photographs and audio visual works.

Copyright law recognizes the following categories of works: literary works, musical works, artistic works and dramatic works[8] and also recognizes contrivances used to perform or present certain works (e.g., CDs to perform music). The works included in various categories are not rigid and have been expanded by the courts to include new technologies and new forms of expression. The fact that copyright law applies to virtually all the types of works available on the Internet has significant implications for all users of the Internet.

Many materials available on the Internet, such as multimedia, consist of a number of different types of works. For example, a computer game might contain sound recordings, musical works, artistic works (photographs, drawings), literary works (text, software) and may itself be a dramatic work (the story line and scenic arrangements). Works that contain multiple elements are called compilations and come into the same category of work as the individual components. For example an encyclopedia consisting of many text elements is a literary work. Compilations for which the various components come into different categories of works are considered the type of work which dominates the compilation.

Many Web sites use databases to provide services or information. Special issues surrounding the protection of databases which are considered compilation works are discussed in section 5.2 (e)(iv), below.

---

[8]   In the United States the main categories are literary works, musical works, dramatic works, pantomimes and choreographic works, pictorial, graphic and sculptural works, motion pictures and audiovisual works, sound recordings and architectural works.

In Canada, the Information Highway Advisory Council expressed the view in its final report[9] that all digital works, including multimedia works, already have sufficient protection based on the existing categories of works under the *Copyright Act*.[10]

## (a)  Requirements for Copyright Protection

There are only limited requirements that must be met for a work to be protected by copyright. A key feature of copyright law is that works created which meet the criteria discussed in sections (i) through (iv) below will automatically be entitled to copyright protection. There are no other formalities required to create the right. However, certain advantages are obtained by the use of copyright notices (see section 5.2(a)(vii)) and by the registration of copyright (see section 5.2(a)(ix)).

### (i)  *Characteristics of the Author or Place of Publication*

In Canada, the author must be, at the date of creation of the work, a citizen, subject or resident of a treaty country,[11] or a citizen or subject of a Country to which the Minister has extended protection by notice in the *Canada Gazette*.[12] Alternatively, copyright will subsist in a cinematographic work if the maker is a corporation having its head office in a treaty country.[13] A published work will also be protected in Canada if it was first published in a treaty country.[14]

Since the Berne Convention includes over 100 countries, most authors of works found on the Internet will qualify for copyright protection in Canada. The Berne Convention provides for the

---

[9]    September 1995, Published by the Information Highway Advisory Council Secretary, Industry Canada.

[10]    *Ibid*; at Page 37.

[11]    A "treaty country" is defined in section 2 of the *Copyright Act* to mean a Berne Convention country, a UCC (Universal Copyright Convention) country or a WTO (World Trade Organization) member.

[12]    Protection was extended to United States nationals well before the United States acceded to the Berne Convention.

[13]    Section 5(1)(b), *Copyright Act* (Canada).

[14]    Section 5(1)(c), *Copyright Act* (Canada).

principle of "national treatment," and accordingly, any author who is a national of any country that belongs to the Convention, or whose work is first published in such country, will be entitled to copyright protection in other Berne Convention countries.

### (ii)  Character of the Work

The work must come within the broad class of original literary, dramatic, musical and artistic works.[15] The courts have interpreted these classes to be very broad and not limiting of new forms of expression. Protection is also granted to performers in respect to their performances, makers in respect to sound recordings, and broadcasters in respect to their signals.

### (iii)  An Original Work

The work must be original. For copyright purposes, "original" means that the work emanates from the author and is not copied from another person's work. The work must be the product of his or her labour and skill and an expression of his or her thoughts and creativity. A minimum amount of creativity is required.[16] Copyright is only concerned with the form of expression and it is this form which must be original. The ideas underlying the form of expression need not be original.

### (iv)  Requirement of Fixation

The work, to be capable of copyright protection, must be fixed in a tangible form. It appears that most works available on the Internet will satisfy this requirement since they will be "fixed" in some form of magnetic, optical or other medium.

---

[15]  In the United States the main categories are literary works, musical works, dramatic works, pantomimes and choreographic works, pictorial, graphic and sculptural works, motion pictures and audiovisual works, sound recordings and architectural works.

[16]  For US purposes "even a slight amount" of originality is sufficient. See *Feist Publications, Inc. v. Rural Telephone Service Co. Inc.*, 499 US 340 (U.S. S.C.). For a recent discussion of the requirements of creativity under Canadian law, see the decision of the Federal Court of Appeal in *Tele-Direct (Publications) v. American Business Information*, [1997] F.C.J. No. 1430, leave to appeal to Supreme Court of Canada refused, May 21, 1998.

### (v)  Ownership

The starting principle under section 13(1) of the Canadian *Copyright Act* is that copyright will vest with the author of the work. The main exception is that where the author is an employee and the work is created in the course of his or her employment, then under section 13(3) of the *Copyright Act*, the employer will be the first owner of copyright. This will mean that where a Web site is developed by a consultant who is not an employee, then in the absence of an agreement to the contrary, the Web designer will own any copyright-protected elements (such as Web page graphics) prepared for the customer.

Where an engraving, photograph or portrait is ordered by a person and is made for valuable consideration, unless there is an agreement to the contrary, the party commissioning the work will own the copyright.

Similar exemptions to the general principle that copyright will reside with the author of the work are applicable under US copyright law which utilizes the concept of "works made for hire." This concept applies to works that are prepared by an employee within the scope of his or her employment, or works specially ordered or commissioned for use in a contribution to a collective work or as one of eight enumerated classes of works.[17] With respect to the enumerated eight classes of works, the parties must agree in writing that the works are to be considered works for hire.

### (vi)  Term

The general rule, for most works, is that copyright will subsist for the life of the author plus the end of the year in which the author dies plus 50 years.[18]

Because of the long term for copyright protection, there may be cases where the author and/or copyright holder of the materials may not be known. If the identity of the author is unknown, the term of copyright in the work will be the earlier of the end of the year of first

---

[17]  See 17 U.S.C. s. 201 (a) and (b).

[18]  See section 6, *Copyright Act* (Canada); in the US see s. 302(a) 17 U.S.C. providing the term of life of the author and fifty years after the author's death.

publication of the work plus 50 years, or the end of the year of the making of the work plus 75 years.[19]

### (vii) Notice

Many works on the Internet do not contain copyright notices. The lack of a copyright notice does not preclude the existence of copyright since, in Canada, no notice is required to create copyright. In the US, no notice is required on works created after March 1, 1989, the date when the US joined the Berne Convention.

Placement of a copyright notice on the work may expand the scope of the rights that may be exercised by the copyright holder in many countries including the United States. In *Religious Technology Centre v. Netcom Online Communications Services, Inc.*,[20] an important factor that lead to the court's finding that the Internet Access Provider, Netcom, should be liable for contributory infringement was the existence of copyright notices in favour of the plaintiff in materials posted on the Internet.

The Berne Convention (described in section 5.2(a)(viii), below) provides for automatic copyright protection without formalities for works of nationals of Berne Convention countries. While the United States has been a member of this Convention since March 1, 1989, US copyright law prior to that date imposed various requirements for copyright notices and other formalities. Because of this requirement, it may be assumed by many people in the US that a work which is not accompanied by a copyright notice is not protected by copyright. Accordingly, it is advisable to place an appropriate copyright notice prominently on each copy of the work. That notice should comply with the US domestic rules,[21] and with the requirements set forth in the Universal Copyright Convention (UCC), which is described in more detail below.

---

[19]    Section 6.1, *Copyright Act* (Canada); in the US anonymous works, works for hire and pseudonymous works have a term of copyright of 75 years from first publication or 100 years from creation, whichever comes first. See 17 U.S.C. s. 302(a).

[20]    907 F. Supp. 1361, 37 U.S.P.Q. 2D 1545 (N.D. Cal. 1995).

[21]    See 17 U.S.C. s. 401.

Both the US domestic law and the UCC requires the following form of copyright notice to be prominently displayed on a work:

© year of publication, name of owner

An example of the notice is:

© 1998 Alan Gahtan, Martin Kratz, Fraser Mann

The © symbol is specifically mandated by the UCC. The year is the year of first publication of the work. The name is the identity of the copyright owner.

Since the © symbol is not a standard ASCII character and might not be placed on all documents or materials placed on the Internet an alternative is to substitute the word "copyright" for this symbol. This substitution will not satisfy the requirements of the UCC, but will satisfy the domestic US requirements.[22] It may also be advisable to add "All Rights Reserved" following the name(s) of the author(s).

### (viii)  The Berne and Universal Copyright Conventions

The Convention for the Protection of Literary and Artistic Works made in Berne (the "Berne Convention") provides for automatic copyright protection to nationals of each member country without any requirement of formalities.

The United States acceded to the Berne Convention in late 1988, effective March 1, 1989. The placement of the author's name on a work creates a presumption (which will apply in the absence of proof to the contrary) that the author is the copyright holder.

As previously discussed, the UCC is another treaty that provides for the international recognition of copyright. Under the UCC, a form of copyright notice is a condition precedent to a claim of rights. The placement of a notice on a work in the form prescribed by the UCC does not impair the ability to claim rights under the Berne Convention.

---

[22]  See 17 U.S.C. s. 401 which permits use of "copr." or "copyright".

### (ix)  Registration

In Canada, there is no formal requirement for registration or notification in order for a copyright to subsist in an appropriate work. As discussed above, the principle of automatic copyright protection without formalities is a feature of the Berne Convention.

There is a register for copyrights in Canada, but its value is evidentiary in nature. Under Section 34.1 of the *Copyright Act* (Canada), registration provides certain useful presumptions which would assist in an action enforcing the right.[23] Registration in the US is now also permissive although it is a prerequisite to bringing a suit for copyright infringement.[24]

## (b)  Specific Rights Under Copyright Law in the Context of the Internet

In this section, we review the specific rights that are granted under copyright law. In each instance, we review the types of activities involving the use of works on the Internet that would come within the rights of the copyright owner, as well as any activity that may be covered by an implied licence granted by a copyright owner upon posting materials to the Internet to be available without restriction to Internet users.

### (i)  Reproduction Right

The copyright owner has the sole right to reproduce the work or any substantial part thereof in any material form whatsoever.[25] This right applies to any work such as a computer program, graphic images, text files and other digital representations, such as, for example, of a song or a book.[26] This right is exercised when the

---

[23]    Details on the rules governing and the procedure involved in registration of copyright may be found in *Protection of Copyright and Industrial Design*, Carswell, Practice Guide, 1995.

[24]    See 17 U.S.C s. 408 (a) and 412.

[25]    See section 3 (1), *Copyright Act* (Canada); for the US provision corresponding to this right see 17 U.S.C. s. 106.

[26]    See, for example, *University of London Press v. University Tutorial Press*, [1916] 2 Ch. 601 involving copying of examinations; *Football League v. Littlewood's Pools Ltd.*, [1959] 1 Ch. 637; [1959] 2 All. E.R. 546 (Ch. D) involving copying of a schedule of games of a professional sporting association; and *Apple Computer Inc. v. MacIntosh Computers Ltd.*, (1986) 8 C.I.P.R. 153, 10 C.P.R. (3d) 1, 3 F.T.R. 118, [1987] 1 F.C. 173, 28 D.L.R. (4th)

copyright owner posts an e-mail message or document that incorporates the work on the Internet. Another person may make further copies or postings of the work only if given authorization (express or implied) by the owner or if an exemption applies. The right of an Internet user to engage in incidental reproduction of a work for the purpose of browsing may be permitted as an implied right granted to the user arising from the posting of materials on the Internet in circumstances where they are availiable without restriction. See discussion in section 5.2(e)(i), (ii) and (iii).

The act of loading a computer program into the memory of a computer has been held to be a reproduction for copyright purposes.[27] Some cases in which the court found that there was a violation of the reproduction right include *Sega Entertainment Ltd. v. Maphia*[28] where a BBS operator was restrained from posting reproductions of Sega's video game software on the BBS and *Marobie-Fl, Inc. v. National Association of Fire Distributors*[29] where unauthorized copies of clip art were made available from a Web site.

### (ii)  Public Performance Right

The copyright owner has the sole right to perform the work or any substantial part thereof in public.[30] This provision permits a copyright owner to restrict any unauthorized performance of various works (e.g., a musical work) in public. In addition, copyright is deemed to be infringed by any person who, for his private profit, permits a theatre or other place of entertainment to be used for the

---

178 (Fed. T.D.) aff'd (1987) 16 C.I.P.R. 15, [1988] 1 F.C. 673, 44 D.L.R. (4th) 74, 81 N.R. 3, 18 C.P.R. (3d) 129 (Fed. C.A.), affirmed 110 N.R. 66, [1990] 2 S.C.R. 209 (1990), 71 D.L.R. (4th) 30 C.P.R. (3d) 257, [1990] 2 R.C.S. 209, 36 F.T.R. 159 (note) (S.C.C.) involving copying of machine-readable versions of a computer program.

[27]  See, for example, *MAI Systems Corp. v. Peak Computer, Inc.*, 991 F. 2d 511 (9th Cir. 1993) which found that copying of a computer program occurs when it is loaded into RAM memory.

[28]  867 F. Supp. 679 (N.D. Cal. 1994).

[29]  The decision is available at <http://www.bna.com/e-law/cases/marobie.html>.

[30]  See section 3(1), *Copyright Act* (Canada); in the US See also the Digital Performance *Right in Sound Recordings Act of 1995*, Pub. L. 104-39 which provides a right to publicly perform digital music by audio transmission.

public performance of the work without the consent of the owner of the copyright, unless that person was not aware, and had no reasonable ground for suspecting, that the performance would be an infringement of copyright.[31]

It is unlikely that any person would be permitted, based either on the terms of any implied licence granted by copyright owner, or any exemption set out in the *Copyright Act*, to perform in public any material which is posted to a Web site; the explicit authority of the copyright holder would be required for such conduct.

### (iii)  Publication Right

The copyright owner has the sole right, if the work is unpublished, to publish the work or any substantial part.[32] This provision gives the copyright owner the right to determine when an unpublished work should be released to the public. Since a Web site may be accessed by members of the public, the posting of a work on a site may be considered as a publication of the work. Any further publication of that work (e.g., by a posting to another site) would require the permission of the owner or would have to be made under an exemption.

The *Copyright Act*[33] provides that it is an infringement of copyright to distribute infringing copies of a work that a person knows or should have known infringes copyright to such an extent as to affect prejudicially the owner of the copyright. The distribution of infringing copies of a work without the owner's permission may prejudice the rights of the copyright holder (even if no payment is demanded). While the posting of a work to a Web site by a copyright owner may represent an implied authorization for a limited distribution of the work, the further distribution (e.g., by posting the work to other sites) may not come within the terms of such implied authorization.

---

[31]  These further rights are provided by section 27(5) of the *Copyright Act*.

[32]  See section 3(1), *Copyright Act* (Canada); See the corresponding US right in 17 U.S.C. s. 106.

[33]  See section 27(4), *Copyright Act* (Canada).

### (iv) Translation Right

The copyright owner has the sole right to produce, reproduce, perform, or publish any translation of the work.[34] This provision gives the owner of the copyright of a work, such as a book, the right to control the making of unauthorized translations.[35] Such conduct would likely not come within the scope of any implied authorization granted by the copyright holder who posts materials to a Web site. The making of a translation of the work would require the explicit authority of the copyright holder.

### (v) Adaptation Right

The copyright owner has the sole right, in the case of a dramatic work, to convert it into a novel or other nondramatic work,[36] or in the case of a novel or other nondramatic work, or of an artistic work, to convert it into a dramatic work.[37] For example, the copyright owner of a book (a literary work) has the right to adapt the book into a movie (a dramatic work).

This right would be exercised by converting an e-mail message or document describing the elements of a play into a novel or nondramatic message. This right would also be exercised upon converting an e-mail message or document describing a nondramatic document (e.g., a story) into a dramatic work (e.g., a screenplay). Such conduct appears not to be included in the implied conduct authorized by the copyright holder who directly or indirectly posts materials to a Web site. Making an adaptation of the work into

---

[34] See section 3(1)(a), *Copyright Act* (Canada).

[35] The issue of whether the act of converting a computer program from one computer language to another is a translation under the *Copyright Act* (Canada) has received some judicial consideration. In *Apple Computer Inc. v. MacIntosh Computers Ltd.* (1986) 8 C.I.P.R. 153 10 C.P.R. (3d) 1, 3 F.T.R. 118, [1987] 1 F.C. 173, 28 D.L.R. (4th) 178 (Fed. T.D.) aff'd (1987) 16 C.I.P.R. 15 [1988] 1 F.C. 673, 44 D.L.R. (4th) 74, 81 N.R. 3, 18 C.P.R. (3d) 129 (Fed. C.A.), affirmed 110 N.R. 66, [1990] 2 S.C.R. 209, (1990) 71 D.L.R. (4th) 95, 30 C.P.R. (3d) 257, [1990] 2 R.C.S. 209, 36 F.T.R. 159 (note) (S.C.C.) the trial judge found the change constituted a translation, while some justices of the court of Appeal found that it was not a translation; the Supreme Court held that it was not necessary to decide the issue.

[36] See section 3(1)(b), *Copyright Act* (Canada); see a broader US right to control the making of derivative works in 17 U.S.C. s. 106.

[37] See section 3(1)(c), *Copyright Act* (Canada).

another form of work would require the explicit authorization of the copyright holder.

### (vi)  Mechanical Reproduction Right

The copyright owner has the sole right, in the case of a literary, dramatic or musical work, to make any sound recording or cinematographic recording work by means of which the work may be mechanically performed.[38]

The law gives the owner of the mechanical reproduction right control over the making of copies of a device such as a compact disc (CD) which contains a musical work.[39] This right is exercised when a person records an e-mail message, image, musical work or document in a form in which it can be performed.

Where the digital file is provided by the copyright holder in circumstances where the user is expected to download and sample the music, and no express restrictions are imposed by the copyright holder, then there may be an implied licence to make the copy by means of which the musical work can be performed. Making additional copies or distributing copies would appear to be outside the scope of any implied licence. In addition, use of the work for any purpose other than personal use at home would likely not be implied and would require the consent of the copyright holder.

### (vii)  Cinematographic Presentation Right

The copyright owner has the sole right, in the case of any literary, dramatic, musical or artistic work, to reproduce, adapt and publicly present the work by cinematograph.[40] This provision gives the owner of the copyright control over the unauthorized reproduction or presentation to the public by cinematograph. This right would be exercised when a person adapts, or uses for purposes of such a

---

[38]  See section 3(1)(d).

[39]  Note, however, that the grant of a licence to make a public performance of a work does not imply any licence or right to make a mechanical reproduction of a work for the purpose of exercising the right to perform the work in public: see *Bishop v. Stevens*, 72 D.L.R. (4th) 97, [1990] 2 S.C.R. 467, 31 C.P.R. (3d) 394, 111 N.R. 376, [1990] 2 R.C.S. 467 (S.C.C.).

[40]  See section 3(1)(e), *Copyright Act* (Canada); for the corresponding right in the US (i.e., the right to perform audio visual works in public), see 17 U.S.C. s. 106.

presentation, material available on the Internet such as graphic images or a movie. Such conduct appears not to be included in the implied conduct authorized by the copyright holder who directly or indirectly posts materials to a Web site. The making of a cinematographic presentation based on the work or that includes the work would require the explicit authority of the copyright holder.

### (viii)  Communication Right

The copyright owner has the sole right, in the case of any literary, dramatic, musical or artistic work, to communicate the work to the public by telecommunication.[41] This provision gives the copyright owner the right to control any transmission of, for example, a musical work to the public by any means of telecommunication. Persons who occupy apartments, hotels rooms or dwelling units situated in the same building are deemed to be part of the public and even a communication intended to be received exclusively by such persons is a communication to the public.[42] On the other hand, if the only role of any person is to provide the means necessary for another person to communicate the work to the public, the person does not by that act alone communicate the work to the public.[43]

Copyright law provides that the broadcaster has a copyright in the communication signal[44] that he or she broadcasts. This right gives the broadcaster the right to fix the broadcast in a tangible form, to reproduce a fixed copy of the broadcast, to perform the communication signal to the public, to re-transmit the communication signal and to authorize any of these sole rights.

---

[41]  See section 3(1)(f), *Copyright Act* (Canada); the US law provides a right to distribute copies of a work to the public by sale, rental, lease, lending or any transfer of ownership. An exclusive transmission right is contemplated in US House Bill 2441. This legislation also contemplates a new set of provisions to prohibit the making, distribution or use of devices to circumvent copyright protection, or management systems which may be used to "meter" copyright usage in the future.

[42]  See section 2.4(1)(a), *Copyright Act* (Canada).

[43]  See section 2.4(1)(b), *Copyright Act* (Canada).

[44]  See *Copyright Act* (Canada), section 21(1). A communication signal consists of radio frequency waves transmitted for reception by the public without the benefit of an artificial guide.

### (ix)  Exhibition Right

The copyright owner has the sole right to present in a public exhibition, for purposes other than for sale or hire, an artistic work created after June 7, 1988, other than a map, chart or plan.[45] This provision gives the owner of the copyright in an artistic work (for example, a painting, engraving, photograph) control over any unauthorized display of the artistic work in a public place except where the display is for the purpose of sale or rental. It could be argued that the posting of materials consisting of graphic images on the Internet, and particularly the World Wide Web, where they may be displayed to members of the public, would require the authorization of the copyright owner under section 3(1)(g).

### (x)  Rental Right

Copyright law grants rental rights for sound recordings and computer programs. The copyright owner of a musical work also has the right to rent out a sound recording of that work.[46]

In the case of a computer program, the rental right applies to a program that can be reproduced in the ordinary course of use, other than by reproduction during execution in conjunction with a machine, device or computer.[47]

Such conduct appears not to be included in the implied conduct authorized by the copyright holder who directly or indirectly posts materials to a Web site. The explicit authority of the copyright holder would be required for any such rental.

### (xi)  Commercial Action/Importation

Copyright in a work, sound recording, communication signal or fixation of a performer's performance may be infringed by any person who: (a) sells or rents out, (b) distributes copies to such an extent as to affect prejudicially the owner of the copyright, or (c) by way of

---

[45]   See section 3(1)(g), *Copyright Act* (Canada); for the US right providing for a right to display or exhibit works in public see 17 U.S.C. s. 106.

[46]   See section 3(1)(i), *Copyright Act* (Canada); for the US right providing for a right to rent works see 17 U.S.C. s. 106.

[47]   See section 3(1)(h), *Copyright Act* (Canada).

trade exhibits in public, distributes, exposes or offers for sale a copy of any such work that the person knows or should have known infringes copyright.[48] It is also an infringement of copyright in a work, sound recording, communication signal or fixation of a performer's performance to possess it for the foregoing purposes[49] or to import it into Canada for any of these purposes.[50] The mere act of posting the work to a Web site should not by itself be considered granting any implied authorization for engaging in such activities.

The copyright owner or an exclusive distributor of books has certain rights to control the parallel importation of new and some used copies of the books in Canada.[51] Such conduct appears not to be included in the implied conduct authorized by the copyright holder who directly or indirectly posts materials to a Web site. In fact, the shipment of a digital file representing a book would seem to bypass any effort to control importation of such books.

For purposes of the foregoing discussion, any implied rights in respect to any acts reserved to the copyright holder would not apply where the copyright holder has stipulated specific terms in relation to what might be done with the applicable material. Any express notice or licence would supersede any implied licence.

### (c)  Liability for Infringing Acts

For the various rights granted to a copyright holder, as discussed above, it would be an infringement for any person to do anything which only the copyright holder is entitled to do. The various types of infringement, and the tests to be applied in determining whether infringement occurs are discussed below.

---

[48]  See section 27(2), *Copyright Act* (Canada); for the US right providing for a right to distribute works by sale, rental, lending, loan or any transfer of ownership see 17 U.S.C. s. 106.

[49]  See section 27(2)(d), *Copyright Act* (Canada).

[50]  See section 27(2)(e), *Copyright Act* (Canada).

[51]  See section 27.1, *Copyright Act* (Canada).

### (i)  Direct Infringement

It is an infringement of the copyright in a work if a person, without the consent of the owner of the copyright, does any act that only the copyright owner has the right to do.[52] In the United States, direct infringement occurs when a person exercises any of the exclusive rights of the copyright holder.[53] It is no defence either under Canadian[54] or US[55] copyright law that the infringement is innocent.

As previously discussed, unauthorized loading of a computer program into the memory of a computer has been held to be reproduction for copyright purposes.[56] In *Sega Entertainment Ltd. v. Maphia*[57] a BBS operator was restrained from posting reproductions of Sega's video game software on the BBS.

In *Religious Technology Centre v. Netcom Online Communications Services, Inc.*[58] neither the Internet Access Provider, Netcom, nor the BBS operator, Klemesrud, was found liable for direct infringement where another person posted allegedly infringing materials to the BBS which was connected to and available through Netcom's network. The judge found Netcom and Klemesrud's role to be the same as every Usenet server, a role which did not amount to direct infringement.[59] There was no positive role or action by the access provider or operator whereby the subscriber makes a copy automatically by visiting the site.

---

[52]  See section 27(1), *Copyright Act* (Canada).

[53]  See 17 U.S.C. s. 106, 501.

[54]  See, for example, *Compo Co. v. Blue Crest Music Inc.*, (1979), [1980] 1 S.C.R. 357, 45 C.P.R. (2d) 1, 105 D.L.R. (3d) 249, (*sub nom. Blue Crest Music Inc. v. Compo Co.*) 29 N.R. 296 (S.C.C.).

[55]  See, for example, *DeAcosta v. Brown*, 146 F. 2d 408 (1944), cert. Denied, 325 US 862 (1945).

[56]  See, for example, *MAI Systems Corp. v. Peak Computer, Inc.*, 991 F. 2d 511 (9th Cir. 1993) which found that copying of a computer program occurs when it is loaded into RAM memory.

[57]  867 F. Supp. 679 (N.D. Cal. 1994).

[58]  907 F. Supp. 1361, 37 U.S.P.Q. 2D 1545 (N.D. Cal. 1995).

[59]  See *Netcom* at page 1553.

In *Playboy Enterprises, Inc. v. Frena,*[60] the court found that the operator of a BBS was not liable for violation of the reproduction right where users uploaded .gif files containing images scanned from Playboy's publications to a BBS allowing other users to download copies of those images. However, the court found the defendant Frena, liable for direct infringement of Playboy's display right and distribution rights.

In *Marobie-Fl, Inc. v. National Association of Fire Distributors*[61] the Internet Access Provider was not liable for infringement in a case where unauthorized copies of clip art were made available from a Web site. The court found that the ISP itself did not carry out the infringement.

### (ii)  Indirect Infringement

A person may be liable for copyright infringement if they provide other persons with the means to carry out infringing acts. Various early cases considered the liability of Internet Service Providers, bulletin board service operators or other service providers who assist users to gain access to or use the Internet in circumstances where the users carry out infringing acts. The issue is to what extent and in what circumstances should the service providers be liable for acts carried out by such other persons.

The Information Highway Advisory Council noted that, under current Canadian copyright law, such operators may be liable for copyright infringement. The Council noted that only common carriers who function[62] solely in that capacity are exempt from copyright liability.

---

[60]   839 F. Supp. 1552 (N.D. Fla. 1993).

[61]   D.C. N.Ill. November 13, 1997, The decision is available at <http://www.bna.com/e-law/cases/marobie.html>.

[62]   A typical example are the telecommunication carriage services provided by the telephone company. In traditional voice communications the telephone company merely provides connectivity between the people who are communicating and has neither any ability to control the content of what is communicated nor any liability for such communications. For example, the telephone company does not screen calls to prevent defamatory statements being made and similarly, has no liability if such statements are communicated by telephone.

The Information Highway Advisory Council suggested that operators of Web sites and BBS systems should remain liable for copyright infringement that occurs on the systems for which they are responsible with the proviso that such liability should not arise where the operator "did not have actual constructive knowledge that the material infringes copyright" or "they acted reasonably to limit potential abuses." This approach is consistent with the findings in the *Netcom* case in the United States. This may already be the position under current Canadian law and, in this regard, the Information Highway Advisory Council noted that no major changes were required in Canadian law to deal with the challenges provided by the Internet.

In this respect, the Information Highway Advisory Council in Canada followed the path set by the Information Infrastructure Task Force formed by President Clinton in the United States. On July 7, 1994, the Information Infrastructure Task Force released its preliminary report for extensive consultation. That consultation was included in a conference which addressed a variety of copyright and related issues. They concluded that a major overhaul of current copyright laws was not required. Instead the Information Infrastructure Task Force recommended:

> "[w]ith no more than minor clarification and limited amendment, the *Copyright Act* will provide the necessary balance of protection of rights — and limitations on those rights — to promote the progress of science and the useful arts. Existing copyright law needs only the fine tuning that technological advances necessitate, in order to maintain a balance of the law in the face of onrushing technology. There must be, however, an effort in three disciplines — law, technology, and education — to successfully address the intellectual property issues raised by the development and the use of the N.I.I."[63]

---

[63]    "Information Infrastructure Task Force, Intellectual Property and the National Information Infrastructure: The Report of the Working Group on Intellectual Property Rights 7" (1995), page 17. For a more complete summary of the N.I.I. Task Force Report and the Canadian Information Highway Advisory Council Report, see J. Fraser Mann, "Reports of the Canadian Information Highway Advisory Council and the United States National Information Infrastructure Working Group on Intellectual Property: A Comparison" 1 *I.T.L.* 2.

The Information Infrastructure Task Force considered but rejected arguments that changes should be made to limit the copyright liability of service providers. The Information Infrastructure Task Force concluded that the existing copyright restrictions are necessary in order for the Information Highway to achieve its full potential. The existing balance of rights must be maintained and should not be readjusted in the context of the Internet. On this point they noted:

> "[c]reators and other owners of intellectual property rights will not be willing to put their interests at risk if appropriate systems — both in the US and internationally — are not in place to permit them to set and enforce the terms and conditions under which their works are made available in the N.I.I. environment. Likewise, the public will not use the services available on the N.I.I. and generate the market necessary for its success unless a wide variety of works are available under equitable and reasonable terms and conditions, and the integrity of those works is assured.[64]

In Canada, the sole rights of the copyright holder may be infringed by a person who authorizes another person to carry out the infringing act.[65] US copyright law recognizes that a defendant may be vicariously liable for copyright infringement if he has under his control the means by which infringement may take place and benefits from any infringement[66]. In *Netcom*, the receipt of access fees paid by users was sufficient benefit for the Internet Access Provider to be found liable based on a theory of vicarious liability.[67] It might be argued, based on this theory, that an Internet Service or Access Provider or a BBS system operator should be vicariously liable where

---

[64]    *Ibid*, page 10 and page 11.

[65]    Section 3(1), *Copyright Act* (Canada). See, for example, *Moorehouse v. University of New South Wales*, [1976] 6 A.L.R. 193 (Aust. H.C.) for a case where the University library was found liable for authorizing an infringement made by a student at a photocopier in the library. It is important to note that the student was not called and the fair dealing exemption was not argued.

[66]    See, for example, *Dreamland Ballroom, Inc. v. Shapiro, Bernstein & Co.*, 36 F. 2D 354 (7th Cir. 1929) and *Fonovisa, Inc. v. Cherry Auction, Inc.* 1996 WL 26912 (9th Cir. 1996).

[67]    see page 1555 of *Netcom*.

the site in question contains links to a site containing infringing materials.[68] This issue is discussed in more detail in Chapter 6.

### (iii)  Contributory Infringement

US copyright law provides a remedy for contributory infringement.[69] The elements of this cause of action are that the defendant, to his or her knowledge, materially contributes to, induces or causes the infringing acts of others.[70] There is no such cause of action under Canadian law, although the course of action of authorizing infringement has certain similarities.

In *Religious Technology Centre v. Netcom Online Communications Services, Inc.*[71] the Internet Access Provider, Netcom, was found liable for contributory infringement in respect to the posting of infringing materials by a disgruntled church member to a Usenet newsgroup hosted by Netcom. While Netcom did not control or approve of the postings, the item continued to be available through Netcom's network after Netcom had been given formal notice (but not proof) of the plaintiff's copyright claim. It was the knowledge of a potential copyright claim and possible infringement, and the failure by Netcom to take prompt action to stop such conduct, that gave rise to liability on the part of Netcom under this theory. The court did not accept Netcom's position that the plaintiff should have proved its ownership of copyright; instead, it was sufficient to show that the posted materials contained copyright notices in favour of the plaintiff and that Netcom failed even to investigate the claim by looking at the posted material.

---

[68]    See, for example, *The Shetland Times Ltd. v. Wills and Zetnews Ltd.*, October 24, 1996 Court of Sessions, Edinborough where a hot link to another's site was considered copyright infringement.

[69]    This form of liability arises under US case law rather than under any specific wording in the US *Copyright Act*. See, for example, *Sony Corp. v. Universal City Studio, Inc.*, 464 US 417 (1984 US S.C.) which recognized this form of infringement.

[70]    See, for example, *Gershwin Publishing Corp. v. Columbia Artists Management, Inc.* 443 F. 2d 1159 (2nd Cir. 1971) and *Netcom*, infra, 907 F. Supp. at page 1373.

[71]    907 F. Supp. 1361, 37 U.S.P.Q. 2D 1545 (N.D. Cal. 1995).

As previously mentioned, in *Sega Entertainment Ltd. v. Maphia*,[72] it was held that uploading Sega games onto a BBS so they could be downloaded by others resulted in liability for contributory infringement.

Also, as previously mentioned, in *Marobie-Fl, Inc. v. National Association of Fire Distributors*[73] the Internet Access Provider was not liable for contributory infringement in a case where unauthorized copies of clip art were made available from a Web site since the ISP did not monitor or control the Web site of the person who conducted the infringement.

### (iv)  Test For Analysis of Infringement

Some of the factors that are considered in determining whether a work infringes the reproduction right for another work are the following:

* Does copyright subsist in the plaintiff's work?[74]

* Did the defendant have access to the plaintiff's work?[75]

* Did the defendant copy the plaintiff's work?[76]

---

[72]  867 F. Supp. 679 (N.D. Cal. 1994).

[73]  D.C. N. Ill. November 13, 1997, The decision is available at <http://www.bna.com/e-law/cases/marobie.html>.

[74]  Given the low level of creativity and originality required under Anglo-Canadian copyright law this step is often satisfied. Note that the US cases deal with some of the issues of common sources, stock items and the like under a *scenes a faire* doctrine which limits the existence of copyright (at the first step of analysis). See, for example, *Autoskill Inc. v. National Education Support Systems Inc.*, 26 U.S.P.Q. 2D 1828 (10th Cir. 1993); *Data East U.S.A. Inc. v. Epyx Inc.*, 862 F. 2D 204 (4th Cir. 1988); and *Atari Inc. v. American Philips Consumer Electronics Corp.*, 672 F. 2D 607 (7th Cir. 1982). Canadian copyright deals with this issue at the last step of the analysis, namely, by finding that similarity in such items is due to causes other than copying.

[75]  Access may suggest copying. Independent creation is a defence under copyright law.

[76]  In many cases the plaintiff may not be able to provide actual evidence of copying. However, where the plaintiff can show substantial similarity, the courts will find a presumption of copying. The onus will be on the defendant to show that the similarity is due to causes other than copying.

- Are the defendant's work and the plaintiff's work substantially similar?[77] and

- Did the defendant have justification for his conduct? Is the similarity due to causes other than copying?[78]

### *(v)  Remedies*

A full range of remedies, both civil and quasi-criminal, is available for the infringement of copyright in a work.[79] The civil remedies for copyright infringement include an injunction, damages and accounting for profits.[80] Such remedies also include the right to obtain delivery of infringing copies and plates used to make the infringing copies.[81]

Copyright legislation also provides for summary remedies, representing quasi-criminal penalties for certain types of infringing conduct. For example, in Canada, it is an offence for a person

---

[77]    The test of substantial similarity under Anglo-Canadian copyright law involves an analysis of whether substantial elements of the plaintiff's work are also found in the defendant's work. The US test is more complex and involves a dissection of the works into copyright and non-copyright subject matter. Under the Anglo-Canadian approach issues of non-copyright subject matter (such as common sources or factual elements) are addressed in the last step, i.e., as part of the analysis of whether the similarity is due to causes other than copying.

[78]    Under this stage of the test the court looks at whether or not similarity is due to a wide range of factors that may cause or require works to be similar to each other. Some of such factors include design constraints which require a similar look (i.e., architectural controls on building plans); requirements for a work to meet compatibility standards; the use of common sources (i.e., both works are based on some external facts such as a historical event); the use of elements which are common in the industry or trade (i.e., elements which are available to all authors.). The US approach tends to deal with the issue of common source or common elements at an earlier stage in the infringement analysis. The issue is also addressed as part of US doctrines such as that of merger of idea and expression (see, for example, *Apple Computer Inc. v. Microsoft Corporation*, 24 U.S.P.Q. 2D 1081, aff'd 32 U.S.P.Q. 2D 1087 (9th Cir. 1994) and *Kregos v. The Associated Press*, 19 U.S.P.Q. 2D 1161 (2nd Cir. 1991) and the *scenes a faire* doctrine (see, for example, *Autoskill Inc. v. National Education Support Systems Inc.*, 26 U.S.P.Q. 2D 1828 (10th Cir. 1993); *Data East U.S.A. Inc. v. Epyx Inc.*, 862 F. 2D 204 (4th Cir. 1988); and *Atari Inc. v. American Philips Consumer Electronics Corp.*, 672 F. 2D 607 (7th Cir. 1982)). This doctrine has not been generally accepted in Canadian jurisprudence.

[79]    See sections 34(1), 35 and 26 of the *Copyright Act* (Canada). For remedies under the US *Copyright Act*, including damages, accounting of profits, attorney fees, see 17 U.S.C. s. 501 et seq.

[80]    See section 38 of the *Copyright Act* (Canada).

[81]    See section 43 of the *Copyright Act* (Canada).

knowingly to make for sale or hire, by way of trade offer for sale or hire, or distribute (so as to prejudicially affect the copyright owner) any infringing copy of a work in which copyright subsists. If found guilty, the defendant may be liable, on summary conviction, to a maximum fine or $25,000 or 6 months imprisonment or both, or on indictment, to a maximum fine of $1,000,000 or 5 years imprisonment or both. The *Copyright Act* also creates offences with respect to certain types of public performances, possession and suppression of title or name.

Canadian copyright law provides that a plaintiff may recover statutory damages for certain types of infringement.[82] The statutory damages will be between $500 and $20,000, with provisions to permit the courts to reduce the statutory damages where there is more than one work in a single medium and the amount would be grossly out of proportion to the infringement. The courts can also award punitive damages in an appropriate case. The law also provides that a collective society may elect to recover between 3 and 10 times the applicable royalties payable to the collective.

In the US, statutory damages may range from US $500 to $20,000 as the court considers appropriate.[83] In cases of willful infringement the court can increase the statutory damages to US $100,000.

## (d)  Defences

There are various exemptions or limitations to a copyright holder's rights. It will generally not be an infringement for a person to perform any act which comes within the exclusive rights of the copyright holder in the following circumstances:

(1) *Express or implied permission granted by copyright holder*

A document made available on the Internet may be accompanied by a notice giving permission for copying the work or for engaging in another activity which is otherwise restricted. If the document contains the terms under which it

---

[82]   See section 38.1, *Copyright Act* (Canada). As of the date of writing, these provisions have not yet been proclaimed in force.

[83]   See 17 U.S.C. s. 504(c).

may be copied or otherwise used, then the user can rely on such permission provided that it is given by or under the authority of the copyright owner.[84]

Alternatively, the user may seek permission at the time of carrying out such copying or other activity.[85] For the reasons discussed above, it may be argued that the act of making a work freely available on a Web site constitutes an implied permission to make a copy of the work for private purposes. However, such permission would not be implied if a notice expressly states that users are not permitted to make copies. In any event, any commercial sale of copies of the work would be outside the scope of any implied permission.

(2) *Works for which term has expired*

It would not be an infringement of copyright to reproduce any work or otherwise to exercise any right reserved to the copyright owner in circumstances where the term of copyright (in most cases 50 years following the end of the year in which the author dies) has expired. For example, if a person posted the text of Shakespeare's *Hamlet,* the copyright in that play would have expired and it may be used by any person. However, the term of copyright would not have expired for most works presently on the Internet.

---

[84]   Many works contain a copyright notice or copyright information. See, for example, the copyright page of a book, licence provisions for many computer programs, or notices in many films and video presentations. Any doubt should be resolved by contacting the copyright owner.

[85]   Generally, it is not difficult to obtain permission from a copyright holder to make copies for non-commercial or non-competitive uses. Most major content providers such as newspapers and media outlets employ staff to assist third parties in processing requests for copyright permissions. The permission should be recorded in writing with a confirming letter providing specifics of the terms of the permission and the works which may be copied. If one cannot locate the copyright holder the Copyright Board can in some circumstances give the permission to copy.

(3) *Works created and first published in countries not members of copyright treaties with Canada*[86]

In view of the number of countries which are members of the Berne Convention, there are few countries to which this exemption would apply. An example would be Singapore which has no copyright treaty with Canada; accordingly, a work created and published by a national in Singapore and not concurrently published in Canada or another Berne Convention country may be unprotected under Canadian copyright law.

(4) *The copying of an non-substantial part of a work*

It is not an infringement of copyright to make a copy of a non-substantial part of a work. The determination of what is a "substantial part" must be made based on the quality and not just the quantity of what is taken, and in many cases, a small part of a work may be considered a substantial part.

(5) *Use of ideas, etc.*

Copyright does not extend to protect ideas, facts, processes or methods, or useful features of works.

(6) *Infringement for which limitation period has expired*

A court may not award a remedy in respect of any infringement unless the proceedings are commenced within 3 years after occurrence of the infringement or within 3 years after the plaintiff knew or should have known of the infringement.[87]

---

[86]  See *Protection of Copyright and Industrial Design*, Carswell, Practice Guide, 1995, for a review of the operation of these treaty provisions and a listing of treaty members.

[87]  See Section 41, *Copyright Act* (Canada).

(7) *Exemption for Internet Access Provider under the* Communications Decency Act[88]

Certain provisions in the *Communications Decency Act* may exempt ISPs from liability.

(8) *Non-protectable elements*

It would not be an infringement of copyright to use common elements which are not sufficiently original to be protected by copyright,[89] or where two works are similar due to external constraints.[90]

### (i) Specific Exemptions

While there are numerous exemptions under the *Copyright Act* (Canada), most apply only in very specific and limited situations. The more important exemptions that may be applicable to uses arising in the context of the Internet are the exemptions for fair dealing (or fair use in the United States), home copying and educational use. These and some other exemptions are discussed below.

---

[88]    See, for example, *Zehran v. America Online, Inc.*, decided November 12, 1997, 4th Cir. 1997. In this case, AOL was provided immunity for liability in respect of third party information under s. 230 of the *Communications Decency Act*. The court also provided a lengthy review of the impracticality of making Internet Service or Access Providers liable for third party infringements due to the virtual impossibility of reviewing, assessing and dealing with the volume of information posted and exchanged on the Internet on a daily basis.

[89]    For example, see *Warren Publishing, Inc. v. Microdos Data Corp.*, 52 F. 3D 950 (11th Cir. 1995) vacated in hearing en banc, 67 F. 3D 276 (11th Cir. 1995), 11th Cir. decided June 10, 1997, where the court found the data elements in a cable fact book were unprotectable (relying on *Feist Publications, Inc. v. Rural Telephone Service Co. Inc.*, 499 US 340 (U.S.S.C.)) and further found that the particular arrangement of the information, which the lower court found creative and protectable, was not sufficiently creative since the selection was made by the computer.

[90]    See, for example, *NEC Corp. v. Intel Corp.*, 10 U.S.P.Q. 2d 1177 (N.D. Cal. 1989) for limited choices available for microcode. See also *Mitel, Inc. v. Iqtel, Inc.* decided September 22, 1997, (10th Cir. 1997) where the court found that codes used in programming call controllers were not copyrighted on the grounds that they were common in the industry and had *de minimus* creativity. The decision can be seen at <http://www.law.emory.edu/10circuit/sept97/95-1394.wpd.html>. Note that Canadian law may reach a similar result but would do so through a different approach. See discussion in section 5.2 (d)(1)(g).

## (1)  *Fair Dealing*

The *Copyright Act* permits a person to copy a work or to engage in another restricted act without the permission of the copyright holder, when such act constitutes a fair dealing with the work and is made for one of certain specified purposes. These purposes include research or private study;[91] or criticism, review or news reporting if the source (and if given in the source, the name of the author of a work, performer of a performance, maker of a sound recording or broadcaster of a communication signal) are mentioned.[92]

While little case law exists on this point, it would appear that at least in some circumstances, where no harm would likely be done to the commercial interests of the copyright holder, a single copy of a work may be taken for one of the purposes specified above under the fair dealing exception.[93] Factors which may be taken into consideration in determining if the conduct is fair dealing include: (1) the type of work; (2) the purpose for which the copy is made; (3) the impact of the copying on the copyright owner's economic interests; and (4) the amount and extent of the copying. In each case, the court must look at all the circumstances of the copying to determine if fair dealing is made out.[94]

The question of whether browsing may come within the fair dealing exemption has not been clearly determined. If it comes within the exemption, it would not be necessary to rely on an implied licence and a user could browse material without regard to whether it was posted by or with the authority of the copyright owner.

---

[91]  See section 29, *Copyright Act* (Canada).

[92]  See section 29.1, *Copyright Act* (Canada), for the criticism or review exemption and Section 29.2 for the news reporting exemption.

[93]  Nimmer, 3 *Nimmer on Copyright*, s.13.05 [A], 1993, suggests that the US fair use exemption will generally not permit taking of an entire copy of a work. But see *Sony Corp. v. Universal City Studios, Inc.*, 464 US 417 (1984 US S.C.) where copying of the entire work was fair use in a case involving little harm to the copyright holder.

[94]  See, for example, in the US *Campbell v. Acuff-Rose Music, Inc.*, 114 S. Ct. 1164 (1994 U.S.S.C.).

As previously mentioned, in *Religious Technology Centre v. Netcom Online Communications Services, Inc.,*[95] a lawsuit was brought alleging copyright infringement of certain materials made available on the Internet. The District Court considered browsing by a user visiting a Web site or BBS to be an exempt activity based on the fair use provisions of the US *Copyright Act.*

(2) *Private Copying of Sound Recordings*

Modern copyright law seeks to address the issue of the widespread reproduction of copyright-protected works by various means. One approach that has been followed for sound recordings is to grant a limited exemption for home or private copying. A second approach is to facilitate the common administration of copyright interests by providing for the formation of collectives to hold and manage such rights for numerous authors.

The home or private copying exemption provides that it is not an infringement of copyright to copy onto an audio recording medium:

(a) a musical work in a sound recording;

(b) a performer's performance of a musical work in a sound recording; and

(c) a sound recording in which a musical work or a performer's performance of a musical work is embodied,

if in each case, the copy is for private use.[96]

This exemption recognizes the widespread home copying activity that occurs in Canada[97] and provides a means to

---

[95]   907 F. Supp. 1361, 37 U.S.P.Q. 2D 1545 (N.D. Cal. 1995).

[96]   See section 80(1), *Copyright Act* (Canada). As of the date of writing, the exemption has not yet been proclaimed in force.

[97]   It also brings Canadian law closer to United States law with respect to musical works. The United States has a broader "fair use" exemption which permits some home copying activity. See, for example, *Universal City Studios v. Sony Corp. of America* 104 S. Ct. 774 [1984] (U.S.S.C.) in which the US Supreme Court found that the home taping of television programs for purposes of "time shifting" was exempt under the US copyright law. The

compensate authors, performers, makers and other rights holders through the levy of a royalty on blank audio recording media (presently cassette tapes) sold in Canada. The manufacturer or importer of the recording media collects the levy, which is then remitted to the applicable collective[98] for distribution to the eligible authors, performers and makers.

However, this levy may be of limited effectiveness insofar as it may be bypassed where the sound recording is available in a digital form through the Internet.[99] Where a digital copy of a sound recording is downloaded from a Web site, the digital file may be stored in a computer memory or disk. However, the blank media royalty is not applicable to the sale of such digital media.

It is important to note that the exemption is only available for private use. Copying for commercial purposes, including rental or sale of the copy, would still be infringing. This exemption does not permit the communication of a copy to the public by telecommunication.

## (3) *Educational Exemptions*

An important use of the Internet is for teaching and education. Copyright law provides certain limited exemptions for educational purposes.[100] One such exemption is that it is not

---

private copying exemption also provides compensation to the rights holders affected.

[98] A collective is a society or other organization which represents the interests of a large group of copyright holders. Collectives facilitate the distribution of this new royalty but also provide blanket consents to use of material in the repertoire of the collective. Rates charged by collectives are subject to approval by the Copyright Board. See section 83, *Copyright Act* (Canada).

[99] In the US also see *Digital Performance Right in Sound Recordings Act of 1995*, Pub. L. 104-39, enacted November 1, 1995.

[100] Prior to the changes provided by S.C. 1997, c. 24, (Bill C-32) section 27(2)(d), of the *Copyright Act* (Canada) (the "educational exemption") provided that "short passages", from sources in which copyright subsists from works not intended for use in schools, suitably acknowledged, do not infringe in school use, so long as "not more than two of such passages from works by the same author are published .... within five years" This was a very limited exemption and of little use to most educational institutions. This exemption is generally preserved in the revised law but supplemented by additional exemptions.

an infringement of copyright for an educational institution or a person acting under its authority to make a copy of a work:

(a) onto a dry-erase board, flip chart or any other thing on which written material may be displayed, or

(b) as an image projected on an over-head projector or similar device

for the purposes of education or training on the premises of an educational institution.[101] This exemption could be invoked by an educator who finds the work on a Web site or discussion group, and makes a copy of the work for the specified educational purposes.

A limited exemption permits the use of a work for a purpose related to the giving of an assignment, test or examination on the premises of an educational institution, including for purposes of setting the questions and communicating the questions and answers to the persons completing the assignment or taking the test or examination and answering the questions by those persons.[102]

Limited exemptions also permit the performance of the following acts if they are done on the premises of an educational institution for educational or training purposes and not for profit, before an audience consisting primarily of students of the educational institution, instructors acting under the authority of the educational institution or any person who is directly responsible for setting a curriculum for the educational institution: (a) the live performance in public, primarily by students of the educational institution, of a work; (b) the performance in public of a sound recording or of a work or performer's performance that is embodied in a sound recording; and (c) the performance in public of a work or other subject-matter at the time of its communication to the public by telecommunication.[103]

---

[101] See section 29.4(1), *Copyright Act.*

[102] See section 29.4(2), *Copyright Act.*

[103] See section 29.5, *Copyright Act.*

Teachers of social studies or other topical subject matters are granted certain rights to use current affairs information available through news programs, which may include news provided by a Web site or service. The teacher or other authorized person with an educational institution may (a) make, at the time of its communication to the public by telecommunication, a single copy of a news program or a news commentary program (other than documentaries), for the purposes of performing the copy for the students of the educational institution for educational or training purposes; and (b) perform the copy in public, at any time or times within one year after the making of a copy under paragraph (a), before an audience consisting primarily of students of the educational institution on its premises for educational or training purposes.[104] The copy may not be kept for more than 30 days and royalties may be payable for such use. A complex administrative record keeping and marking process is imposed on the educational institution under these provisions.[105]

### (ii)  Public Policy Exemptions

In some cases, courts have found that a person may use materials in a manner that would otherwise infringe copyright based on grounds of public policy. One circumstance in which this defence or exemption may be applicable is where legal materials, such as statutes, regulations and judicial decisions, are used for purposes of legal proceedings or activities. The grounds for the exemption is the public interest policy for any person to have the means of knowing the law which would take precedence over the interests of the

---

[104]  See section 29.6 (1) *Copyright Act* (Canada). Not yet in force as of the date of publication.

[105]  See sections 29.5 through 29.9, *Copyright Act* (Canada).

copyright holder.[106] The rationale for this principle, as cited in various judicial decisions, is stated as follows:[107]

> "(1) In a democracy where the widest possible public dissemination of materials of public interest is considered vital:
>
> (a) expositions of the law (statutes, judicial opinions and legislative histories) cannot be copyrighted because everyone is presumed to know the law and no one can be given a monopoly on publishing their expositions;
>
> (b) materials generated by government employees and initially printed should be given the widest, least expensive distribution, which is possible only if no one can monopolize the publication or republication of an item."

The principle that works created at public expense should be freely available without copyright restrictions is expressly set out in the US copyright law which expressly excludes copyright in statutory materials and government documents.[108] French legal doctrine appears to follow a similar approach to that of the US.[109]

The approach followed in the United Kingdom is to set out, by way of general notice,[110] the circumstances in which government materials and statutory materials may be reproduced. This notice

---

[106]   See, for example, *B.C. Jockey Club v. Standen* [1983],4 W.W.R. 537, 146 D.L.R. (3d) 693, 73 C.P.R. (2d) 164 (B.C.S.C.), aff'd (1985) 22 D.L.R. (4th) 467, 66 B.C.L.R. 245, [1985] 6 W.W.R. 683, 8 C.P.R. (3d) 283 (B.C. C.A.) where the court expressed the view that judicial opinions may be published on public policy grounds.

[107]   Brian Price, "Copyright in Government Publications: Historical Background, Judicial Interpretation and Legislative Clarification" (1976) 74 *Mil. L. Rev.* 19 at p. 36.

[108]   In the United States, there is no copyright protection for government works. The US *Copyright Act* of 1895, Act of June 12, 1895, c. 23, 28 Stat. s. 52 and US *Copyright Act* of 1909, Act of Mar. 4, 1909, c. 320, 35 Stat. s. 7 contain express statutory bars. See also *Nash v. Lathrop* 142 Mass. 29, 6 N.E. 559 (1886). The present US *Copyright Act* states in s. 105 that: "copyright protection under this title is not available for any work of the United States Government."

[109]   H. Desbois, *Le Droit d'Auteur en France*, 2nd ed. Paris, Dallotz, 1966, para. 41.

[110]   Gen 75/76-Crown Copyright dated August 12, 1975.

applies to Bills, Acts of Parliament, statutory rules, orders, statutory instruments, other Parliamentary papers and Hansard.

Canada has followed this approach by confirming the right to make broad use of federal legal materials. The Canadian provision states:

"Whereas it is of fundamental importance to a democratic society that its law be widely known and that its citizens have unimpeded access to the law;

And whereas the Government of Canada wishes to facilitate access to its law by licensing the production of federal law without charge or permission;

Therefore His Excellency the Governor General in Council, on the recommendation of the Minister of Canadian Heritage, the Minister of Industry, the Minister of Public Works and Government Services, the Minister of Justice and the Treasury Board, hereby makes the annexed Reproduction of Federal Law Order:

REPRODUCTION OF FEDERAL LAW ORDER

Anyone may, without charge or request for permission, reproduce enactments and consolidations of enactments of the Government of Canada, and decisions and reasons for decisions of federally constituted courts and administrative tribunals, provided due diligence is exercised in ensuring the accuracy of the materials reproduced and the reproduction is not represented as an official version."

An incidental problem that arises under Canadian law with respect to the copying of materials that may be permitted by end users under the fair dealing exemption or based on public policy grounds is whether the exemption also applies where the copy is made by an intermediary. The classic example of this issue involves librarians who make a copy of a work for an end user who may qualify for the fair dealing exemption (i.e., the copy is to be used for private study or research). The librarian makes no productive use of the work yet may be liable for infringement.[111] This problem has been addressed by specific legislative protection for librarians in Canada.[112]

Another example of a public policy exemption is a House of Lords decision that recognized such an exemption to the copyright claim of an automobile manufacturer permitting the making of spare parts.[113]

### (iii)  Other Exemptions

Other common exemptions include:[114]

(1) making a copy of a computer program by the user for archive purposes only or to adapt the computer program for use on a different computer system;[115]

(2) the incidental and unintentional inclusion of a work in another work;[116] and

(3) the reproduction of a work at the request of a person with a perceptual disability into a format designed for such persons.[117]

## (e)  Special Problems

Copyright law provides many rights applicable to various uses of works available on the Internet. The very nature of the Internet, as discussed above, gives rise to some special issues involving the use of copyright works which are discussed in this section. These issues include the use of the Internet for browsing, for caching and for reproducing works onto mirror sites. To understand the significance

---

[111]  See, for example, *Moorehouse v. University of New South Wales*, [1976] 6 A.L.R. 193 (Aust. H.C.) for a case where the University library was found liable for authorizing an infringement made by a student at a photocopier in the library. It is important to note that the student was not called and the fair dealing exemption was not argued.

[112]  See sections 29.5 through 29.9, *Copyright Act* (Canada).

[113]  See *British Leyland Motor Corp. Ltd. v. Armstrong Patents Co. Ltd.*, [1986] 1 All E.R. 850 (H.L.).

[114]  See section 32.1, *Copyright Act* (Canada), and the sections that follow for further exemptions.

[115]  See section 30.6, *Copyright Act* (Canada).

[116]  See section 30.7, *Copyright Act* (Canada).

[117]  See section 32, *Copyright Act* (Canada).

of these activities, it is important to consider the concept of implied licence and the implications of posting materials to a Web site. Another special issue involves the scope of protection available for databases.

### (i) Implied Licence Arising from Posting Copyright Materials on the Internet

By its very nature, the Internet is a forum for the sharing of data and information. A person who owns copyright in certain material and makes that material available by various means involving use of the Internet may be considered as understanding the normal uses that are made of such material. On this basis, the person would likely be found to have granted an implied right to permit users to engage in such ordinary uses of the material.[118] The existence and scope of the implied licence may vary according to the terms of any express notices given to users or agreements made with such users.

The scope of the rights granted under such an implied licence would depend on the circumstances. For example, the act of posting a message on a Listserv gives rise to an implication that the system operator is authorized to reproduce and distribute the message to others. If a copyright holder wishes to impose limitations or conditions other than those that are likely to be implied based on common Internet practice (as discussed below), then such limitations or conditions should be expressly set out in a notice accompanying the messages.

Certain materials are made available on the Internet in a fashion similar to the shareware concept, which developed as an approach to software distribution in the early 1980s. A software developer or vendor would make software available to the marketplace to be copied by users. A user who liked the software and wished to use it was encouraged to send in a payment. A variation of this approach was to distribute software that was limited in features or functionality. Once the user paid for the licence, the full programs were provided or complete features enabled. The shareware approach was followed as a means for the vendor to offer free samples to encourage

---

[118] See, for example, Stolowitz, "Copyright in the Internet: A short primer for business lawyers", 1996, at <http://www.techlaw.com/TextOnly/WhatsNew/copyright.html>.

customers to sample their wares or services. Many Web sites on the World Wide Web work in a similar manner by offering "free samples," such as digital sound recordings, graphic images, information or software. The free samples may be offered to encourage users to subscribe for the more complete version of the product or the provision of the product or service on an ongoing basis.

Where the owner of copyrighted materials makes these materials available on the Internet, the permitted uses of these materials would have to be determined based on the express agreement made with each user, or failing such an agreement, the terms that a court would find that the parties might have made in an agreement had they considered it. Some of the factors that a court may consider to determine the reasonable contemplation of the parties include the following:

- What would be the natural and reasonable expectations of a person in the position of the user;[119]

- Did the owner of copyright reserve any rights or uses in making the material available;[120]

- Where the issue relates to use of a work in a certain format or media, what technology is available for use of the work

---

[119]   See, for example, *ADI Ltd. v. J.L. Destein* (1982), 41 N.B.R. (2d) 518, 107 A.P.R. 518, 68 C.P.R. (2d) 262, 141 D.L.R. (3d) 370, (N.B.Q.B.) where the owner of a building that settled sued ADI, who designed the building, and won damages. The building was then sold to the defendant who hired ADI to redesign the building. ADI provided prints but no reproducible copies. The defendant Destein reproduced the plans to carry out the reconstruction. Destein did not dispute that ADI held the copyright or that ADI did not grant express permission to reproduce the plans but claimed an implied right to reproduce the plans. The court found that the purchaser had an implied licence to copy the plans for purposes of permitting the legitimate repair of a structure, being the use for which the plans were prepared and commissioned by the purchaser. In the absence of an express agreement by the parties, the court implied the terms of the licence.

[120]   See, for example, *Warner Bros. Pictures v. Columbia Broadcasting Systems*, 216 F. 2D 945 (9th Cir. 1954) where the court found that since use of certain characters and names was never specifically mentioned, such use was reserved by the licensor.

and what might have been anticipated by the parties given their relative skills;[121]

•   Did the party making the material available even have the right to authorize the uses which are asserted.[122]

With all of these factors the court must then decide who gets the benefit of any doubt or uncertainty. One line of cases suggests that a user may exercise all rights that reasonably flow from the grant[123] while other cases suggest that any use not expressly granted is reserved.[124]

It is suggested that if the copyright owner posts material to a Web site and does not expressly provide for certain prohibitions, then users should be found to have those limited rights which represent the natural and reasonable uses of the information on the site. These uses should include the browsing and review of the material, being the specific purposes for which the information is posted.[125] By contrast, the implied rights would not extend to the use of corporate

---

[121]   See, for example, *Ettore v. Philco Television Broadcasting Corporation*, 229 F. 2D 481 (3rd Cir. 1956), cert. Denied, 351 US 926 (1956) where a court found that a professional prize fighter would not have known about the value of movie rights in 1936, and accordingly such use was not read into a broad grant of rights. See also *Bartsch v. Metro-Goldwyn-Meyer, Inc.*, 391 F. 2D 150 (2nd Cir. 1968), cert. Denied, 393 US 826 (1968) where an experienced businessman accepted a broad grant of rights, which was found effective to cover certain uses which were not expressly mentioned.

[122]   See, for example, *Bishop v. Stevens*, 72 D.L.R. (4th) 97, [1990] 2 S.C.R. 467, 31 C.P.R. (3d) 394, 111 N.R. 376, [1990] 2 R.C.S. 467 (S.C.C.) where a grant by the public performance rights collective was held not to imply any exercise of the mechanical reproduction right (which was not held by the performing rights collective).

[123]   See, for example, *Platinum Record Co. v. Lucasfilm, Ltd.*, 566 F. Supp. 226 (D.N.J. 1983) which held that a grant to "exhibit, exploit, market, and perform perpetually throughout the world by any means now or hereafter known" included use of video cassettes and video disks to distribute the musical works.

[124]   See, for example, *Rey v. Lafferty*, 990 F. 2D 1379 (1st Cir. 1993). In *Data Products, Inc. v. Reppart*, 18 U.S.P.Q. 2D 1058 (D. Kan, 1990), the court refused to permit use of a computer program by corporate subsidiaries outside the express provisions of a licence by a successor to the licence.

[125]   See *Foresight Resources Corp. v. Pfortmiller*, 719 F. Supp. 1006 (D. Kan. 1989) in which a licensee adapted software where the licence agreement did not prohibit such conduct. The judge permitted such adaptations and quoted from the Final Report on New Technological Uses of Copyrighted Works as follows: "Should proprietors feel strongly that they do not want rightful possessors of copies of their programs to prepare such adaptations, they could, of course, make such desires a contractual matter."

logos or other identification of the Web site owner or host, nor would it include other commercial activities.[126]

The fact that material posted to a Web site, with the authority of the copyright holder, becomes publicly available (unless certain measures are taken to restrict access) means that users may also be entitled to exercise certain limited rights to use such materials under certain exemptions granted by copyright law. One such exemption is that of fair dealing which may permit the copying of work, or a substantial part of the work, for purposes of private study or research, or for the purposes of criticism, review or newspaper summary if the source and the author's name (if given in the source) are mentioned.[127]

If a copyright owner wishes to limit the scope of an implied licence that may be found, or the rights arising from any exemption in the *Copyright Act*, the owner may use various means of restricted distribution available for works on the Internet.[128] Similarly, a copyright holder may also set out the express terms of licences for the online use of materials on the Internet.

The issue of whether "browsing" may be an infringing act or may come within one of the exemptions in the *Copyright Act* is discussed below.

---

[126] In *Ryan et al v. The Uncover Company and Knight-Ridder Information, Inc.* a complaint was filed by writers whose published articles (in which they appeared to hold copyright) were made available for users to copy for a fee from a database system operated by the defendant. The class action suit alleges that no authorization was given for the conduct of the defendants. See the complaint filed Oct. 22, 1997 in N.D. Cal. at <http://www.jmls.edu/cyber/cases/carl1.html> but see also *Tasini v. New York Times*, 93 Civ. 8678 (SS) (S.D.N.Y. Aug. 13, 1997) where the court held that a publisher may place articles written by freelance writers into a database without specific permission.

[127] S. 107 of the U.S copyright law provides for a broader fair use defence. This is discussed in more detail in section 5.2 (iv) below.

[128] Some of these methods involve use of passwords, digital signatures or other unique identifiers provided to a user in order to obtain access to the full text of the information or materials. For example, a Web site may permit the downloading of software with limited functionality. If a user wants the fully functional version of the software, then he or she would subscribe and may be provided with the fully functioning software by courier or other physical delivery, or electronically by being provided with access (through the use of a password, digital signature or other means) to a restricted portion of the Web site.

### (ii) Browsing

Most people visit Web sites on the World Wide Web by using a Web browser such as Netscape's Navigator or Mircosoft's Explorer. These computer programs permit the user to view the material on the Web site in a manner appropriate to the standards applicable to that software.

The act of visiting a Web site causes the browsing software to load a copy of the Web page or pages into the browser software for viewing by the user. Intermediate copies may be made as the digital file is copied from the Web site and passes through various nodes and gateways on the Internet to the viewer's computer. These are transitory copies (subject to the discussion on caching in section 5.2(e)(iii) below). The viewer can then scroll through that material and print it out, store it to disk or continue his or her quest by following links to other Web sites or pages of interest to the user. For the purposes of the present discussion, "browsing" means the act of loading a copy of Web pages into the browser software, thereby making a transitory copy of the material. Such acts should be distinguished from the printing or downloading of copies of the Web pages or other materials located on the Web site.

Unless one of the exemptions provided by copyright law applies, it is clear that the reproduction of a substantial portion of a work without the copyright owner's authority is an infringement. The act of loading a computer program into the memory of the computer has been held to be reproduction for copyright purposes.[129]

In Canada, the final report of the Information Highway Advisory Council[130] made the following recommendations:

   (1)  Browsing should be an activity defined in the *Copyright Act*;

---

[129]  See, for example, *MAI Systems Corp. v. Peak Computer, Inc.*, 991 F. 2d 511 (9th Cir. 1993) which found that copying of a computer program occurs when it is loaded into RAM memory. Other authorities have suggested that a reproduction occurs only when there is a certain degree of permanence to the reproduction: see Canada's blueprint for copyright reform, the *Charter of Rights for Creators*, 1985, (P. 42). However, the *Charter of Rights for Creators* did not fully anticipate the importance of digital works and the present status of the Internet.

[130]  September 1995, published by the Information Highway Advisory Council Secretary, Industry Canada.

(2) The *Copyright Act* should provide a definition of a "publicly available" work to address when a work may be generally available through the Internet; and

(3) It should be left to the copyright owner to determine whether and when the browsing activity should be permitted on the Internet and to identify such portions of the work as would be available for browsing activity.

Some commentators have interpreted these recommendations to mean that the *Copyright Act* should be changed to create special rights and limits on such rights with respect to browsing on the Internet. Such changes might include a requirement for the copyright owner's authorization to browse materials made available on a Web site. However, because browsing is fundamental to the operation of the World Wide Web portion of the Internet, a legislative change that would expressly prohibit such activity would change the way the Internet operates.

Browsing may also be permitted as an exempt activity based on the fair dealing provisions of the Canadian *Copyright Act* (or the similar fair use provision in the US *Copyright Act*). In *Religious Technology Centre v. Netcom Online Communications Services, Inc.,*[131] a lawsuit was brought alleging copyright infringement of certain materials made available on the Internet. The District Court considered browsing by a user visiting a Web site or BBS to be an exempt activity as follows:

> "There could hardly be a market for licensing the temporary copying of digital works onto computer screens to allow browsing. Unless such a use is commercial, such as where someone reads a copyrighted work online and therefore decides not to purchase a copy from the copyright owner, fair use is likely. Until reading a work online becomes as easy and convenient as reading a paperback, copyright owners do not have much to fear from digital browsing and there will not likely be much market effect."[132]

---

[131]   907 F. Supp. 1361, 37 U.S.P.Q. 2D 1545 (N.D. Cal. 1995).

[132]   37 U.S.P.Q. 2D at page 1558. Note that this appears to be an *obiter dictum*, not necessary to the decision.

Because material posted to a Web site may be accessed by many users, the act of making such work available by this means may also constitute a communication of the work to the public by telecommunication. This issue is considered further in section 5.4 below.

In summary, browsing activity should be deemed to be authorized when a copyright holder either personally posts or authorizes another person to post copyright material to a Web site since the copyright holder is thereby authorizing other persons to come and view the posted material. Arguably that authorization should extend to making a copy of the posted material for purposes of private study or research, although this activity may be covered by the fair dealing exemption in any event.[133] As a result, the issues that should properly be addressed are (i) determining the proper scope of the authorization and (ii) what happens if the posting party is neither the copyright holder nor a person acting with the authority of the copyright holder.

The issue should not be the regulation of browsing, but to ensure authorization for the posting of material to the Web site. If a copyright owner does not wish his or her materials to be browsed, then the owner should employ various means of restricted distribution available on the Internet.[134] Of course, there would be no right to "browse" materials in violation of such restrictions. The owner may also restrict the scope of the activities of a user by means of an express agreement made with the user or by means of a prominent notice that appears when the work is displayed.

### (iii) Caching and Mirror Sites

Access to popular Web sites may be difficult to obtain if many users seek to use common gateways or network links to gain access to the sites. In order to facilitate more rapid access to a Web site or materials provided on the Internet, some of the materials are stored or cached at intermediate points or nodes on the Internet. Further,

---

[133] See discussion of the fair dealing exemption in section 5.2(d)(i)(a) above.

[134] See Fites and Kratz, *Information Systems Security: A Practitioner's Reference*, 1993 Van Nostrand Reinhold, N.Y., N.Y. ISBN 0442001800 for examples of use and implementation of such methods.

many Web Browser programs, such as Netscape's Navigator or Microsoft's Explorer, keep a transitory copy in a cache file so that the user can more quickly retrace his or her links to a previously visited Web site or pages. For purposes of the present discussion, the term "caching" means the act of loading a copy of the Web page or pages into either the browser software or onto an intermediate location of the Internet for more rapid access.

It is helpful to review both types of caching separately. Where the browser software retains the transitory copy of Web pages in a cache file, such conduct should be consistent with the limited uses made of a work by a user who browses and/or downloads the work for purposes of private study. Such use may be considered as coming within the scope of the implied authorization granted by the copyright holder who posts his or her materials on the Internet. The only issue in such a case should be where the material has been posted to the Internet without the authority of the copyright holder. The user gains no additional rights to the use of such materials.

The caching of materials at intermediate locations on the Internet, provided that such activity is solely for the purpose of providing more rapid access to the materials, in some circumstances may also come within the scope of the implied authorization granted by the copyright holder.[135] However, if a person caches large volumes of materials made available by others on the Internet and seeks to make use of such materials for commercial purposes, then the implied authorization of the copyright holder may be exceeded.

A person who makes material available on Web sites may impose technological means to prevent other persons from caching the material on intermediate servers. The taking of such steps would preclude any argument that the content provider has granted an implied authorization for the caching of material on the intermediate server.

---

[135] However, in some cases, particularly where a Web site is advertising supported, intermediate caching may result in a loss of revenues to the operator of the original Web site due to a failure to record access to the sites that were accommodated from cached copies of the Web site. In such cases, intermediate caching may be argued to be inappropriate.

Another approach to relieving the congestion to a popular Web site is to create a duplicate site at a different address, which is usually made available by traversing down less congested gateways and network links. This is called a mirror site which usually contains an exact duplicate of the original site. A mirror site is normally created based on the terms of an express agreement made between the person responsible for the creation of the content on the original site and the party hosting the mirror site. Accordingly, the question of whether the operation of a mirror site comes within the terms of an implied authorization does not normally arise.

### (iv)  Protection of Data and Databases

Databases contain information of many types that is organized, stored and retrieved by users. Many Web sites contain databases which are used to provide services or access to information. Databases are considered compilation works under copyright law. Significant work is often involved in the creation of such compilations. In Anglo-Canadian law, which does not have a tort of unfair competition as exists under United States law, the test that has been applied to determine whether copyright protection is available for compilations is whether labour, skill and judgment were expended in the assembly of the compilation.[136]

Because databases are so important in the context of the Internet, we review the protection available for the data elements and the database as a whole.

### (1)  Protection of Data Elements

The individual data elements making up a database will be protected by copyright only if they satisfy a certain minimum standard of creative expression so as to be considered to be works separate from the database as a whole. Some cases suggest that the amount of creativity required for a short series of words or symbols to be protected by copyright may be minimal. However, copyright protection is generally not available for a single word, even if it is a

---

[136]  See, for example, *Football League Ltd. v. Littlewood's Pools Ltd.* (1959), 1 Ch. 637 (Ch. D.) where a football league play schedule was protected by copyright, based, among other factors, on the labour and effort involved in constructing the schedule.

result of labour, skill and judgment, where that word was not intended to convey information, or provide pleasure or entertainment.[137] Courts have found copyright, however, to exist in a grid of numbers and lines generated by computer.[138] Similarly, copyright has been found in tables of numbers, words and the like and also in encrypted messages.[139]

### (2) The Database Itself

In various Canadian cases dealing with compilations, Canadian courts reached beyond the form of expression to consider aspects of the structure or sequence of the work.

In *Kelly v. Morris*,[140] the court granted an injunction to restrain publication of a directory or guide book. The court in that case rejected the argument that, once published, the material in such compilations became public knowledge and could be used without restriction by others. The court found instead, that the compiler of a work is not entitled to spare himself the labour and expense of original inquiry by adapting and republishing the information contained in previous works on the same subject, even if the underlying information may be identical if correctly given because it comes from the same external sources.[141]

In *Underwriters Survey Bureau Ltd. v. American Home Fire Assurance Co.*,[142] the court found that a compilation of data in an

---

[137] See, for example, *Exxon Corp. v. Exxon Insurance Consultants International Ltd.*, [1981] 3 All E.R. 241; *Francis Day & Hunter Ltd. v. Twentieth Century Fox Corp.*, [1939] 4 D.L.R. 353, [1939] 4 All E. R. 192, [1940] A.C. 112 (J.C.P.C.). In the US, titles, for example, are not protected by Federal or state copyright. *Arthur Retan & Associates Inc. v. Travenol Laboratories, Inc.*, 582 F.Supp. 1010 (N.D. Ill. 1984); *Gordon v. Warner Bros. Pictures, Inc.*, 269 Cal.App. 2d 31, 74 Cal. Reporter 499 (Cal. App. 1969).

[138] *Express Newspapers PLC v. Liverpool Daily Post & Echo PLC*, [1985] 3 All E.R. 680 (Ch. D.).

[139] *D.P. Anderson & Co. Limited v. The Lieber Code Company* (1917), 2 K.B. 469.

[140] *Kelly v. Morris* (1866), L.R. 1 Eq 897; see also *Cox v. Land & Water Journal Co.* (1869), L.R. 9 Eq 324.

[141] In *Kelly v. Morris* and also in *Cox v. Land and Water Journal Company* injunctions were granted. Of significance in both cases is the fact that certain errors and outdated facts of the original works were reproduced in the derived works.

[142] [1939] 4 D.L.R. 89, [1939] Ex. C. R. 296 (Can Ex. Ct.).

insurance manual was protected by copyright. While the individual components might not have been original, the particular grouping of related information and the presentation were original. In that case, the plaintiff's assembly of data was original and there was no common source from which the defendants could derive a similar work.

A more recent case is *British Columbia Jockey Club v. Standen.*[143] In that case the Jockey Club had assembled, after considerable effort, a publication containing information relating to horse racing activities. The individual components were not original to the plaintiff. The defendant produced another publication which reproduced information from the plaintiff's publication and in addition, contained considerable additional information collected by the defendant. The defendant argued that he was entitled to take the bare information from the plaintiff's publication and after expending his own labour and skills present that information in his own style and with added information of his own.

On appeal, the court found that the trial judge was correct in relying on the following extract from *The Modern Law of Copyright*:

> "... The copyright in such a work may be infringed by appropriating an undue amount of the material, although the language employed be different or the order of the material be altered. Were the law otherwise, copyrights in compilations would be of little or no value. The point is distinctly stated in two dicta which have frequently been approved: "No man is entitled to avail himself of the previous labours of another for the purpose of conveying to the public the same information;" and "The true principle in all these cases is that the defendant is not at liberty to use or avail himself of the labour which the plaintiff has been at for the purpose of producing his work; that is, in fact, merely to take away the result of another man's labour or, in other words, his property."[144]

By contrast to these decisions, more recent cases have focused on whether a compilation reflects originality in the overall arrangement of the various components of the work. In *Slumber-Magic Adjustable*

---

[143]    (1985), 66 B.C.L.R. 245, 22 D.L.R. (4th) 467, [1985] 6 W.W.R. 683, 8 C.P.R. (3d) 283 (B.C. C.A.).

[144]    Laddie, Prescott & Victoria, *The Modern Law of Copyright* (1980), Para. 2.65, p. 41, quoted at 22 D.L.R. (4th) 467 at 470.

*Bed Co. v. Sleep-King Adjustable Bed Co.,*[145] Madam Justice McLachlin, as she then was, applied the following test:

> "It is established that compilations of material produced by others may be protected by copyright, provided that the arrangement of the elements taken from other sources is the product of the plaintiff's thought, selection or work. It is not the several components that are the subject of copyright, but the over-all arrangement of them which the plaintiff through his industry has produced. The basis of copyright is the originality of the work in question. So long as the work, taste and discretion have entered into the composition, that originality is established. In the case of a compilation, originality requisite to copyright is a matter of degree depending on the amount of skill, judgment or labour that has been involved in making the compilation; *Ladbroke (Football) Ltd. v. William Hill (Football) Ltd.*, [1964] 1 All E.R. 465 (H.L.)."

In *Tele-Direct (Publications) Inc. v. American Business Information, Inc.*, the Federal Court of Appeal[146] affirmed the finding of the Trial Division[147] that copyright did not subsist in certain components of a Yellow Pages telephone directory. The court in that case was not asked to rule on whether copyright subsisted in the directory as an entire compilation, since this had been conceded by the respondent. The issue, instead, was whether copyright subsisted in certain "fragments" of the directory, namely, the in-column business listings which constituted a sub-compilation.

In affirming the decision of the Trial Division that these components of the directory were not protected by copyright, Décary J.A. relied on the fact that in 1993, the *Copyright Act* was amended to include a new definition of a "compilation" insofar as it relates to the "selection or arrangement of data". The court found that this definition, which was enacted to implement the North American Free Trade Agreement ("NAFTA"), had the effect of deciding the battle between partisans of the creativity doctrine whereby compilations must possess some minimal degree of creativity, and partisans of the

---

[145]   (1984), 3 C.P.R. (3d) 81, [1985] 1 W.W.R. 112 (B.C. S.C.).

[146]   (1997), 221 N.R. 113, 154 D.L.R. (4th) 328, 76 C.P.R. (3d) 296, 134 F.T.R. 80 (note) (Fed C.A.); see 1 *I.T.L.* at 83, leave to appeal to the Supreme Court of Canada refused (May 21, 1998).

[147]   (1996), 27 B.L.R. (2d) 1, 113 F.T.R. 123, 74 C.P.R. (3d) 72 (Fed. T.D.), affirmed.

industrious collection or "sweat of the brow" doctrine where copyright is seen as a reward for the work that goes into compiling facts.

In interpreting this new definition, Décary J.A. relied on Article 1705 of NAFTA, which requires each Contracting Party to protect works "that embody *original expression*" within the meaning of the Berne Convention, and in particular, to protect compilations of data and other material that "by reason of the selection or arrangement of their contents constitute *intellectual creations*". [*Emphasis added.*]. He found that these expressions meant that compilations of data should be protected based on standards of intellect and creativity. Since these standards were already present in Anglo-Canadian jurisprudence, the Canadian Government, in signing NAFTA, and the Canadian Parliament, in amending the *Copyright Act*, must have expected the courts to follow the "creativity" rather than the "industrious collection" school of cases. Moreover, the amendments simply reinforced "in clear terms what the state of the law was, or ought to have been: the selection or arrangement of data only results in a protected compilation if the end result qualifies as an original intellectual creation."

In determining whether the sub-compilation was protected, Décary J.A. referred to the traditional test that has been applied by the courts, namely, whether "skill, judgment or labour" was expended in creating the work. The court found, however, that whenever the word "or" was used in these cases, it was meant to be used in a conjunctive rather than disjunctive sense. Accordingly, a considerable level of labour will not be sufficient in most situations if it is combined with only a negligible degree of skill and judgment.

Décary J.A. found that copyright legislation protects and rewards only the "intellectual effort" of the "author", and the word "author" conveys a sense of creativity and ingenuity. Accordingly, any cases which in the past adopted the "sweat of the brow" doctrine should not be read as meaning that the amount of labour itself would be a determinative source of originality. Moreover, any cases following such an approach would be wrong and irreconcilable with the standards of intellect and creativity set out in NAFTA and endorsed in the 1993 amendments to the *Copyright Act,* and that were already recognized in Anglo-Canadian law.

Applying these principles to the facts of the current case, the court found that the sub-compilation in question was not a "new product of inventive labour" and did not amount to an "intellectual creation" within the meaning of Article 1705 of NAFTA. Instead, the compilation of in-column listings was of such an obvious and commonplace character as to be unworthy of copyright protection.

Décary J.A. found further that in view of his finding that there was no copyright in the sub-compilation, it was not necessary to consider the issue of infringement.

Décary J.A. indicated that the 1993 amendments permitted Canadian courts to seek assistance from authoritative US decisions. This did not mean that the courts should depart from fundamental principles of Anglo-American jurisprudence, but only that Canadian courts should not hesitate to adopt an interpretation that satisfies both the Anglo-Canadian and American standards. It was of some significance that Article 1705 of NAFTA and the added definition of a compilation in the Canadian *Copyright Act* tracked to a certain extent the definition of a "compilation" in the US *Copyright Act*. After reviewing the US jurisprudence, the court concluded that "there is a fortunate similarity in matters of compilation of data between the American approach and our own."

## 5.3 MORAL RIGHTS

A work protected by copyright may be an expression of the author's personality, and accordingly, an author may wish to restrain certain uses of the work that may adversely affect the author's reputation. Accordingly, the *Copyright Act* provides for certain "moral rights" to protect the author's personality and reputation. An author retains moral rights even after a sale of any tangible embodiment of the work and even after an assignment of copyright in the work.

The moral rights may be described as (i) a right to claim authorship, (ii) an integrity right, and (iii) an association right. The moral rights apply even if the author is not the owner of the copyright in the work (e.g., where the work was created by an employee in the course of employment so as to make the employer the first owner of copyright). The author may waive the moral rights but such rights may not be assigned to another person.

The full range of remedies is available for an infringement of moral rights in a work.[148] In addition, certain types of conduct for which there are statutory defences to a copyright infringement action are also defences to a moral rights infringement action.[149]

Limitations on enforcement of moral rights include the requirement to bring action within three years of the cause of action.[150]

### (a)  Right to Claim Authorship

The author has the right to require his or her name to be associated with the work if reasonable in the circumstances. Further, where reasonable in the circumstances, the author has the right to be associated with the work under a pseudonym or the right to remain anonymous.[151]

Violation of this right could arise where a person links to another person's Web page in such a way as to lead a user to believe that the work belongs to the person making the link.

### (b)  Integrity Right

The author has the right to object to or restrain certain uses of or dealings with a work if the use or dealing involves a distortion, mutilation or other modification of the work that would prejudice the honour or reputation of the author.[152]

This right was found to have been violated where a mall owner placed Christmas ornaments on the necks of a flying Canada Geese

---

[148]  See section 34(1.1), *Copyright Act* (Canada) which provides remedies by way of injunction, damages, accounts or delivery up and otherwise are available to the moral rights claimant.

[149]  See, for example, sections 64.1(1), *Copyright Act* (Canada), providing that application of useful features of a utilitarian article is not an infringement of either copyright or moral rights in the work or design which is applied to the article.

[150]  See section 41, *Copyright Act* (Canada).

[151]  See section 14.1, *Copyright Act* (Canada), see also *New Brunswick Telephone Co. v. John Maryon International Ltd.* (1982), 43 N.B.R. (2d) 469, 113 A.P.R. 469, 141 D.L.R. (3d) 193 (*sub nom. John Maryon International Ltd. v. New Brunswick Telephone Co.*) 24 C.C.L.T. 146 (N.B. C.A.) leave refused (1982), 43 N.B.R. (2d) 468, 113 A.P.R. 468, 46 N.R. 262 2 S.C.R. viii (S.C.C.).

[152]  See section 28.2, *Copyright Act* (Canada).

sculpture even though the mall owner owned the sculpture.[153] It has also been suggested that this right could be infringed upon the modification of a computer program and its graphic display.[154] In many cases, however, there may be an implied right for the owner of any tangible expression of a work, such as in the case of engineering drawings or plans, to modify the work.[155]

### (c)  Association Right

The author has the right to object to or restrain any use of a work in association with a product, service, cause or institution where such conduct would be to the prejudice of the honour and reputation of the author.[156] For example, the use of a design or style of art for which an author is well-known in association with a disreputable business may damage the author's reputation.

The association right might be violated by establishing a link to a Web site and by suggesting an association or connection to that site, where such suggestion would be harmful to the reputation of the author of the material located on the site to which the link is made.

## 5.4  PERFORMERS' RIGHTS

Neighbouring rights are certain rights related to the existence or creation of copyright in a work. These rights apply to various industries that are largely based on the use of copyright materials. The neighbouring rights consist of performers' rights, broadcasters' rights and rights of makers of sound recordings and related provisions. The rationale for protecting the performers' rights is that the interpretation that a performer may give to a copyright protected work (e.g., a musical work, or a dramatic work) may itself be a reflection of considerable creative expression. A "performer's performance" means (i) a performance of an artistic work, dramatic work or musical work, whether or not the work was previously fixed

---

[153]  *Snow v. Eaton Centre Ltd.*, (1982) 70 C.P.R. (2d) 105 (Ont. H.C.).

[154]  See *Nintendo of America Inc. v. Camerica Corp.*, (1991) 34 C.P.R. (3d) 193, 42 F.T.R. 12, affirmed (1991) 36 C.P.R. (3d) 352, 127 N.R. 232, 44 F.T.R. 80 (note) (Fed. C.A.).

[155]  See *Netupsky v. Dominion Bridge Co. Ltd.*, [1972] S.C.R. 368, [1972] 1 W.W.R. 420, 3 C.P.R. (2d) 1, 24 D.L.R. (3d) 484 (S.C.C.).

[156]  See section 28.2(1)(b), *Copyright Act* (Canada).

in any material form, and whether or not the term of copyright protection for the work under the *Copyright Act* (Canada) has expired,[157] (ii) a recitation or reading of a literary work, whether or not the work's term of copyright protection under the *Copyright Act* (Canada) has expired,[158] or (iii) an improvisation of a dramatic work, musical work or literary work, whether or not the improvised work is based on a pre-existing work.[159] The definition of performance includes any acoustic or visual representation of the performer's performance. These rights may be of some importance with respect to performances that might be available on Internet Web sites.

A key feature of performer's rights is the existence of a pre-existing work. Depending on the circumstances, this pre-existing work may be a literary, artistic, dramatic or musical work. Further the performer may acquire rights in a performance of the pre-existing work even if that work is no longer the subject of copyright protection.

After conclusion of the Uruguay round of the General Agreement and Tariffs and Trade, Canada agreed to provide for protection of performers' rights.[160] These rights were enacted by amendments to the *Copyright Act*, which came into force on January 1, 1996.[161] Canada subsequently expanded the scope of the performers' rights and provided protection for other neighbouring rights,[162] including broadcasters' rights and rights of makers of sound recordings so as to permit Canada to join the Rome Convention.

The following are the elements of performers' rights: (a) a fixation right, (b) a reproduction right, (c) a communication right, (d) a performance right and (e) a rental right. These rights may be

---

[157]   Section 2, *Copyright Act* (Canada).

[158]   Section 2, *Copyright Act* (Canada).

[159]   Section 2, *Copyright Act* (Canada).

[160]   For more details see *Final Act Embodying the Results of the Uruguay Round of Multilateral Trade Negotiations*, done at Marrakech, Morocco, April 15, 1994, annex 1C: *Agreement on Trade-Related Aspects of Intellectual Property Rights*, April 15, 1994.

[161]   *An Act to implement the Agreement Establishing the World Trade Organization*, S.C. 1994, c. 47.

[162]   *An Act to Amend the Copyright Act*, S.C. 1997, c. 24, proclaimed law April 25, 1997.

applicable to the performance of materials that may be accessed or exchanged by means of the Internet. The specific rights are described below.

## (a)  Fixation Right

The owner of the performer's right has the sole right to fix the performer's performance, or any substantial part thereof, in any material form.[163] This right would appear to include making a digital copy of the performance.

## (b)  Reproduction Right

If the performer's performance is fixed, the owner of the performer's right has the sole right to reproduce an unauthorized fixation,[164] or for authorized fixations the right to reproduce any reproduction of the fixation so long as such reproduction was made for a purpose other than that for which the consent of the owner of the performer's right was obtained.[165] This provision would give the owner of the performer's right a degree of control over unauthorized copies of a digital file containing the performer's performance of a musical work. Depending on the circumstances, the right to make a reproduction of a fixed performance may be implied if the performance is placed on a Web site by or with the authority of the owner of the performer's right with a view to permitting users to "sample" the work.

## (c)  Communication Right

If the performer's performance is not fixed, the owner of the performer's right has the sole right to communicate the performer's performance, or any substantial part thereof, to the public by telecommunication at the time of the performer's performance.[166] If

---

[163]  See section 15(1)(a)(iii) of the *Copyright Act* (Canada). The concept of record, perforated roll or other contrivance is replaced with sound recordings.

[164]  See section 15(1)(b)(i), *Copyright Act* (Canada).

[165]  See section 15(1)(b)(ii) and section 15(1)(b)(iii), *Copyright Act* (Canada).

[166]  See section 15(1)(a), *Copyright Act* (Canada). See also section 2.4(1) of the *Copyright Act* which sets out certain limits on what is a communication to the public by telecommunication.

the posting of material to a Web site is considered to be a public communication (see section 5.2(b)(viii)), then the simultaneous display of a performance on a Web site at the time of performance would be included in this right of the performing rights holder.

### (d) Performance Right

The owner of the performance right has the right to perform the performance in public where it is communicated to the public by telecommunication other than by communication signal.[167] This right might be exercised where the performance is performed by execution of a computer program to "play" a digital file containing the performance.

### (e) Rental Right

The owner of the performer's right has the sole right to rent out a sound recording of the performer's performance.[168] This right would limit further dealings with a sample performance posted on a Web site.

Some substantial defences or limits on performers' rights are as follows:

(1) any fair dealing with the performer's performance, a fixation thereof or a reproduction of the fixation, so long as such dealing is for the purposes of private study or research, and, if certain conditions are met, for purposes of criticism, review or newspaper summary;[169]

(2) the making of a fixation or reproduction of a performer's performance that is performed live or a sound recording performed at the same time as the performer's performance (e.g., a simultaneous Web broadcast and performance);[170]

---

[167] See section 15(1)(a)(ii), *Copyright Act* (Canada).

[168] See section 15(1)(c), *Copyright Act* (Canada).

[169] See sections 29, 29.1 and 29.2, *Copyright Act* (Canada); see also the discussion of implied licence under section 5.2(v)(a).

[170] See section 30.8, *Copyright Act* (Canada).

(3) the making of a reproduction of a performer's performance embodied in a sound recording solely to provide it in a format suitable for broadcasting;[171] and

(4) if use of a performance is authorized in a cinematographic work then the performer may no longer authorize the fixation right, communication right or performance right.[172]

## 5.5  TRADE SECRETS

### (a)  Nature of Protection

Information, data, ideas, plans, designs or concepts, whether technical or business in nature, may be protected under the law protecting trade secrets. Such protection may be available for any type of information or data, such as business plans, technical data, and secret processes.[173] The rights may be lost by disclosure of confidential information on the Internet.

Trade secrets may be protected based on a breach of confidence action (as discussed below) which gives the person to whom the obligation of confidence is owed the right to restrain any unauthorized use or disclosure of the information.[174] An additional or separate cause of action may exist for the protection of trade secrets based on a contractual or fiduciary relationship[175] between the "owner" of confidential information and a person who is subject

---

[171]  See section 30.9, *Copyright Act* (Canada).

[172]  See section 17(1) *Copyright Act* (Canada) and the relevant provisions of section 15(1), *Copyright Act*.

[173]  See, for further background, *Saltman Engineering Co. v. Campbell Engineering Co. Ltd.*, (1948), 65 R.P.C. 203 [1963] 3 All E.R. 413 (note) (Eng. C.A.); and *Seager v. Copydex Ltd.*, [1967] 1 W.L.R. 923, [1967] 2 All E.R. 415 (Eng. C.A.) and the cases cited therein.

[174]  See, for example, *International Corona Resources Ltd. v. Lac Minerals Ltd.*, (1989), 6 R.P.R. (2d) 1, 44 B.L.R. 1, 35 E.T.R. 1, (*sub nom. LAC Minerals Ltd. v. International Corona Resources Ltd.*) 69 O.R. (2d) 287, 26 C.P.R. (3d) 97, 61 D.L.R. (4th) 14, 101 N.R. 239, 36 O.A.C 57, [1989] 2 S.C.R. 574, [1989] 2 R.C.S. 574 (S.C.C.).

[175]  An obligation of confidence arises in a fiduciary relationship. Note that the fiduciary also has other obligations owed to the party who has the benefit of the fiduciary relationship. See, for example, *Phipps v. Boardman*, (1996), (*sub nom. Boardman v. Phipps*) [1967] 2 A.C. 46, [1966] 3 ALL E.R. 721 (U.K.H.L.) where the fiduciary was prevented from making any use of the information he acquired for his own benefit.

to restrictions on the use of such information.[176] In this chapter we will refer to the person to whom the obligation of confidence is owed as the "owner" of the trade secret.

### (b)  Breach of Confidence: Nature of the Action

The elements to be met to bring an action for breach of confidence include the existence of a relationship of confidence, the existence of specific confidential information and the fact that detriment will arise from any unauthorized disclosure. These elements are discussed below:

### (i)  *A Relationship of Confidence*

There must be a relationship between the person who owns the confidential information and the person who is to be bound by the obligation of confidence. The obligation of confidence may arise from a variety of relationships, including: (1) where the recipient has undertaken an express obligation of confidence such as in a non-disclosure agreement;[177] (2) where an obligation of confidence is implied, such as during pre-contractual negotiations;[178] or (3) in circumstances where the obligation of confidence arises as an incident of other legal obligations, such as in a fiduciary relationship or in a relationship between an employee and an employer.[179] In

---

[176]  Technically, under present Canadian law, the person to whom the obligation of confidence is owed does not appear to "own" "property" in the sense contemplated by the Criminal law: See *R. v. Stewart*, (1983), 42 O.R. (2d) 225 S.C.C.C. (3d) 481, 3 S.C.R. (3d) 105, 149 D.L.R. (3d) 583, 74 C.P.R. (2d) 1, 24 B.L.R. 53 (Ont. C.A.), reversed (1988) 41 C.C.C (3d) 481, 39 B.L.R. 198, 50 D.L.R. (4th) 1, 19 C.I.P.R. 161, 21 C.P.R. (3d) 289, 85 N.R. 171, 28 O.A.C. 219, 63 C.R. (3d) 305, 65 O.R. (2d) 637 (note), [1988] 1 S.C.R. 963, [1988] 1 R.C.S. 963 (S.C.C.).

[177]  See, for example, *Eli Lilly Can. Inc. v. Shamrock Chems. Ltd.*, (1985) 6 C.I.P.R., 4 C.P.R. (3d) 196 (Ont. H.C.). For several examples of non-disclosure agreements see the appendices to *Obtaining Patents*, 1995, Carswell, Practice Guide, Toronto.

[178]  See, for example, *Seager v. Copydex Ltd.*, [1967] 1 W.L.R. 923, [1967] R.P.C. 349, 2 All E.R. 415 (Eng. C.A.); *International Corona Resources Ltd. v. Lac Minerals Ltd.*, (1989), 6 R.P.R. (2d) 1, 44 B.L.R. 1, 35 E.T.R. 1, (*sub nom. LAC Minerals Ltd. v. International Gorona Resources Ltd.*) 69 O.R. (2d) 287, 26 C.P.R. (3d) 97, 61 D.L.R. (4th) 14, 101 N.R. 239, 36 O.A.C. 57, [1989] 2 S.C.R. 574, [1989] 2 R.C.S. 574 (S.C.C.). In each such case there were circumstances suggesting the existence of obligations of confidence.

[179]  See, for example, *Phipps v. Boardman*, (1966), (*sub nom. Boardman v. Phipps*) [1967] 2 A.C. 46, [1966] 3 All E.R. 721 (U.K. H.L.).

circumstances where there is a further relationship between the owner and the recipient of the information, the recipient may have legal obligations which are additional to the obligation of confidence.

### (ii)  Confidential Information

The information in question must have the necessary quality of confidence.[180] Accordingly, any publication or other action by the owner which results in the information becoming available to the public will preclude this cause of action. This must be considered when making patent applications or seeking other forms of protection where the application, or if granted, the registration, is available to the public. Disclosure of confidential information in a discussion group or chat room to members of a Listserv or on a Web site will result in a loss of the confidential character of the information.

### (iii)  Detriment

In order to be actionable, the unauthorized use or disclosure must be to the detriment of the owner of the confidential information.[181] This is usually not difficult for the plaintiff to establish since loss of control over the information will by itself cause detriment to the owner, such as by loss of the headstart associated with knowledge and control of the information.[182] It is actionable for a person owing an obligation of confidence to disclose or misuse the confidential information or any part thereof without the consent of the

---

[180]  *Saltman Engineering Co. v. Campbell Engineering Co. Ltd.,* (1948), 65 R.P.C. 203, [1963] 3 All E.R. 413 (note) (Eng.C.A.); *Shauenburg Industries Ltd. v. Borowski,* (1979), 25 O.R. (2d) 737, 101 D.L.R. (3d) 701, 8 B.L.R. 164, 50 C.P.R. (2d) 69 (Ont. H.C.).

[181]  *International Corona Resources Ltd. v. Lac Minerals Ltd.,* (1989), 6 R.P.R. (2d) 1, 44 B.L.R. 1 35 E.T.R. 1, *(sub nom. LAC Minerals Ltd. v. International Corona Resources Ltd.)* 69 O.R. (2d) 287, 26 C.P.R. (3d) 97, 61 D.L.R. (4th) 14, 101 N.R. 239, 36 O.A.C. 57, [1989] 2 S.C.R. 574, [1989] 2 R.C.S. 574 (S.C.C.).

[182]  *Chevron Standard Ltd. v. Home Oil Co. Ltd.,* [1980] 5 W.W.R. 624, 11 B.L.R. 53, 50 C.P.R. (2d) 182, 22 A.R. 451 (Alta. Q.B.) aff'd. [1982] 3 W.W.R. 427, 64 C.P.R. (2d) 11, (1982) 19 Alta. L.R. (2d) 1, 35 A.R. 550 (Alta C.A.) leave to appeal to S.C.C. refused [1982] 2 S.C.R. vi.

owner.[183] The full range of remedies is available for any breach of confidence.[184]

An innocent third party who acquires confidential information without notice of a breach of an obligation of confidence but is subsequently informed of the breach is also bound by the obligation of confidence so long as the information is not yet published.[185] However, it may be difficult to enforce this right for information wrongfully disclosed by means of the Internet in view of the difficulties in determining who obtains access to such information.

The equitable nature of the breach of confidence action gives rise to certain limitations on the action. The fact that there must be a relationship between the owner of the confidential information and the person bound by the obligation of confidence means that the rights are only *in personam*, not *in rem*. No obligations are imposed on "strangers", and accordingly, various kinds of industrial espionage activity may not be caught by this action.[186]

---

[183]  See, for example, *Coco v. A.N. Clark (Engineers) Ltd.*, (1968), [1969] R.P.C. 41, [1968] F.S.R. 415 (Eng. Ch.D); *Slayutych v. Baker* (1975), [1976] 1 S.C.R. 254, 2 N.R. 587 at 595, 38 C.R.N.S. 306, 75 C.L.L.C. 14, 263, 55 D.L.R. (3d) 224, [1975] 4 W.W.R. 620 (S.C.C.); and *R.L. Crain Ltd. v. Ashton*, 8 Fox Pat. c. 269, [1949] O.R. 303, 9 C.P.R. 143, [1949] 2 D.L.R. 481 affd. (1949), 9 Fox Pat. c. 201, 11 C.P.R. 53, [1950] O.R. 62, [1950] 1 D.L.R. 601 (Ont. C.A.).

[184]  A very common form of relief is an interlocutory injunction and then permanent injunction, see *International Tools Ltd. v. Koller*, [1968] 1 O.R. 669, 38 Fox Pat. C. 66, 54 C.P.R. 171, 67 D.L.R. (2d) 386 (Ont C.A.); Other forms of relief available include: (a) damages, see *Seager v. Copydex Ltd.* (No. 2), [1969] 2 All E.R. 718, (Eng.C.A.), *Shauenburg Industries Ltd. v. Borowski*, (1979), 25 O.R. (2d) 737, 101 D.L.R. (3d) 701, 8 B.L.R. 164, 50 C.P.R. (2d) 69 (Ont. H.C.); (b) an account of profits, see *Peter Pan Manufacturing. Corp. v. Corsets Silhouette Ltd.*, [1963] 3 All E.R. 402 (Eng. Ch. Div.) (c) a constructive trust, see *Pre-Cam Exploration & Development Ltd. v. McTavish*, [1966] S.C.R. 551, 56 W.W.R. 697 57 D.L.R. (2d) 557, 50 C.P.R. 299 (S.C.C.); and (d) an order for delivery-up, see *International Corona Resources Ltd. v. Lac Minerals Ltd.*, (1989), 6 R.P.R. (2d) 44 B.L.R. 1 35 E.T.R., (*sub nom. LAC Minerals Ltd. v. International Corona Resources Ltd.*) 69 O.R. (2d) 287, 26 C.P.R. (3d) 97, 61 D.L.R. (4th) 14, 101 N.R. 239, 36 O.A.C. 57, [1989] 2 S.C.R. 574, [1989] 2 R.C.S. 574 (S.C.C.).

[185]  See, for example, *Wheatly v. Bell*, [1984] F.S.R. 16 (S.C. N.S.W.).

[186]  See, for example, *Franklin v. Giddins*, [1978] 7d R. 72 (S.C. Brisbane); *R. v. Stewart*, (1983) 42 O.R. (2d) 225, 5 C.C.C. (3d) 481, 35 C.R. (3d) 105, 149 D.L.R. (3d) 583, 74 C.P.R. (2d) 1, 24 B.L.R. 53 (Ont. CA) reversed (1988), 41 C.C.C (3d) 481, 50 D.L.R. (4th) 1, 39 B.L.R. 198, 19 C.I.P.R. 161, 2 C.P.R. (3d) 289, 85 N.R. 171, 28 O.A.C. 219, 63 C.R. (3d) 305, 65 O.R. (2d) 637 (note), [1988] 1 S.C.R. 963, [1988] 1 R.C.S. 963 (S.C.C.).

Other circumstances in which there may not be a cause of action include (1) the information is no longer confidential;[187] (2) there is a just cause or excuse for the disclosure;[188] (3) the disclosure is required by law such as in legal proceedings, in investigation by a regulatory body,[189] for purposes of securities regulation, or in patent or other applications; or (4) the court exercises the discretion to deny certain relief because the action is an equitable remedy.

In principle, an obligation of confidence can last indefinitely as long as the information is maintained as secret.

## (c) Special Problems

### (i) Participation in Usenet and Discussion Listservs

Obviously, the communication of confidential information to another person in any forum without obligations of confidentiality applicable to all parties is likely to result in loss of the secret. As a result, participation in an Usenet forum or a chat group can destroy trade secret protection for confidential information disclosed by a participant. There are no restrictions on other participants in such services and no practical means to identify the persons who may obtain access to the information. Accordingly, no confidential information should be disclosed in any forum open to the public on the Internet if trade secret protection is desired to be maintained.

### (ii) Use of Search Engines and Potential for Monitoring

It is possible for third persons to intercept and to monitor e-mail communications. Although the law is not clear on this point, it would seem that since most messages transmitted on the Internet use telephone services, the laws restricting the interception and monitoring of telephone communications should be applicable. It would be prudent in any event not to disclose highly sensitive or

---

[187]   See, for example, *Attorney General v. Times Newspapers Ltd.*, [1973] 3 All E.R. 54, [1973] 3 W.L.R. 298, [1974] A.C. 273 (U.K. H.L.).

[188]   See, for example, *Canadian Javelin Ltd. v. Sparling*, (1978) 4 B.L.R. 153, 59 C.P.R. (2d) 146 (Fed. C.A.); affd (1978) 22 N.R. 465, 91 D.L.R. (3d) 64, 59 C.P.R. (2d) 165 (Fed. C.A.) and *Lennon v. News Group Newspapers Ltd.*, [1978] F.S.R. 573 (C.A.).

[189]   See, for example, *Competition Act*, R.S.C. 1985, c.C-34; *National Energy Board Act*, R.S.C. 1985, c. N-7; *Investment Canada Act*, R.S.C. 1985, c. 28.

confidential information in e-mail communications unless encryption or other technical measures are taken to protect the information.

## 5.6  TRADEMARKS

Trademarks are often used in association with materials available on the Internet and particularly on sites on the World Wide Web. A trademark may also be used as part of the address for a Web site or the electronic address of a user. Both aspects are discussed below, after a brief introduction to trademark principles. Also discussed below is the use of trademarks in the context of online marketing and promotional activities. General legal considerations concerning these activities are discussed further in Chapter 6.

### (a)  Introduction

A trademark is a way of distinguishing one person's product or service from that of another person. Trademarks can be in various forms such as a name ("NETSCAPE"), slogan ("Where Do You Want To Go Today"), a logo or design (i.e., the unique Apple logo of Apple Computers) or a unique shape. The function of a trademark is to indicate the source or origin of any person's products or services[190] and to distinguish the products or services of one person from those of another.

Trademarks protect the goodwill and reputation associated with a product[191] or service. Unlike other forms of intellectual property, rights in trademarks arise only upon their use, rather than upon their creation.

---

[190] US trademark law tends to follow the approach set out in an article by Frank I. Schechter, "The Rational Basis of Trademark Protection", 40 *Harv. L. Rev.* 813 (1927), which suggested that the true function of a trademark is to identify the source of a product and thereby promote purchases by the consumer. Under this theory, any use of a trademark, even on non-competing goods, is seen as whittling away or diluting the identity and appeal of the trademark in association with the product.

[191] R.S.C. 1985, C. T-13, as amended. It should be noted that although the *Trade-Marks Act* refers to wares, the terms "products" or "wares" are used interchangeably in this text.

Registered trademarks are protected under the *Trade-Marks Act*.[192] Trademarks, including unregistered marks, may also receive a certain level of protection under the common law passing off action, or under the provisions of Section 7 of the *Trade-Marks Act*. Other remedies may be available depending on the circumstances. Certain rights related to trademark rights are granted with respect to an individual's personality.[193]

### (b)  Scope of Rights

A trademark registered under the *Trade-Marks Act*[194] provides the owner with an exclusive right, in the country of registration, to use the trademark in association with the products or services for which it was registered. The registration of the trademark provides the following rights: (a) the exclusive right to use the trademark; (b) a right to restrict use of a confusingly similar trademark by another person; and (c) a right to restrict use of the mark by another person in a manner that may depreciate the goodwill attached to the mark. These rights are described below:

### (i)  *Exclusive Use*

The owner of a trademark registered in Canada has the sole right throughout the country to use the trademark in association with the products and/or services for which it was registered.[195] For trademark purposes, "use" means, in relation to a product, the placement of the trademark on the product or on its packaging at the point of sale or when possession is passed to a customer,[196] and in

---

[192]  R.S.C. 1985, c. T-13, as am. For the Unites States see the *Lantham Act*, 15 U.S.C. (See, for example, s. 32 (1) for Federal trademark infringement; s. 43 (a) for Federal unfair competition; s. 1114 (1), 1125 (a) and 1125 (c) for elements of the *Federal Trademark Dilution Act of 1995*).

[193]  Rights in a person's likeness, voice, appearance, shape or other attributes of personality may obtain a degree of protection under the common law and certain provisions of privacy legislation in some provinces. In some cases copyright, moral rights and/or performer's rights may also play a role in protection of rights in a person's likeness, voice or other attributes of the person's personality.

[194]  Details on making a trademark application may be found in White, *Selection and Protecting Trademarks*, 1994, Canada Practice Guide, Carswell, Toronto.

[195]  Section 19, *Trade-Marks Act*.

[196]  Section 4(1), *Trade-Marks Act*.

relation to services, means the use of the trademark incidental to the provision of the services or in advertising the services.[197]

### (ii)  Confusion

The owner of the registered trademark has the right to be free of any use of a confusingly similar trademark or trade name.[198] Confusion may be determined by reference to a number of factors[199] such as the channels of trade, nature of the products, type of customers and other related factors.[200]

In *Peinet Inc. v. O'Brien*,[201] a passing off action was brought to preclude use of "pei.net" as a domain name on the grounds that the domain name was confusing with the plaintiff's corporate name. The court found that the plaintiff did not meet the requirements for injunctive relief. There was evidence by the defendant of a lack of confusion. The court also considered that the domain name was all lower case and separated by a period (i.e., pei.net) whereas the corporate name was "Peinet."

### (iii)  Depreciation of Goodwill

The owner of a registered trademark has the right to restrict other persons from using the trademark in a manner that is likely to have

---

[197]  Section 4(2), *Trade-Marks Act*.

[198]  See section 20, *Trade-Marks Act*.

[199]  The issue of whether or not there is confusion is guided by s. 6(5) of the *Trade-Marks Act*. See also *Forum Corp. of North America v. Forum Ltd.*, 14 U.S.P.Q. 2d 1950 (7th Cir. 1990) which sets out seven factors which should be weighed to determine a likelihood of confusion under US trademark law.

[200]  Section 6(5) of the *Trade-Marks Act* sets out a number of factors which may be considered having regard to all of the surrounding circumstances in determining whether the trademarks are confusing. Those factors are: (1) The inherent distinctiveness of the trademarks or trade names and the extent to which they have become known; (2) The length of time the trademarks or trade names have been in use; (3) The nature of the wares, services or business; (4) The nature of the trade; and (5) The degree of resemblance between the trademarks or trade names in appearance or sound or in the ideas suggested by them.

[201]  (1995), 61 C.P.R. (3d) 334, 40 C.P.C. (3d) 58, 130 Nfld. 6 P.E.I.R. 313, 405 A.P.R. 313, 405 A.P.R. 313 (P.E.I. T.D. [In Chambers]).

the effect of depreciating the value of the goodwill attached to the mark.[202]

### (iv)  Authorization

The owner of the registered trademark also has the right to authorize others to carry out any of the acts contemplated above.[203] The trademark owner may license another person to use the trademark, but the owner must have the capability, either directly or indirectly, of controlling the character and quality of the wares and/or services provided by the licensee in association with the trademarks.[204]

### (v)  Dilution

In the US, the *Federal Trademark Dilution Act*[205] provides a special remedy to protect famous trademarks from certain uses by other persons which, strictly speaking may not be infringement of the trademark, but which tend to dilute the reputation or value of the trademark. The Act provides only for injunctive relief, except in the case of the wilful conduct by the defendant, which will entitle the trademark owner to a broader range of remedies. Ownership by the defendant of a trademark registered on the US Federal register is a complete bar to action under the *Federal Trademark Dilution Act*.

The *Federal Trademark Dilution Act* preserves fair use of famous trademarks in comparative commercial advertising or promotion for purposes of identifying the competing goods or services of the owner

---

[202]  See section 22, *Trade-Marks Act.* Also relevant is section 22(2) which provides that in an action in respect of use of a trademark contrary to section 22(1) the court may decline to order the recovery of damages or profits and may permit the defendant to continue to sell wares marked with the trademark that were in his possession or under his control at the time notice of the complaint was given to him by the owner of the registered trademark. Issues of liability under section 22 are discussed in more detail in Chapter 6.

[203]  See section 50, *Trade-Marks Act.* Under Canadian law in force until June 8, 1993, the owner of a registered trademark could only permit others to use the trademark if a registered user's appointment was filed at the trademarks office. Failure to take this precaution could have resulted in loss of the registration for the trademark.

[204]  See section 50(1), *Trade-Marks Act.*

[205]  Signed into law January 16, 1996, Pub. Law 104-98. This Act created a new section 43(c) of the *Lantham Act*, 15 U.S.C. 1125.

of the famous trademark. Noncommercial uses and all forms of news reporting and news commentary are also exempt.

Canada does not have a similar right under its trademark law.

## (c) Defences

Some substantial defences to an infringement action or limits on the enforceability of a registered trademark, are as follows:

(1) any defect in registration;

(2) any adverse change in the distinctiveness of the trademark;[206]

(3) loss of distinctiveness through unlicensed use of the trademark by others;[207]

(4) failure to use the trademark;[208]

(5) failure to bring action within the applicable limitation period.[209]

The full range of remedies is available for an infringement of trademark.[210] An action for infringement of a registered trademark may be brought in either the Federal Court or in a provincial court

---

[206] See, for example, section 12(1)(b) of the *Trade-Marks Act* which requires that the trademark not be descriptive of the wares or services with which it is associated. Over time, a trademark may become descriptive rather than distinctive of the wares or services with which it is associated. See, for example, *Canadian Shredded Wheat Co. v. Kellogg Co.,* [1938] 1 All E.R. 618, [1938] 2 D.L.R. 145 55 R.P.C. 125 (Ontario P.C.) which found SHREDDED WHEAT to be an apt description of the defendant's product.

[207] Since a trademark must distinguish the wares or services of its owner, use of the same trademark by another trader for substantially the same wares or services would result in the trademark becoming no longer distinctive of the original owner's wares or services. Exceptions are use licensed under Section 50, *Trade-Marks Act* or use by infringers where the owner takes reasonably prompt action to restrain such unauthorized use.

[208] If the owner does not use the trademark as registered for a substantial time (generally more than 3 years) without a reasonable excuse then the registration of the trademark may be expunged for lack of use. See section 45, *Trade-Marks Act.*

[209] The *Trade-Marks Act* does not contain an express limitation period. As a result the applicable limitation period under provincial law or under the Federal Court procedure may apply. See Vaver, "Limitations in Intellectual Property: The Time is Out of Joint" (1994) 73:4 *Canadian Bar Rev.* 451 for a discussion of these issues.

[210] See section 53.2, *Trade-Marks Act* which provides that remedies by way of injunction, damages, accounts or delivery up and otherwise are available to the owner of the trademark.

of superior jurisdiction. An action to expunge or amend a registration of a trademark must be brought in the Federal Court.

### (d) Special Problems

#### (i) Use of the Trademark

"Use" for trademark purposes means, in relation to a product, the placement of the mark on the product or on packaging for the product at the point of sale or when possession is passed to the customer,[211] or in relation to services, the use of the mark incidental to the provision of the services or use in advertising the capability of providing services.[212]

On the question of whether the placement of a trademark on a Web site or on the Internet is "use" for trademark purposes, it has been found that an access code on a computer screen represents use for trademark purposes.[213] "Use" in relation to services would likely be made out to the extent that the trademark is used in advertising the service from a Web site. It is unlikely that mere advertising on a Web site is "use" in relation to products.[214]

A further issue is whether trademark use would be found to infringe rights in each jurisdiction from which a user may access the Web site.

The mere use of a domain name, particularly if the distinctive element of the domain name is a famous trademark of another person, may be infringing conduct[215]. Similarly use of a trademark in a domain name has been held to satisfy the "in commerce" requirement to bring action under the *Federal Trademark Dilution Act*.[216]

---

[211]    Section 4(1), *Trade-Marks Act*.

[212]    Section 4(2), *Trade-Marks Act*.

[213]    See *BMB Compuscience Canada Ltd. v. Bramalea Ltd.* (1988), 20 C.I.P.R. 310, [1989] 1 F.C. 362, 23 F.T.R. 149, 22 C.P.R. (3d) 561, [1989] 1 C.F. 362 (Fed. T.D.).

[214]    However, if products are actually sold through the Web site then, in some circumstances, this may constitute use.

[215]    See, for example, *Intermatic Inc. v. Toeppen* (1996), 40 U.S.P.Q. 2d 1412 (Illinois D.C.) in which Toeppen registered 240 domain names.

[216]    See *Intermatic Inc. v. Toeppen*, 40 U.S.P.Q. 2D 1412 (N.D Ill. 1996).

### (ii)   Trademarks and Domain Names

Often a URL or Internet site address will contain a trademark as the second level domain and as a unique identifier of a business. For example, a generic Internet URL may be in the form: <http://www. trade-name.com> where the "trade-name" element may be the business's trademark.

A problem arises from the basic principles of trademark law and the nature of a domain name. As an address, each domain name must be unique, and only one person can have a particular name for its Internet address.[217] Since most elements of the URL are generic, it is the second level domain name (the "trade-name" in our example) that must be unique. On the other hand, trademark law permits more than one person to use the same trademark so long as the trademarks are used for different products or services and create no likelihood of confusion.[218]

Since two or more businesses may be using the same trademark in a legitimate manner, the issue arises as to which entity is entitled to use the trademark as part of its Internet address. This problem is compounded by the fact that when used as part of a domain name, there may be literally hundreds of legitimate uses of the identical trademark worldwide. The complex interaction of trademark law and the domain name system is discussed in Chapter 3.

---

[217]   For example, <http://www.abc.com>, <http://www.abcinc.com>, <http://www.abc_inc.com> and <http://www.abc_us.com> are all unique addresses but all of which include the same common distinctive element "abc". Technically all such domains can co-exist. An issue arises if there is dilution or confusion with another person's trademark due to the manner of promotion or use of similar addresses particularly where the distinctive element that is common to both addresses is also used as a trademark.

[218]   For example, <http://www.xyz.com>, used by a grocery retailer who carries on business under the trade name or trademark "xyz" may not be confusing with <http://www.xyzinc.com> used by an automobile manufacturer selling a sport utility vehicle under the trademark "xyz". The channels of trade, nature of the products, type of customers and other factors are sufficiently different that there would be no likelihood of confusion. The issue of whether or not there is confusion is guided by S. 6(5) *Trade-Marks Act*. See also *Forum Corp. of North America v. Forum Ltd.*, 14 U.S.P.Q. 2d 1950 (7th Cir. 1990) which sets out seven factors which should be weighed to determine a likelihood of confusion under US trademark law.

### (iii)  Links and Frames as Passing Off

The use of a link or frame to point to a Web site and the materials of another person may give rise to trademark consequences particularly if there is a suggestion, express or implied, that there is some connection or relationship between the linked site and the site to which the link is made. Such conduct may give rise to trademark infringement or more likely an action in common law for passing off.[219]

The common law action for passing off seeks to prevent one trader from representing its goods and services as those of another. This action requires a misrepresentation causing confusion or a risk of confusion as to an association or connection between traders.[220] The following are the elements of this action:

#### (1)  Reputation in the Market

In order for rights to exist the trader must have a distinctive reputation in the marketplace. Traders who adopt common or descriptive terms for carrying on business will be less likely to satisfy this requirement.

#### (2)  Misrepresentation

There must be a misrepresentation by the defendant to a prospective customer or to the actual customer of goods or services supplied by the plaintiff. The misrepresentation can take a variety of forms. For example, it could include the use of a link or frame that obscures the identification of the ownership of the site to which the link is made and suggests that the products, services or information available on that site originate with the owner of the site creating the link. The test is whether consumers would reasonably believe that there is a connection between the

---

[219]  It is reported that the Government of Canada required a recruiting company to cease using logos and materials on its Web site that suggested a connection or endorsement of a company's services by the Federal Government. Calgary Herald, January 16, 1998.

[220]  *Walt Disney Productions v. Triple Five Corp.* (1994) 17 Alta. L.R. (3d) 225, 113 D.L.R. (4th) 229, [1994] 6 W.W.R. 385, 149 A.R. 112, 63 W.A.C. 53 C.P.R. (3d) 129 (Alta. C.A.), leave to appeal dismissed [1994] 7 W.W.R. l xix (note), 20 Alta. L.R. (3d) xxxix (note), 114 D.L.R. (4th) vii (note), 55 C.P.R. (3d) vi (note), 178 N.R. 160 (note), 162 A.R. 319 (note), 83 W.A.C. 319 (note) (S.C.C.).

wares, services or business of the plaintiff and those of the defendant.[221]

(3) *Intention to Deceive*

The lack of an intention to deceive is not relevant where the representation is factually false. If a plaintiff has warned the defendant of the plaintiff's rights, some cases have found that any continued use of the name may raise an inference of fraud.

Some Canadian courts have found passing off to exist where the defendant misrepresents some association between the plaintiff and defendant even where the fields of business of the plaintiff and defendant are quite different.[222] For example, in *National Hockey League v. Pepsi-Cola Canada Ltd.*,[223] the court stated that there are two types of passing off. The traditional passing off action involves competitors in a common field of activity where the defendant has named, packaged or described its product or business in a manner likely to lead the public to believe that the defendant's product or business is that of the plaintiff.[224] The other form is where the defendant has promoted its product or business in such a way as to create a false impression that such product or business is approved, authorized or endorsed by the plaintiff or that there is a business connection between the plaintiff and defendant. By these means a defendant may hope to "cash in" on the goodwill of the plaintiff.[225] Where there is no common field of business between two sites for which a link has been

---

[221] *Walt Disney Productions v. Triple Five Corp.*, (1994) 17 Alta.L.R. (3d) 225, 113 D.L.R. (4th) 229, [1994] 6 W.W.R. 385, 149 A.R. 112, 63 W.A.C. 112, 53 C.P.R. (3d) 129 (Alta. C.A.) leave to appeal dismissed [1994] 7 W.W.R. 1 xix (note), 20 Alta.L.R. (3d) xxxix (note), 114 D.L.R. (4th) vii (note), 55 C.P.R. (3d) vi (note), 178 N.R. 160 (note), 162 A.R. 319 (note), 83 W.A.C. 319 (note)(S.C.C.).

[222] *Consumers Distributing Co. v. Seiko Time Canada Ltd.* (1980) 29 O.R. (2d) 221 11 B.L.R. 149, 112 D.L.R. (3d) 500, 50 C.P.R. (2d) 147 (Ont. H.C.) affirmed (1981) 34 O.R. (2d) 481, 60 C.P.R. (2d) 222, 128 D.L.R. (3d) 767 (Ont. C.A.) (C.A.) reversed on other grounds [1984] 1 S.C.R. 583, 1 C.P.R. (3d) 1, (*sub nom. Seiko Time Canada Ltd. v. Consumers Distributing Co.*) 10 D.L.R. (4th) 161, 54 N.R. 161, 29 C.C.C.T. 296, 3 C.I.P.R. 223, 10 D.L.R. (4th) 161 (S.C.C.).

[223] (1993), 28 B.C.A.C. 316, 47 W.A.C. 316 (B.C. C.A.).

[224] (1993), 28 B.C.A.C. 316, 47 W.A.C. 316 (B.C. C.A.).

[225] (1993), 28 B.C.A.C. 316, 47 W.A.C. 316 (B.C. C.A.).

made, the extended passing off action may be applicable. If there is no foreseeable likelihood of the public being deceived or confused, then there is no basis for recovery."[226]

In addition to the common law rights there may be a cause of action under section 7 of the *Trade-Marks Act*. This provision sets out a code of statutory rules related to this subject, as follows:

"No person shall

(a) make a false or misleading statement tending to discredit the business, wares or services of a competitor;

(b) direct public attention to his wares, services or business in such a way as to cause or be likely to cause confusion in Canada, at the time he commenced so to direct attention to them, between his wares, services or business and the wares, services or business of another;[227]

(c) pass off other wares or services as and for those ordered or requested;

(d) make use, in association with wares or services, of any description that is false in a material respect and likely to mislead the public as to:

    (i)   the character, quality, quantity or composition,

    (ii)  the geographical origin, or

    (iii) the mode of the manufacture, production or performance of the wares or services; or

---

[226] From R.G. Howell, *Character Merchandising: The Marketing Potential Attaching to a Name, Image, Persona or Copyright Work*, (1991) 6 *I.P.J.* 197.

[227] In *Westfair Foods Ltd. v. Jim Pattison Industries Ltd.* (1990), 45 B.C.L.R. (2d) 253, [1990] 5 W.W.R. 482, 68 D.L.R. (4th) 481, 30 C.P.R. (3d) 174 (B.C. C.A.) the court of Appeal refers to the rights under section (b) as nothing more than a statutory statement of the common law tort of passing off. Some doubt was expressed as to the constitutional validity of this section in a number of cases but the recent decision of the Federal Court of Appeal in *Asbjorn Horgard A/S v. Gibbs/Nortac Industries Ltd.* (1987), 13 C.I.P.R. 263, [1987] 3 F.C. 544, 80 N.R. 9, 38 D.L.R. (4th) 544, 14 C.P.R. (3d) 314, 12 F.T.R. 317 (note), [1987] 3 C.F. 544 (Fed. C.A.) reconsideration refused 14 C.I.P.R. 17, 16 C.P.R. (3d) 112 (Fed. C.A.) found section 7(b) to be valid.

(e) do any other act or adopt any other business practice contrary to honest industrial or commercial usage in Canada."[228]

As a result, it is important for each operator of a Web site or other person making a link to another person's Web site or information on the Internet to ensure that it does not pass off its wares and services as being connected or associated with those of the other person.

---

[228]  In *MacDonald v. Vapor Canada Ltd.* (1976), [1977] 2 S.C.R. 134, 22 C.P.R. (2d) 1, 66 D.L.R. (3d) 1, 7 N.R. 477 (S.C.C.) the Supreme Court of Canada held that Section 7(e) was outside the constitutional competence of the Federal Government. The constitutional validity of "the remaining provisions of section 7 was, however, supported in the decision of the Federal Court of AppeaL in *Asbjorn Horgard A/S v. Gibbs/Nortac Industries Ltd.* (1987), 13 C.I.P.R. 263, [1987] 3 F.C. 544, 80 N.R. 9, 38 D.L.R. (4th) 544 14 C.P.R. (3d) 314, 12 F.T.R. 317 (note), [1987] 3 C.R. 544 (Fed. C.A.) reconsideration refused 14 C.I.P.R. 17, 16 C.P.R. (3d) 112 (Fed. C.A.).

# 6

# Use of Web Site for Advertising
# and Promotion

## 6.1 INTRODUCTION

The Internet is a remarkable new medium of communication. It creates new challenges and opportunities for promoting and marketing products and services using this new channel. This chapter provides an introduction to some of the legal restrictions and other constraints on the use of the Internet for these purposes.

A 1993 computer industry newsletter, *The Computer Times*, carried as its cover story "The Internet is Commercial", decrying the fact that the Internet, originally a defense research and academic project founded in 1969,[1] was being transformed through the increasing participation of commercial users. Up to this time, the Internet was largely the private reserve of educators, academics, researchers and computer technology professionals. The users of the Internet had built their own culture and unwritten codes of conduct based on the agreed use of common protocols. Many resented and continue to resent the "intrusion" of business into this realm.

A number of factors lead to the accessibility of the Internet to a much wider audience. These factors can be summarized as:

- Ease of entry — the development of the World Wide Web ("WWW") meant that the unsophisticated user could use a relatively simple graphical user interface ("GUI") to access information sites on the Internet. This opened up the Internet to a substantially larger audience;

---

[1] ARPANET — an Advanced Defense Research project is the generally acknowledged precursor of the Internet.

- The development of Web sites on the Internet was facilitated by the adoption of standardized protocols and programming language, including hypertext markup language (HTML) for writing content for Web sites and the availability of cross-platform Web browsers providing accessibility to users regardless of their operating system;

- The use of third party access providers to facilitate the management of technical details of access to the Internet; and

- Breakdown of the distinction between publishers and users. The ability of any person not only to obtain access to material but also to create new material which can be accessed by others has greatly expanded the level of participation in the Internet.

These factors, among others, have resulted in an explosion of interest in the Internet as a new communications vehicle. Evidence cited before the United States Supreme Court[2] indicated that in 1996, there were over ten million computer systems[3] connected to the Internet providing its infrastructure and computer Web site framework and there were at least 40 million users connected to the Internet. The Supreme Court of the United States heard evidence that the number of users connected to the Internet was expected to grow to 200 million by the year 1999.

Marketing surveys[4] generally suggest that the average Internet user is in the age range 25 to 30, of above average education, with above average salary (household income above $50,000.00). While approximately two thirds of users are male, the number of female participants on the Internet is rapidly increasing.

---

[2]   *ACLU v. Reno* (No. 96-511, June 26, 1997) U.S. S.C., 929 F. Supp. 830-31 (E.D.Pa. June 11, 1996).

[3]   More recent evidence suggests there are approximately 16,100,000 Internet host computers and that the average world wide percentage increase in the number of host computers is approximately 60% per year as of January, 1997. It is interesting to note, however, that the annual percentage increase of Internet hosts is substantially higher in Asia where the percentage increase on an annual basis in Malaysia is close to 400% and in Hong Kong close to 200%. See *The Economist*, July 26, 1997, pg. 56.

[4]   International Data Corporation Canada, Internet WWW Survey: Consumers for Internet Commerce 1996.

Such a market is bound to attract the attention of businesses who wish to market and advertise their products and services. There is, however, another factor which makes use of the Internet for marketing and advertising activities very appealing: the user pays essentially all the costs of obtaining access to the marketing information. Since such costs are low, one of the themes governing the Internet is "build it and they will come."

Unfortunately, there are other themes on the Internet, including: "buyer beware," and an etiquette for use of the Internet (or "Netiquette") which is enforced in a decentralized and unregulated manner by self-styled guardians of the Internet as we will see below.

For many years, traditional marketing and advertising companies struggled to understand the Internet and, perhaps because of their general lack of technical sophistication, were slow to catch the wave. At present, however, online marketing and use of Web sites have become an essential part of an integrated marketing and advertising campaign for many businesses. However, the failure of some advertising and marketing agencies to understand the Net's "culture" or the operational and legal problems that arise and the nature of the Internet can create problems for the businesses for whom they are providing marketing and/or advertising services. Accordingly, this chapter seeks to review some of these issues.

## 6.2  TYPES OF ADVERTISING OR MARKETING ACTIVITIES ON THE INTERNET

The following is a summary of the various Internet applications that may be used in connection with advertising or promoting the products or services that may be offered by a business:[5]

- **World Wide Web** (WWW) — Each World Wide Web site has an unique address that usually includes the corporate name or other identifier for the business responsible for the site. Any such site is easily accessible through Web browser software such as Netscape Navigator or Microsoft Explorer. The World Wide Web can provide linkage between documents and sites using the hypertext markup language (HTML). The World Wide Web is

---

[5]   See Chapter 1 for additional discussion regarding these applications.

easy to use and its rapid growth has overshadowed some other aspects of the Internet. The ability to establish sites focused on a company, or its products or services, and to provide appealing multimedia works to attract visitors to the site have made the World Wide Web one of the key elements in the marketing and/or advertising strategies for most businesses using the Internet.

- **Usenet** — This is a network that provides the capability of carrying out detailed discussions or conferences on focused topics. Usenet is generally accepted as a forum for unregulated free speech. Topics discussed on the Usenet may include information about the products or services of a particular manufacturer, information about various hobbies or information about certain types of music.[6] Since the participants in a Usenet service will all share an interest in the topic, the users represent an already qualified target group for marketers and advertisers. Unfortunately, irresponsible conduct such as spamming carried out by some marketers and advertisers, has created a negative reaction among members of the Usenet community to marketing or advertising activities.[7]

A variation of Usenet are the many Listserv systems which facilitate a similar discussion using e-mail of facilities. Listserv services are also frequent targets for spam.

- **File transfer protocol** (FTP) — This facility permits the transfer or downloading of files containing computer software, graphics, text or other information. FTP may be used with a search tool such as Archie which may be accessed through Telnet, e-mail, the World Wide Web or Gopher. The capability of using FTP to provide "free samples" of software, sound recordings and other products makes FTP a useful marketing tool.

- **Gopher** — This facility permits users to obtain information located at various sites on the Internet. Somewhat like FTP,

---

[6]   The most notorious sites on the Usenet can be found under the "alt" or "alternative" hierarchy and typically include discussions regarding sexually explicit material or provide a forum for exchange of sexually explicit material, opinions and the like.

[7]   This topic is discussed later in this chapter under the topic of spamming, and in connection with the informal regulation or nonlegal regulation of conduct on the Internet by self-styled Internet guardians.

Gopher (and the variant TurboGopher) is a standard for file and data retrieval. A complementary service to Gopher is Veronica which provides a searching capability. The use of Gopher applications has diminished significantly since the advent of the Web.

- **Electronic mail** — Electronic mail is one of the most widely used services on the Internet. It provides an inexpensive and efficient means of communication between users located anywhere in the world. The ability to reach a large number of individuals by electronic mail permits directed or focused marketing activities.

- **Internet Relay Chat (IRC)** — This facility provides a method of communicating with other users of the Internet in real time. A number of users form groups (or channels) to discuss specific subjects. Users may also carry out private communications. IRC may find use in some interactive promotional or marketing activities or as a means of providing access to a vendor's support staff.

Some of the major types of marketing or advertising activities conducted on the Internet include:

- A **World Wide Web site**, established and operated by a business which focuses on a particular product or service. This is the most popular form of marketing carried out on the Internet. Since a user determines what sites to visit, the operation of a site for this purpose generally does not create controversy;

- A **Banner ad** which may be placed on popular Web sites. Banner ads typically provide a click-through link to the advertiser's site which contains detailed information about a particular product, service, company or brand;

- Use of so-called "**push technology**" which allows a user to select the type of information to be delivered to that user (often at the "cost" of requiring the user to also receive advertising);[8]

---

[8]    Pointcast is perhaps a classic example of this approach. <http://www.pointcast.ca> and <http://www.pointcast.com> provide the software which can be used to track current market, news or other activity of interest. Updates are periodically downloaded to the user's computer. Other popular examples of push technology are **backWeb** (<http://www. backWeb.com>) which provides information packages which can be displayed as

- A **frame** which is created by dividing a user's screen into multiple windows. One window or frame is filled with advertising while the main window or frame is filled with content of interest to the user. This technique can be used to frame content located on the site which creates the frames or from a site operated by an unrelated entity. If the frames are established in such a manner that another person's trademarks are either used or concealed without authorization then legal consequences may arise; and

- **Spam,**[9] which is the widespread sending of unsolicited bulk commercial electronic mail messages via the Usenet or e-mail systems. This is seen as an imposition on users who receive the junk e-mail and can be disruptive to the business of Internet Access or Service Providers. At the same time, due to the large number of people that can be reached, even if only a very small percentage of persons who receive the "spam" respond to the sales pitch, this may be a very cost effective advertising vehicle. To date, spam has been predominantly used to advertise "get rich quick" schemes, sex sites or long distance phone cards. Most businesses do not engage in spamming activity due to the very adverse reputation their trademarks and products may acquire through use of such a marketing approach;

Marketing studies appear to suggest that brand value can be enhanced through the construction and maintenance of interesting and informative Web sites as well as the placement of banner

---

animations popping up on the screen, audio messages, desktop wallpapers and screen savers and **Afterdark** (<http://www.afterdark.com>) which offers news and features from a variety of sources such as *Wall Street Journal, Sports Illustrated Online*, and *U.S.A. Today.* Sports scores and stocks scroll by in a ticker format. The tradeoff for access to these services is that the material sent to the user will often contain advertisements for third party products or services. Most users find this to be a very acceptable compromise and see it as akin to the traditional radio or television which provide free content in exchange for having that content interspersed with advertising material.

[9]    With apologies to the manufacturer of the successful and popular trademarked canned meat product, Hormel Foods, whose very successfully registered trademark "Spam" for a packaged pork and ham meat product, has been satirized and popularized in the infamous Monty Python skit and now has come to describe the practice of sending unsolicited bulk e-mail. The use of spam is one of the most objectionable marketing tactics conducted on the Internet. In fact, it appears to be have been popularized by the infamous lawyers Cantor and Siegel who, in 1994, repeatedly sent out a message to almost all Usenet news groups offering legal services to help enter the United States green card lottery.

advertisements on popular Web sites. These types of marketing activities are analogous to traditional forms of advertising and are not regarded negatively by most users.

Operators of legitimate Web sites expend considerable funds to develop their sites to communicate messages to promote their products or services.

Unfortunately the contents of a Web site may be easily copied. While copying of content or other unauthorized use would likely involve both trademark and copyright infringement, there may be practical difficulties in seeking legal remedies. To date such activities have been dealt with by embarrassing the pirates who set up the mirror site, commencing civil and/or criminal action in the appropriate jurisdictions, and/or using the wide range of "self help" techniques available on the Internet, such as engaging in "cyber warfare" against the counterfeit sites.[10]

## 6.3  LOCATING THE WEB SITE

A critical issue for owners of a Web site is to ensure that it can be located by potential customers. Various search engines are available for users to carry out searches. Examples of some of the popular search engines are AltaVista,[11] Excite,[12] Hotbot,[13] Lycos,[14] Infoseek,[15] and Yahoo.[16]

Search engines commonly use a program, known as a "Web spider," to crawl through the World Wide Web. As the Web spider passes through pages, it indexes the contents and follows the links to other Web pages. Therefore, any Web site that is referenced (with a link) from other indexed Web sites will automatically be indexed. Operators of Web sites can also proactively register their Web sites

---

[10]   More detail on some such activity in the context of spamming is found in subsection 6.5 below which deals with limits on marketing and advertising activities on the Internet.

[11]   <http://www.altavista.digital.com>.

[12]   <http://www.excite.com>.

[13]   <http://www.hotbot.com>.

[14]   <http://www.lycos.com>.

[15]   <http://www.infoseek.com>.

[16]   <http://www.yahoo.com>.

with many directories and search engines. Services such as Register-IT![17] or Submit It![18] allow a single submission to be sent to a variety of different search engines or directories.

A Web site might therefore be located by means of a keyword search conducted using a search engine. However, search engines may identify thousands of sites in response to a particular request. An operator of a Web site can improve the odds of their site being ranked closer to the top of such a list by providing descriptive information which is incorporated into invisible portions of their Web pages (called meta tags) which can be read and acted upon by some search engines. In fact one problem being experienced by some businesses is the use of their marks as meta tags by competitors to divert potential customers to Web sites operated by these competitors.

Web masters or Web site owners who wish to check the popularity of their site may do so with automated tools available on the Internet. For example, Rank this![19] provides a tool which checks a variety of search engines and will inform the Web master if the particular Web address is located in the top ten or two hundred positions with each search engine. This provides an effective diagnostic tool to permit fine tuning of the Web site to increase the number of "hits."

Many businesses will also place the Web address of their Web site on advertisements, product brochures and other types of promotional material.

## 6.4  INTERACTIVE FEEDBACK FROM A WEB SITE

A unique feature about advertising and marketing activity on the Internet is that there is a means of verifying the effectiveness of the Web site. Operators of Web site can record the number of "hits" or visits to their Web site (or even to each page on their Web site) thereby measuring the popularity of the site or for gauging interest in the various content made available on the site.

---

[17]  <http://www.register-it.com>.

[18]  <http://www.submit-it.com>.

[19]  <http://www.rankthis.com>.

Unlike information gathered through traditional polling techniques which are used to identify the size of the audience potentially exposed to the advertising or marketing message, the information collected for Internet advertising provides more accurate information and is generally accessible in a very timely manner, at a low cost, and can allow fine tuning of the Web site very quickly with measurable results.

Web sites use various techniques to gather additional information about users. One technique is to upload information to the user's computer (called a "cookie") which can then be queried on subsequent visits.

Many Web sites also encourage users to register with the site in order to obtain access to the site or to participate in promotions or contests.

In addition to obtaining direct and immediate feedback about a user, the Web site advertiser can use the information provided by a user to customize or personalize the presentation of the Web site for that particular user, even on subsequent visits. The use of cookies allows this to occur even if the actual identity of the user is not konwn. Such capability is unavailable with all traditional forms of marketing or advertising activity and provides a basis for building a closer relationship between the advertiser and the user/customer.

The capability of tracking visitors to a Web site raises concerns about personal privacy. Many Web browsers provide a feature which allows a user to be warned when a Web site is seeking to set a cookie. Some Web sites obtain explicit permission from the user before setting or accessing cookies.

The *New York Times* Web site[20] illustrates the strength of Web advertising. The *New York Times* boasts to advertising executives that it "is the first and only media site of its kind to target advertisements based on 100% user supplied information." They note that their demographic databases are based on actual information supplied by registered users as opposed to statistical or other less reliable approaches. As a result, the *New York Times* notes that it can

---

[20]    <http://www.nytimes.com/adinfo>.

customize online advertising to specific demographic characteristics, thereby providing more effective targeting than is available with many traditional forms of advertising or marketing activity.

In summary, the Internet is a unique medium which, for a relatively small cost, permits an advertiser to reach a potential audience in the millions with favourable socioeconomic demographics such as above average education and income. Further, a Web site provides an opportunity to encourage repeat visits, to provide information which can be continuously updated and to develop an interactive and more meaningful relationship with the consumer market. As a result, while many advertisers and marketers initially misunderstood and, indeed, were fearful of the Internet, it has now been embraced by that industry as an effective new channel to complement existing channels.

## 6.5  LIMITS ON MARKETING OR ADVERTISING ACTIVITIES

There are generally two types of limits or restrictions on marketing or advertising activity on the Internet. One type of restriction arises from the enforcement of so-called Netiquette by individuals or organizations who seek to preserve the "purity" of the Internet, in many cases for altruistic, but in other cases, for malicious purposes. The second type of restriction arises from legal rules which apply to the conduct of any advertiser or marketer on the Internet.

Marketing activities on the Internet may also need to comply with guidelines issued by industry associations. For instance, the Canadian Direct Marketing Association's "Code of Ethics and Standards of Practice" contains rules that must be observed by member companies, including rules that are specific to electronic media such as the Internet.[21]

## 6.6  NON-LEGAL ISSUES

The Internet has an evolving and self-enforced code of conduct of which advertisers and marketers should be aware. For instance, persons who express unpopular opinions in Usenet chat sessions may

---

[21]    <http://www.cdma.org/new/ethics.htm/>.

be flamed.[22] Sales pitches or direct sales solicitations on Usenet and Listservs are also generally not well accepted. Some moderators of Listservs have developed procedures for communication of commercial messages to subscribers. Companies wishing to send direct commercial messages through a Listserv discussion group should first ascertain the accepted practices in the group and, where practical, consult with the group moderator regarding their intended use. Marketers and advertisers should be aware that the reaction on the Internet to what may be considered as offensive activity, such as spamming, is swift and vigorous and may be significantly damaging to the reputation of the advertised or marketed product and may even give rise to a boycott.

## 6.7  SPAM

A large amount of adverse attention has been focused on "spamming." As previously noted, spamming is the sending of bulk unsolicited e-mail with commercial messages to many news groups on the Usenet or subscribers of Listservs. Spam may include circulation of "get rich quick" schemes, sex ads, or the promotion of legitimate products or services. In some cases self-styled Internet guardians, will take proactive measures to combat spam. Recipients of spam may also react.

Reasons often cited by anti-spamming guardians for their actions include that the spammers typically do not pay the real costs incurred by their activities, the volume of spam e-mail may be such that it can clog servers and the network and slow down communications between legitimate users and perhaps most importantly, the spam messages are unwanted by a large majority of recipients with the result that it makes use of the Internet less beneficial. In effect, spamming is like "junk fax" which imposes a cost and burden on recipients by utilizing their access time, memory and other resources without permission to do so. A major difference between junk fax, which may consume resources printing several pages each day, and

---

[22]  Flaming is any form of abusive comments made by one or more participants in Usenet against a particular individual. This activity may, of course, constitute defamation and be otherwise actionable.

spam, is that the Internet Service or Access Provider may be bombarded by millions of such messages each day.[23]

Various self-help "approaches" have been developed to combat spamming. Some of these approaches are described below.[24]

### (a) Self-Help Approaches to Spam

Users can reduce their exposure to receiving spam messages by taking a number of proactive steps. Some of these steps are:

- users can verify that its Internet Service Provider or Internet Access Provider is not providing or operating a background computer program[25] which can be used by Web servers to obtain the user's ID and that the provider is not permitting spammers to operate on its servers;

- users can restrict the exposure of their e-mail addresses by not participating in directories or by disguising their addresses. A further alternative is to obtain a disposable forwarding address;[26]

- users can search e-mail directories and "look-up" services to find where their addresses are registered, and request removal of their addresses. Legitimate businesses will usually accommodate such requests; and

- users and/or Internet Service or Access Providers may use screening software to reduce the volume of spam that reaches their system.[27]

---

[23]  For example, in *America Online, Inc. v. Cyber Promotions, Inc.* C.A. No. 96-5213, November 26, 1996 (E.D. Penn 1996) AOL's servers were receiving over 1,900,000 spam E-mail messages each day.

[24]  For much more detail on this subject see Junkbusters — <http://www.junkbusters.com>.

[25]  Often known as an "identd demon."

[26]  Disposable forwarding addresses may be obtained from companies like NetAddress at <http://www.netaddress.com> or Bigfoot at <http://www.bigfoot.com>.

[27]  For example, in *America Online, Inc. v. Cyber Promotions, Inc.* C.A. No. 96-5213, November 26, 1996 (E.D. Penn 1996) AOL used an E-mail screening tool which it called the "PreferredMail-The Guard Against Junk E-Mail" which permitted each of its 7,000,000 users to choose whether or not they wished to receive spam by making a positive choice on a screen saying "I want junk e-mail!". The court found this approach to be legitimate conduct by AOL.

In addition to these steps, users may also respond directly to unwanted messages. In the infamous Canter and Siegal case,[28] many users who received the unwelcome messages responded by "letter bombing" the server used by Canter and Siegal. It is still common for users to provide negative feedback to the spammer. An alternative used by many users is to "ping" the system to check network connections. A so-called "ping attack," if carried out by a sufficient number of users, may flood the server. However, this type of response may also harm innocent parties, such as the Internet Service or Access Provider (assuming the provider did not authorize the use of the account for spam) and other users of the affected servers.[29]

Spammers will often seek to avoid the identification of their marketing material as such by using false headers or disguising their return address.[30] Where spammers provide a means of communicating a positive response to the advertising message (such as a 1-800 number), a person frustrated with the interference of the spamming activity may seek to tie up the 1-800 line as retribution.

Another alternative for victims of a spam is to forward the spam to the Web master of the particular Internet Service Provider with a view to causing the spammer's account to be terminated.[31] Another approach is to establish filters to automatically delete mail from the same sender in the future.[32]

---

[28]   This was the case where two US lawyers sent a number of spam messages advertising for clients for an upcoming US Immigration green card lottery. The messages were posted to numerous Usenet groups and provoked a very vocal and angry reaction from users who found the blatant advertising on the Internet in bad taste, objectionable or offensive.

[29]   See, for example, *Cyber Promotions, Inc. v. Apex Global Information Services, Inc.* (E.D. Pa., decided September 30, 1997) where the Court found that a ping attack was not an act of God and the ISP was aware of the risk of such a response to the plaintiff spammer's activities. A copy of the judge's decision is available at <http://www.parrhesia.com/cyberpromo.html>.

[30]   The "return" address may often be directed at an innocent victim or one of the more vocal critics of spamming. In Canada, there appears to be direct criminal consequences from such reckless and/or intentional interference with another user's account by falsifying part of the message. See below for more details.

[31]   Many spammers use private Internet access accounts under terms which prohibit the use of the account for any commercial activity. The violation of such conditions typically permit the cancellation of a spammer's Internet access account.

[32]   These features are already found in many popular e-mail software programs such as EudoraMail Pro, Net Manage, Netscape Communicator, and Claris e-mail.

Blacklists of advertisers have been developed as a mechanism to enlist consumer support in combatting spamming and other offensive marketing activity on the Internet. Such lists may provide any person who is listed with a limited period of time to cease carrying out the offensive activity before their products and services are made subject to a boycott.

Another approach used by some "cyber guardians" is the use of "cancel" messages. In fact, automated systems (or "cancelbots" which cancel all messages that meet specific criteria) have been developed for use on the Internet. In response, some spammers seek to disguise their identities or the identification of the messages, in effort to evade the operation of the cancelbot. One of the dangers of cancel or kill messages, or the use of filters, is that some legitimate messages may be disrupted. An approach the courts appear to sanction is the use of screening or filtering software to give users a choice of whether or not to receive junk e-mail.[33] It is likely that these various self-help activities will continue until there are effective enforcement mechanisms available at law to deal with the transmission of unsolicited advertising on the Internet.

### (b)  Legal Sanctions for Spam — Civil Causes of Action

There are various legal issues associated with many of the activities of spammers and the "self-help" activities used by self styled guardians of the Internet. These will vary from one jurisdiction to another. The rights and obligations of the parties will also depend on the terms of access agreements between the Internet Access or Service Provider and users.

One technique used by some recipients of spam messages is to seek to establish a contract with the spammer by agreeing to receive spam messages for a fee. The user may offer to review unsolicited commercial messages for a fee, and allege that the spammer's conduct in continuing to send spam messages after receiving such an

---

[33]   For example, in *America Online, Inc. v. Cyber Promotions, Inc.*, C.A. No. 96-5213, November 26, 1996 (E.D. Penn 1996), the court approved the use of such a tool to give users a choice of whether or not to receive the spam and also permit the system operator (AOL) to protect against 1,900,000 unsolicited spam messages impacting the servers each day.

offer results in a contact being made by the actions of the spammer in continuing with the spam conduct.[34]

Another approach is to rely on any applicable legislation that prohibits unsolicited fax or similar marketing activity. Unfortunately, Canada lags behind the United States and other jurisdictions in protecting consumers from these types of marketing activities.[35]

In the United States, the courts have found that Internet users do not, by virtue of their constitutional right of freedom of speech, have the right to use another person's network, servers or system without compensation to send millions of unsolicited messages each day.[36]

Many spammers obtain a temporary private user account from a commercial service or access provider as a base from which to send their spam messages. Such accounts are typically subject to contractual terms that restrict users from making use of the account for spamming. The rationale for such restrictions is that the use of the Internet access account for spamming purposes may have the effect of shutting down or severely limiting the network connection, thereby denying legitimate users access to the Internet. An Internet Access or Service Provider that seeks to cancel a user's account should review its rights to terminate before doing so in order to avoid a claim for breach of contract.[37]

---

[34]   For more details on this approach, see <http://www.junkbusters.com/ht/en/spam.html>.

[35]   There may be protection from unsolicited fax communications in the United States under the *Telephone Consumer Protection Act*, the *Electronic Communication Privacy Act*, *Lanham Act*, or other legislation. The state of Nevada is reported to have introduced an anti-spam bill which would require a spammer to identify himself and remove recipients from the database on request.

[36]   See the decision in *America Online, Inc. v. Cyber Promotions, Inc.* C.A. No. 96-5213, November 26, 1996 (E.D. Penn 1996) where the court rejected the defendant's claim of a constitutional right to send millions of spam messages each day to AOL's 7,000,000 customers.

[37]   See, for example, *Cyber Promotions, Inc. v. Apex Global Information Services, Inc.*, (E.D. Pa., decided September 30, 1997) where the plaintiff spammer sued the Internet service provider for breach of contract. The plaintiff had purchased a number of T-1 lines from the ISP. The contract required 30 days notice before the defendant could terminate the service. The defendant cancelled the plaintiff's account after a substantial ping attack on the defendant's network. The court found the ping attack was not an act of God and the ISP was aware of the risk of such a response to the plaintiff's activities. Further the defendant had provided ongoing connections to other spammers and only targeted the plaintiff for cancellation of the Internet access. A copy of the decision is available at

Other consequences may also arise. Where the spammer's commercial conduct violates the Internet service provider's Internet access rules or agreement, then civil liability may arise.[38] Or, where a spammer uses a database acquired from another person without permission or authority, it may face action for copyright infringement, trespass, misappropriation and unfair competition.

Sending spam may be an actionable tort in some jurisdictions as data and business may be lost by other users and by Internet Service or Access Providers. A spammer may also be liable where it uses another's name as the "from" address.[39]

### (c)  Legal Sanctions for Spam — Criminal Sanctions

Legislative efforts have been made in some jurisdictions to curb the sending of unsolicited telecommunications, however, Canadian law has not fully addressed the issue.

It is possible that certain provisions of the *Criminal Code* dealing with computer crimes may provide a remedy for spamming or similar intrusive marketing activities. In Canada, the provisions of the

---

<http://www.parrhesia.com/cyberpromo.html>.

[38]  See, for example, *Typhoon, Inc. v. Kentech Enterprises, Paging America et al.* (S.D. Ca., Complaint filed August 20, 1997) where an Internet Service Provider sued a paging company that is alleged to have accessed the plaintiff's mail server without consent to send thousands of spam messages. The defendant's mail return address was invalid. The next day, the plaintiff's servers were allegedly accessed without authority to send thousands of similar messages. The plaintiff installed a spam filter and allegedly recorded thousands of attempts to write messages using the plaintiff's system. Thereafter the defendant is alleged to have sent further spam messages through another Internet access account using a nonexistent account with the plaintiff as a return address. Further messages were directed to the plaintiff who sued, claiming misappropriation of name and identity, trespass to chattels, unjust enrichment, unfair competition and violation of both S. 43(a) *Lanham Act* and provisions of the *Electronics Communication Privacy Act*. A copy of the complaint may be obtained at: <http://www.jmls.edu/cyber/cases/typhoon1.html>.

[39]  See, for example, *Seidl v. Greentree Mortgage Company* (D.C. Col., complaint filed August 1997) where a spammer is alleged to have used a false "from" designation in his messages and the return path targeted the plaintiff as the source of the message. The plaintiff sued, alleging a number of causes of action including deceptive trade practices, trespass to chattels, negligence, invasion of privacy, violation of a right of privacy, false light invasion of privacy as well as alleged breach of *Colorado's Deceptive Practice Act* and 47 U.S.C. s. 227. A copy of the complaint may be found at <http:///www.cs.colorado.edu/~seidl/lawsuit/complaint.html>.

*Criminal Code*[40] dealing with abuse or misuse of computer systems and data that may have some application to such forms of advertising and marketing activity on the Internet are reviewed below.

In the United States, repeated transmission of unsolicited e-mail may violate federal trademark law and various computer crime statutes.[41] Some states, such as Nevada, have also enacted legislation which prohibits the transmission of unwanted advertising on the Internet.[42]

### (i)  Unauthorized Use of a Computer System

Section 342.1 of the *Criminal Code* of Canada provides as follows:

(1)  Everyone who fraudulently and without colour of right,

    (a)  Obtains, directly or indirectly, any computer service;

    (b)  By means of an electromagnetic, acoustic, mechanical or other device, intercepts or causes to be intercepted, directly or indirectly, any function of a computer system; or

    (c)  Uses or causes to be used, directly or indirectly, a computer system with an intent to commit an offence under (a) or (b) or an offence under Section 430 in relation to data or a computer system,

is guilty of an indictable offence and is liable to imprisonment for a term not exceeding 10 years, or is guilty of an offence punishable on summary conviction.

(2)  In this Section,

"computer program" means data representing instructions or statements that, when executed in a computer system, causes the computer system to perform a function;

---

[40]  R.S.C. 1985, c. C-46, as amended.

[41]  See *America Online Inc. v. Prime Data Systems Inc.*, Civil Action 97 — (E.D. Virginia, October 21, 1997).

[42]  SB13, enacted July 1997, effective July 1998.

"computer service" includes data processing and the storage or retrieval of data;

"computer system" means a device that, or a group of interconnected or related devices, one or more of which;

(a) Contains computer programs or other data, and

(b) Pursuant to computer programs:

(i) Performs logic and control, and

(ii) May perform any other function;

"data" means representations of information or of concepts that are being prepared or have been prepared in a form suitable for use in a computer system;

"electromagnetic, acoustic, mechanical or other device" means any device or apparatus that is used or is capable of being used to intercept any function of a computer system, but does not include a hearing aid used to correct abnormal hearing of the user to not better than normal hearing;

"function" includes logic, control, arithmetic, deletion, storage and retrieval and communication or telecommunication to, from or within a computer system;

"intercept" includes listen to or record a function of a computer system, or acquire the substance, meaning or purport thereof."

Because this section applies to any fraudulent act of obtaining any computer service or intercepting any function of a computer system, it may apply to certain types of spamming activities in which a user carries out unauthorized acts that impair an Internet Service or Access Provider's computer system.[43] The use of an Internet access account without consent (such as where an individual or private Internet access account is used in violation of express prohibitions on commercial use), may also represent an unauthorized use of a computer system for purposes of section 342.1(1)(c). The use of a

---

[43]    See, for example, the decision in *America Online, Inc. v. Cyber Promotions, Inc.*, No. 96-5213, November 26, 1996 (E.D. Penn 1996).

computer system without authorization may also constitute an offense in US jurisdictions.

### (ii)  Mischief in Relation to Data

Subsection 430 (1.1) of the *Criminal Code* provides as follows:

"Everyone commits mischief who wilfully

(a)  destroys or alters data;

(b)  renders data meaningless, useless or ineffective;

(c)  obstructs, interrupts or interferes with the lawful use of data; or

(d)  obstructs, interrupts or interferes with any person in the lawful use of data or denies access to data to any person who is entitled to access thereto."

Subsection (5) provides that this provision is also a hybrid offence, and in the case of a conviction on indictment, carries a maximum term of imprisonment of five years. Subsection (8) provides that "data" has the same meaning as in section 342.1.

Traditional spamming activity may be caught by this provision insofar as it may delay, impede or limit the rights of other users to obtain timely access to their messages and otherwise use the Internet for its intended purposes. In this regard, a user will likely be charged for access time by his or her Internet Access Provider while reviewing or discarding spam messages. The user may consider this unauthorized imposition to be an interference in use of the Internet (which itself is a computer system). Such an interference in lawful use of data may constitute an offence if such conduct is carried out "wilfully." There may also be an unlawful interference with data, where a spammer disguises the message, uses false "From" headings or takes other steps to disguise the source of the message. The case is more compelling where millions of spam messages impinge on the servers of the Internet Access or Service Provider.[44]

---

[44]  See *America Online, Inc. v. Cyber Promotions, Inc.*, C.A. No. 96-5213, November 26, 1996 (E.D. Penn 1996).

In *Turner v. The Queen*,[45] (a case decided prior to the enactment of section 430(1.1)), the court held that the unauthorized encrypting of data on magnetic tapes in such a manner that the data could not be properly accessed or used by its owner could constitute mischief in relation to property since there was an interference with the use of the tangible property on which the data was contained. In that case the judge referred to the provisions of subsection 387 (1.1) (now s. 430(1.1)) above, which were, at that time, before Parliament but not yet enacted into law. In an *obiter dictum*, the judge noted that the conduct of the defendants in encrypting data and thereby essentially destroying the access to it by its legitimate owners could also fall within the then draft provision.

The use of cancelbots and/or cancel or kill messages or files may constitute intentional interference with data. This may be a source of some risk to the self-styled Internet guardians. A key question is whether the unauthorized intrusive messages sent by spammers are "lawful." US courts have found no inherent right either under the constitution or under antitrust law to permit a spammer to make free use of another's computer service and facilities.[46] Accordingly, an Internet Access or Service Provider is entitled to use screening or similar tools to protect the network while giving users a choice of whether to receive the spam messages.

### (iii) Theft of a Telecommunication Service

Section 326 of the *Criminal Code* (Canada) provides as follows:

"(1) Everyone commits theft who fraudulently, maliciously, or without colour of right,

...

    (b) Uses any telecommunication facility or obtains any telecommunication service,

(2) In this section and in section 327, "telecommunication" means any transmission, emission or reception of signs, signals, writing,

---

[45]  (1984) 27 B.L.R. 207, 13 C.C.C. (3d) 430 (O.H.C.).

[46]  See *America Online, Inc. v. Cyber Promotions, Inc.*, C.A. No. 96-5213, November 26, 1996 (E.D. Penn 1996).

images, sounds or intelligence of any nature by radio, visual, electronic or other electromagnetic system."

The deceptive use of a private Internet access account to send bulk commercial e-mail in contravention of an Internet access agreement could be found to be obtaining a telecommunication facility "fraudulently, maliciously, or without colour of right."

## 6.8  GENERAL LEGAL ISSUES

Advertising and marketing activities carried out by means of the Internet raise some of the same legal issues as those that arise from other marketing activities. These include defamation, copyright law, and various laws against misrepresentation.[47] As a result, the Internet marketer must take all of the traditional precautions to avoid liability for misleading practices.

A further factor that complicates any Internet marketing is that the material is available on a world wide basis. Material that may be considered appropriate or lawful in one jurisdiction (such as where the Web site is physically located) may be offensive, illegal or otherwise objectionable in another jurisdiction. As a result, the marketing business should review and monitor the development of the law in all major markets in which customers access the Web.

The following discussion is an illustrative list of some key legal concerns for any Internet based marketing campaign.

### (a)  Rights to Use the Advertising or Marketing Content

#### (i)  Copyright

The graphic designs, logos, art work, computer programs, textual materials, sound and/or audio visual recordings, Web site designs and other content used on Web sites or exchanged on the Internet are protected by copyright law.

---

[47]  See, for example, Young & Fraser, *Canadian Advertising & Marketing Law*, 1997, which provides an overview of the traditional legal issues.

Since international treaties provide for the automatic protection in Canada of works created by nationals of most other countries,[48] marketing and advertising businesses should assume that most material available on the Internet is protected by copyright.[49] As a result, any reproduction, display to the public or other acts restricted by copyright law with respect to such publication of materials[50] could result in liability for copyright infringement. Such actions could give rise to claims for statutory damages and possible criminal liability.

As noted in detail in Chapter 5, the *Copyright Act*[51] of Canada also provides for certain moral rights, namely the rights to be named as the author of the work, the right of integrity, and the right to restrict use of the work in association with a product or service that would prejudice the honour or reputation of the author. These moral rights are personal rights of the authors and may not be assigned, although they may be waived. Given the ease with which a work available on the Internet may be modified or combined with other works, considerable caution should be exercised to avoid moral rights liability in any marketing or advertising campaign. Appropriate waivers should be obtained from the author.

## (b)  Unfair Competition

Since the Internet is unregulated, there is no central body to ensure that the information conveyed is accurate or truthful, nor is there central editorial control over the content. Consequently, some businesses may misrepresent their products or services. In one case, a business carried out a campaign to promote magazine subscriptions and in doing so used e-mail to create fictitious messages from satisfied customers.[52]

---

[48]  See the provisions of the *Berne Convention for the Protection of Literary and Artistic Works* (1886) and its several revisions.

[49]  For more details on some of the limits to such protection see *Protecting Copyright and Industrial Design*, (Toronto: Carswell Practice Guide, 1995).

[50]  See Chapter 5.

[51]  R.S.C. 1985, c. C-42, as amended.

[52]  See, for example, *People of the State of New York v. Lipsitz* (N.Y. Sup. Ct. 1997) where the Court found the defendants conduct violated New York consumer fraud and false advertising laws.

The following is a summary of some of the major legal rules that prohibit such false or misleading advertising in Canada.

### (i)  Competition Act

Material misrepresentation in advertising is an offense under section 52 of the *Competition Act*,[53] which provides as follows:

> 52(1) "No person shall, for the purpose of promoting, directly or indirectly, supply or use of a product or for the purpose of promoting, directly or indirectly, any business interest, by any means whatever,
>
> (a)    make a representation to the public that is false or misleading in a material respect;
>
> 52(4) in any prosecution for a contravention of this section, the general impression conveyed by representation as well as the literal meaning thereof shall be taken into account in determining whether or not the misrepresentation is false or misleading in a material respect.

An example of misrepresentation on the Internet involves a business that promoted visits to Web sites to encourage viewing of adult images. Users were advised that the adult images were free to view and download, but that a special viewer was required. Upon installation, the "viewer" software would terminate the modem connection without the knowledge of the user, and then would automatically dial an international long distance number for which the operator of the Web site received a kickback.[54]

All advertising campaigns, and in particular any comparative advertising, should be reviewed for accuracy to ensure that all claims made regarding the business's own product or service and those regarding any competitor are true, provable and defensible.[55]

---

[53]    R.S.C. 1985, c. C-34, as amended.

[54]    See such a case in *The Federal Trade Commission v. Audiotex Connection, Inc.* (E.D. N.Y. 1997). A copy of the complaint, filed November 1997, is located seen at <http://www.ftc.gov/os/9711/Adtxamdfcmp.htm>. A copy of the consent decree and order is located at <http://www.ftc.gov/os/9711/Adtxprmford.htm>.

[55]    More detailed information on the *Competition Act* and related issues of concern to marketers and advertisers may be found in Young & Fraser, *Canadian Advertising & Marketing Law*, 1997.

### (ii)  Unfair Trade Practices Act

Many provinces also have statutory regimes to protect consumers. For instance, section 4(d) of the *Unfair Trade Practices Act*[56] of the Province of Alberta states that "any representation or conduct that has the effect, or might reasonably have the effect, of deceiving or misleading a consumer or potential consumer constitutes an unfair act or practice." The Act provides a number of specific examples of unfair trade practices, including a representation that the goods or services have sponsorship, approval, performance, characteristics, accessories, ingredients, quantities, uses or benefits that they do not have.

Under section 11 of the *Unfair Trade Practices Act* of Alberta, a consumer who has entered into a consumer transaction and has suffered damage or loss due to an unfair act or practice, may commence an action in court for relief against any supplier who engages in or acquiesces to the unfair act or practice.[57]

Liability under the *Unfair Trade Practices Act* or similar statutory rules should be considered, especially in cases of advertising, since it is more likely that the claim regarding the advertiser's product or services will be carefully scrutinized by any competitor and/or consumer.

### (iii)  Passing Off

A common practice on the Internet is to use hypertext links to direct a user visiting one Web site or page to other information of interest that may be found on another person's Web site or page. The destination Web site owner has no control over the hypertext link nor over the way in which the hypertext link is described on the referring Web site. The way in which the hypertext link is presented may suggest a connection between the two sites or the underlying businesses.

---

[56]   R.S.A. 1980, c. U-3, as amended.

[57]   In Ontario, see the *Business Practices Act*, R.S.O. 1990, c. B.18.

A common law action for passing off can prevent one trader from representing his goods and services as those of another. Further, section 7 of the *Trade-Marks Act*,[58] also states:

"No person shall:

(a) make a false or misleading statement tending to discredit the business, wares or services of a competitor;

(b) direct public attention to his wares, services or business in such a way as to cause or be likely to cause confusion in Canada, at the time he commenced so to direct attention to them, between his wares, services or business and the wares, services or business of another;

(c) pass off other wares or services as and for those ordered or requested;

(d) make use, in association with wares or services, of any description that is false in a material respect and likely to mislead the public as to:

(i) the character, quality, quantity or composition,

(ii) the geographical origin, or

(iii) the mode of the manufacture, production or performance of the wares or services; or

(e) do any other act or adopt any other business practice contrary to honest industrial or commercial usage in Canada."

In view of these provisions, and comparable provisions in other jurisdictions, it is important for a business on the Internet to ensure that it does not pass off its wares or services as being connected or associated with the wares or services of another business and particularly a competitor. Special caution should be exercised in the case of making hypertext links to the Web sites of other businesses to avoid any suggestion that the destination Web site is providing any sponsorship or approval of the referring Web site's business, products, services or activities.

One concern regarding hypertext links is the use of another business trademarks on the hypertext link. This may give rise to a

---

[58] R.S.C. 1985, c. T-13, as amended.

potential risk of trademark infringement and passing off.[59] One approach to mitigate the risk of such liability is to state clearly that, any trademarks of the other person belong to that person. An explicit disclaimer may state that the advertiser's product is not approved, associated or otherwise connected with the other party.

A business which conducts advertising or marketing activities on the Internet should also ensure that such activities do not violate the other provisions of section 7 of the *Trade-Marks Act*. However, note that the constitutional validity of section 7(e) has been cast in doubt by the case *McDonald v. Vapour Canada Ltd.*[60]

### (iv)  Trade Libel

It is actionable to challenge a trader's right or title to sell his or her goods and services or make other statements calculated to injure the trader's business.[61] Such an action requires that a false and harmful statement or suggestion regarding the trader be made to a third party. Thus false and damaging statements made by e-mail or in Usenet discussion groups regarding another's product or service may be actionable.

### (v)  Fraud

Outright fraud, deceit and other dishonest conduct whether on a Web site, by e-mail message or otherwise are likely to give rise to civil and possible criminal liability in Canada or the United States.[62] It is actionable to make a false statement with the intention that another person will rely on it to his or her detriment. Although an action in tort for deceit requires fraudulent intent, a contractual misrepresentation is actionable without a specific fraudulent intent.[63]

---

[59]    Liability for use of links and frames is discussed in section 6.10.

[60]    [1977] 2 S.C.R. 134, 22 C.P.R. (2d) 1, 66 D.L.R. (3d) 1, 7 N.R. 477 (S.C.C.).

[61]    See Salmond on *The Law of Torts*, 18th Ed., Sweet & Maxwell.

[62]    For an example under US State false advertising provisions see, *People of the State of New York v. Lipsitz* (N.Y. Sup. Ct. 1997).

[63]    See Fleming, *The Law of Torts*, 6th Ed. The Law Book Company Limited.

## (c)  Trademark Infringement[64]

A business should ensure that it does not use the trademark of a competitor or other business in association with its products or services and that it does not use a confusingly similar trademark for such purposes. In Canada those actions may result in liability under sections 19 and 20 of the *Trade-Marks Act*, respectively.

Liability under section 19 may arise from the use of a registered trademark belonging to another person. Such improper use might include use on a hypertext link to another site, particularly if the party originating the hypertext link is engaged in the sale of products or services of the same class as those of the trademark owner.

Section 22 of the *Trade-Marks Act* states that:

"No person shall use a trademark registered by another person in a manner that is likely to have the effect of depreciating the value of the goodwill attaching thereto." [65]

Liability under section 22 with respect to the use of a trademark that is confusingly similar may arise from use of a parody of a trademark in association with products or services similar to those for which the trademark is registered. Liability may arise under this section from use of some variation of a registered trademark on a Web site as part of a hypertext link.

The right to use another person's trademarks for purposes of comparative advertising is, in some cases, constitutionally protected in the United States, but may be prohibited in other countries. In many countries including Canada, comparative advertising which involves use of a competitor's trademark must be carried out in strict compliance with applicable law.

---

[64]  The topic of trademarks in the Internet context has been covered in Chapter 5 and the special issues arising from use of trademarks in domain names is discussed in Chapter 3.

[65]  There has been considerable case law regarding what constitutes "use" which is beyond the scope of this publication.

## 6.9  CONTESTS AND PROMOTIONS

The use of promotional contests on the Internet can be a powerful tool for attracting attention to a Web site.[66] However, running a contest, especially on the Internet, can create a legal headache for the contest promoter if not done properly. The promoter of any contest run on the Internet needs to conform to the laws of not only the place of business of the promoter, but also of the countries from which contestants are permitted to enter.

Contests and sweepstakes on the Internet may be subject to a wide variety of legislation in different jurisdictions. Many jurisdictions require extensive disclosure.[67] In some jurisdictions, sweepstakes must be registered and a bond posted to cover the value of the prizes. In addition, the overall impression conveyed must not be misleading.

Different rules may apply to games of pure chance, such as lotteries or sweepstakes, as opposed to games of real skill, such as competitions. "Hybrid" contests, in which there is a mixture of chance and skill, may be subject to the same rules as games of chance. While it is generally permissible to impose an entry fee as a condition of participating in a contest, charging a fee or other consideration[68] as a condition of entering a game of chance or of "mixed chance and skill" may violate gambling laws aimed at illegal raffles and lotteries. It is therefore important to provide an alternative

---

[66]    For example, contests in the direct marketing business have been proven as being responsible for the sale of more products and services than any other marketing and promotional techniques.

[67]    The information required to be disclosed may include, among other things, the anticipated number of participants, the approximate value of prizes, the odds of winning, the full cost of the chance to win each prize and any other fact known to the promoter that may materially affect the chances of winning.

[68]    "Consideration" may, but need not be, a cash payment. Any detriment to the contestant, such as trying out a software program, or enrolling as a trial member in an online service, may constitute consideration. However, there can be a distinction between conducting a contest among people who are existing customers, as opposed to inducing non-customers to become customers by the lure of the contest. In some circumstances, even the latter may be permitted. For instance, in an Alberta case involving Canada Trust's "Burn Your Mortgage" contest (*Regina v. The Canada Trust Company* (unreported), July 20, 1984 (C.A.)), it was held that the interest paid by the mortgagors on their mortgages was not consideration for entering the contest. However, in that case, Canada Trust was able to show (1) that the interest rates were unaffected by the costs of the contest (i.e., they were market rates) and (2) that the contest was funded from a promotional/advertising budget.

method for a consumer to enter a sweepstake other than through the purchase of a product or service.[69] In some jurisdictions, additional restrictions may be applicable to certain types of promotions or industries.[70]

Promotional contests (in which any form of property is given away to promote a business interest) are not in themselves illegal in Canada, but must be carefully conducted so as not to violate two federal statutes, the *Criminal Code* and the *Competition Act*. A contest conducted in the Province of Quebec or open to residents of Quebec, would also have to comply with the specific Quebec legislation governing lotteries and contests and with the legislation governing the use of the French language. To date, other provinces have not enacted any specific legislation governing promotional contests, nor do they impose any "official language" requirements.

## (a)  The Element of Skill and No Consideration

Under Canadian criminal law, it is illegal for anyone other than a government-licensed lottery operator to award prizes by pure chance.[71] For this reason, promotional contests in Canada include an element of "skill"[72] this is usually done by requiring the contestant who is selected by a random draw to answer a "skill-testing question" (usually mathematical[73]) in order to become the "winner."

Even a game of "mixed chance and skill," however, is illegal in Canada if the contestant or competitor "pays money or other valuable

---

[69]  For example, a *Prodigy Internet "Make it Yours"* sweepstakes which had permitted contestants to install the Prodigy software and enrol in Prodigy Internet prior to December 31, 1996, also provided an alternative "write-in" method of enrolment. Presumably this was done so as to not characterize the sweepstake as requiring consideration and therefore constituting an illegal lottery.

[70]  Examples are telemarketing, gasoline promotions and use of 900 numbers.

[71]  *Criminal Code* s. 206(1) (a) to (d).

[72]  This element of skill must be real and actually test a skill or aptitude. A test that is simply a formality may not be sufficient.

[73]  In the previously mentioned *Canada Trust* decision, the court confirmed that a four step mathematical question that involved multiplication, division, addition and subtraction, which had to be answered within a limited time, required a degree of skill sufficient to avoid characterization of the contest as an illegal lottery.

consideration."[74] For this reason, Canadian promotional contests usually provide in the contest rules that "no purchase is necessary."

In some US jurisdictions, courts dealing with similar issues have interpreted "consideration" to mean money or something of economic value beyond some effort by a participant.[75] A requirement to purchase a product as a condition of contest participation would therefore be illegal.[76] This has resulted in many contests accepting a "reasonable hand drawn facsimile" in lieu of a proof of purchase of a particular product. In other jurisdictions, courts have found that even when no money is paid, "consideration" can consist of some act that must be performed by the participant, such as a requirement to visit the sponsor's establishment[77] or to register coupons sent through the mail and to deposit such coupons at the nearest supermarket.[78]

To minimize the risk of criminal liability the prudent sponsor will therefore minimize the actions required to participate. A free alternative for entry should be provided. For example, Prodigy Internet ran a sweepstake where everyone who installed their software and enrolled was automatically entered.[79] An alternative, "write in" method was also provided.

Even filling out a questionnaire in order to enter could be considered consideration. Visitors to a Web site should be allowed to enter the contest by simply providing minimum information about themselves. In a contest called Office 97 Launch Poll, run by Microsoft Canada, visitors to Microsoft's Web site who completed a particular poll form were automatically entered in the contest. However, Microsoft only required the name and address section of the form to be completed in order to participate in the contest.

---

[74]    *Criminal Code* s. 206(1)(f).

[75]    For example, *California Retailers v. Regal Petroleum Corp.*, 50 Cal. 2d 844 (1958).

[76]    However, this is not the case in all jurisdictions. For instance, see the *Canada Trust* case.

[77]    *Knox Indus. Corp. v. State*, 258 P.2d 910 (Okla. 1953).

[78]    *Luck Calendar Co. v. Cohen*, 19 N.J. 399 (1955).

[79]    See footnote 69.

## (b)  Necessary Disclosures

Most jurisdictions impose some sort of disclosure obligation on the operation of contests. In Canada, adequate and fair disclosure is required by the *Competition Act*.[80] In the US, disclosure obligations may be imposed by a variety of federal and state regulations. Examples of the types of information that may need to be disclosed depending on the jurisdiction, include:[81]

- the number and approximate value of prizes[82] and any regional allocation;[83]

- the anticipated number of participants;

- the chances of winning;

- the full cost of the chance to win each prize;

- the date the contest closes, and the date and place of the draw; and

- any other fact known to the advertiser that materially affects the chances of winning.[84]

Depending on the jurisdiction in which the contest is offered, additional disclosure requirements may apply. For example, such requirements may be imposed under certain trade practices and consumer protection legislation, particularly in the US.

Disclosure should be made in a reasonably conspicuous manner prior to the potential entrant being inconvenienced in some way or committed to the product or to the contest. The onus is on the advertiser to provide adequate information rather than on the entrant to obtain details about the contest. In the case of a contest conducted online, potential entrants should be advised of the contest rules and other disclosure requirements early in the contest entry process rather

---

[80]  Section 59.

[81]  However, it should be noted that these are not all necessarily required in Canada.

[82]  *Competition Act* s. 59(1)(a).

[83]  For example, if draws are held on a regional basis and each entry is only eligible to win in one draw, it would not be correct to say that there are multiple chances to win (*R. v. Kraft Foods Ltd.* (1972), 11 C.C.C. (2d) 406, 36 D.L.R. (3d) 376, 11 C.P.R. (2d) 240 (Quebec Court of Appeal)).

[84]  *Competition Act* s. 59(1)(a).

than after they have been asked to fill out online forms or have been presented with multiple online advertisements.

A standard practice has not yet developed concerning the need for potential contest entrants to scroll through the contest rules and regulations as part of the entry process rather than being provided with access to the rules from a descriptive hypertext link. However, it would be prudent for organizers of online contests to utilize a "click-through" agreement pursuant to which the participant confirms reading the rules and complying with the contest requirements.

### (c)  Other Considerations

Promotional contest organizers should ensure that there is no undue delay in distributing the prizes.[85] As well, the selection of participants or distribution of prizes is required to be made on the basis of skill or by random draw.[86]

### (d)  Quebec

Quebec imposes somewhat more stringent rules governing contests than do other North American jurisdictions.[87] Many contests that are run by US promoters routinely exclude residents of Quebec from such contests. However, contests run by Canadian corporations usually attempt to include Quebec due to the importance of the Quebec market and a wish to make the contest national.

The significant differences applicable to most contests involving Quebec residents are that: (i) a fee must be paid by the contest promoter based on the value of the prizes offered to Quebec participants;[88] and (ii) a form must be filed in advance, along with the text of the contest regulations and associated advertising. There is a further requirement to post security in some circumstances,

---

[85]   *Competition Act* s. 59(1)(b).

[86]   *Competition Act* s. 59(1)(c).

[87]   These are contained in *An Act respecting lotteries, racing, publicity contests and amusement machines*, R.S.Q. c.L-6 and Rules issued by the Registrar of Lotteries.

[88]   If the total value of the prizes exceeds $1,000 then this fee must be paid 30 days before the contest is advertised. Otherwise, it must be paid 5 days before the contest is advertised.

particularly if the contest promoter does not have a place of business in Quebec.[89]

## (e)  Some US Contest Requirements

The following materials are provided to illustrate some of the potential requirements that may be applicable to the operation of contests in the United States. The specific requirements and issues to be considered will vary depending on the state and the nature of the contest.

### (i)  Federal Requirements

The Federal Trade Commission ("FTC") has enacted rules and regulations applicable to contests conducted by specific industries, such as the food retailing and gasoline industries,[90] or specific types of campaigns. Advertisements for pay-per-call services that offer a prize, award, or service or product at no cost or reduced cost may be required to disclose the odds of receiving the prize or similar item, or the factors used in calculating the odds applicable to the awarding of such a prize.

### (ii)  State Requirements

State law mandating specific kinds of disclosure may also be applicable to advertisements which urge callers to place calls to 900 numbers and which advertise a prize or award in connection with sweepstakes.[91] For example, in California, if a 900 number is used in the conduct of a sweepstake, a free alternative entry mechanism must also be provided and adequately promoted.[92] Operators of such sweepstakes may also be required to register with the Department of Justice.[93]

---

[89]  This is done to ensure that prizes won by residents of Quebec are properly remitted and that the required post-contest report is filed confirming, among other things, that the prizes were awarded.

[90]  16 C.F.R. s. 419.

[91]  16 C.F.R. s. 308.3(c).

[92]  *Cal. Bus. & Prof. Code* s. 17539.5(d)(1). This is also the case in Canada.

[93]  *Cal. Bus. & Prof. Code* s. 17539.55.

In some jurisdictions, certain types of records concerning a contest, including names and addresses of contestants, number of prizes, and names and addresses of winners, must be maintained for a minimum length of time after all prizes are awarded.[94] Therefore, records of promotional contests conducted on the Internet should be retained for the required period of time.

### (f)  Potential Liability of Internet Service Providers

The foregoing regulations governing contests should be of concern not only to businesses placing promotional material on the Web, but also to third party providers of Web hosting services. For example, a party that knowingly provides Web hosting services to the advertiser of an illegal lottery could be found liable as a person who "makes, prints, advertises or publishes ... a scheme ... for disposing of property by ... any mode of chance".[95] An Internet Access Provider who knows that its service is being used to provide access to a Web server located at a customer's site that contains material related to the operation of an illegal lottery could potentially be liable as a person who "knowingly sends, transmits ... or allows to be sent, transmitted ... or knowingly accepts for transport ... any article that is used or intended for use in carrying out any device, proposal, scheme or plan for ... disposing of any property by any mode of chance."[96] Normally the ISP will seek to protect itself by restricting use of its facilities for such purposes.

### (g)  Contest Rules

The following guidelines should be considered in any contest or promotion carried out by means of the Internet[97]:

- State whether multiple entries submitted by the same entrant are void. Where multiple entries are accepted, it may be desirable to limit the number of prizes that can be won by any one entrant.

- Disclaim responsibility for any errors in the operation of the contest.

---

[94]    *Cal. Bus. & Prof. Code* s. 17539.2.
[95]    *Criminal Code* s. 206(1)(a).
[96]    *Criminal Code* s. 206(1)(c).
[97]    However, note that these may not all be legally effective.

- State that prize winners will be determined in a random drawing (or other means) from among all eligible entries.

- State whether winners will be required to sign publicity releases (i.e., releases to permit use of name and/or photograph without payment or compensation) or other releases or disclaimers (i.e., statements releasing content promoters from liability).

- State, if applicable, that the chances of winning depend upon the number of eligible entries received.

- Reserve a right to terminate the contest early in case of technical or other problems. State where notice of such termination will appear (for example, posted on a certain Web site).

- Clearly define who is eligible to enter (e.g., only residents of certain countries, persons who meet certain minimum age requirements). Set out any categories of people who may not be eligible to enter, such as employees of the sponsor or the contest organization and members of their families. Consider using a "click-through" or other online agreement which requires participants to confirm they meet eligibility requirements.

- State that the contest is being conducted in compliance with all federal, provincial/state and local laws (i.e., in the jurisdictions identified in rules accompanying the contest) and that the contest is not open to residents of other jurisdictions.[98]

- State whether winners are responsible for any payments (i.e., where the prizes consist of airline tickets, are winners responsible for their own ground transportation, meals, gratuities, insurance and other personal or incidental expenses). In certain cases taxes may be applicable and the sponsor may want to state that any tax payable on a prize is the sole responsibility of the winner.

- In certain cases the value of prizes may need to be expressed as a range. For example, the value of airline tickets may vary depending on the winner's point of departure and destination. The

---

[98] The contest promoter should determine where the contest is legal.

value of hotel accommodations may vary depending on the hotel and time of year.[99]

- State whether prizes are non-transferable and whether prize substitutions or cash alternatives will be provided.

- Discuss how winners will be notified (e.g., by mail) and any conditions that must be met before an entrant will be declared a winner (e.g., answering skill-testing question, signing declarations or releases). State how the names of winners will be announced (e.g., by posting the names on a specific Web page).

- State that entries become the property of the sponsor.

- State which jurisdiction's law shall govern the contest.

- Disclose the name of the sponsor.

- Set out if the information collected from the entrants might be used for other purposes (such as development of marketing lists).

- Provide for any other information or disclosure required by any of the applicable jurisdictions.

## 6.10  LIABILITY FOR LINKS AND USE OF FRAMES

### (a)  Links as Infringement

The Web uses a page formatting language called hypertext markup language ("HTML") to format the various elements that appear in the documents making up the pages of a Web site. One such element is a hypertext link which may point to a file or document located on the same or a different Web server. When a user clicks on a hypertext link (which can be a marked portion of the text or a graphic image), the Web browser program initiates loading of the Web page associated with that link. In many ways, a link is simply a pointer like an entry in a library catalogue or a listing in a telephone directory. A particular Web document may contain numerous links to other Web documents and may itself be the destination of many similar links contained on other pages. The use of links is fundamental to the operation of the World Wide Web.

---

[99]   For more information on adequate and fair disclosure, see a commentary on section 59(1)(a) of the *Competition Act* published by the Federal Department of Industry.

Linking is normally encouraged on the Web because it can be used to connect material on related topics, even if such material is located on different Web sites, and because it provides an effective system for browsing the vast content available on the Internet. It is common for links to be created to documents belonging to others without seeking their prior consent. In most cases, the operator of a Web site will want pages on its site to be the destination of as many links as possible. Information is placed on the Internet in order to facilitate dissemination and more links will likely result in greater visibility. However, some persons object if links are made to their Web sites from sites which contain inappropriate materials or if inappropriate methods of linking are used.

HTML supports two general types of links. The first type, known as a hypertext reference link (HREF), works by associating a portion of text[100] or an image with another document, which is loaded into the browser's window and replaces the current document when that link is selected. If the link is not selected then the referenced document is not loaded.

A hypertext reference link consists of two components. The first, which is visible, is the highlighted text that serves as a reference or description of the document being linked. The other component which is not normally visible is the Universal Resource Locator or Web address of the linked document.[101] A hypertext reference link therefore serves a function analogous to a footnote in an article — it provides a reference to a related document.

The second type of link is an inline link, which allows embedding of images, background sounds or objects into a specific location in an HTML document.[102] Each such embedded object possesses its own unique URL which can be examined by viewing the HTML codes contained in a particular document. However, embedded objects appear as part of the document and only the document's URL is shown.

---

[100]  Such text is distinguished from regular text by use of a special colour or formatting such as underlining.

[101]  Some Web browsers will display the URL associated with a hypertext link in a special information portion of the browser when the cursor is positioned over a particular hypertext link.

[102]  An example is the IMG tag to reference an image.

### (i)  Links to Infringing or Inappropriate Materials

In the US, it has been argued that the maintenance of links to sites carrying infringing content (such as unauthorized copies of copyrighted software) constitutes contributory infringement under the US *Copyright Act* on the grounds that such links assist the infringing activity.[103]

In an action filed by Adobe Systems against Tripod Inc.,[104] the plaintiffs claimed contributory copyright infringement by an Internet Service Provider for its role in making available "cracker tools" from its Internet server.[105] The plaintiffs also claimed that:

> "by allowing links to pirated copies of plaintiffs' software products to remain at [the defendants'] site, where they are readily accessible, the defendants implicitly authorized persons who access [the defendants'] site to go to the linked sites and download copies of the plaintiff's computer programs".

In another case, the UK media[106] reported that police in the UK decided not to bring forward a charge following a complaint against the Lesbian and Gay Christian Movement in Britain for including a hypertext link on their Web site to a US based Internet site containing a poem by James Kirkup.[107] However, the complaint, filed by the group Reform, a conservative evangelical lobby group which was involved in a campaign within the Church of England against homosexuality, had lead to an 18-month investigation by the police.

---

[103]  See Chapter 5 for a discussion of the US doctrine of contributory infringement. Canadian copyright law does not provide for this type of infringement but has a similar concept known as "authorizing infringement".

[104]  *Adobe Systems, Incorporated, Claris Corporation, and Traveling Software, Inc. v. Tripod Inc. and Bo Peabody*, No. 96CV30189 in the United States District Court for the District of Massachusetts, October 7, 1996. See Software Publishers Association press release of November 15, 1996 at <http://www.spa.org/piracy/releases/settled.htm>. See also *Adobe v. C2Net*, Civil Action C-96-20833, filed October 7, 1996 in the US District Court for the Northern District of California.

[105]  "Cracker tools" are software programs specifically designed to remove or by-pass technical means implemented in other programs to prevent unauthorized use.

[106]  See <http://www.xs4all.nl/~yaman/linkpoem.htm>

[107]  The poem titled "The love that dares to speak its name" had been at the centre of a successful blasphemous libel prosecution.

In June 1997, three freelance journalists, hoping to expose a flawed investigation, placed a confidential report on child abuse in Nottingham County (UK) on their Web site.[108] The Nottingham County Council claimed they were the copyright holder and obtained an injunction forcing the journalists to remove the report from their site and any links to other sites containing the report.[109] Over 30 mirror sites quickly appeared carrying copies of the report. Some of these mirror sites removed the report following legal threats from the council. However, the operators of other sites, including a professor of law at Case Western Reserve University Law School in Ohio,[110] refused. After an unsuccessful two month attempt to suppress the online publication of the report, the Nottinghamshire Country Council withdrew their complaint.

Links to other types of inappropriate materials may also result in liability. For example, if links are made to child pornography, hate literature (i.e., material which advocates hatred or violence towards an identifiable group) or other types of illegal content, the provision of the link may be construed as facilitating the commission of an offence or as promoting the availability of the illegal content. Links to defamatory materials[111] or other infringing material may also raise concerns as to whether the person making the links is facilitating the improper or illegal activity.

In at least one dispute, the threat of litigation was based solely upon the presence of a link to a US-based Web site containing a trademark registered in Canada. The Year 2000 Information Center,[112] a Web site operated in Canada by deJager & Co., Ltd., was reportedly threatened by legal action to remove a link to a Web site operated by Project 2000, Inc., a US-based company offering shirts and baseball caps commemorating the effort of computer professionals in addressing the year 2000 computer problem. Lawyers representing Year 2000, Inc., the owner of a Canadian trademark on

---

[108] Joint Enquiry Team Report.

[109] The argument was that if the material to which a link is made infringes copyright, then the link facilitates the infringement.

[110] <http://samsara.law.cwru.edu/comp_law/>.

[111] Defamatory materials are those which contain a false statement about another person or entity that is damaging to their reputation.

[112] <http://www.year2000.com/>

the term "Year 2000", which plans to market products related to the millennium event, claimed that the link on the Year 2000 Information Center Web site constituted a violation of Canadian trademark law by illegally displaying the protected "Year 2000" mark via the Internet link.

The operators of the Year 2000 Information Center Web site removed the link to avoid involvement in the dispute. However, the Year 2000 Information Center had become the premier source of information on the computer date crisis, also known as the "millennium bug" and was the best location to advertise Project 2000's products, even in respect to the US market.

In the absence of any case law on the subject, it is unclear whether the party making a link to another site has an obligation to review the contents of the site to which the link is made, and if so, whether there is an ongoing obligation to monitor such content. It is also unclear whether such an obligation may arise following notification being given to the operator of a Web site regarding the infringing or improper nature of materials located at the site to which the link is made. One view is that the provision of a hypertext reference link is analogous to providing a library classification number for a book, and, as such, should not constitute the basis for any liability.

### (ii)  Links to Commercial Web Sites

In most cases, links are welcomed as they benefit the destination site by attracting additional visitors. However, linking by third parties directly to sub-pages (subsidiary pages other than the home page) on a site is becoming of increasing concern to operators of Web sites that depend on revenues from commercial advertising. Bypassing a site's home page by navigating to a specific sub-page can result in a loss of advertising opportunities.[113]

One of the first cases to deal with liability on this basis arose in the Shetland Islands, off the coast of Scotland. *The Shetland Times*

---

[113]   In most advertising-supported Web sites, each page on the site contains advertising banners. The more pages on the site a potential visitor must go through in order to reach the desired content, the more advertising revenue is earned. This aspect of the Web creates an incentive to make it more difficult rather than less difficult for a visitor to find information being sought at such sites.

made available on the Internet various materials, including photographs, which appeared in its printed editions. Each item contained a heading identical to that used in the printed issue.

A local competitor, an Internet-based newspaper called *The Shetland News*, created a Web site which contained verbatim reproductions of some of the headlines from *The Shetland Times*, along with links which provided direct access to the text of each item without requiring the user to access *The Shetland Times* front page. However, *The Shetland News* site also contained hundreds of pages of original content and was not simply a repackaged version of *The Shetland Times*.

*The Shetland Times* claimed that the bypassing of its front page meant that users would miss any advertising material which appeared on that page. *The Shetland Times* obtained an injunction to prevent *The Shetland News* from providing hypertext links to its Web site.[114] However, the decision was based on certain unique provisions of the UK *Copyright, Designs and Patents Act* 1988 dealing with cable transmissions and, therefore, the case provides very little precedent value on the question of whether linking constitutes copyright infringement.

Disputes involving links have also arisen in North America. When Microsoft launched its Seattle Sidewalk Web site,[115] the first of a number of planned city-oriented sites, the site contained information about events taking place within Seattle, and where appropriate, mentioned that tickets for such events were available from Ticketmaster.[116] A link was also included to the location on Ticketmaster's Web site containing ordering information for the particular event. This allowed visitors from the Seattle Sidewalk Web site to bypass Ticketmaster's home page and numerous intermediate pages (each containing paid advertising) that they would otherwise need to click through before coming to the page containing

---

[114] *Shetland Times Ltd. v. Dr. Jonathan Wills and Zetnews Ltd.*, (Lord Hamilton, J., Court of Sessions, Edinburgh, Scotland, October 24, 1996) in which an interim injunction was issued.

[115] <http://seattle.sidewalk.com/>

[116] Ticketmaster is a vendor of tickets to entertainment events through North America and operates a Web site which provides listings of upcoming events and allows the purchase of tickets by phone or online.

information in respect of the particular event. Ticketmaster objected to such linking and sought an injunction and damages against Microsoft.[117]

Ticketmaster also turned to technical means to block traffic originating from "unauthorized" external links. This was accomplished by constantly changing the names of all Web pages on the Ticketmaster site other than the home page.[118] The result was to require any external links to be made only to the home page. However, a disadvantage of this approach is that it renders ineffective any indexing of the sites's content by popular Internet search engines, such as Alta Vista, Excite, Infoseek or Lycos.

It is unlikely that the mere provision of a link to another person's site constitutes an infringement of copyright of material contained on the site. Hypertext linking is a fundamental characteristic of the Web.[119] An argument can be made that placing content on the Web is an implied consent for others to make a link to such content. The counter-argument is that creating a link directly to a sub-page or an element (such as a graphic, audio or video clip) can interfere with the owner's ability to place notices around such content or may lead viewers to incorrectly attribute ownership to the party who created the link.[120]

The seamless transition from one Web site to another that occurs when a link is activated may blur the distinction between the proprietary content of the linking site and that of the site to which the link is made. This blurring may cause users to assume incorrectly that

---

[117] *Ticketmaster Corporation v. Microsoft Corporation*, Civ. 97-3055 DDP (C.D. Cal. April 12, 1997). The suit was commenced after negotiations between the parties concerning sharing of revenue in respect of such linking had broken down.

[118] The "home page" is the page intended by the Web site operator to function as the front door or starting location for accessing the other content on the Web site. The home page typically contains a description of the entity operating the Web site and links to other sections of the site.

[119] One commentator described the Web as "a medium whose very existence and viability is defined by its hyperlinking capabilities.": David G. Post, "Plugging In," *The American Lawyer*, July-August 1997.

[120] Operators of Web sites should ensure that copyright and other proprietary notices are added to each page of a Web site.

there is an affiliation or association between the two sites and may support a claim for false designation of origin.[121]

Most advertisement-supported Web sites welcome links, even to sub-pages. A well designed advertisement-supported site can take advantage of a visitor accessing a sub-page by placing advertisements on each page, including sub-pages, and by placing links on such sub-pages to other interesting or related content available on that site and thereby capturing a visitor's attention and encouraging the visitor to explore other pages on the site.[122]

However, in the *Ticketmaster* case, visitors to the Seattle Sidewalk site were being directed to the Ticketmaster site for a very specific purpose and were not as likely to explore other pages. Ticketmaster therefore had a stronger interest in ensuring that users would view as many advertisements as possible before providing them with access to the specific information that they wished to access.

### (iii)  Use of Images for Hypertext Links

Infringements of copyright or trademark can occur due to the manner in which hypertext links are made. For instance, the use of an image (such as a logo) as a link to another site may constitute copyright infringement unless authorization is obtained from the owner of the copyright in such image. Likewise, it may be argued that the use of a trademark (which may be a word or design mark) belonging to another entity, even if used to highlight a link to a site operated by the trademark owner, may require the authorization of the trademark owner.[123]

### (b)  Composite Web Pages

As previously discussed, objects can be embedded into a document from the same Web site or from a different Web site using an inline link. Embedded images appear within the body of the document in the same way as photographs appear in a newspaper. The creator of

---

[121]   15 USC s. 1125(a).

[122]   For instance, each page on CNET's Web site contains references and links to CNET's home page, other services and sites operated by CNET and, more importantly, links to related articles or other content on CNET's site. <http://www.cnet.com/>.

[123]   See discussion in Chapter 5.

a document containing embedded images can also use various HTML formatting instructions to control various attributes of how such images will appear in the document.[124] A user viewing a Web page containing embedded objects from other Web sites would not normally know that such objects are being retrieved from a different Web site and would assume that they are being provided by the same entity as the owner of the Web page on which they appear.

Unless special steps are taken to limit access to images or other objects, other entities can embed these objects into their documents merely by inserting an appropriate tag in their documents containing the URL address for those objects.

From a technological perspective, a Web site may incorporate embedded objects from another Web site without reproducing the embedded objects; instead, the objects can be loaded from the original site directly into the Web browser's display. However, the act of instructing a visitor's Web browser to display an image belonging to one person within a page and under a URL belonging to another entity may constitute reverse passing off.[125] As well, such activity may infringe the exclusive right of the copyright owner of that image to create a derivative work or adaption of the original work. Moreover, to the extent that such activity facilitates infringement, it may constitute an authorization of infringement in Canada and contributory infringement in the United States.[126]

In some cases, users link directly to specific elements such as images on a Web page in order to bypass the loading of time-consuming advertising or other content on the page. For example, Intellicast, MSNBC's weather service provides weather maps and weather forecasts in the form of graphic images.[127] The pages containing these images also contain advertising banners. Intellicast found that some Internet users were bookmarking the desired images directly in order to bypass the advertising, corporate logos and copyright information intended to be displayed adjacent to the image.

---

[124] For instance, their size and alignment with the text contained on such Web page. The image can even be defined as a hypertext link to another document.

[125] Reverse passing off occurs when someone else's work is passed off as one's own. This is in contrast to "passing off" where a person passes off their work as that of someone else.

[126] See Chapter 5 for a more detailed discussion.

[127] <http://www.intellicast.com/>.

Intellicast responded by "tweaking" its servers to accept requests only from pages originating at its own site.[128]

The unauthorized referencing or use by one site of the content including images, audio, video, Java applets and other elements located at another site, places additional load on the server running the Web site on which such content is stored, as well as consuming a portion of the bandwidth of such site.

Server restrictions of the type imposed by Intellicast are likely to become more prevalent in the future. Sites which depend on advertising revenue are likely to prohibit access to any element except a complete Web page. Specialized products are also being developed to help prevent unauthorized referencing of content by other sites.[129]

The use of inline links to the comic strip "Dilbert" has already been the subject of threatened legal action by United Media against the operator of a Web site incorporating an inline link to Dilbert-related images. The dispute was settled by the removal of the inline link after the operator of the Web site had received a cease and desist letter.

### (c)  Unauthorized Framing

A third method of linking is to utilize a feature which can be activated on most Web browsers to divide the browser's screen into multiple, scrollable windows or frames, each of which can be made to operate independently and can be instructed to load content from the same or a different Web site. The frames feature is analogous to the picture-in-picture feature available on some television sets.

The frames feature provides the operator of a Web site with the ability to create a smaller separate window containing navigation tools, such as a table of contents, which will remain on the user's screen. Selecting a particular heading from this window can cause the associated document to be loaded into a larger main window or frame.

---

[128]  "Intellicast Smartens Up to Banner Bypass," *Wired News*, March 28, 1997 <http://www.wired.com/news/technology/story/2844.html>.

[129]  For instance, see WebReferee from Maximized Software.

However, the frames feature can technically also be used by the operator of one Web site to incorporate another entity's Web site, or specific components, into its own Web site. The Web browser will only display the URL of the original site and any such foreign content incorporated into a Web site will appear as if it had originated from the original site.

Framing material from another entity's Web site can raise issues of copyright infringement, misappropriation, trademark infringement, trademark dilution, passing off, defamation and other possible causes of action.

On October 17, 1996, TotalNEWS launched a Web site[130] as a clearinghouse to the various news sources available on the Internet. In early 1997, a number of news service providers[131] with Web sites commenced a suit[132] against TotalNEWS, claiming the defendants were engaged in the Internet equivalent of pirating copyrighted material from a variety of famous news sources and repackaging those stories to advertisers as part of a competitive publication or program.

The suit alleged misappropriation, trademark dilution, trademark infringement, false representations and false advertising, unfair competition, deceptive acts and practices, copyright infringement and tortious interference. This was the first case in North America involving litigation over Web links and the use of the frames technology.

TotalNEWS derived its revenues from advertising which was wrapped around the content displayed from the many linked sites. Selecting a link from the TotalNEWS site resulted in content from the selected site being displayed in one frame while TotalNEWS' URL, logo and Java-based advertising were displayed simultaneously in other frames.[133]

---

[130]  <http://www.totalnews.com/>.

[131]  The Washington Post Co., Time Inc., Cable News Network, Inc., Times Mirror Company d/b/a Los Angeles Times, Dow Jones & Co., Inc., and Reuters New Media Inc.

[132]  *The Washington Post Co. v. TotalNews Inc.*, 97 Civ. 1190 (SDNY, Feb. 20, 1997).

[133]  For instance, buttons to news providers such as USA Today, The Washington Post, CNN and Reuters, were placed in a frame or window on the left margin of the screen. Pressing the buttons located on this directory frame resulted in the contents from the selected Web site being displayed in a second frame to the right of the directory frame. This functionality

As noted above, many Web sites, especially those supported by advertising, welcome the opportunity to attract more visitors to their sites. Additional "hits" mean increased advertising revenues. However, there are significant disadvantages when such visitors view the site through a frame on a composite page located on someone else's Web site.

When frames are used on a Web page, the URL at the top of the Web browser program continues to show the Web address of the composite page and not any individual page displayed in a frame. This has two implications. The first is that Web users may not even realize that they have left the original site or are viewing material from another site.[134] The second is that since the URL for only the composite page is displayed by the browser, any attempt to bookmark (i.e., add an entry for that site in a directory contained in the browser program to facilitate a return visit) a Web site displayed in a frame results in a bookmark being added for the Web site containing the composite page instead.

The appearance of content from the framed site on the same page as content from the site containing the composite page can lead some users to believe that the material displayed in a frame has been licensed to the host of the composite page. Any copyright notices on the composite page may mislead viewers into thinking that they are applicable to the contents found at the framed site. Also, any notices setting out limitations on the use of the materials located on the framed site may be bypassed.

Combining materials from two Web sites on the same screen may also lead to an incorrect inference that the owner of one site is endorsing the goods or services of the other party, or that some type of affiliation or business relationship exists between the owners of the two sites. As well, trademarks contained on pages at the framed site will appear in conjunction with materials including ads that are displayed in other frames on the composite page. This may constitute "use" of the trademark with other products or services leading to dilution of the mark.

---

is analogous to a car radio with pre-selected radio station buttons.

[134] This creates the potential for violation of moral rights of the authors of the materials on the framed site. See Chapter 5 for a discussion on moral rights.

The presentation of a framed site typically results in a distortion of the presentation. Although the displays used by Web users are not uniform in size, most users utilize a screen that is at least 640 x 480 pixels in size. Web sites design their arrangement of content based on this assumed minimum screen size. The frame used by TotalNEWS to display its directory buttons took up slightly more than 15% of the page width. This resulted in the framed site being presented through a narrower window that had to be scrolled in order to view the entire content. Accordingly, the form in which the pages from the framed Web sites appeared varied from that intended by their owners.

The display of content from the framed sites through a window smaller than the assumed minimum screen size may also result in advertising on the framed sites being obscured. Advertisers may buy space based on an expectation that their advertisement will appear in a certain location and be free from the clutter of competing advertisements.

In the *TotalNews* case, even if the plaintiffs' advertisements were not partially or totally obscured, they faced competition from advertisements placed elsewhere on the TotalNEWS composite page. In some cases, such advertisements were for competing products. TotalNEWS may have made the plaintiffs' performance of their advertising contracts more burdensome and interfered with the benefits that advertisers on the plaintiffs' Web sites had bargained for.

Another problem faced by the framed sites was that TotalNEWS utilized rotating ads which changed approximately one per minute. This resulted in new ads being continually loaded from the TotalNEWS site and a reduction in the available bandwidth. As a result, it took longer for content from the framed sites to be loaded.

The plaintiffs stated in their complaint that they had expended substantial resources to gather and display the content placed on their Web sites and that much of their content was time-sensitive. The plaintiffs alleged that the defendant's actions constituted common law misappropriation of their valuable commercial property and unfair competition under New York state law.

The plaintiffs also alleged multiple counts of trademark infringement and dilution. They claimed that the display of content belonging to the plaintiffs in the composite page created by TotalNEWS was likely to cause confusion and to deceive visitors as to the source or origin of the content and advertising depicted at the site. They claimed that the portrayal of content from their Web sites through TotalNEWS' composite page diluted and detracted from the distinctiveness of their famous trademarks. As well, they claimed that some users could mistakenly believe that there was an affiliation between the plaintiffs and the defendant or that the defendant had obtained permission from the plaintiffs to utilize their content.

The TotalNEWS site contained a disclaimer page which stated that no relationship existed between TotalNEWS and the third party owners of the Web sites being accessed and that the trademarks and copyrights for these sites were owned and controlled exclusively by the third parties. The trademarks owned by the plaintiffs utilized in TotalNEWS' directory frame were also referenced to their appropriate owners. However, visitors to the TotalNEWS site were not required to view this disclaimer page and the link to the disclaimer page was placed at the bottom of TotalNEWS' home page — an area not likely to be viewed by most users.

The plaintiffs also claimed that TotalNEWS' actions constituted copyright infringement. The use of frames to pull in content from other Web sites does not involve direct copying of such third party content by the operator of the composite page (and accordingly there should be no direct copyright infringement). However, to the extent that the instructions issued to the browsers of the individual Web users may result in unauthorized copying of content from the framed sites, such activities may constitute contributory infringement in the US or authorization of infringement in Canada. Such loading of content by the browser programs of visitors to the TotalNEWS site would be an infringement only if such activities do not come within the scope of any implied or express licence otherwise granted by the plaintiffs to visitors to their Web sites to download and view such content.

The plaintiffs' claims against the defendant might have been strengthened had they employed a "Terms of Service" agreement that prohibited users from downloading the contents of their site unless the user was visiting their site exclusively, or that prohibited the display of their pages in a frame less than the entire size of the display space on a browser program.

Some technical solutions may also be available to prevent unauthorized framing. For instance, one of the plaintiffs, CNN, subsequently employed a special code in its Web pages which checked if the content was being viewed from within a frame, and if so, caused the unauthorized composite page to be replaced with the CNN page on the entire screen. However, this solution was far from perfect. It took up to a minute or more to take effect, and even then, a pop-up window inviting users to return to the TotalNEWS site could still be superimposed on the CNN Web site.

The lawsuit against TotalNEWS was settled in June, 1997. The terms of the settlement included a licence to permit TotalNEWS to provide links to the plaintiffs' Web sites. The difference between linking and framing is that linking results in the linked site filling up the user's entire screen without the previous site retaining control over the Universal Resource Locator ("URL") displayed at the top of the screen and without any advertisements from the previous site being displayed in the linked site.

Pursuant to the settlement, TotalNEWS was permitted to provide links to the plaintiffs' Web sites subject to certain conditions. The links could only consist of the names of the linked sites in plain text. TotalNEWS was not permitted to utilize any of the plaintiffs' proprietary logos or other distinctive graphics as hyperlinks. As well, the links could not be done in any manner that would be reasonably likely to (i) imply affiliation with, or endorsement or sponsorship by, any plaintiff; (ii) cause confusion, mistake or deception; (iii) dilute the plaintiffs' trademarks; or (iv) otherwise violate state or federal law.

TotalNEWS agreed to permanently cease framing the plaintiffs' Web sites in the manner complained. Specifically, TotalNEWS agreed not to cause, directly or indirectly, any plaintiff's Web site to appear on a user's computer screen with any material supplied by or associated with TotalNEWS or any third party. Such material includes a URL, text, graphics, a pop-up window, audio, video or other content.

The terms of the settlement did not prohibit TotalNEWS from continuing to frame any of the approximately 1,400 sites, other than those belonging to the plaintiffs, to which links had been established by TotalNEWS. The owners of some of the other sites appear to welcome the extra traffic directed to their sites notwithstanding the use of frames by TotalNEWS.

The Stipulation and Order of Settlement and Dismissal was comprehensive and attempted to block TotalNEWS from reverting to its previous practices. For instance, while TotalNEWS is not restricted from linking to any other Web site which does not include any proprietary content of any plaintiff, or is not owned or operated by a plaintiff, TotalNEWS may not link to any third party's Web site that purposefully or overtly encourages users to link to any plaintiff's Web site in a manner forbidden to TotalNEWS.

Within days of the settlement, TotalNEWS introduced a personalization function to allow users to add sites to their "personal links." Any such site, which could include a site owned by one of the plaintiffs, would then show up within TotalNEWS' view window and continue to be framed with TotalNEWS advertising.

While the TotalNEWS lawsuit and subsequent settlement does not provide any legal precedent, as no decision was issued by a court, it does signal that Web site operators should review their use of frames and weigh any inappropriate use against the risk of a lawsuit and potential liability.

### (d)  Reducing the Risk of Liability

The law concerning the use of links and frames is still developing and no definitive precedent currently exists. However, cautious operators of Web sites can take certain steps to help reduce the risk of liability and the expense of defending a lawsuit. The following is a list of recommended steps:

### (i)  Do Not Use Trademarks or Headlines as Links

While descriptive names may be used for links, the use of another entity's logos, trade names or trademarks as a link should be avoided.[135] As well, in the case of news stories, use of the identical headline should also be avoided.

### (ii)  Seek Permission or Link to Home Page

Risk of liability or the inconvenience of a lawsuit may be avoided by seeking permission before linking to content located on another entity's Web site. Affiliated commercial sites may enter into a "linking agreement" to set out the standards and other terms applicable to the establishment of such links. If this is not feasible, consideration should be given to providing links to the home page of another entity's Web site. In this way, advertising supported sites are more likely to welcome the link. The disadvantage is that the home page of the other site may provide limited guidance on how to access material related to the content at the original site.

### (iii)  Clearly Indicate Source

Ideally, any link made to another entity's Web site should result in the new site filling the entire screen (i.e., that there is no use of frames). If frames are to be used, steps should be taken to avoid confusion as to the source of materials appearing on the screen at any time.

### (iv)  Do Not Imply an Affiliation

An indication of an affiliation with another entity should be avoided unless such affiliation actually exists or permission has been obtained to indicate such affiliation. The use of links to imply that another entity has sponsored or endorsed goods or services could result in liability for unfair competition, or passing off. This may be the case in the absence of an express endorsement if consumers are likely to be misled.

---

[135] For example, if such use is found to detract from the value of a "famous" trademark as a means of identifying and distinguishing goods or services then liability can arise in the US under the *Federal Trademark Dilution Act* (15 USC s. 1125 [c]).

### *(v)  Do Not Copy a Collection of Links*

Many Web sites contain a collection of links to related resources. While an individual link may not contain sufficient originality to be protected by copyright, a collection of links may be copyrightable as a compilation.

### *(vi)  Use of Disclaimers*

Some Web site operators have taken steps to reduce their potential liability for links to inappropriate material. For instance, by selecting any external links referred to on the *New York Times* Web site, a notice will be displayed stating that the links are to external Web sites which are not part of the *New York Times* and that the *Times* has no control over their content or availability.

The Vancouver Stock Exchange (VSE) also seeks to create an electronic contract with visitors to disclaim any responsibility for information at external sites operated by its members and for which links have been made from the VSE.[136] The VSE advises visitors that they are about to leave the VSE Web site, that the information provided at a member's Web site is issued by the member and is the responsibility of the member, that the VSE does not verify such information or make any representations, warranties or guarantees concerning such information and that the VSE shall not be held responsible for any losses arising from any visitor obtaining access to the other sites. A visitor to the VSE Web site must click on "I Accept the above terms" in order to proceed to the list of external sites.

## 6.11  SPECIAL RULES FOR SPECIFIC INDUSTRIES

Information placed on a Web site may also be regulated by industry-specific regulations. For example, US airlines must comply with US Department of Transportation regulations.

Virgin Atlantic Airways, Ltd. placed a series of fare advertisements on its Web site.[137] The advertisements listed a "21 day APEX" fare of US $499 for a weekly round trip flight between

---

[136]   See <http://www.vse.com/memberfirms.html>.
[137]   See <http://www.fly.virgin.com/atlantic>.

New York and London during certain travel periods. Separately, in a section above the listed price, the advertisement contained a disclaimer which stated, "Please check with reservations or your local travel agent for latest fare, availability and any taxes, charges or restrictions."

In a telephone call to Virgin Atlantic by an investigator from the Office of Aviation Enforcement and Proceedings, the investigator was told that the listed fare was not available at the time and that the lowest fare was US $518. In addition, the investigator was told that the advertised fare did not include US $38.91 in unspecified taxes.

Virgin Atlantic's Internet advertisement was found to have violated a regulation which provides that "any advertisement or solicitation by a direct air carrier ... for passenger air transportation ... that states a price for such air transportation ... [is considered] to be an unfair or deceptive practice, unless the price stated is the entire price to be paid by the customer to the air carrier, or agent, for such air transportation."[138]

Virgin Atlantic's Internet advertisements failed to disclose both the type and amount of the applicable taxes and fees. The Department of Transportation stated that a general disclaimer regarding additional charges, such as the one included in Virgin Atlantic's advertisements, was insufficient notification of per passenger taxes and fees. Furthermore, at least one Internet advertisement listed a fare that was not available at the advertised price and this constituted a separate offense.

Virgin Atlantic settled the matter by agreeing to pay US $14,000 in penalties and agreeing to other terms contained in a consent order.[139]

## 6.12  QUEBEC LANGUAGE REQUIREMENTS

Businesses operating in Quebec who maintain Web sites may need to ensure that the contents of their Web sites comply with Quebec's

---

[138]  14 CFR 399.84. Any violation of this regulation also constitutes a violation of 49 U.S.C. s. 41712 which prohibits "unfair or deceptive practices or unfair methods of competition."

[139]  Department of Transportation order 95-11-37 (Nov. 21, 1995) <http://www.dot.gov/general/orders/19954qtr/ord951137.html>.

language laws. Article 52 of the *Charter of the French Language* requires that catalogues, brochures, leaflets, commercial directories and other publications of that nature be in the French language. A translation may be provided as long as French is given equal prominence. The *Office de la langue francaise* (OLF) has taken the position that this definition is broad enough to include content placed on Web sites, or sent by fax or electronic mail.

According to a notice[140] issued by the OLF on June 21, 1997, all companies which have a place of business or an address in Quebec are required to provide Quebec consumers with a French language version of any commercial publication appearing on their Web sites. A company which does not have a base of operation in Quebec (i.e., neither a place of business nor an address in Quebec) will not be compelled under Quebec laws to use French on its Web site.

Micro-Bytes, a computer retailer located in Pointe Claire, received a warning letter from the OLF in late May 1997, advising that the company's Web site violated Quebec's language law. In response, Micro-Bytes took down most of the content on its site until it was able to prepare French language translations.

These requirements do not apply to non-commercial messages such as those of a religious, political, ideological or humanitarian nature which may be published in a language other than French. Cultural or educational products may also be advertised exclusively in the language used in the product without a French version.

The OLF has disputed claims that its inspectors are surfing the Internet for possible language violations. Although the OLF has indicated that it may decide to act on its own initiative, it has stated that in practice, its investigations are based almost exclusively on complaints received from the public.

The OLF has acknowledged that the Internet is being used by many companies as a means of advertising products for the global market and that Web sites are not necessarily intended for the Quebec market. Accordingly, a French language version of advertisements

---

[140]   See <www.olf.gouv.qc.ca/charter.html>.

posted on the Web site of a company located in Quebec is required only for products that are available in Quebec.[141]

There may be an issue as to whether the OLF is exceeding its jurisdiction by applying Bill 101 to the Internet because telecommunications is under federal jurisdiction in Canada. However, the Quebec government has taken the position that it has a right to control commercial Web sites on the Internet as part of the province's responsibility over consumer protection and advertising.

Other jurisdictions, including France, have similar language requirements that may be applicable to content placed on Web sites. The Georgia Institute of Technology in France was sued by French-language rights organizations because its Web site had offered information in English only. The lawsuit was dismissed on procedural grounds.

## 6.13  META TAGS

Another area of concern is the unauthorized use of "meta tags".

Searching for information on the Web usually involves turning to Internet directories such as Yahoo!, or search engines such as Alta Vista or Hotbot. Search engines scan the entire content of a Web site and generate indexes based on the full text of documents.

Many search engines also index information contained on meta tags inserted in the Web documents to assist the search engines in classifying and describing the contents of the various sites. Information inserted in such meta tags is not normally visible when a document is viewed by a browser program, but can be displayed if the user instructs the browser program to show the "source document."

Certain Web sites have learned to manipulate the search results produced by the Internet search engines by placing the names of their competitors or popular search topics in their meta tags. This technique can be used to divert interest from their competitor's site.

The legality of this practice has been questioned. Oppedahl & Larson, a law firm specializing in intellectual property law and

---

[141]  According to the June 21, 1997 notice mentioned previously.

operator of a popular Web site, launched an action against a Web site that had incorporated their firm name into meta tags used on their site.[142]

## 6.14  OTHER CONSIDERATIONS

The global reach of the Internet may also necessitate a review of symbols and other images used on a site with a view to ensuring that they do not offend potential customers of various cultural or religious backgrounds. As an example of the type of advertising that should be avoided, in 1997, Nike Inc. introduced a new logo on its Nike Air basketball shoe that was intended to look like flames. However, to many Muslims, the logo looked like the Arabic word for God, Allah, and its use on a shoe was very offensive. Nike averted a boycott by apologizing, recalling 30,000 pairs of shoes, reorganizing its design department and pledging to foster greater sensitivity to Muslim concerns.[143]

---

[142] See *Oppedahl & Larson v. Advanced Concepts* (97-2-1592, Colarado). See also *Playboy Enterprises, Inc. v. Calvin Designer Label* 44 US P.Q. 2d 1157 (N.D. Cal. Sept. 8, 1997) <http://www.ljx.com/LJX files/metatagsuit.html>. See also *Insituform Technologies Inc. v. National Envirotech Corp.*, Civil Action No. 97-2064 (E.D. La. final consent entered Aug. 27, 1997).

[143] The *Toronto Star*, July 27, 1997 at A4.

# 7

# Electronic Commerce

## 7.1 INTRODUCTION

The United States government has released "A Framework for Global Electronic Commerce," a strategy paper intended to help accelerate the growth of global commerce across the Internet.[1] The paper outlines five principles to guide the US government in supporting the evolution of electronic commerce:

(1) The private sector should lead. The Internet should develop as a market driven arena, not a regulated industry.

(2) Governments should avoid undue restrictions on electronic commerce. There should be minimal intervention by the government. The government should also refrain from imposing new and unnecessary regulations or taxes on commercial activities conducted on the Internet.

(3) Where government involvement is needed, its aim should be to support and enforce a predictable, minimalist, consistent and simple legal environment for commerce.

(4) Existing laws and regulations that may hinder electronic commerce should be reviewed and revised or eliminated to reflect the needs of the new electronic age.

(5) Electronic commerce on the Internet should be facilitated on a global basis.

The paper also makes the following recommendations:

---

[1]   Available at <http://www.iitf.nist.gov/eleccomm/ecomm.htm>.

- No new taxes should be imposed on Internet commerce (existing taxes would still be applicable).

- In the near future, case-by-case monitoring of electronic payment experiments is preferable to regulation.

- The US supports the development of an international uniform commercial code to facilitate electronic commerce. Such a code should encourage recognition of electronic contracts, and the development of consistent international rules for acceptance of electronic signatures and other authentication procedures. The code should also promote the development of alternative dispute resolution mechanisms, set predictable rules for exposure to liability and streamline the use of electronic registries.

- Clear and effective intellectual property protection is necessary to protect against piracy and fraud. The administration will review the system of allocating domain names in order to create a more competitive, market-based system.

- The US government recognizes the importance of privacy and supports private sector efforts to implement self-regulatory privacy regimes. The government will work with industry and privacy advocates to develop appropriate solutions to privacy concerns that may not be fully addressed by the industry through self-regulation and technology.

- The Internet must be secure and reliable. The administration, in partnership with industry, will promote the development of a market-driven, public key infrastructure that will promote the general public's trust in encryption.

- In many countries, telecommunications policies are hindering the development of advanced digital networks. The US will work internationally to remove barriers to competition, customer choice, lower prices and improved services.

- With respect to content, the administration encourages industry self-regulation, the adoption of competitive content rating systems, and the development of effective, user-friendly technology tools (e.g., filtering and blocking technologies).

- The marketplace, not governments, should determine technical standards and other mechanisms for interoperability on the Internet.

Electronic Commerce has also been an important agenda item for the Canadian government. An Industry Canada Task Force on Electronic Commerce has been reviewing various aspects of electronic commerce. The Task Force issued a report[2] in January 1998 (the "report") which recommends new legal measures for the protection of personal information. The report is discussed in detail in section 7.7 below. The report is the first in a series of reports in which Industry Canada is seeking comments on clear and predictable rules to facilitate the growth of electronic commerce.

## 7.2  EDI AND ELECTRONIC COMMERCE

Many early EDI applications utilized the services of a value-added network (VAN) for message exchange. These VANs performed a number of services, including storage, logging, translation and interconnection with other VANs. However, traditional forms of EDI which utilize the services of VANs have been slow to catch on. Only a small percentage of business currently utilize EDI and many EDI trading partners are now evaluating or experimenting with the use of the Internet instead of the much more expensive services of VANs.

Messaging standards on the Internet are currently based on X.400 protocols (as well as the more common SMNP Protocol). Vendors of X.400 products may soon make available for use on the Internet certain value-added services provided by traditional VANs such as delivery reports, priority service, date/time stamping and multiple or alternative recipients. There are also efforts within the Internet community to develop supplemental protocols for handling EDI transactions over the Internet.

With traditional EDI applications, a trading partner agreement was used to create a contractual relationship between the parties. However, the ease of setting up new electronic relationships using the

---

[2]    Industry Canada Task Force on Electronic Commerce. *The Protection of Personal Information — Building Canada's Information Economy and Society*, January 1998. A copy of the report is available on Industry Canada's Strategis site at <http://strategis.ic.gc.ca/privacy>.

Internet will require new, more responsive mechanisms to create such relationships. These may come from legislative reforms or through use of online contracting mechanisms.

## 7.3  PAYMENT MECHANISMS

### (a)  Transmission of Payment Information

Because business transactions are increasingly being conducted electronically, new forms of payment mechanisms are required to support online transactions between parties that do not have established trading partner agreements.

There is currently no single payment mechanism in use for transactions conducted through the Internet. The most frequently used method is the transmission of credit card information either through an encrypted electronic channel using the Internet, or through an off-line alternative such as a voice telephone call or a fax transmission. In the latter case, most of the information concerning the transaction is exchanged online, and the information provided off-line to effect payment must be matched to the online transaction.

In the above mentioned payment mechanisms, the credit card information is sent to the merchant for processing like a mail order or phone order transaction. An alternative model for electronic payment is for the bank or credit card organization to participate in the transaction in a manner that precludes the need for providing the credit card number to the merchant. Instead, the information is transmitted either directly or by means of an encrypted envelope sent via the merchant's system to the bank or credit card company which then issues a confirmation code to the merchant.

It is expected that a major impetus that will facilitate payment mechanisms used for electronic commerce over the Internet will be the Secure Electronic Transaction (SET) protocol sponsored by MasterCard and Visa. SET can be utilized to create a multi-layered encrypted communication channel between a purchaser and a merchant. This is accomplished by utilizing symmetric cryptography to encrypt individual messages,[3] public key cryptography for key

---

[3]  A 1,024-bit random key is utilized as a session key.

exchange[4] and authentication message digests[5] to ensure the integrity of messages and digital signatures[6] as a form of electronic signature.[7]

## (b)  Electronic Money

Electronic money may take the form of stored value smart cards. These may take the form of multi-purpose cards, which are open systems that can be used to buy goods or services from several providers or transfer e-money from one cardholder to another. They may also take the form of more private "digital money," which are single-purpose cards or closed systems that can be used to purchase goods or services from one supplier or a limited number of suppliers.

Electronic money is based on public key encryption technology that creates a block of digital data that can represent money and be used for payment. In general, there are two distinct forms of electronic money: identified electronic money and anonymous electronic money. Identified electronic money contains information that can reveal the identity of the person who was issued the money from the bank. Some forms of identified electronic money also allow the issuing bank to track the electronic money as it moves from one person to another. By contrast, anonymous electronic money cannot be tracked by the issuing bank and can be spent or transferred without leaving a transaction trail.

---

[4]  The session key is encrypted with the recipient's public key so that it can only be extracted and utilized by someone in possession of the corresponding private key.

[5]  A message digest is created using a one way hashing function which is a one-way transformation that results in a digital fingerprint of a particular message. A message digest can confirm that a message was not altered during transmission but cannot be used to reconstruct the original message.

[6]  A digital signature is created by encrypting a message digest with a sender's private key. A recipient can confirm that a message was sent by a particular sender by decrypting the message digest using the sender's public key and then checking the message digest against the message to which it was attached. This procedure validates the sender because only someone who possesses the corresponding private key could have encrypted the message digest.

[7]  For more details on the use of cryptography, digital signatures and public key encryption schemes, see *Information System Security: A Practitioner's Guide*, Van Nostrano Reinhold, 1994, New York.

Certain electronic money schemes permit person-to-person transfer, like real cash, while others require that the money be transferred by a consumer directly to a merchant as payment for an online transaction. Certain electronic money schemes also require access to an online network when the money is transferred, while others permit transactions to occur off-line without the involvement of the bank. The most complex form of electronic money is anonymous electronic money that can be transferred off-line because some sort of mechanism is necessary to prevent double-spending.[8]

With some forms of electronic money, specifically a tokenized system where the real electronic money is transmitted electronically, a loss of the digital representation of the money can result in a real loss to the owner. With other systems, the electronic money is simply a notational system or record rather than the money itself. In the latter case, the money can be returned to the consumer upon the bank being notified of its loss or destruction.

The extent of risk to be assumed by financial institutions engaging in electronic cash transactions will depend on whether the liability of consumers is limited under the provisions of any consumer protection legislation. If none apply, then the rights and liabilities of the issuer and consumer will be primarily determined by their contractual agreements entered into at the start of the relationship and general common law principles.

Governments also have a number of concerns related to the use of electronic money. Trade in drugs and the taking of profits from organized crime as well as other types of criminal activities generate money that must be integrated into the financial systems for criminals to make use of the money. Law enforcement agencies have historically relied upon the intermediation of banks and other financial institutions to provide choke points through which funds must pass. Therefore a major concern regarding the use of electronic money, especially anonymous electronic money, is the potential that

---

[8]    Anonymous money can be structured to accumulate information as it travels from person to person. The system can be structured so that the transaction trail will only be revealed if the electronic money is spent on more than one occasion. If the money is not double-spent then the bank will not have sufficient information to determine the identity of the original spender or reconstruct the path taken as the electronic money moves from one person to another.

it will be utilized for money laundering purposes.[9] However, some of the anonymous electronic money schemes allow at least one of the parties to be identified so that the resulting tender does not become a useful tool for criminals.

Some governments have the authority to issue orders to require banks to detect, detain and report international funds transfers from designated "blocked entities" which may be countries, corporations or individuals to assist in the confiscation of funds from those entities. Electronic money may be used to defeat such orders.

The growth of electronic money may also undercut government monetary policy. Digital money could circulate outside the central banking system and therefore would become untraceable and unmeasurable. As such, it would undermine the historic control of central banks over the money supply.

Electronic money would likely not be held to constitute "legal tender" because it is not a medium of exchange that is authorized, adopted or backed by the government. E-money is only backed by the issuer's promise to pay. Electronic money may, however, constitute "money" because parties are free to make contracts based on a medium of exchange of their choosing.

There is currently no legislation specifically applicable to electronic money as a payment mechanism. If electronic money is issued by entities other than financial institutions, the current system of regulation and protection may not apply.[10]

An issuer of electronic money that holds money from a customer pending transfer to a third party following the customer's use of the

---

[9]    Anonymous card-to-card systems, or those digital money systems that utilize numbers only and provide a high level of privacy, could be used to facilitate money laundering. Many attributes of such systems are similar to those associated with the use of cash. However, electronic data is easier to conceal and to transfer across borders than is cash. See 62 Fed. Reg. 278 90 (May 21, 1997) issued by the US Department of the Treasury that would apply the *Bank Secrecy Act* to electronic banking. The regulations would require ascertaining the identity of parties and the maintenance of records which would be accessible to the government.

[10]    For a detailed review of regulatory issues related to electronic money see Thomas P. Vartanian, Robert H. Ledig and Alison G. Conver, "A Survey of Selected Federal Regulatory and Legal Developments in Electronic Financial Services" in *The Business Lawyer*, vol. 53, November 1997 at 251.

electronic money may be deemed to be engaged in the business of taking deposits and therefore may be a regulated financial institution. However, if an electronic money scheme does not require the issuer to hold any funds on behalf of the customer for transfer to a third party, the issuer might not be deemed to be engaged in any regulated financial activity.

Finally, the failure of an electronic money issuer could undermine public confidence in e-money systems, cause a run on such systems, and have a detrimental affect on the traditional financial system. As a result, there may be a need for regulatory intervention based on public policy considerations.

To deal with these issues, regulators are considering various options. These include establishing a regulatory authority to designate that certain electronic money arrangements should be subject to government oversight. The regulatory scheme that would be imposed as a result of designation could involve a requirement that electronic money issuers be separately regulated entities with limits on investment powers, that they be closely supervised, and that they hold paper currency in escrow accounts to ensure stability and/or have guarantees from sponsors. As an alternative, there could be a less intrusive form of regulation based on disclosure.

## 7.4  FORMATION OF ENFORCEABLE ELECTRONIC CONTRACTS

The ability to form enforceable contracts online is a fundamental requirement to the growth of electronic commerce on the Internet. The fact that the Internet is an electronic marketplace means that unlike other commercial transactions, there may not be a paper document executed by the parties or a paper trail of the transaction.[11]

In some cases, the parties may contract electronically for the acquisition of goods or services to be delivered or performed through other channels. In other cases, it is possible for the entire transaction,

---

[11]    In the case of EDI, the parties usually have a pre-agreed contractual framework which governs their transactions. However, in the case of Internet-based commerce, the parties may not have a prior relationship or an enforceable agreement which sets out their rights and obligations.

including both the formation and the performance of the contract, to take place online.

The legal requirements for a contract made by means of the Internet are the same as for any other contract. Generally, an enforceable contract can be formed by oral or written agreement and may be implied from the conduct of the parties. Key requirements for the formation of an enforceable contract include the communication of an offer and the communication back of an acceptance of that offer. An offer and acceptance can be communicated orally or by written documents, or can be transmitted electronically through the Internet. Many of the legal issues that arise with respect to contract formation are no different than those encountered with other electronic means of communications such as telephones, fax and telex machines.

Contracts which involve the sale of goods (including services provided incidentally to the sale of goods) are generally governed by sale of goods legislation.[12] The fact that an electronic medium, such as the Internet, is used to form the contract does not change the applicability of such legislation. Contracts for services, or intangible goods not otherwise falling within the scope of the applicable sale of goods legislation, are governed by common law rules which vary from jurisdiction to jurisdiction.

Contracts for the sale of goods made between persons located in different countries will generally be governed by the UN Convention on the International Sale of Goods ("the Vienna Convention") unless the parties expressly agree that the Convention is not to apply.

## (a)  Making Offers Online

An offer may be communicated orally or in writing. An offer may also be published or transmitted electronically through the Internet. For example, an offer may be published on a Web site, posted to a Usenet newsgroup or an electronic mailing list (or listserv) or sent by e-mail to a specific recipient.

A company carrying on business through the Internet will generally wish to ensure that Web site promotional material, like

---

[12]    In the US these are governed by the *Uniform Commercial Code* (UCC).

advertisements placed in traditional media, are treated as an "invitation to treat" rather than an offer. The offer itself may be communicated separately by e-mail once a user signifies a wish to acquire the product or service that is advertised on the Web site. This will permit the merchant to set out precise terms governing the contractual relationship with a user, including the terms as to the time the contract comes into effect and the location where the contract is made. The location where the contract is made, in turn, may determine what laws will apply and which courts will have jurisdiction. Therefore, a merchant will usually want to ensure that any material placed on the Web should not be capable of being construed as an offer.[13] The only exception to the rule will be for the terms and conditions contained on the legal notice page which the operator will wish to impose for the use of the Web site.

### (b)  Acceptance in Online Transactions

The formation of an enforceable contract requires, at a minimum, the acceptance of an outstanding offer. Other requirements include that valuable consideration must be given and there must be an adequate description of the subject matter. Certain terms, if not addressed by the parties, may be implied by the court.

### (i)  Electronic Acceptance

As a general rule, in order to accept an offer, the offeree must communicate his or her acceptance back to the offeror or someone authorized by the offeror to receive it. Unless the offer expressly states otherwise, an offer may be accepted by the same mode of communications used to make the offer or a more reliable mode. In the US, an offer may be accepted "in any manner and by any medium reasonable in the circumstances."[14] Therefore, an offer received by e-mail may also be accepted by e-mail unless the offer

---

[13]    Advertisements are not generally considered offers. However, if the terms of the advertisement are sufficiently definite, and in particular, if the advertisement specifies the quantity and price of the particular item available, the advertisement may constitute an offer.

[14]    UCC, s. 2-206(1)(a). However, other factors to be considered include any prior course of dealing between the parties or usage of trade. The offeror may also specify a required form of acceptance.

specifies some other mode of acceptance. The transmission of the acceptance by electronic means should not be an impediment to formation of an enforceable contract, as long as the basic requirements for acceptance are met.[15] A more difficult issue will be whether an offer received by another mode of communication such as by post or fax may be accepted using e-mail communication.

### (ii)  Web-Wrap or Click-Through Agreements

An acceptance leading to an enforceable contract can generally be manifested by some form of conduct specified by the offeror as well as by verbal or written agreement. The method of acceptance generally followed for online contracts is to require the customer to scroll through the terms of the agreement. The user is asked to signify acceptance by clicking on a particular button (e.g., the button marked ACCEPT) or hypertext link, or by entering a particular symbol or code in a box on a Web form. The acceptance of a contract through such conduct is analogous to the acceptance of a shrink-wrap software licence agreement by opening the cellophane wrapping surrounding the package or envelope containing the diskettes.[16]

The following is a sample clause:

"Before you click on the "Accept" button at the end of this document, carefully read the terms and conditions of this Agreement. By clicking on the "Accept" button, you are consenting to be bound by and are becoming a party to this Agreement. If you do not agree to all of the terms of this Agreement, click the "Do Not Accept" button and do not use the software."

---

[15]  The basic requirements are that the person intending to accept the offer must:
   (1)  know of the offer and intend to accept it;
   (2)  be a person to whom the offer was made;
   (3)  accept the offer unequivocally and without qualifications (which would have the effect of turning the purported acceptance into a counter offer); and
   (4)  generally give the offeror timely notice of his or her acceptance.

[16]  In the US, shrink-wrap software licence agreements have been accepted as enforceable contracts. See *ProCD, Inc. v. Zeidenberg*, 86 F.3rd 1447 (7th Cir. 1996) where a shrink-wrap licence agreement in respect of a yellow page directory was held enforceable notwithstanding that it was not visible on the package. See also, *Hill v. Gateway 2000 Inc.*, 105 F. 3d 1147 (7th Cir. 1997)

The use of "click-through" licence agreements is becoming quite prevalent. For example, users of PointCast software[17] are advised in the course of installation that the right to use the software and the information provided by means of the software is limited by the terms and conditions of a "scrollable licence agreement" that follows.[18]

The licence agreement is then presented in a scrollable window with buttons marked "Agreed" and "Not Agreed" located at the bottom of the window. Users are instructed to click on "Agreed" if they agree to the terms of the licence agreement or otherwise click on "Not Agreed".

As with many other licence agreements that are provided online, the PointCast Licence Agreement states that the licensor may change the terms or add new terms, and may change the conditions or impose new conditions on the use of the software. The Agreement states that these changes become effective immediately upon notification by any means that gives the licensee actual knowledge. The Licence Agreement states that the use of the software after such notice shall be deemed acceptance of the new terms by the licensee.

Some financial institutions have also commenced use of "click-through" or "Web-wrap" agreements for certain types of transactions. For instance, First Union, a US bank, offers an online application for a home equity loan. Part of the application procedure includes a notification of certain terms and conditions. To complete the process, applicants must click on a button marked "I understand and accept the above terms and conditions." A similar procedure is used by Bank of Montreal to process online applications for MasterCard products.

To date, the enforceability of a "Web-wrap" or "click-through" online agreement has not been fully tested by a court in North America.[19] Nevertheless, certain steps may be taken in preparing and

---

[17]    Version 1.4.

[18]    In reality, the software is downloaded and installed before users are actually presented with the licence agreement. However, the failure to click on the "Agreed" button would result in the user being denied access to the software.

[19]    However, see *Hotmail Corporation v. Van Money Pie Inc. et al.*, C98-20064 (N.D. Cal., April 20, 1998) where the issue was considered in the context of a preliminary injunction.

presenting such an agreement to strengthen the case so that it will be found to be enforceable.

(1) The user should be required to scroll through the actual terms before being presented with the mechanism to accept. However, this procedure is not always followed in practice. Many Web sites use forms where an offeree is given the opportunity to view the terms by clicking on a hypertext link from a highlighted word such as "rules" or "terms and conditions," but such terms are not actually presented unless the offeree takes such further action.

(2) The offeree should be given a clear method to accept or decline and the offeree's actions should be logged as part of a business process.[20] It is important that a permanent log be maintained so that evidence of acceptances may be available.

(3) Any promotional material on the Web site for the product or service in question should contain conspicuous references to the online agreement.

(4) The online agreement should be drafted in "plain English" language that can be easily understood by a typical consumer.

(5) Any unusual or onerous provisions not normally found in the type of contract in question, and provisions that limit or exclude liability for damages, should be emphasized or otherwise brought to the user's attention. If the products or services are to be made available to users located in the Province of Quebec, consideration should be given to the Civil Code which requires certain types of provisions to be brought specifically to the attention of the other contracting party.

(6) The user should be required to repeat the acceptance process any time there is a change in the provisions of the Agreement.

Where click-through agreements are to be used between parties who engage in repetitive transactions or who have an on-going relationship (such as a financial institution and its customer), the parties may expressly recognize the procedures used in click-through

---

[20] For greater certainty, a user could be asked to confirm his or her acceptance by clicking on a second button or by requiring the user to enter certain information as part of the acceptance process.

agreements for specific transactions by means of a signed written agreement (such as an operation of account or a trading partner agreement) that serves as a "master" agreement.[21]

Click-through agreements should also be considered as a means to supplement copyright protection or to provide protection in circumstances where copyright protection is not available. In *ProCD v. Zeidenberg*,[22] the defendant purchased and mounted a copy of ProCD's "yellow pages" CD-ROM directory on the Internet. Relying on the US Supreme Court decision in *Feist*,[23] the defendant claimed that the data contained on the CD-ROM was not protected by copyright. The defendant also wrote his own search program to avoid use of ProCD's search program that was protectable by copyright.

The court agreed with the defendant on the copyright issue and found that the ProCD listings did not show the necessary originality in their selection and arrangement to qualify for protection. However, the court held that the ProCD product was protected from unauthorized reproduction by reason of a shrink-wrap licence agreement which accompanied the product.[24]

Some Web sites purport to impose terms and conditions upon visitors by including a legal notice page on the Web site which states that use of the Web site will constitute acceptance of the terms and conditions listed on that page. However, in such cases, there may be an issue as to whether the terms and conditions are brought to the attention of the offeree, so as to become a binding contract. Moreover, if continued viewing of the content on the Web site is engaged in by the offeree without contractual intent, such action might not constitute acceptance of the offeror's terms.

Another important consideration is the determination of the terms to be applicable to a contract formed online. At common law, the

---

[21]   This would be similar to the use of a trading partner agreement between participants using EDI.

[22]   908 F.Supp. 640 (W.D. Wis. 1996). See <http://zeus.bna.com/e-law/cases/procd.html>.

[23]   *Feist Publications, Inc. v. Rural Telephone Service Co. Inc.*, 111 s.ct. 1282, 20 I.P.R. 121, 499 U.S. 340 (1991).

[24]   However, courts may be less inclined to find that such agreements are enforceable where a pre-existing agreement exists between the parties. See *Step-Saver Data Systems v. Wyse Technology*, 939 F. 2d 91 (3d Cir. 1991).

formation of an enforceable contract requires the offeree to accept the terms of the offer without modification. Any change made by the offeree terminates the original offer and results in a counter-offer which may then be accepted or rejected by the original offeror. Some jurisdictions have altered this strict rule.[25]

One general caveat is that any offer should state that it may only be accepted without modification. Another general caveat is that where an offer is made on a Web site for acceptance by a visitor to the site, it may be advisable to refrain from providing any comment or note field so that the offeree does not have an opportunity during the "acceptance" process to insert any additions or proposed changes.

Another issue that should be considered is that a Web-wrap or click-through agreement is likely to be characterized as "contract of adhesion" due to its "take it or leave it" nature. If a contract of adhesion contains terms that are unfair under the circumstances, or terms which are very onerous or unusual which have not been brought to the attention of the other party, then courts are more likely to hold such contracts as unenforceable under the doctrine of unconscionability.

### (iii)  Timing and Place of Acceptance

General rules of contract formation should be applicable to Internet-based commerce. One such rule is that a contract is formed when the acceptance is communicated to the offeror.[26] However, an exception to this rule has developed in the case of contracts made through the mail. Under the "mail box" rule, acceptance is effective when mailed even if it never reaches the offeror. The timing of acceptance is important because an offer can generally be revoked until it is accepted.

It is not clear whether or not the mail box rule will be held applicable to the types of electronic communications used on the Internet. In the US, the *Restatement of Contracts (Second)* provides that acceptances given by telephone or other medium of substantially instantaneous two-way communication are governed by principles

---

[25]    For instance, section 2-207 of the UCC.

[26]    However, this rule may not be applicable to international transactions.

applicable where the parties are in each other's presence (i.e., that a contract is formed when the message signifying acceptance is received). The rationale for this rule is that in such a case, the offer can be accepted without the offeree being in doubt as to whether the offeror has attempted to revoke before receiving the acceptance. Proposed draft revisions to the UCC would reject the mail box rule for electronic communications.[27]

However, the logic supporting the rejection of the mail box rule for instantaneous communications does not appear applicable where a message is being sent by a one-way form of electronic communications. Parties communicating electronically using the Internet are not usually engaged in a real-time conversations such that the sender knows immediately if the message has reached the recipient. In a real-time two-way communication, both parties usually make a statement at the same time to signify the end of the conversation. This is not the case with many types of Internet-based communications.

The issue of timing with respect to fax transmissions was recently considered by an Ontario Court. In *Bickmore v. Bickmore*,[28] the court drew an analogy between offers made by facsimile and offers made by mail. An offer made by mail implicitly entitles the acceptance to be made in a like manner. Where an offer made by mail is accepted by mail, the contract is made at the time of mailing, *whether or not* it is ever received. The court stated that this same rule applies to telegrams. The court therefore reasoned that a similar approach should be adopted for fax transmissions where the offer to settle is silent as to the method of acceptance. Since receipt of a fax transmission is virtually simultaneous with transmission, the court found that acceptance of the offer occurred at the time of sending the fax transmission.

---

[27]   See the proposed revision dated March 21, 1997 to the current section 2-208 and the proposed revision dated January 20, 1997 to section 2B-206 of the UCC. The applicable provision in the ABA Model Electronic Data Interchange Trading Partner Agreement is also contrary to the mailbox rule. A more current version of the proposed Article 2B is available at <http://www.law.upenn.edu/library/ulc/ulc.htm>.

[28]   (1996), 7 C.P.C. (4th) 294 (Ont. Gen. Div.).

An offeror, wishing to avoid assuming the risk of becoming bound to a contract without knowledge of the acceptance (i.e., in a jurisdiction where the mail box rule is applicable), should make clear in the online offer that the contract will only be made when the offeror has received the communication containing the acceptance.

Merchants may find it desirable to state that the contract is made at the location where the acceptance is received by the merchant. This, together with a governing law clause, should mean that the contract will be governed by the laws of the jurisdiction where the merchant is located.

### (c)  Ascertaining Identity of Other Party and Role of Digital Signatures

Electronic communications, and the Internet in particular, present opportunities for an imposter to assume the identity of another person or to assume a fictional identity. Therefore, before entering into an electronic agreement with another party, and commencing performance, a party will be well advised to verify or authenticate the identity of the other party.

This issue should also be of concern to parties who may be subject to legal claims as a result of electronic communications engaged in by other persons. Under some circumstances, an imposter (such as an employee, former employee or hacker) may gain access to confidential passwords or other means of authenticating messages, and may thereby seek to bind the impersonated party or subject the impersonated party to a claim in negligence.

It is likely that digital signatures will be increasingly used to authenticate transactions conducted over an electronic communication medium such as the Internet. A digital signature may be defined as an electronic identifier, created by computer, and intended by the party using it to have the same force and effect as a manual signature.[29] It is anticipated that the growth of electronic commerce will lead to an increasing use of digital signatures to replace traditional paper-based signatures.

---

[29]    California Gov. Code s. 16.5.

Digital signatures may be given legal effect through legislation, or by court decision, or through a written contract whereby the parties acknowledge the validity of the use of digital signatures in subsequent transactions. Digital signature legislation has been enacted in some jurisdictions and is being considered in others. For example, the Utah *Digital Signature Act*[30] authorizes the use of digital signatures in commercial transactions. In Utah, a digitally signed document is recognized as valid as if it had been written on paper. Other jurisdictions, such as California, have taken a more incremental approach and only provide recognition to digital signatures used in communications with a public entity.

The American Bar Association Committee on Science and Technology has issued draft Digital Signature Guidelines (October 5, 1995) and the United Nations Commission on International Trade Law has proposed guidelines to expand the recognition of digital signatures as valid signatures.

In Canada, the Uniform Law Conference of Canada established, in late 1996, an Electronic Commerce Project with the objective of removing legal obstacles to electronic commerce. The ULCC is considering various steps, such as implementing the UN Model Law on Electronic Commerce, and establishing rules for digital signatures.

Another initiative is one by the Canadian Federal government to establish a public key infrastructure for electronic filings to be made with the government. This infrastructure involves the use of public key/private key cryptography. A person has a public key which is shared with other parties and which can be used to decrypt or encrypt messages, and a private key which is not shared with others. Designated third parties will have the responsibility of providing certification as to ownership of the keys used for electronic communications. It is hoped that the federal initiative will serve as a model for the provinces and the private sector.

---

[30]    Utah Code Ann. ss. 46-3-101.

## (d) Legal Requirements for Contracts to be "In Writing" and to be "Signed"

While many types of contracts may be formed through the exchange of electronic communications across the Internet, many jurisdictions require certain types of contracts or consents to be "in writing" and in some instances to be "signed."[31] These requirements may arise from common law or statutory requirements commonly referred to as "statute of frauds" requirements. The rationale underlying such requirements is the need to protect a party from fraud or deceit by requiring that there be a reproducible record of certain types of agreements. The following are examples of the types of agreements for which there may be a "writing" requirement depending on the jurisdiction:

(1)  a contract of an executor or administrator to answer for a duty of the decedent;

(2)  a contract to answer for the duty of another (i.e., guaranteeing the performance of another, such as a repayment of a loan);

(3)  a contract made upon consideration of marriage;

(4)  a contract for the sale of an interest in land; and

(5)  a contract that is not to be performed within one year from the making thereof.[32]

In the US, the UCC also requires a "signed writing" for contracts involving the sale of goods valued at over $500 and those not capable of being performed within one year.[33] Compliance with this requirement may mean that a customer must be asked to print out, sign and mail in a copy of an agreement or consent form, even if certain elements of the transaction may be completed online.

---

[31]  "Statute of Frauds" legislation in many jurisdictions requires that certain contracts be in writing and signed by the person against whom enforcement is sought. It may be possible to rely upon certain exceptions such as performance or the doctrine of equitable estoppel as a substitute for a writing.

[32]  *Restatement (Second) of Contracts*, s. 110 (1979) (US). Similar requirements apply in Canada.

[33]  Section 2-201. Note, however, that draft revisions to the UCC may eliminate the writing and signature requirements set out in this provision. Also, the general rule may be different when both parties to the transaction are merchants.

In Canada, there are various legal requirements for certain types of contracts or consents to be "in writing" and in some instances to be "signed". It is also important to review the federal and any applicable provincial "Interpretation Act."[34] Other legislation may also be relevant depending on the nature of the transaction. For instance, in Ontario, the *Consumer Reporting Act* provides that no person shall request or obtain a consumer report, in certain circumstances, unless that person first gives written notice of the fact to the consumer.

The Act also provides that, where a person proposes to extend credit to a consumer, and a consumer report containing credit information only is being or may be referred to in connection with the transaction, the person shall give notice of the fact to the consumer in writing at the time of the application for credit, or if the application is made orally, orally at the time of the application for credit.

The Act does not set out what constitutes written notice. It is not clear whether this would include notification through the viewing of a Web page. Since the Act permits verbal notification at the time of the application for credit where such application is made orally, it seems reasonable that such legislation should be amended to permit analogous treatment of electronic transactions.

Another issue that must be considered is that some statutes require certain documents to be filed in a "prescribed form." There may be a concern that the word "form" may be interpreted narrowly to refer only to paper.

### (i)  Writing Requirements

The underlying policy objectives for requiring certain documents to be "in writing" may be satisfied by an electronic message. In some jurisdictions, evidence of an electronic transmission, including tangible written text produced by computer retrieval, may be sufficient to satisfy "in writing" requirements. Some courts have also

---

[34]    In Ontario, section 35 of the *Interpretation Act* defines a writing as a "writing," or any term of like import, and includes words printed, typewritten, painted, engraved, lithographed, photographed or represented or reproduced by any mode of representing or reproducing words in visible form.

held telexes, telegrams and facsimiles as being sufficient to satisfy "in writing" requirements.

In some cases, the writing requirement will be met if the message can be reduced to a tangible form. For example, with respect to the sale of goods in the US, the UCC definition of a writing includes printing, typewriting or any other intentional reduction to a tangible form. However, other types of messages, such as those exchanged on an Internet Relay Chat (IRC) facility or online chat facility will not likely have sufficient permanence to constitute a writing.

Any requirement that the message be in a tangible form may be met if the message is reduced to tangible form by either the sender or the recipient. Therefore a party engaging in electronic commerce who wishes to comply with a requirement that the electronic messages be in writing should ensure that the messages are printed out or otherwise archived in some sort of tangible or permanent form.

In the US, the National Conference of Commissioners on Uniform State Laws (NCCUSL) has undertaken the task of defining the scope of a proposed uniform law to address electronic contracting.[35] The NCCUSL has recommended that any law that requires information to be in writing, should state that the requirement may be met by an electronic message if the information contained therein is accessible so as to be usable for subsequent reference.[36]

### (ii) Signature Requirements

A requirement for a signature does not necessarily mean that only a handwritten signature will be sufficient. For example, a signature is defined by the UCC as "any symbol executed or adopted by a party with present intention to authenticate a writing."[37] Similarly, the US *Restatement (Second) of Contracts*, in section 134, provides

---

[35]    The American Bar Association's Section of Business Law formed an Ad Hoc Task Force which published a memorandum dated December 10, 1996 (the "ABASBL Memorandum"). It sets forth issues and concerns that NCCUSL may find useful as it commences its work. A copy is located at: <http://www.abanet.org/buslaw/cyber/nccusl.html>.

[36]    S. 9(d).

[37]    UCC s.1-201(39). The draft revision to UCC Article 2B also takes a similar approach but uses the term "authenticate" in lieu of "signature".

that a signature may be "any symbol made or adopted with intention, actual or apparent, to authenticate the writing as that of the signor." A commentary to this provision provides that a signature may include "an arbitrary code sign."[38]

A process which requires an individual to type his or her name in a specified field or to click on a particular button may constitute a signature where the individual has been advised that such action will be treated as expressing an intent to "sign" the document or form being presented electronically. There does not currently appear to be a requirement that a signature meet any particular standard of reliability prior to being given legal effect. However, the use of a confidential password or personal identification number may be advisable so that the "signature" can be more persuasively attributed to a particular person. A signature provided electronically may also need to be tested against a reliability standard in order to conform to the requirements of the UNCITRAL Model Law.

The legal effect of digital signatures has not been judicially addressed in most jurisdictions. Furthermore, most consumers do not currently have digital signatures and generally are not technically sophisticated enough to understand the use of digital signatures.

Pending any changes that may be made to Canadian legislation to facilitate electronic commerce, various companies in Canada are adopting alternatives to meet any signing or writing requirement and also to authenticate the identity of the sender of electronic messages. It is advisable, at least for certain consumer and financial transactions, to have the transactions documented by some form of written and signed document. Some financial institutions, for example, allow customers or potential customers to apply for a loan over the Internet. The loan transaction is approved in principle by electronic means, but a signed agreement may still be required before the loan transaction is finalized.

---

[38]    See *Hessenthaler v. Favzin*, 564 A. 2d 990 (PA Super. Ct.1989) which held that a mailgram satisfied the requirement for a signature under the statute of frauds in Pennsylvania. See also *Doherty v. Registry of Motor Vehicles*, 97 CV0050 (Dist. Ct., Suffolk Co., 1997) which accepted a notation made by a State trooper as sufficient to satisfy the state's perjury statute signature requirement.

The writing requirement has also lead some merchants to use the Internet to provide a copy of an agreement which must then be downloaded, printed, signed and mailed in by an applicant. However, there is a risk in such circumstances that an applicant may modify the contents of the agreement prior to printing, and the modification may not be detected by the merchant.

### (e)  Competency and Authority to Enter into a Transaction

#### (i)  Competency

A prerequisite to the formation of an enforceable agreement is that both parties must be legally competent (i.e., have the required mental capacity) to enter into an agreement for a particular transaction. For example, for certain types of contracts, such as those for the purchase of non-necessities, defences to the enforcement of the contract may be available to minors and individuals suffering from mental disability. Although minority or mental disability is not always ascertainable even in face-to-face transactions, it becomes even less apparent when transactions are conducted electronically.

#### (ii)  Actual Authority

One of the issues that arises with respect to online contracts is whether a user within a corporate organization who accepts the contract by clicking the "accept" button or by some other conduct is authorized to bind the corporation. It would be advisable to put a statement in the contract stating that the person accepting the agreement has the authority to do so.

For significant contracts, the authority of the person purporting to act on behalf of a corporation should be verified in the same manner as for non-electronic agreements. However, such verification may reduce the benefits otherwise available from the use of electronic commerce.

#### (iii)  Apparent Authority

Even if an individual lacks actual authority, an enforceable agreement may still be formed if the individual is vested with apparent authority to act on behalf of a corporation. Apparent authority can be established where a corporation has provided an individual with sufficient "indicia of authority" that would lead others to believe that the individual has authority to act on behalf of the corporation. In the "physical world," such apparent authority may be established through the use of business cards, access to a corporation's letterhead, use of an office belonging to the corporation, use of the corporation's telephone system to take calls, and other acts that would lead other persons to believe that the individual occupies a position of sufficient authority to bind the corporation generally or with respect to a particular type of transaction. In such circumstances the corporation will be bound notwithstanding the lack of actual authority.

In the context of the Internet, the above-mentioned indicia may be missing from the online world. However, other electronic identifiers may be found to constitute sufficient indicia to establish apparent authority. For example, an e-mail address identifiable with a corporation (i.e., which incorporates a domain name corresponding to the corporate name) may be the electronic equivalent of a business card.[39]

Headers attached to e-mail messages may contain additional information such as the name of the corporation where the message originated and optional information such as the sender's job title. To the extent that such header information may be modified by company employees, then this could be equivalent to allowing employees to print their own business cards.

Information contained on a corporation's Web site might also be used to identify a particular individual as being associated with the corporation and as occupying a position that would customarily be associated with the authority to bind the corporation. From this perspective, the information contained on a corporation's Web site can have significant legal consequences.[40]

### (f)  Computer-Generated Offers and Acceptances

Historically, contracts were formed through the direct actions of two individuals acting on their own behalf or on behalf of the

---

[39]   This demonstrates the need for caution before an entity provides clients, customers or other third parties with mailboxes on its Internet-accessible e-mail system.

[40]   For this reason, it is important to make prompt revisions to a Web site to delete references to employees who are no longer associated with the company.

corporations which they represent. However, the increasing use of computers, including for order processing on the Internet, can result in contractual transactions being effected with little or no direct human intervention.

In some cases, an offer or acceptance or both may be generated as a pre-programmed response by a computer system. For example, in an EDI transaction, a purchaser's computer system may respond once the inventory level of a particular item is below a specified threshold, and automatically send an EDI message containing an order to a supplier's computer system. The supplier's computer system may then send an acknowledgment back confirming acceptance of the order. A similar process may occur in a consumer transaction or in a transaction between entities that do not have any prior dealings. For example, a new customer may visit a supplier's Web site, scroll through an online catalogue and then place an order. The order may then be acknowledged (i.e., accepted) and processed automatically by the supplier's computer system.

Pending draft revisions to the UCC would give legal recognition to computer generated offers.[41] Such revisions would clarify that an enforceable contract may be formed notwithstanding that no individual representing either party was aware of or reviewed the initial message or response or took any action signifying acceptance.

## (g)  Jurisdictional Issues

The Internet is a global network. The provider of certain goods or intellectual property, such as software offered by means of the Internet, may be located in one jurisdiction, the service provider(s) through which access is provided may be in another jurisdiction and the purchaser or licensee of intellectual property may be in still another jurisdiction.

An enforceable contract is formed when an offer is accepted. If a contract does not designate an appropriate forum for resolving disputes between parties located in different jurisdictions, an important factor that will be considered in determining the forum will

---

[41]    UCC, section 2-208 (March 21, 1997 draft). See also the proposed revision to section 2B-206 (January 20, 1997 draft). For an update on the current status of the Article 2B revisions, see <http://www.ljx.com/internet/ir_ucc.html>.

be the location where the contract was formed. Such location will also be an important factor used by the courts to decide what laws will govern the agreement where the same is not set out in the contract. It should be noted that the jurisdiction whose laws govern an agreement may not coincide with the forum used to resolve a dispute, and a court in one jurisdiction may, where appropriate, apply the laws of another jurisdiction.

The choice of the jurisdiction whose laws will govern a contract and where any dispute will be resolved can have a major impact on the resolution of the dispute. Different jurisdictions may have different requirements for certain types of transactions and may provide different protections for certain types of parties (for example, consumer protection legislation). As well as differences in substantive law, different jurisdictions may apply different procedural rules and limitation periods which can bear on the outcome of a dispute.

A more detailed discussion of jurisdictional issues related to the Internet is found in Chapter 10.

### (h)  Regulatory Developments

The global nature of electronic commerce is challenging the effectiveness of traditional boundaries (i.e., provincial/state or country borders) as logical division points for different rules applicable to contract law. This is being recognized and work is being undertaken to achieve harmonization.

For instance, the work of the National Conference of Commissioners on Uniform State Laws was mentioned previously. In Canada, uniform legislation may be developed by the Uniform Law Conference of Canada (ULCC) as part of its Electronic Commerce Project. Also, as previously mentioned, Industry Canada's Task Force on Electronic Commerce is reviewing steps the federal government can take to facilitate electronic commerce.

Electronic commerce on the Internet often includes transactions where the parties are located in different countries. For this reason, it would be desirable if the laws governing electronic contracting in one country were compatible with the laws of other nations. The

United Nations' proposed model law on Electronic Commerce[42] may therefore provide the framework for development of such laws by many countries.

## 7.5 CONSUMER PROTECTION

Many jurisdictions have enacted legislation to deal specifically with transactions involving consumers. The legislation may provide for certain statutory warranties and conditions governing the sale of goods or services and state that these warranties and conditions may not be disclaimed by agreement of the parties. The legislation may provide for a cooling off period for certain types of transactions, during which time the consumer may rescind the transaction. Consumer protection legislation may also restrict a supplier from limiting liability, may require contracts to be drafted in plain language, and may prevent the imposition of "unfair" or unconscionable terms. In certain circumstances, consumers may also be provided with a right to rescind a transaction.

Certain jurisdictions have also enacted legislation dealing specifically with mail order transactions. This legislation may require persons engaged in such transactions to provide the name and address of the person carrying on the business. Such legislation may be applicable to online sales transacted through the Internet.

The European Union is also considering the adoption of a common directive in respect to distance contracts.[43] The draft directive as currently proposed would cover most forms of direct marketing and should encompass Internet-based marketing using the Web or e-mail. Some of the important provisions of the proposed directive are that:

- consumers must be given certain minimum information both at the time that the contract is solicited and at or near the time of delivery;

---

[42]   UNCITRAL Model Law on Electronic Commerce. United Nations Commission on International Trade Law (UNCITRAL) draft Model Law on legal aspects of Electronic Data Exchange and related means of communications. Published April 24, 1996.

[43]   Common Position (EC) No 19/95 of the European Parliament and of the Council on the protection of consumers in respect of distance contracts, 1995 O.J. (c 288/1).

- subject to certain exceptions, consumers must be given a "cooling off" period; and

- solicitations may not be made through telephone, fax or e-mail unless the consumer has provided his or her consent.

On January 1, 1997, *California Business and Professions Code* Section 17538 went into effect. This law requires vendors conducting business through electronic communications, including the Internet, to meet certain requirements. These requirements include the obligation to provide specific information to buyers, such as the vendor's return and refund policy, the legal name under which the business is operated and a complete street address for the business. Vendors must also deliver goods and services by certain deadlines, failing which they are obligated to provide refunds. Any business offering products or services on the Internet that is accessible to persons in California may be affected by the legislation.

## 7.6  TAXATION OF ONLINE COMMERCIAL TRANSACTIONS

### (a)  Overview

In most jurisdictions, the basic tax rules governing individuals and businesses have not been changed to deal with the exchange of products and services over the Internet. However, the unique nature of the Internet and the intangible and direct means by which electronic products and services can be delivered virtually instantaneously anywhere in the world create new stresses on the tax system.

Many jurisdictions tax on the basis of residence[44] or the citizenship or nationality[45] of the taxpayer. In the context of the Internet, two fundamental issues have vexed taxing authorities. The first issue involves seeking to apply to the Internet rules developed in the context of physical residence or nationality. The second issue deals with the ability to verify and audit electronic transactions. The following addresses some aspects of the first issue.

---

[44]    See section 2 (2) *Income Tax Act*, R.S.C. 1985, c. 1 (5th Supp.), as am.

[45]    This is a major basis of taxation in the US.

## (b)  Basis of Taxation in Cyberspace

Traditional concepts of residence have little significance when a substantial business may be operated from a Web site for which the location of the Web server is essentially irrelevant to and likely also unknown to most consumers. A Canadian taxpayer, being a resident of Canada, is taxed on worldwide income. Where a business or person is not resident in Canada and is not carrying on business in Canada[46] that person may be outside the scope of Canada's tax law.[47]

Tax authorities in Canada and other industrialized nations must address the tax implications arising from the ability to conduct a worldwide business from a server which may be located in almost any location.[48] Where physical or tangible products are shipped based on orders taken from a Web site, traditional rules do provide some guidance. The matter becomes more complex when intangible goods (such as software, or graphic images in digital form) are provided or when electronic services are provided from a Web site.

The OECD conducted a study on Electronic Commerce[49] which sought to identify the initial issues involved in preparation of major industrialized economies for an electronic commerce age. The section of the report on taxation recommended the application of principles of taxation based on the residency of the business and the source of the products (whether tangible or not). The report also suggested that the tax systems applied to transactions conducted over the Internet should be consistent, workable and not discriminatory. The report suggested that an international tax regime will need to be developed

---

[46]  See section 253, *Income Tax Act* which defines when a non-resident carries on business in Canada and may therefore be subject to Canada's tax jurisdiction. See also Interpretation Bulletin IT-420R3 which seeks to elaborate on this definition.

[47]  There are complex rules dealing with liability for tax in Canada and in most countries. These matters are outside the scope of this brief introduction. A further concern for any business is to consider how and to what extent the tax laws of various jurisdictions may intersect and which may lead to double taxation.

[48]  For a good introduction to this area see Brennan, Macaulay, *Emerging Tax Issues for Electronic Commerce*, Paper presented at the Canadian Institute NETLAW '97 conference September, 1997 in Calgary, Alberta

[49]  See Electronic Commerce Opportunities and Challenges for Government, June 12, 1997, OECD, Paris.

based on co-operation among governments. Suggestions of a "bit tax," to apply to the data exchange process, would eliminate the present advantages available to tax haven jurisdictions but may not reflect the inherent value exchanged and may be easily bypassed.

Because the US dominates the Internet, its views on the manner in which tax law will be applied in cyberspace are of fundamental importance. The present US policy[50] is to favour a market-oriented non-regulatory approach to the Internet. This approach is intended to permit the Internet to flourish. The US government proposes to examine whether this approach will lead to a decline in state and municipal revenues and will seek to address those issues using traditional tax principles[51] to ensure that similar forms of income are treated in a similar manner by tax authorities.

Australia has undertaken a review of tax issues of electronic commerce from a local perspective.[52] Among the issues examined by this report: the special risks of money laundering, the possibility of aggressive tax planning, the increasing internationalization of business and the growth of the cash economy.

Canada has generally taken a look and see approach and plans to develop a policy in response to major international initiatives and any unique issues which arise in Canada. Early steps by Canada include the formation of an Advisory Committee on Electronic Commerce.[53] Some of the special issues being considered in Canada include the application and enforcement of GST obligations with respect to the sale of products and services from Web sites. Even non-residents of Canada are liable for GST if they carry on any business in Canada.

Some of the factors a court might consider in determining if a business is carrying on business in Canada include where the Web

---

[50]    *A Framework for Global Electronic Commerce*, July 1, 1997, released by President Clinton. The report is available at <http://www.whitehouse.gov/WH/New/Commerce>.

[51]    See also *Selected Tax Policy Implications of Global Electronic Commerce*, November 1996, Department of the Treasury, Office of Tax Policy for further details on US tax policy.

[52]    See *Electronic Commerce Project*, Australian Taxation Office.

[53]    See *Advisory Committee on Electronic Commerce*, Revenue Canada Backgrounder, April 10, 1997, Ottawa.

site server is located, where the contract is made and where payment is accepted.

Where physical goods are imported into Canada, Revenue Canada will collect GST and applicable duties and customs charges on importation. There is, however, no practical mechanism to either identify or levy charges on imports of electronic goods such as software, digital images or digital music files.

Given the zeal of tax authorities in looking for new ways to extract revenue and the explosive growth of electronic commerce activity on the Internet, new regulatory approaches will develop in the next few years. In the meantime, the traditional rules apply and the operator of a Web site must review his or her tax exposure and obligations.

### (c)  Minister's Advisory Committee on Electronic Commerce

One component of the Canadian federal government's strategy for electronic commerce is contained in *Electronic Commerce and Canada's Tax Administration: A Report to the Minister of National Revenue from the Minister's Advisory Committee on Electronic Commerce*[54] (the "report"). The scope of the report covers numerous aspects of electronic commerce, as well as its implications for tax administration.

The Advisory Committee recognized that electronic commerce is putting pressure on traditional approaches and rules involved in tax administration. Electronic cash and payment systems that do not have a paper trail present problems similar to those raised by the underground economy. Disintermediation results in a loss of compliance/collection points. Furthermore, the ease of access to international markets, customers and service providers challenges the revenue collecting abilities of governments around the world.[55] The report therefore makes a series of recommendations on what can be done to ensure that electronic commerce does not result in any undue erosion of tax revenue, and that appropriate revenues from electronic commerce activities are collected.

---

[54]  April 1998. Available at <http://www.rc.gc.ca/ecomm/>.

[55]  Forward to the Report.

The report begins by examining the growing importance of electronic commerce for promoting knowledge-based economies and the role of the Internet as a platform for facilitating such activities. Various factors and statistics are reviewed which indicate a strong potential for the growth of electronic commerce. However, they also highlight some concerns about doing business on the Internet and point to the need for an effective strategy that will address issues such as privacy, security and consumer protection.

The report reviews international initiatives by national governments and international organizations in respect to electronic commerce. A Canadian strategy to facilitate electronic commerce is proposed. The elements of such a strategy include the need to (i) facilitate universal access and interoperability, (ii) build trust in the electronic marketplace and (iii) foster a favorable legal framework.

The Advisory Committee identified the need for rapid action in the area of privacy protection and consumer protection laws; security (ensuring the identity of contractual parties and the integrity of certification authorities); and ensuring the integrity of information systems. It indicated that an important first step in stimulating electronic commerce is for Internet users to have confidence that their private data is properly protected, and that they have legal recourse in the event such data is misused. Virtually all of the industry representatives that were canvassed indicated a clear intention to inform consumers of how their personal information is being stored, in what circumstances it might be released and how it is used. Similarly, industry is prepared to offer consumers a way to limit the use and reuse of their personal data, and otherwise take active steps to protect their privacy. The Advisory Committee noted that the Ministry of Industry and Justice, after consultations with the provinces and other stakeholders, will bring forward proposals for a legislative framework governing the protection of personal data in the private sector.

The Advisory Committee also addressed issues related to trust in respect to transactions conducted electronically. It stated that the use of digital signatures, based on public key cryptography, could provide businesses and consumers with appropriate certainty in their electronic dealings. However, it recognized the acceptance of a public key infrastructure (PKI) would require identification of appropriate entities capable of acting as trusted third parties or certification authorities. Financial institutions, telecommunications companies and governments were suggested as possible candidates.

The Advisory Committee also recommended that the various levels of government articulate a clear plan and implement the necessary measures for defining the necessary legal framework for electronic commerce. According to the Advisory Committee, such a framework would need to ensure effective intellectual property protection for a digital environment; clear rules on jurisdiction, applicable law, and enforcement and on liability and contractual obligations involved in electronic transactions; and a fair, equitable and transparent tax regime for electronic commerce.

The growth of electronic commerce will be hampered without clear commercial rules and effective dispute resolution processes, including a clear understanding of liability. Laws governing commercial contracts may need to be tweaked to remove barriers and uncertainty in respect to contracts concluded electronically. Possible elements to be addressed include default rules on the formation and governance of electronic contracts, characteristics of valid electronic writings and original documents, legal recognition of digital signatures and electronic evidence rules. Many of these issues are being addressed by the Uniform Law Conference of Canada's Electronic Commerce Project which is considering model legislation including the adoption of the UNITRAL model law on electronic commerce.

The report makes a number of general recommendations for government aimed at promoting the development of electronic commerce in Canada, including:

- leadership by the private sector of the management, promotion and development of electronic commerce in recognition that electronic commerce is driven by market forces and by new and rapidly developing technologies;

- recognition by the federal government that, in co-operation with other governments in Canada, it should assist businesses in the pursuit of electronic commerce activities by providing a tax and commercial environment that would be viewed as a model of co-operation around the world;

- advocation of a tax neutral position with regard to electronic commerce transactions;

- further study concerning the risk of loss of revenue, and the extent of those losses, resulting from electronic commerce activities before any new policies or taxes are introduced;

- the creation by governments of a favourable policy and legal environment for the growth of electronic commerce;

- immediate action by the Government of Canada, including Revenue Canada, to clarify and communicate the application of existing government policies and practices to electronic commerce activities;

- promotion of consistency in electronic commerce polices among all levels of government in Canada, and among national governments around the world; and

- acceptance by governments of the role of model users of the Internet and electronic commerce.

The report discusses the implications and risks for Canada's tax administration that are posed by the expansion of electronic commerce. What emerges are seventy-two detailed recommendations in the area of income taxes, commodity taxes, custom duties and tariffs. These include:

- working to minimize the incidence of non-compliance (e.g., tax evasion);

- issuance of an interpretation bulletin to clarify Revenue Canada's position with respect to which electronic commerce activities may constitute "carrying on business" in Canada;

- review of existing rules regarding the allocation of income in order to minimize double taxation and ensure a fair allocation of taxable income between multiple jurisdictions;

- review of existing provisions regarding withholding taxes for goods and services being delivered electronically so that those transactions are treated as equivalent to the purchase of tangible goods;

- addressing issues related to consumption taxes and custom duties/tariffs that are raised by the transformation or recharacterization of goods and services to intangible property; and

- addressing issues related to records retention.

## 7.7  PRIVACY IN CYBERSPACE

### (a)  Introduction

There are at least two privacy interests that may be of concern for purposes of activity on the Internet. The first is the expectation of users that messages that they send by means of an employer's or a third party's computer system or network will not be intercepted. Although corporate LAN Administrators and Internet Access Providers ("IAPs") have a legitimate interest in ensuring that their systems are not used for unlawful or improper purposes, the interception of messages may be in violation of users' rights of privacy.

The second privacy interest that may be of concern relates to the collection, use and disclosure of personal information by Web site operators about visitors to their site. Web site operators may collect such information by requiring or encouraging visitors to register certain personal information in order to obtain access to the site as a whole or to certain parts of the site. Visitors may be asked to provide their name and e-mail address, and in some cases, actual address (including postal code), phone number and areas of interest. Web site operators may obtain additional information by monitoring the specific pages visited on the site[56] or other activity conducted on a site (for instance, logging of searches conducted).

The activities of particular users, even those carried out during different online sessions, can be tracked through the use of "cookies." A "cookie" refers to small pieces of information or identifiers to which an operator has access on a particular user's PC which can then

---

[56]   Web servers typically create a statistical log that captures information as to each page accessed at a particular Web site and the IP address of the computer that requested the page. Although an IP address does not identify an individual, many ISPs provide a facility which permits a remote host to query the name or e-mail address of the subscriber to whom a particular IP address was issued.

be interrogated on a subsequent visit.[57] The information provided by a cookie can tell the operator of a Web site which pages on that site were viewed by a visitor on a prior visit and any preferences expressed by that visitor.

The information captured by cookies and Web site logs may or may not provide personal information about identifiable individuals. However, when combined with information obtained during the registration process, or potentially provided by the ISP, such information can permit the creation of a comprehensive profile of a particular user. Additional information may be gathered from the many online phone directories and other databases available on the Internet. The profile can then be sold to advertisers and other interested parties without the consent or knowledge of individual users and can be used to direct targeted advertising to particular users.[58]

A small minority of Web sites permit users to request that the personal information they provide during the registration process will not be shared with others. However, other Web sites advise users in their legal notices page that use of the site shall constitute the user's consent for their personal information to be shared with other parties. Such a notice may be an inconspicuous part of the legal terms and may not set out explicitly what is contemplated. Many Web sites are silent as to what uses may be made of any information provided by visitors and whether such information will be shared with others.

The inappropriate collection of personal information on the Internet may constitute unfair and deceptive trade practice. For instance, the US Federal Trade Commission (FTC) investigated KidsCom, a Web site that invited children to sign up for prizes and a pen-pal service. KidsCom collected names, home addresses, birth

---

[57]    Cookies are small pieces of data sent to a user's hard drive by Web servers to track usage from one session to the next. Leading Web browsers, including Netscape Communications Corp.'s Navigator and Microsoft Corp.'s Internet Explorer, accept cookies automatically but can be configured to notify users of an incoming cookie.

[58]    An ability to capture demographic information about visitors to their site can allow Web site operators to direct specific types of advertisements to visitors having a particular demographic characteristic.

dates and information about products and activities of interest. Some of the information was aggregated and sold as marketing data.

The FTC found that such practices were a violation of FTC rules and likely constituted unfair and deceptive practices. Specifically, the FTC stated that it was a deceptive practice to collect personally identifiable information from children for one purpose without notifying parents that the data may be used for other purposes. Web sites must also notify parents before they release personally identifiable information to third parties.

Privacy rights may be protected by various means, such as by common law causes of action, privacy legislation affecting the public or private sector, self regulation, and criminal legislation, Internet-specific legislation has also been proposed.

### (b)  Privacy-Related Common Law Torts

In various countries, certain privacy-related torts are recognized which, under appropriate circumstances, might be relevant to the use and disclosure of information on the Internet. The following torts have been recognized in the US *Restatement of Torts*:

- disclosure of private facts of a kind that would be highly offensive to a reasonable person and not newsworthy;

- misappropriation of personality[59] (name or likeness);

- placing another person in a false light (falsely associating an individual with activities that would be highly offensive to a reasonable person); and

- unreasonable intrusion upon another's seclusion or solitude, or into his or her own private affairs (which may include the collection of personal information).

---

[59]  The tort of misappropriation of personality may be involved where a person's name or likeness is appropriated for commercial use (i.e., in association with goods or services). It must be distinguished from a right of publicity which prevents others from publicizing a person's name and likeness without consent. In April 1998, Corel Corp. was sued by Hedy Lamarr, a glamorous movie star of the 1930s and 1940s, for allegedly using her likeness without permission. Ms. Lamarr alleges that a stylized picture of her appears on the cover of Corel Draw 8 and on Corel's Web site. The lawsuit was filed in Florida where Ms. Lamarr resides.

Although the common law in Canada has been less receptive to providing equivalent rights to privacy, courts in Ontario have recognized that there may be a common law cause of action for invasion of privacy. In *Saccone v. Orr*,[60] the Ontario County Court awarded damages for the defendant's use of a tape recording of a private conversation involving the plaintiff. In *Palad v. Pantaleon*,[61] the plaintiff was awarded $2,500.00 for invasion of privacy where the defendant creditor had harassed the plaintiff by making frequent phone calls and appearing at the debtor's home and workplace.

In determining whether the use or disclosure of either the contents of messages sent by users on a network or information generated by the network (i.e., the identity of the sender and recipient of messages) could constitute an unjustified invasion of privacy giving rise to civil damages, a court will examine all of the circumstances of the use or disclosure, and consider the damages suffered by the user. The risk of liability of a network operator would be substantially increased if messages were intercepted for purposes unrelated to the exercise of control over the use and operation of the network.

Various other causes of action may be relied upon at common law to protect rights to privacy, but the protection granted may be limited in scope. For example, in the case of an action for defamation, it must be shown not only that the information which is disseminated is untrue, but also that the dissemination has caused damage to an individual's reputation.[62] In general, such a cause of action does not enable an individual to prevent the collection or the dissemination of information which is accurate, nor does it enable the individual to control the uses that may be made of such information.[63]

There may also be obstacles to the application of an action based on breach of confidence. Such an action may be restricted to information of a confidential nature that was communicated in circumstances giving rise to an obligation of confidence. The type of

---

[60]    (1981), 34 O.R. (2d) 317, 19 C.C.L.T. 37 (Ont. Co. Ct.).

[61]    (June 14, 1989), York 266930/86 [unreported].

[62]    Special damages may be assumed with certain types of defamation, such as libel or slander *per se*.

[63]    However, defamation is not a privacy tort *per se*. Defamation is discussed in more detail in section 8.2.

information generally collected by Web sites is not usually of a confidential nature (for instance, a person's name and address). Furthermore, the information may not be communicated in circumstances which give rise to an express or implied duty of confidentiality.

Another quasi-privacy tort is a right of publicity which permits a person to limit the public use of his or her name or likeness. For instance, the State of New York recognizes a right of publicity but contains an "incidental use" exemption for news services. In 1994, Howard Stern, a nationally recognized talk show host, television personality and author, announced his candidacy for governor of New York. Delphi, an online service, ran an ad for the service that included an emphasis on a special discussion group it had set up on the service to discuss Stern's candidacy and included a picture of Stern's bare posterior that was taken from the back cover of his book. Stern sued for violation of his right to privacy.[64] Delphi claimed its actions fell within an "incidental use" exception. The court held that companies engaged in the news business have a broad right under the First Amendment to advertise their news services and may utilize pictures of famous personalities in the news in such advertising without resulting in a breach of the personality's right of publicity. It found that Delphi was either a newspaper or news distributor, that its bulletin board function was the equivalent of a "letters to the editor" section of a newspaper and that Delphi qualified for the incidental use exception as a news distributor.

## (c)  Statutory Rights of Privacy

### (i)  Public Sector

Most Canadian provinces have enacted privacy legislation specifically applicable to public sector entities. For instance, in the Province of Ontario, government "institutions," such as provincial and municipal ministries, boards, commissions and agencies, are subject to the provisions of the *Freedom of Information and Protection of Privacy Act*[65] or the *Municipal Freedom of Information and*

---

[64]  *Stern v. Delphi*, 626 N.Y.S.2d 694 (Sup. Ct. 1995).

[65]  R.S.O. 1990, c. F.31.

*Protection of Privacy Act*[66] (collectively referred to as the "Privacy Acts"). The Privacy Acts govern the collection, use and disclosure of information by such institutions and may apply to a wide variety of computer systems and networks that may be operated by such institutions, ranging from the bulletin boards operated by school boards to the systems used to store motor vehicle registration information. Federal institutions in Canada are governed by the *Privacy Act*.[67]

### (ii) Private Sector

Some Canadian provinces have enacted legislation creating a statutory tort for one person to violate the privacy of another. For instance, the legislation enacted by British Columbia,[68] Manitoba,[69] Newfoundland[70] and Saskatchewan[71] make it a "tort, actionable without proof of damages, for a person, wilfully and without a claim of right, to violate the privacy of another." The interception of messages or the disclosure of the existence of messages sent by means of a computer network may be a violation of such legislation, even if such conduct may not be a violation of any criminal legislation.[72] However, the above-mentioned statutes do not define the term "privacy" and have left the interpretation of what constitutes an invasion of privacy to the courts.

Some jurisdictions have also adopted legislation to provide specific protection for personal information in the private sector. For example, the 1995 *EC Directive on the Protection of Natural Persons*

---

[66]    R.S.O. 1990, c. M.56.

[67]    R.S.C. 1985, c. P-21.

[68]    *Privacy Act*, R.S.B.C. 1979, c. 336.

[69]    *Privacy Act*, R.S.M. 1987, c. P125.

[70]    *An Act Respecting the Protection of Personal Privacy*, R.S.N. 1990, c. P-22.

[71]    *An Act Respecting the Protection of Privacy*, R.S.S. 1978, c. P-24.

[72]    In *Ferguson v. McBee Technographics Inc.*, [1989] 2 W.W.R. 499, 24 C.P.R. (3d) 240, 58 Man. R. (2d) 119 (Man. Q.B.), it was held that listening to and recording a telephone conversation with the knowledge of only one of the participants was a *prima facie* violation of the Manitoba *Privacy Act* (S.M. 1987, c. P125, C.C.S.M. c. P125). This was the case notwithstanding that section 184 of the Canadian *Criminal Code* provides that it is not an offence to record a conversation where the consent of only one of the parties to the communication is obtained.

*in Regard to the Processing of Personal Information and the Free Dissemination of that Information* (the "Privacy Directive"), imposes certain obligations on entities collecting, retaining, using and communicating information that concerns a natural person. The Privacy Directive also provides for the establishment of a regulatory framework for the protection of personal data by prohibiting transfers of such data to non-Member States unless they are deemed to provide "an adequate level of protection" of that data.

In Canada, the Province of Quebec has adopted *An Act respecting the protection of personal information in the private sector* (the Act).[73] This Act sets out detailed rules governing the purposes for which any private enterprise may collect personal information, the uses to be made of such information, and the purposes for which the information may be communicated to third persons. The Act also sets out the rights of any person about whom personal information is collected to obtain access to that information and to exercise certain recourses arising from any inaccuracies in the information or any improper use of the information.

The Act will have a significant effect on the collection and use of personal information collected through a Web site located in Quebec. Business entities that collect personal information from residents in Quebec may also need to consider the applicability of this legislation to their activities if they have a substantial presence or otherwise operate in Quebec.

Certain industries such as insurance companies may be subject to industry-specific statutory requirements.  For example, the Alberta *Financial Consumers Act*[74] provides that personal financial information provided by a consumer for the purpose of obtaining advice about or investing in certain financial products may be used only for the purpose for which it was given, unless the consumer otherwise consents.

Most Canadian provinces have legislation regulating consumer reporting agencies (companies that collect credit and other information about individuals and provide consumer reports to third

---

[73]    S.Q. 1993, c. 17. See ss. 27 to 41. See also articles 35-40 of the *Civil Code* of Quebec.

[74]    S.A. 1990, c. F-9.5.

parties for certain specified purposes such as granting credit). As an example, Ontario's *Consumer Reporting Act*[75] requires such businesses to register, sets out conditions under which information may be disclosed and imposes certain notice obligations.

Another example of industry-specific regulation is federal legislation governing financial institutions. For instance, section 157(2) of the *Bank Act* requires banks in Canada to establish procedures to restrict the use of confidential information.[76] The Canadian government has also proposed regulations which would require federally-regulated financial institutions to adopt a code of practice to protect the privacy of personal information.[77]

### (iii) Industry Canada's Task Force on Electronic Commerce

Industry Canada's Task Force on Electronic Commerce has issued a report recommending new legal measures for the protection of personal information.[78] The report reviews why current forms of legal protection are not sufficient, and sets out the principles that must be followed in designing a new privacy law.

The report is in furtherance of the Canadian government's previously announced commitment to enact legislation to protect personal information by the year 2000.

The report notes the need for such legislation to strike a balance between two competing objectives, namely, the business need to gather, store and use personal information, and the consumer need to be informed about how that information is used and to be assured that the information will be protected.

The report notes that, apart from legislation to protect personal information held by the public sector, and legislation enacted by Quebec to protect personal information in the private sector, legal protection of personal information in Canada is sporadic and uneven.

---

[75]   R.S.O. 1990, c. C. 33.

[76]   *Bank Act*, S.C. 1991, c.46.

[77]   Government of Canada, Department of Finance, *1997 Review of Financial Sector Legislation: Proposal for Changes* (Ottawa, June 1996).

[78]   Industry Canada Task Force on Electronic Commerce, "The Protection of Personal Information — Building Canada's Information Economy and Society" January 1998.

Many industries are not subject to any rules, while others are subject to a "patchwork" of laws and regulations that fail to establish common principles. Among the factors that necessitate new legislation to protect personal information are: advances in technology that permit information to be distributed over networks and information from various sources to be combined, the growth in the amount of information held by the private sector, and the convergence of cable and telephone communication technologies. Such legislation is also required to ensure that Canada is not at risk of having data flows from the European Union blocked for failing to provide an adequate level of protection for personal information.

The report considers several issues that must be addressed in designing new privacy legislation. One such issue is to ensure uniform protection of personal information across Canada, including protection for information held by those private sector entities such as the telecommunications and banking sectors that are federally regulated, and other sectors such as health care and education that are provincially regulated. The report notes that the different levels of government in Canada must work together to achieve a uniform approach to protection. In this regard, the Uniform Law Conference of Canada ("ULCC") is expected to prepare a draft *Uniform Act* in 1998.

A further issue considered by the report involves a review of the principles on which any new law should be based. The Report suggests the principles embodied in the Canadian Standards Association (CSA) *Model Code on the Protection of Personal Information* (Model Code) would be an appropriate starting point since they represent a consensus among key stakeholders, they provide flexibility and they are technologically neutral. However, various provisions of the Model Code may have to be made more precise when embodied in legislation. Moreover, the new law may have to include certain obligations not contained in the Model Code, while certain types of information may have to be excluded from the legislation.

A further issue considered by the report is whether sectoral codes should be recognized in the new law. The report notes that some jurisdictions treat sectoral codes as legally binding, while others provide for industry codes to provide guidance in the interpretation of the law. Responsibility for approving an industry code could be given to a government body that would be responsible for verifying that the code complies with the law.

The report also considers what provisions should be included in the new law to ensure compliance and to redress complaints. The report suggests that it may be appropriate to have a variety of oversight bodies, which would be responsible for determining whether various entities are complying with the law, for handling complaints and for providing recourses to affected persons. A central authority or privacy commissioner may also be given responsibility for monitoring compliance and for issuing recommendations to deal with new technologies and practices.

In conclusion, the report notes that Canadians must find a balance between the need of business for access to the information necessary for functioning in a knowledge-based economy and the rights of individuals to privacy and security of personal information. While Canadians still have the opportunity to design the kind of system required to safeguard information privacy, the report notes the need for establishing a legislative framework before the issues discussed in the report move beyond the control of Canadians.

### (iv)  Developments in Other Jurisdictions

Some of the laws governing the protection of personal information also include rules governing the manner in which the information may be collected. For example, under the UK *Data Protection Act* (1984),[79] persons asked to provide personal information must be informed of the identity of the entity collecting the data, the purpose of the collection and the persons to whom the data may be disclosed. Such notice must be provided before the information is collected. This requirement would limit the right of an entity operating a Web site to require visitors to register and to provide name and address information before obtaining full access to the Web site. Instead, the operator would have to provide certain information[80] to any visitors before information from them is collected.

---

[79]    1984, c. 35.

[80]    This information would include the name of the entity collecting the information and the purpose for which the persons to whom the information may be disclosed.

In the United States, a number of statutes may provide privacy protection for Internet-based communications including:[81]

- *Electronic Communications Privacy Act*[82]
- *Computer Fraud and Abuse Act*[83]
- *Privacy Protection Act*[84]
- *Privacy Act*[85]
- *Fair Credit Reporting Act*[86]
- other information privacy acts and state statutes

Internet-specific legislation has been proposed in the United States. The "Consumer Internet Privacy Protection Act of 1997" (Bill HR 98) would seek to regulate the use by interactive computer services of personally identifiable information provided by subscribers to such services.[87] If enacted, this Act would prohibit an interactive computer service from disclosing to a third party personally identifiable information provided by a subscriber to such a service without the subscriber's informed prior written consent. As well, a subscriber must be permitted to revoke a consent and upon such revocation, the service must cease disclosing any personally identifiable information to a third party.

An interactive computer service would be prohibited from knowingly disclosing to a third party any personally identifiable information provided by a subscriber that has been falsified. In addition, subscribers are granted the right to obtain access to their personally identifiable information so that they can verify or correct such information. Finally, the Act would require the service to provide the subscriber upon request with information concerning the

---

[81]    See Susan E. Gindin, "Lost and Found in Cyberspace: Informational Privacy in the Age of the Internet," 34 *San Diego Law Review*, August-September 1997.

[82]    Pub. L. No. 99-508, 100 Stat. 1848, codified in various sections of 18 U.S.C.

[83]    18 U.S.C. section 1030.

[84]    42 U.S.C. section 2000aa.

[85]    5 U.S.C. section 552a.

[86]    15 U.S.C. section 1681.

[87]    See <http://zeus.bna.com/e-law/docs/hr98.html> for more information on Bill HR 98.

identity of any third party recipients of the subscriber's personally identifiable information.

### (d) Voluntary Codes

In response to the growing use of computer systems and electronic networks, model codes have been developed. As noted above, the Canadian Standards Association ("CSA") has issued a *Model Code on the Protection of Personal Information* (the "Model Code").[88] The Model Code is intended as a voluntary standard that may be adopted by any organization concerned about the protection of personal information. Once the Model Code is adopted, the provisions containing prescriptive language become requirements. An organization may tailor the Model Code to meet its particular circumstances, such as by developing an organization-specific code and by providing organization-specific examples. The Model Code addresses the manner in which personal information is collected, used, protected and disclosed, and the rights of individuals to obtain access to that information and where necessary, to have it corrected.

The Model Code is based on the *Guidelines on the Protection of Privacy and Transborder Data Flows*, adopted by the Organization for Economic Co-operation and Development (the "OECD"), consisting of some 19 European countries together with Canada, United States, Japan, New Zealand and Australia (the "guidelines").[89] The guidelines do not have any binding legal effect, but instead represent a voluntary code with which member states are expected to comply. The guidelines provide for the principle of free flow of data between countries, subject to certain basic standards being adopted to provide for the protection of personal data in relation to both the public and the private sectors.

Some industry associations have also issued codes of ethical conduct which contain provisions intended to protect privacy. While compliance with such codes may be mandatory for members of such

---

[88]    For a full decision of the Model Code, see J. Fraser Mann, *Recent Developments in Information Privacy: A Proposed Model Code for Legislative Reform*, 1 *I.T.L.* 6.

[89]    *Guidelines on the Protection of Privacy and Transborder Flows of Personal Data*, Annex to Recommendation of the Council, September 23, 1980, Organization for Economic Co-operation and Development, Paris, 1981.

associations, membership in the association itself may be voluntary. One such example is the *Code of Ethics and Standards of Practice* of the Canadian Direct Marketing Association (CDMA). CDMA's code contains provisions which permit consumers to control the use of their personal information and to reduce the amount of direct marketing material sent to them.

A number of initiatives to develop voluntary privacy codes specific to the Internet have been advanced. One such initiative is TRUSTe (formerly eTRUST), a program initiated on January 1997 by the non-profit Electronic Frontier Foundation.[90] TRUSTe operates as an online equivalent of a "Good Housekeeping Seal of Approval." Sites registered with TRUSTe display icons (or "trustmarks") which indicate what they will and will not do with information obtained from users. Such sites are then subject to audit. The TRUSTe program has been relatively successful and has been transferred to a for-profit entity.

To participate, a site must agree to abide by a stringent set of privacy guidelines developed by TRUSTe. The guidelines require Web sites to set out their information gathering practices, what personal identifiable data they collect, the purposes for which the information is used, and the persons with whom it will be shared. Users must be allowed to correct, update and delete personal identifiable information. Monitoring of personal communications between users is also prohibited.

A more recent standard, the Open Profiling Standard,[91] was proposed in the early part of 1997 by Netscape Communication Corp. and backed by 60 other high-tech firms. Netscape's proposal was quickly followed by Microsoft's endorsement of the Platform for Privacy Preferences, also known as P3, which was proposed by the World Wide Web Consortium. The latter is an extension of the more established Platform for Internet Content Selection (PICS).

---

[90]    See <www.truste.com>.

[91]    Under OPS, a user creates a personal profile, which might include the person's name, address, sex, marital status, phone number, e-mail address, hobbies and similar information, which is stored on the user's hard drive. When that user then visits a Web site that requests personal information, the user can decide whether to disclose the requested data.

Under the P3 standard, users define the information that they are willing to have collected about them. If a Web site attempts to collect more information than that defined by the user, a pop-up message would alert the user who would then either leave the site or consent to the collection of the additional information.

A number of other self-imposed regulations or guidelines may also be applicable to the collection or use of personal information. Many trade associations and industry groups (for instance, the Canadian Bankers Association) have established voluntary codes of compliance and in some cases, companies have established company-specific privacy policies and guidelines.[92]

Some companies with extensive operations on the Internet are developing their own self-imposed privacy policies. For instance, McGraw-Hill, publisher of Business Week and operator of approximately 70 Web sites, has adopted a policy which prohibits the distribution of certain types of private information, such as Social Security numbers and medical records, to third parties and imposes limits on the collection of personal data.

Privacy on the Internet is of concern to many users. If the voluntary industry initiatives are not successful in allaying people's fears, then new legislation or regulations may be adopted. A survey[93] released in June 1997, found that 58 percent of computer users who were surveyed wanted the government to pass laws on how personal information can be collected and used. However, for the time being at least, the US Administration and the Federal Trade Commission appear willing to give voluntary industry initiatives a chance before resorting to new regulation.

In June 1997, the Federal Trade Commission held public hearings on consumer privacy. It concluded that Congress should not adopt

---

[92]    For example, the Bank of Montreal, a Canadian chartered bank, has a booklet entitled "Your Privacy" which sets out the Bank's commitment to protect the privacy and confidentiality of certain types of personal information collected from customers. The Bank also has an internal Confidentiality of Information Policy. All directors and personnel are required to be aware of the Policy and designated personnel are also required to acknowledge their understanding of the Policy in writing.

[93]    Conducted by Privacy and American Business, a privacy journal and research service. Released June 10, 1997.

new legislation governing the collection and use of personal information. Instead, the Commission expected operators of Web sites to monitor how they collect and use personal data. The Commission also indicated that it expected a substantial majority of Web sites to post privacy policies.

### (e)  Criminal Legislation

In certain countries, the interception of private communications may be a violation of criminal legislation. For instance, in Canada, section 184(1) of the *Criminal Code*[94] makes it an offence for any person to use a device to wilfully intercept a private communication. Any wilful use or further disclosure of an unauthorized interception may also constitute a separate offence.

However, criminal prohibitions against unauthorized interception of private communication may not apply to all types of interception of communications. For example, transmission logs captured by the system may be distinguished from the contents of messages and may not constitute "communications" for the purposes of criminal legislation. Accordingly, the monitoring or logging by an IAP of sites visited by its users, or the logging of certain routing information concerning e-mail messages, whether for the IAP's marketing purposes or for purposes of assisting a law enforcement agency with a warrantless search, may not attract criminal liability.

This topic is discussed further in Chapter 11.

### (f)  Transborder Data Flow

In many countries, including Canada, no laws of general application have been enacted to regulate the transfer or transmission of computerized data outside the jurisdiction. However, certain laws of this nature may apply to specific industries, such as consumer reporting agencies and banks.[95]

---

[94]    R.S.C. 1985, c. C-46, as amended.

[95]    For example, the Canadian *Bank Act* provides that, subject to certain exceptions, all registers and records required or authorized to be kept by any bank must be prepared and maintained in Canada, and information or data relating to the preparation and maintenance of such records must be both maintained and processed in Canada.

As noted above, some jurisdictions, including the Province of Quebec and many EU Member States,[96] have enacted legislation governing the use of personal information. Such legislation may restrict the export of personal information to countries that do not have an adequate level of protection for such data.

Transborder data flow was also the subject of a declaration adopted by governments of OECD Member countries on April 11, 1985 (the "OECD Declaration").[97] The OECD Declaration acknowledged the economic and social benefits resulting from access to information and the common interest of Member countries in facilitating the free flow of information from one country to another.

An interesting issue is whether the transmission of personal information through the Internet to another country with the requisite level of protection may nevertheless constitute a violation of privacy legislation if the information is routed through another jurisdiction without adequate protection before reaching the destination. This can be a problem because even data exchanged by means of the Internet between two users in the same jurisdiction may pass through another jurisdiction.[98]

---

[96]    For example, the UK *Data Protection Act* (1984) regulates the use of computerized data relating to a living person who can be identified from the data, sets out registration formalities and regulates the categories of people to whom the information may be disclosed. The European Union's *Directive on the protection of individuals with regard to the processing of personal data and the free movement of such data* (Directive 95/46/EC of the European Parliament and of the Council of Europe, October 24, 1995) also restricts the transfer of personal data from an EU-member state to a non-member state. The EC *Data Protection Act* will be effective as of October 29, 1998. For more information see Fiona Carlin, "EU to Install Data Privacy Standards," The National Law Journal, October 27, 1997 at B07. <http://www.ljx.com/internet/1027eudata.html>.

[97]    OECD, "Declaration on Transborder Data Flow", April 11, 1985.

[98]    For example, the path between two users attached to different IAPs may need to cross into another jurisdiction before finding a common route between the two IAPs. Also, one or both users may be using the facilities of a foreign IAP or online service. For example, many Canadian residents utilize America Online, CompuServe or other US-based online services or IAPs to gain access to the Internet. Any communications between two Canadian users may be routed through the service provider located in the US.

# 8

# Web Site Liability Issues

## 8.1  AN OVERVIEW OF LEGAL ISSUES

### (a)  Internet Liability Study

In Canada, an Internet Liability Study (the study) was commissioned by Industry Canada and released in the Spring of 1997.[1] The study is believed to be the first comprehensive report on the specific issues of liability for content on the Internet. It also addressed information controls, privacy issues and the protection of works on the Internet.

The purpose of the study was to assist Internet participants to better understand their potential liability and rights with a view to eliminating or reducing uncertainty as to the current law. The study is different from previous government studies, such as those conducted by the Canadian Information Highway Advisory Council and the United States National Information Infrastructure Task Force, that were primarily concerned with policy issues. The topic areas covered in the study include obscenity, child pornography, hate propaganda, civil liability, trademarks and copyright.

The study was made difficult by the almost complete absence of case law in Canada dealing with the application to the Internet of many traditional legal regulations. Although numerous Internet-related actions have been decided by US courts in recent years, including those dealing with copyright infringement, obscene materials and

---

[1]  Racicot, Hayes, Szibbo and Trudel, *The Cyberspace is Not a No Law Land*, Industry Canada. The study was current as of the Fall of 1996 and does not reflect amendments to the Canadian *Copyright Act* introduced in Bill C-32 or the WIPO Treaties resulting from the Diplomatic Conferences on Certain Copyright and Neighbouring Rights held in Geneva in December 1996, although both are briefly mentioned in the study; see also, Gahtan, Review of *The Cyberspace is Not a No Law Land* in *Information & Technology Law* 2:1 (November 1997).

defamation, the laws of Canada and the US differ in certain areas. For example, with respect to copyright, US law incorporates the concept of contributory infringement which is not found in the Canadian *Copyright Act* (although a somewhat similar concept of "authorizing infringement" exists). Also, US copyright law is subject to "fair use" defences which may be broader in scope than the "fair dealing" defences under Canadian copyright law.

The study assumed that legal liability may arise from activity on the Internet and focused its analysis on who is or should be liable. Liability was analysed on the basis of specific activities carried out by a specific individual rather than based on a more superficial analysis of liability for certain categories of persons.

The study highlights some of the potential problems of applying existing legislation and legal principles to the Internet. For instance, a copyrighted work may be stored in multiple locations and assembled only when the work is accessed. As long as each part is not a "substantial part," the reproduction of each of these parts may not constitute an infringement of copyright. An infringement would only occur if the parts were re-assembled into an entire work. However, due to the hypertext nature of the Web, this may not be necessary in order for the work to be improperly accessed and used.

Some of the conclusions reached by the study were:

- Although an individual hypertext link cannot be copyrighted, there may be copyright in a compilation or collection of links.

- Certain types of "caching" may constitute a reproduction of a copyrighted work.

- Implied licences may cover certain activities involved in accessing an authorized copy of a work.

- In certain situations, intermediaries such as Internet Service Providers and Online Services may be held liable for copyright infringement due to activities of their users and subscribers.

- An operator of a newsgroup, interactive chat group or mailing list could be liable for publication or distribution of obscene material especially if such activity is "moderated."[2]

- The receipt of certain types of content may itself lead to liability. For instance, mere possession of child pornography (possibly even in the cache of a Web browser) may be an offence.

- The gathering of personal information through Web sites may need to be performed in compliance with privacy legislation where potential visitors include residents of jurisdictions that have legislation governing such activities (such as Quebec).

The study is not likely to prompt any quick or radical legislative changes. It advocates a slow, cautious approach to increased regulation. According to the study, laws should only be modified when it becomes clear that changes are necessary. It suggests that where current laws can be reasonably interpreted as applicable, the prudent policy approach would be to wait to determine how courts apply existing laws to Internet-related activities. It also suggests that any necessary amendments should be as narrow in scope as possible and should be made in a technology-neutral manner.

## (b) Obligation to Keep Content Current

Readers of information in printed form understand that the information may not be up-to-date, and therefore are more cautious in relying on such information. However, viewers of material maintained in electronic form and made available using the Internet may expect the information to be up-to-date. Accordingly, any content placed on a Web site that may be relied upon by others should be kept up-to-date or otherwise be accompanied by a notice on each page warning that the contents may not be current and setting out the date of last revision. It may also be advisable in some circumstances to insert a notice that the online version is provided only for guidance and that the official version is located at the organization's office or another designated location.

---

[2]    A "moderated" newsgroup is one where individual messages must be approved by a moderator prior to general distribution.

Operators of Web sites should also keep in mind that most users of the Internet utilize popular Web search engines to locate information on the Internet. These search engines will automatically index all pages contained on a Web site. A search on a particular key word or individual's name using an Internet search engine may cause a user to link directly to a page on an organization's Web site. The information on that page may no longer be valid or current. For instance, if a professional organization or regulatory organization were to post notices of disciplinary actions undertaken against its members, information about suspensions or other disciplinary actions posted to certain pages should be kept up-to-date or otherwise contain a note as to the effective date of the information. The failure to take such steps may result in liability to a user who relies on inaccurate information or to the subjects of such information.

## 8.2  LIABILITY FOR DEFAMATION ON THE INTERNET

"The law of defamation seeks to balance two opposing interests: on the one hand there is freedom of speech; on the other hand, the importance of reputation. In a cyber society or wired world, both of these interests are increasingly important.[3]"

In Canada, the law of defamation outside the Province of Quebec is based on the common law. In the Province of Quebec, protection of an individual's reputation is based on Article 3 of the Quebec *Civil Code* and section 4 of the *Charter of Human Rights and Freedoms*.[4]

An action for defamation typically requires the plaintiff to establish:

- the offending statement was communicated to a third party;

- the offending statement refers to the plaintiff; and

- the offending statement is defamatory (i.e., is false and discredits the plaintiff).

---

[3]    David Potts and Sally Harris, "Defamation on the Internet," *Legal Issues on the Internet* Conference, Toronto, May 14, 1996 at 9.

[4]    R.S.Q. c. C-12.

Once these conditions are established, the plaintiff can benefit from certain presumptions. For instance, subject to evidence to the contrary, it is presumed that the statement was published with malice and that the plaintiff suffered damages. The defendant may avoid liability by establishing that the statements were true or that they constituted fair comment.

There is a risk of substantial damage arising from any defamatory statement made on the Internet. This is due to the fact that the statement may easily be transmitted internationally to a large audience.

In many countries with an English common law background, it is important to determine whether any defamatory statement constitutes either libel or slander. In the case of slander, a plaintiff must usually prove special damages in order to recover, whereas such proof is not necessary in a claim of libel.[5] In the case of statements transmitted on the Internet, this determination will likely be based on the type of service utilized to transmit the statement. Statements contained on a Web site made to an e-mail discussion list and Usenet newsgroup would likely have a sufficient level of permanence for the statement to qualify as libel. However, other Internet services such as Internet Relay Chat (IRC) or real-time audio-visual programming may lack sufficient permanence to support the characterization of a statement as libel.

As noted above, one of the elements of a claim of defamation is communication to a third party. When the Internet is being used to communicate the defamatory statement, some type of proof may be necessary to show that the defamatory statement was actually read by a third party. However, the communication requirement will likely be met when a defamatory statement is sent to third parties by e-mail or list servers or posted to a Usenet news group.

Another Internet-related issue is the extent to which Internet Service Providers may be liable for distribution of the defamatory statement. Under English law, distributors such as booksellers are entitled to protection under an innocent dissemination defence if the

---

[5]  Slander is often defined as a spoken form of defamation while libel is generally defamation in print or in a medium that possess some degree of permanence.

distributor can prove that he or she was not negligent in the distribution. The defence is not available if the distributor knew or should have known of the defamatory statements, or knew or should have known that the publication being sold was of a character that it would likely contain defamatory material. By contrast, a publisher who repeats or republishes any libellous statement is liable in the same manner as the original publisher.

The issue of whether the innocent distributor defence is available may be most relevant with respect to ISPs who provide access to a wide range of Usenet newsgroups.[6] Due to the volume of materials posted each day, it is not feasible to screen the materials coming in on Usenet from other sites. However, many Usenet sites are known for containing statements about identifiable persons that may be libellous.

Interactive communications on Usenet newsgroups are regarded as an important activity on the Internet, and any finding that an ISP in a particular country is liable for Usenet materials coming from other sites would effectively force all ISPs to stop carrying Usenet. On the other hand, an ISP may still be held liable for defamatory statements contained on Web pages hosted by that ISP or on chat facilities provided by that ISP, or contained in Usenet messages originating at that ISP's Usenet server, especially if that ISP is provided with notice of such activity and fails to take action to remove or cancel the offending material.[7] An IAP should not be liable merely for providing networking services to connect a Web server containing libellous material where such Web server is owned and maintained by a customer at the customer's premises.

The potential liability for defamatory statements is a serious concern of ISPs, IAPs and online service operators. Many operate facilities, such as Web hosting, e-mail discussion lists and Usenet newsgroup servers, that can be used by subscribers to publish defamatory statements to third parties.

---

[6]    This defense is discussed in more detail *supra*.

[7]    Offending material carried on a service provider's web server can be removed while offending messages sent through Usenet can be cancelled by sending a cancel message into the Usenet network.

In two Internet-related defamation actions, US courts appeared to establish a proportional relationship between a service provider's liability for libellous statements posted by their subscribers and the amount of editorial control the service provider sought to exercise over such online content.[8] However, legal developments in this direction can discourage service providers from taking any steps to regulate content.

Some jurisdictions have amended their defamation legislation to provide a defence for a party who is not primarily responsible for the publication of the defamatory statement, who has taken reasonable care and who had no reason to suspect that his or her assistance was facilitating the publication of the defamatory statement. For instance, see the UK's *Defamation Act* (1996), cited earlier. Such provisions should mean that ISPs would not be liable for defamatory materials placed on their system where the posting was done by a person over whom they had no effective control. However, such ISPs must still take precautionary steps, such as by publishing and enforcing "use policies" in order to rely on the statutory defence.

In some cases the ISP is put into a Catch-22 situation. On one hand, the very act of exercising editorial control over Internet content may put the ISP in a situation where it will be liable for defamatory statements circulated on the Internet. On the other hand, it may have to exercise such editorial control in order to rely on the defence that it took reasonable care and did not know, or have reason to believe, that it was contributing to the publication of a defamatory statement. A number of ISPs in the UK are lobbying for changes in the law so

---

[8]   In *Cubby, Inc. v. CompuServe, Inc.*, 776 F. Supp. 135 (S.D.N.Y. 1991), the court accepted CompuServe's argument that it was acting as a distributor rather than a publisher and should not be held responsible for libelous statements posted by one of its subscribers. However, in a later case, *Stratton Oakmont, Inc. v. Prodigy Services Co.*, 1995 NY Misc.LEXIS 229, 23 Media L. Rep. 1794, where a service provider attempted to exercise some editorial control over content posted to its system, the service provider, Prodigy, was held liable as a publisher. Prodigy had assumed a duty to screen offensive messages from its service and was liable as a publisher based on its use of content guidelines, using forum leaders who were responsible for enforcing the guidelines, and use of software to pre-screen messages for certain obscenities.

that only the content provider (i.e., the person who uploads the content) will be responsible for ensuring the material is legal.[9]

One issue currently under discussion is whether a different standard should apply to defamatory statements made on the Internet in circumstances where the defamed person may have the same ability to communicate with a large audience as the person making the defamatory statement, and accordingly can rebut the statement or correct an error. Access to the courts is arguably not as necessary when defamed individuals have the capability themselves to set the public record straight and therefore avoid or substantially reduce the potential damage to their reputation. This may be true if the communication was made on a chat facility, Listserv or Usenet. However, if the defamatory statement was made on an electronic newsletter (whether Web-based or using a mailing list) then the defamed person may not have access to the same audience which could number tens of thousands of readers.

Another issue related to defamation on the Internet is the test to be applied to statements which are circulated between different jurisdictions where the laws of such countries apply different standards according to the identity of the plaintiff. For example, the US has applied a narrow definition of defamation to make it compatible with principles of First Amendment free speech. Specifically, an "actual malice" standard[10] is required to find liability in cases involving defamation of public officials or public figures.[11] However, actual malice need not be shown where the plaintiffs are not public figures, have not put themselves in the public eye and are not involved in issues of public concern.[12] The rationale for this distinction is that non-public figures do not have the same level of access to the media to rebut or disprove damaging statements.

---

[9]   Tim Hardy, "UK Internet Services Seek Legal Change," *The National Law Journal* (P. B07) Monday, August 25, 1997 <http//www.ljx.com/internet/0825ukisp.html>.

[10]  Knowledge that the statement was false or reckless disregard of whether it was false or not.

[11]  *New York Times v. Sullivan*, 376 U.S. 254 (1964).

[12]  However, the absence of actual malice can limit awards to actual damages.

In the case of defamatory statements circulated on the Internet, a plaintiff must consider whether it will lose the protection afforded to private citizens by participating in a public discussion such as on Usenet. The Internet provides many forms of discussion facilities including Usenet, mailing lists and chat areas (conference rooms and Web sites where participants can become well-known within a certain group). A defendant to a libel action could argue that the public figure standard should apply and that the defendant should not be liable for false statements made against the plaintiff as long as they were not made with malice or recklessly.

A further issue arising from defamation on the Internet is the determination of the appropriate forum for prosecution of the claim. A defamatory message posted on Usenet or placed on a Web page is accessible from almost any country in the world. This may result in forum shopping by a prospective plaintiff seeking to bring the action in a jurisdiction with strict defamation laws.

Because of the nature of the Internet, it may be difficult for a plaintiff to obtain relief against publishers of defamatory, infringing or other forms of illegal material. For instance, a Web site named "McSpotlight" was launched in February 1996, and provides access to many files containing highly defamatory information concerning McDonalds, including a leaflet published by Helen Steel and David Morris. Although McDonalds was able to obtain a judgment for damages against Steel and Morris in an amount of approximately US $93,000 (at a significant cost to McDonalds), McDonalds was less successful in dealing with the McSpotlight Web site. The McSpotlight Web site is mirrored in a number of jurisdictions, and the volunteers who operate it have vowed to launch new sites if any existing site is shut down.

Similar difficulties were faced by German authorities, who attempted to block a Dutch Web site called "Radikal" which was used by a group of activists to publish subversive material, including instructions on how to sabotage a railway station. Copies of the Dutch Web site were placed on over 40 mirror Web sites before the site could be closed.

## 8.3  ILLEGAL CONTENT

### (a)  Obscenity and Pornography

While the number of sex-related Web sites comprise only 2-3% of the commercial sites available on the Web, industry sources indicate that such sites represent a substantially higher source of revenue than other Web sites. Sex-related searches make up approximately 10% to 20% of visits to Web sites. It is estimated that one-quarter of Internet users have visited an adult-oriented site.[13]

The laws of many jurisdictions contain prohibitions on the transmission or distribution of obscene materials. In some cases, these laws deal specifically with online behaviour. For example, the US *Communications Decency Act* of 1996[14] ("CDA") sought to impose criminal liability on those who knowingly and intentionally use their telecommunications systems or permit such system to be used, for the creation and transmission of obscene, indecent or patently offensive materials to minors. However, on June 26, 1997, the US Supreme Court struck down two key provisions.[15]

Even where legislation regulating the transmission or distribution of obscene materials does not deal specifically with electronic transmissions, such legislation can likely be applied to prosecute an individual who engages in the prohibited activity using the Internet as a transmission medium.

Obscenity is defined in subsection 163(8) of the Canadian *Criminal Code* as any publication whose dominant characteristic is the undue exploitation of sex, or of sex together with crime, horror, cruelty or violence. The question of whether the dominant theme of a publication is the undue exploitation of sex is determined by

---

[13]   *USA Today*, August 20, 1997.

[14]   *The Communications Decency Act* of 1996 ("CDA"), 47 U.S.C. s.223, part of the *Telecommunications Act* of 1996, signed into law Feb. 8, 1996, Pub. L. No. 104-104, codified, as amended, at 47 U.S.C. s.151 (1996). The American Civil Liberties Union ("ACLU") challenged certain sections of the CDA as infringing on First Amendment rights (*ACLU v. Reno*).

[15]   See Chapter 2.

reference to a "community standards test."[16] If it is determined that the material involves the undue exploitation of sex, the portrayal of sex is then examined in context to determine whether it is the dominant theme of the work as a whole, or whether it falls within a "public good" exemption by being essential to a wider artistic, literary or other similar purpose.

The *Criminal Code* contains two distinct offences related to obscenity. Subsection 163(1) prohibits the production or distribution of obscene materials. This provision has been held to be a "strict liability offence". This means that a lack of knowledge that the material in question exceeded community standards will not be sufficient to avoid liability.

Subsection 163(2) of the *Criminal Code* makes it an offence to knowingly sell or expose to public view, or to have possession for the purposes of selling or exposing to public view, obscene materials. In contrast to subsection 163(1), the Crown must prove that the accused had subjective knowledge of the content and nature of the obscene material to prove the elements of a charge under subsection 163(2).

Another related provision of the *Criminal Code* that should be considered is section 163.1, which deals with child pornography. Child pornography is defined in subsection 163.1(1) as any visual representation depicting a minor (i.e., a person under the age of 18 years) engaging in sexual activity, or having as its dominant characteristic the depiction of a minor's sexual organs or anal region, or any written material or visual representation advocating or counselling such sexual activity with a minor. This provision makes it an offence to publish, distribute or possess child pornography unless an applicable defense can be established.

It should be emphasized that the mere possession of child pornography, even if not for the purpose of publication or distribution, is an offence. This means that an Internet user who visits a site that displays child pornography or who downloads and stores

---

[16]   See *R. v. Butler* (1992), [1992] 2 W.W.R. 577, [1992] 1 S.C.R. 452, 134 N.R. 81, 8 C.R.R. (2d) 1, 89 D.L.R. (4th) 449, 78 Man. R. (2d) 1, 16 W.A.C. 1, [1992] 1 R.C.S. 452, 70 C.C.C. (3d) 129, 11 C.R. (4th) 137 (S.C.C.) reconsideration refused [1993] 2 W.W.R. lxi (S.C.C.).

such images on the user's hard disk may be committing a criminal act.

## (b) Hate Messages

The Internet is attracting the attention of many groups who are seeking an efficient and inexpensive means to disseminate hate messages to millions of potential recipients, especially the young, who are heavy users of the Internet. These groups use the Internet to spread their message, recruit new members and even provide instructions on such topics as bomb making.

A number of jurisdictions have enacted legislation to prohibit activities that lead to the incitement of hatred. In Canada, the *Criminal Code* contains three sections dealing with hate propaganda. Subsection 319(1) provides that any one who, by communicating[17] statements[18] in any public place, incites hatred against any identifiable group that is likely to lead to a breach of the peace is guilty of an offence. Subsection 319(2) provides that any one who, by communicating statements, other than in private conversation, wilfully promotes hatred against any identifiable group, is guilty of an offence.

Section 318 makes it an offence to advocate or promote[19] genocide (killing or inflicting conditions to destroy members of a group). In contrast to section 319, this offence is not limited to statements made in a public place or those made other than in private conversation.

A third provision, section 320, permits a court to authorize the seizure of copies of a publication reasonably believed to be hate propaganda. "Hate propaganda" is defined as

---

[17] "Communicating" is defined non-exhaustively in section 319 as including "communicating by telephone, broadcasting or other audible or visible means."

[18] "Statements" is defined non-exhaustively in section 319 to include "words spoken or written or recorded electronically or electro-magnetically or otherwise."

[19] In *R. v. Keegstra*, [1990] 3 S.C.R. 697, 1 C.R. (4th) 129, 77 Alta. L.R. (2d) 193, 117 N.R. 1 [1991] 2 W.W.R. 1, 114 A.R. 81, 61 C.C.C. (3d) 1, 3 C.R.R. (2d) 193, [1990] 3 R.C.S. 697 (S.C.C.) the Supreme Court of Canada interpreted "promotes," in the context of section 319(2), as active support or instigation or something more than mere encouragement or advancement of hatred.

". . . any writing, sign or visible representation that advocates or promotes genocide or the communication of which by any person would constitute an offence under section 319."

Various other federal and provincial laws may also contain prohibitions on communications which promote hatred. For instance, section 13 of the *Canadian Human Rights Act* prohibits the communication of hatred by means of a telecommunications undertaking. Provisions in provincial human rights codes may also be applicable. For instance, section 14(1) of Saskatchewan's *Human Rights Code* prohibits the publication or display of "any notice, symbol, emblem, article, statement or other representation which exposes, or tends to expose, to hatred, ridicules, belittles or otherwise affronts the dignity of any person because of his or her race, creed, religion, colour, sex, marital status, disability, age, nationality, ancestry or place of origin."

Although Canadian courts have not yet considered many of the above-mentioned provisions in the context of the Internet, it appears likely that they would be held to be applicable to Internet-related activities. For instance, a Canadian Human Rights Tribunal hearing in October 1997 had to consider whether Ernst Zundel was responsible for disseminating hate material on a site in California that bears his name and is accessible to Canadians.

### (c)  Publication Bans

Some countries impose legal restrictions on the publication or dissemination of certain types of information in specified circumstances. These restrictions may be for the purpose of ensuring that an accused obtains a fair trial in a criminal matter. For example, a Canadian court prohibited the publication of information from a murder trial in order to protect the rights of the accused person's spouse who was charged with the same offence and whose trial was to be held at a subsequent date.[20] Information relating to the initial proceeding nevertheless became available on a number of newsgroups carried through the Internet in violation of the publication ban.

---

[20]  Murder trials of Paul Bernardo and Karla Homolka.

In other cases, certain points of view or speakers may be the subject of the ban. For example, the UK imposed a broadcasting ban on the transmission of the views of any official representative of the Sinn Fein political party due to its alleged involvement with terrorism.

Another common type of publication ban concerns opinion polls published close to upcoming elections. For instance, the *Canada Elections Act* provides that "no person shall broadcast, publish, or disseminate the results of an opinion survey respecting how electors will vote in an election" within three days of the actual balloting. Violators are subject to a maximum fine of $1,000 or one year in jail.

During the last few days prior to the June 2, 1997 Canadian federal election, a number of Canadian Web sites established associated sites in the United States in order to avoid the prohibition ban. However, the publication or dissemination of the prohibited information through the use of a foreign Web site may not provide full protection. If some of the activities relating to the dissemination of the prohibited information take place in Canada, an offence may still occur in Canada.

In May 1997, *Republique des Pyrenees*, a daily French newspaper, defied a similar law barring publication of opinion polls just prior to national elections. The fine for violation of the French law is approximately US $88,000. However, a number of foreign-based publications published poll results on their Web sites which were popular with French Web surfers.

Other countries such as Belgium, Italy and Spain have similar bans. However, a number of countries, including the United Kingdom and the United States, do not impose any restrictions on the publication of poll results, including in the period immediately prior to an election.

## 8.4  SERVICE PROVIDER LIABILITY ISSUES

As noted in the preceding sections, ISPs and online service providers face potential liability due to not only their own actions, but also those of their subscribers. Such liability may arise under copyright laws, the laws of defamation, export control legislation, and criminal laws applicable to obscenity, indecency, gambling, dissemination of hate materials and other criminal offenses.

Aside from simply providing access to the Internet, many ISPs provide users with the ability to upload materials to a shared Web server that may then be accessed by other users. Many ISPs also operate a Usenet news server which can be used to post or read messages. Some also set up e-mail distribution lists (or list servers) that may be managed by a particular user for an additional fee.

Internet users may take advantage of these facilities to upload unlawful, defamatory or infringing materials. Examples of unlawful material includes hate propaganda, materials which are subject to a publication ban, pornography and obscene material. Infringing materials may include works which infringe copyright, trademark or privacy laws.

In almost all cases, users can upload content directly to the ISP's storage devices without such material being reviewed by the ISP. In the case of a Usenet news server, messages are received from other sites in addition to those that may be posted by local users.

Reviewing or otherwise screening content uploaded by subscribers of even a closed system, such as an online service, is not usually practical. For instance, the number of screens of information transmitted by CompuServe on a weekly basis has approached one billion.[21]

In considering potential liability for materials distributed on the Internet, it is important to distinguish between an operator of a Web site, where material is created and stored, and a service provider, such as an IAP that is simply providing communication of the work. Liability is more likely to be imposed on the former, especially in cases where the operator of a Web site is informed of the presence of harmful materials on its system and does nothing to remove them. In the case of defamatory statements, the Web site operator may be considered to be a re-broadcaster of such statements and liable to the same extent as the author.

---

[21]    Stuckey, Kent D., *Internet and Online Law* p. xxii.

While an ISP that is simply a conduit for content which originates from third parties generally may not be liable for such content, it may be incumbent on the ISP to take reasonable steps to remove such information once it is made aware of its harmful nature. The degree of control that can be exercised by an ISP may be closely correlated to the degree of responsibility that will be imputed by the law.

While civil liability under the common law is centred around duties of diligence, Quebec's civil law approaches liability from the perspective of the prejudice that was suffered. The extent of liability imposed under the civil law may be greater because a person's unreasonable conduct that causes loss or prejudice requires him or her to provide compensation for the damages suffered.

In some jurisdictions, attempts are being made to clarify the liability of ISPs for materials carried on their system. For instance, reforms proposed by the Canadian Advisory Council on the Information Highway in its *Final Report of the Copyright Subcommittee*,[22] included a recommendation that operators of BBSs (and presumably ISPs), should be liable for materials carried on their systems as they are not common carriers. However, the operators should have a defence if they do not have actual or constructive knowledge of the infringing material and acted reasonably to limit abuses.

It is arguable that an ISP could be prosecuted under the criminal law for aiding and abetting in the commission of an offence, such as the distribution of pornography or publication of hate literature. For example, liability could arise for "aiding" in the commission of an offence if the ISP was aware that the network was being used to commit an offence and performed some act for the purpose of aiding the offence. Similarly, liability for "abetting" the commission of an offence can arise if the person encourages its commission; this generally requires prior knowledge that the offence will be committed. If an ISP was aware that the network was being used on a continuing basis for the commission of an offence, and having the

---

[22]   See Information Highway Advisory Council, *Copyright and the Information Highway: Final Report of the Copyright Subcommittee* (Ottawa: Information Highway Advisory Council Secretariat, 1995).

means to do so, took no action to prevent its continuation, the ISP may be liable for having encouraged the commission of the offence.

A guiding principle that should be followed when analyzing the potential liability of online service providers is that liability should be determined based not on how a particular entity is categorized, but rather based on the activities carried on by the entity in the course of transmitting information or otherwise facilitating its availability.

The Canadian Association for Internet Providers (CAIP) has responded to some of the concerns regarding service provider liability in its Code of Conduct.[23] Section 5 provides that CAIP members will not knowingly host illegal content and that CAIP members will share information about illegal content for this purpose. While such rules will not in themselves provide immunity to ISPs, they may help an ISP demonstrate an intention to keep harmful content from being carried on its system.

### (a)  Defamation

A person may be liable for communicating intentionally, or by a negligent act, a defamatory statement to a person other than the person defamed. A person may also be liable for intentionally and unreasonably failing to remove defamatory matter on property in his possession or control. Accordingly, an ISP Web site operator or online service provider may be found to have "published" material provided by third parties if they fail to take reasonable steps to prevent the dissemination of defamatory material.

In August 1997, America Online was named as a co-defendant in a US $30 million libel suit filed by White House aide Sidney Blumenthal against Matt Drudge, whose Internet column, The Drudge Report, was hosted on AOL.[24] The potential of third-party liability for defamation is a serious concern of ISPs, IAPs and online service operators. Many operate facilities, such as Web hosting, e-mail

---

[23]   See <http://www.caip.ca/caipcodf.htm>.

[24]   Matt Drudge had broadcast on August 10, 1997 that the then new advisor to President Clinton, writer Sidney Blumenthal, had a "spousal abuse past" that had been concealed. Although Drudge later retracted the story, Mr. Blumenthal and his wife sued alleging 21 counts of defamation, false light, invasion of privacy and intentional infliction of emotional distress.

discussion lists and Usenet newsgroup servers, that can be used by subscribers to publish defamatory statements.

As noted above, in two Internet-related defamation cases, US courts appeared to establish a proportional relationship between a service provider's liability for libelous statements posted by their subscribers and the amount of editorial control the service provider sought to exercise over such online content.[25]

However, the decision in the *Prodigy* case may have been effectively overruled by the "Good Samaritan" provisions of the CDA of 1996[26] which provides a defence against civil liability for a service provider or user of an interactive service in respect to any action taken in good faith to restrict access to or availability of material that the service provider or user considers to be obscene, lewd, lascivious, filthy, excessively violent, harassing or otherwise objectionable. The CDA also contains a provision that "no provider or user of an interactive computer service shall be treated as the publisher or speaker of any information provided by another information content provider."

The "Good Samaritan" provisions of the CDA were applied in *Zehran v. America Online, Inc.*[27] An unknown person had posted messages on America Online bulletin boards falsely purporting to advertise the availability from Zehran of products glorifying the bombing of the Federal Building in Oklahoma city in which 168 people were killed. Zehran had notified America Online of the messages and they were removed. However, America Online did not take any steps to block further bogus messages from being placed on its system.

Zehran sued America Online claiming the service provider was negligent in allowing the notices to remain and appear on AOL's bulletin board despite having received notice and complaints from

---

[25]  *Cubby, Inc. v. CompuServe, Inc.*, 776 F. Supp. 135 (S.D.N.Y. 1991); *Stratton Oakmont, Inc. v. Prodigy Services Co.*, 1995 NY Misc.LEXIS 229, 23 Media L. Rep. 1794.

[26]  The Good Samaritan provisions are codified at 47 U.S.C. s. 230(c)(1)-(2).

[27]  Civil Action 96-952-A, E.D. Virginia, March 21, 1997. The decision was subsequently upheld by the 4th US Circuit Court of Appeals, 97-1523 (4th Ctr.), 1997 WL 701309 (Nov. 12, 1997). See <http://zeus.bna.com/e-law/cases/zeran.html>.

Zehran following the appearance of the first advertisement. The US District Court held that the CDA preempts a cause of action in negligence against an interactive computer service provider arising from the distribution of allegedly defamatory material through the provider's electronic bulletin board. This preemption is applicable to any cause of action brought after the enactment of the CDA even though the events giving rise to the claim occurred before the CDA became effective.[28]

The "Good Samaritan" provisions may also shield operators of Web sites or other interactive computer services from other forms of liability. In *Doe v. America Online Inc.*,[29] the Circuit Court for the 5th Judicial Circuit (Palm Beach County, Florida) held that claims against AOL based on use of the service by a subscriber to market child pornography were barred by 47 U.S.C. s. 230.

In Canada, the common law recognizes an "innocent dissemination" defense which may be especially important in respect of activities conducted by ISPs. The innocent dissemination can be invoked if:

- the person did not have knowledge of the libel contained in the material being disseminated;

- there was nothing in the material, or in the circumstances in which it was communicated to, or disseminated by the person, that ought to have led the person to suppose that it contained a libel; and

- at the time of the dissemination of the material the person was not negligent in failing to know that it contained libel.

If the foregoing conditions are met, the person who disseminates the work should not be liable for its publication.[30] However, a distributor who is made aware of the harmful nature of the

---

[28] The immunity afforded by the CDA applies to all suits filed after its enactment, notwithstanding when the operative facts arose. Section 230(d)(3) provides, in pertinent part, that "[no] cause of action may be brought and no liability may be imposed under any State or local law that is inconsistent with this section."

[29] Case No. CL 97-63 (June 26, 1997).

[30] Based on Raymond E. Brown, *The Law of Defamation in Canada*, Second Edition at 7.12(6).

information has the duty to withdraw it, failing which, that person may be held liable for the damage caused by the statements.

## (b) Infringement of Third-Party Rights

An ISP may be liable for its role in allowing a subscriber or user to utilize its facilities to infringe the rights of another. For example, under Canada's *Copyright Act*, any person who "authorizes" any act which is an infringement of copyright is deemed to be a party to such infringement. The concept of "authorization" has been judicially defined to include such acts as the countenance, sanctioning or encouragement of infringing activities by other persons.

Recent case law in the United States also suggests that operators and owners of online systems or networks may be liable for infringement of copyright by other parties in certain circumstances. For example, the operation of computer bulletin boards which are used to upload or download unauthorized copies of video games[31] or photographs[32] may constitute copyright infringement. In some cases the courts have stated that a lack of knowledge by the defendant of the specific unauthorized copying or the fact that the systems operator did not copy the infringing material was inconsequential to the question of whether there was copyright infringement. A more specific analysis of liability for copyright infringement can be found in Chapter 5.

Even when the facts do not support a finding that an ISP is liable for direct infringement, the ISP may nevertheless be liable under US copyright laws for contributory infringement. Generally, liability for contributory infringement can be established if a person with knowledge of the infringing activity of another person, induces, materially contributes to, or causes such activity. An ISP may be deemed to have sufficient knowledge to be liable for contributory infringement if it receives notice that a user is infringing the copyright of another person and it takes no action to prevent the continuation of such infringing activity. However, an ISP may not be

---

[31]    *Sega Entertainment Ltd. v. Maphia*, 857 F. Supp. 679 (N.D. Ca. 1994).

[32]    *Playboy Enterprises, Inc. v. Frena*, 839 F. Supp. 1552 (M.D. Fla. 1993) where the BBS operator was held liable for direct infringement of Playboy's display rights, for allowing its users to download infringing copies of Playboy photographs.

liable for infringement in respect of incidental copies automatically made on its system as part of a process initiated by a third party, if the ISP did not take any action to facilitate the unauthorized copying other than installing and maintaining the system. This may be the case, for example, where a Usenet news server exchanges messages with other similar services.[33]

It can be argued that an ISP cannot reasonably be expected to be aware of the contents of the vast amounts of information which may be uploaded to, downloaded from, and accessed through its system, or to know whether, in any particular case, the owner of the copyright has consented to the copying or distribution of any work by means of its system. However, it would be reasonable to expect an ISP to establish rules governing the use of its system, which may include prohibitions against the distribution of material that infringes the rights of third parties. It is also reasonable to expect an ISP to take appropriate steps to remove any infringing material upon learning that such material is stored on its system. Finally, the ISP may also have an obligation to take reasonable steps to restrict access to a particular user who, to the knowledge of the ISP, is obtaining access to infringing materials stored on an interconnected network.

The *Digital Millennium Copyright Act of 1998*[34] would provide limitations on the liability of service providers for online infringement of copyright. If certain conditions are met, ISPs would be shielded from liability for infringement resulting from:

- routing activities
- caching activities
- hosting activities
- operation of searches and facilities

---

[33]  *Religious Technology Centre v. Netcom Online Communications Services, Inc.*, 907 F. Supp. 1361 (N.D. Cal. 1995). In this case, a critic of the Church of Scientology had posted portions of its texts to the Internet "alt.religion.scientology" Usenet newsgroup.

[34]  Bill s. 2037, passed by the Senate May 14, 1998.

### (c) Hosting of Unlawful Materials

#### (i) Hate Messages

Under Canadian legislation dealing with hate material, an ISP could be liable for "communicating statements in any public place" if it permits hate messages to be transmitted on its system. Liability will depend on the scope of access that users have to the system, which will determine, in turn, whether the system could be considered a public place. While the ISP is providing a medium through which others can communicate statements, the question of whether or not the ISP has any responsibility for the contents of such statements will depend on the control that the ISP can exercise over such contents. The ISP may be found liable for "communicating statements" if its representatives are aware of the contents of hate messages being transmitted through the system and they have the capability of deleting such messages but fail to do so.

#### (ii) Publication Bans

Where there is a prohibition against the "publication" of certain information, an ISP could be in violation of the ban, if it permits the distribution on its system of restricted information of which it is aware. This follows from the wide definition of the term "publish" to include acts such as to cause to be seen or read. The making available of a news group containing a large body of unrelated information which includes a small portion of information covered by a publication ban should not constitute an act of publication if the ISP is not specifically aware of the prohibited material. Conversely, highlighting information covered by the ban and calling attention to its availability or making available a news group, the focus of which is a discussion of banned information, may constitute a publication in violation of the ban.[35]

---

[35]    For example, the name of a newsgroup may provide sufficient notice that it may contain discussions or content that is subject to a publication ban.

### (iii)  *Pornographic or Obscene Materials*

Another growing concern for ISPs is liability for pornographic or obscene materials placed on their systems.[36] In some jurisdictions, ignorance of the nature or presence of the obscene material may be a defence if the accused made an honest and reasonable mistake of fact. However, a mistake of law, which causes the accused to believe that material is not obscene, where the person knows the nature or presence of such material, may not be a defence. Unfortunately, there is usually not a simple test for determining whether any given material is obscene within the meaning of relevant legislation governing such conduct.[37]

For the reasons noted above with respect to banned information, an ISP may be liable for having published, distributed or circulated pornographic material where the ISP knows such material is available on its system and the ISP has the capability of deleting or restricting access to such material but fails to do so. For instance, a Canadian ISP could be charged with distribution of obscene material under subsection 163(1) of the *Criminal Code* for its role in facilitating access to such material. It will be a question of fact in each case as to whether the ISP has sufficient knowledge and involvement to be a party to the publication, distribution or circulation of the information. The risk of liability would be greater where the ISP (or another person involved in its operation, such as the moderator of a news group) takes an active role in reviewing the material prior to its distribution on the system. An ISP would be less likely to face liability in respect of materials which are available from other Internet sites and where its only role is to provide connectivity to the Internet.

An ISP can minimize its risk of liability by taking certain steps to help establish a due diligence defense to a charge of publication or distribution under subsection 163(1) of the *Criminal Code*. This

---

[36]  Even if an ISP has the resources and desire to screen its system for pornographic materials, this may not always be possible. Unlike images in paper form, electronic images must be viewed through software which can reconstruct the visual image. There are currently more than a dozen commonly used formats for representing images digitally and countless proprietary formats.

[37]  Another complicating issue is determining which jurisdiction's standards should be applied.

includes implementing an "acceptable use policy" that clearly prohibits the transmission of obscene material by its subscribers. Preferably, this should be incorporated into each subscriber's agreement with the ISP. An ISP should also review any obscene material brought to its attention and respond appropriately to such behaviour.

In some cases a specific exemption may be available to an IAP, an ISP or an Online Service Provider. For example, US-based ISPs may be entitled to rely on a "provider exception" in the CDA which excludes liability for an entity that merely provides connection to a system, facility or network not under the entity's control, including the transmission, downloading, storage or other activities incidental to the provision of access that do not include the creation of the content. The CDA also provides a defence for an entity that has undertaken good faith reasonable measures to prevent access by minors to prohibited materials. The focus of liability under the CDA is on those who create and assist in the distribution of prohibited content. IAPs and online service providers are therefore not made liable for indecent material accessed by means of their services. IAPs, ISPs and online service providers based in the US should take the steps necessary to avail themselves of the defences and exceptions available under the CDA.

Another factor that should be considered in determining the potential liability of an ISP is that most Web browser programs support viewing of images stored in GIF or JPG formats. However, there are dozens of different image file formats which can be utilized to store photographs digitally. Without appropriate software capable of reconstructing and displaying an image, an ISP may not be capable of reviewing the contents of images stored on its system even if it wishes to do so.

# 9

# Information Security and the Internet

In order for electronic commerce across the Internet to reach its full potential, the infrastructure must first be capable of providing the same levels of trust found in traditional business exchanges. This will occur only if the parties involved in Internet commerce can be assured of the confidentiality, security and integrity of the messages transmitted via the Internet.

## 9.1 INFORMATION SECURITY REQUIREMENTS

### (a) Confidentiality and Integrity

Unlike messages sent through an organization's internal system, messages sent through the Internet must pass through a number of intermediate systems. Each stop provides an opportunity for interception.

E-mail messages are especially at risk. These are almost always sent in a plain ASCII text format and can be easily read by anyone who has access to the mail directories of a particular system. They are also susceptible to being scanned or filtered by automatic programs looking for certain key words.

The most effective way to prevent interception of messages transmitted through an open system such as the Internet is to use encryption. Specifically, encryption can provide a "secure form" to protect the confidentiality of messages sent between a user's Web browser and a Web server that is used to collect confidential information.

If a secure form cannot be used, an alternative would be to include a prominent warning regarding the potential loss of confidentiality on any Web form where confidential information is being sought or may be provided. For instance, the National Association of Securities Dealers allows for the submission of complaints against a brokerage firm or one of its brokers using a complaint form that can be filed online. NASD advises anyone wishing to submit a complaint through the Internet that "[e]lectronic transmissions on the Internet are not always secure" and that the person wishing to file a complaint "may wish to communicate only basic information to [NASD] using the Internet, and send any specific confidential or sensitive information by regular mail or [through] a telephone call [...]."

Encryption is a process for scrambling messages to make it difficult and time-consuming for an unauthorized recipient to unscramble and view the contents. The use of encryption can provide assurances regarding the confidentiality of a communication, i.e., to ensure that the message remains private. Encryption can also protect the integrity of a transaction, i.e., to ensure that the communication is not modified in the course of transmission. The protection of message integrity may also involve the utilization of a time-stamping function to provide a means of verifying the time of transmission of a message.

It may be desirable or even necessary to utilize encryption to protect electronic communications for reasons other than to facilitate electronic commerce. Various data protection laws may require those entities maintaining personal information on systems accessible through the Internet to exercise reasonable forms of technological protection to safeguard the confidentiality of such data, including its confidentiality in the course of transmission. For example, the UK Data Registrar has recommended that prior to being asked to provide personal data, Internet users should first be warned that the Internet is not a secure medium, absent the use of strong encryption, and be provided with an opportunity to cancel the transaction.

### (b)  Authentication and Non-Repudiation

The use of an electronic communication system to effect a legal transaction or to serve as an authorization gives rise to several evidentiary issues where no physical document is created, or no original signed document is exchanged between the parties. One such issue is the need to authenticate that an electronic message originated with the person by whom it purports to have been sent; in other words, in the absence of an original signed document, the courts must be satisfied as to the genuineness of an "electronic signature."

Each of the parties involved in a communication or transaction will wish to ensure that the other party may not repudiate that party's actions. The recipient of a message will want to ensure that the sender cannot later deny that he or she had sent a particular message. As well, the sender will want to ensure that the recipient will not at a later date be able to deny receipt of the communication.

Internet e-mail is especially at risk of forgery. A message can be made to appear as if it were coming from a certain party without that party's knowledge or consent. Most Internet e-mail programs, and even the e-mail modules in Web browsers, allow users to specify and change information inserted in the "from" field of an e-mail message.

The authenticity of an electronic message may be established by the use of certain techniques to confirm the identity of the originator. These techniques could include the following: the use of confidential passwords, access codes or personal identification numbers assigned to individual users of the system; the use of smart cards or other physical cards to be used to obtain access to the system; and personal identification techniques involving some personal traits of the person sending the message.

Financial institutions carrying out business activities on the Internet have had to address the increased risk of operating in this new environment. The lack of face-to-face contact and the inability to utilize magnetic-stripped cards with secure ATM networks make it difficult to authenticate instructions from customers. Many financial institutions have responded by modifying their operation of account agreements to shift such risks onto their customers. However, the re-allocation of risk is not always possible and the use of simple passwords is generally not sufficient to confirm the identity of the sender of a transmission.

Financial institutions are also concerned with the authentication issue insofar as it raises questions as to their compliance with the *Proceeds of Crime (Money Laundering) Act* (Canada).[1] The

---

[1]    S.C. 1991, c. 26.

Regulations to the Act require a financial institution to authenticate the identity of its customer and in addition, to obtain a signature card from its customers. It would appear that the existing regulatory regime for money laundering does not yet adequately contemplate the role that the Internet will play in the delivery of financial services. However, changes to facilitate Internet banking are currently under consideration.

In view of the foregoing, attention is now turning to the use of cryptography and "certification authorities" to authenticate the identity of the sender of electronic messages. Such mechanisms provide a means not only for verifying the identify of the sender but also for providing for the non-repudiation of the transaction. These techniques are of particular interest to financial institutions not only because they facilitate financial transactions but also because such institutions may, subject to regulatory constraints, make ideal certification authorities.

## 9.2  CRYPTOGRAPHY AND CERTIFICATION AUTHORITIES

The more common system of encryption, technically referred to as symmetrical cryptography, is based on using a single secret key (i.e., the same password) for both encryption and decryption. However, even if a very secure encryption algorithm is used, symmetrical encryption systems have a number of inherent weaknesses.

The first problem is that both parties to a communication must share knowledge of the secret encryption key or password. This means that each party must trust the other party not to disclose the secret key.

The parties must also trust the method used to distribute secret key information. Key distribution is not a problem if the sender and recipient can meet in person to exchange information about the key or if they both have access to a secure channel for transmission of the secret key. However, key distribution can be a problem where the parties cannot exchange keys in private or where other parties may be involved.

Finally, since the private key is known to both parties, it is difficult to implement a non-repudiation function as the sender of a message can always claim that the message was forged by the recipient or a third party.

An asymmetric or "public key" encryption cryptosystem ("PKE") solves these problems.[2] PKE is based on the use of two mathematically related keys where a message encoded using one key requires the second key for decoding. A party engaged in electronic communication retains a "private" key which is not shared with other persons and which is used to encrypt messages sent electronically. That person creates or is assigned a "public" key which is shared with any persons to whom electronic messages are sent and can be used to de-crypt messages from the sender. While the keys are mathematically related, it is not feasible to determine the private key from knowledge of the public key. A certification authority may also be utilized to provide assurances that the public key really does belong to the person who purports to have published it.

While no system of cryptography can be guaranteed to be completely secure, public key cryptography is based on widely known mathematical algorithms which have been tested to such an extent that their integrity is universally accepted, and can be used as the basis for digital signatures.

General concern by Internet users regarding confidentiality have popularized programs such as Pretty Good Privacy Inc.'s PGP software, and competitive programs such as Entrust Technologies Ltd.'s Entrust/Solo, which utilize public key encryption to provide confidentiality and authentication.

The use of encryption is now prevalent in many Internet related products. Most popular Web browsers can automatically set up encrypted communication sessions when used to access a Web server that supports the use of encrypted communications.[3] They can therefore be used to allow a consumer to send personal information or a credit card number securely to a merchant's Web server.

---

[2]  Public key cryptography was invented by Whitfield Diffie and Martin Hellman of Stanford University in 1976. Details of PKE may be found in *Information Systems Security: A Practitioner's Guide* (Van Nostrand Reinhold, 1994).

[3]  Early versions of Netscape's Navigator Web browser were subjected to a number of attacks and a few flaws were discovered and rectified. However, these flaws were due to the implementation of PKE rather than defects in the underlying algorithms.

## 9.3 EXPORT CONTROLS

The full potential of the Internet for electronic commerce will not be achieved until consumers and users are confident of the security measures taken to protect transmitted information. Encryption is required to protect the confidentiality of private messages transmitted across the Internet and for authentication purposes. However, the import, export or use of encryption is regulated in a number of countries. The original rationale for the regulation of encryption, the Cold War, has long ended but restrictions on encryption have continued. Since most schemes being developed for the use of digital cash[4] or secure payment systems depend on the use of strong encryption, these legal restrictions also pose a threat to the continued commercial development of electronic money.

Most countries have enacted legislation governing the import or export of certain goods. Such restrictions may extend to computer hardware and software, including infrastructure components of the Internet, and may extend to any product that utilizes encryption technology (or even technical information describing the encryption technology). For example, in Canada, the *Export and Import Permits Act*[5] authorizes the Governor in Council to establish a list (called the Export Control List) of articles, the export of which is controlled for any one of several purposes.

The United States has also enacted laws which restrict the export of certain types of encryption technology.[6] Products which utilize weak forms of encryption, (i.e., with a key length of 40 bits or less)

---

[4]    For instance, *DigiCash* from DigiCash Corp and *CyberCash* from CyberCash Inc.

[5]    R.S.C. 1985, c. E-19, as amended.

[6]    US export restrictions on encryption technology are based on the *Arms Control Export Act* (ACEA), 22 U.S.C. S.2778, which allows the President to designate certain items as defense articles or defense services. These items make up the United States Munitions List. The import and export of items on the US Munitions List is controlled by regulations adopted under the ACEA, entitled the *International Traffic in Arms Regulations* (ITAR), 22 C.F.R. Sections 120-130 (1994). Section 121.1 Category XIII(b)(1) covers "components or software with the capability of maintaining secrecy or confidentiality of information or information systems" and therefore encompasses cryptographic software.

can be exported.[7] Products which utilize more powerful encryption cannot be exported without a permit. However, a 40-bit key length is not commercially secure. On January 30, 1997, Ian Goldberg, a graduate student at the University of California at Berkeley, was able to use a network of about 250 workstations to crack a 40-bit algorithm in less than four hours. Longer bit lengths increase the time required to crack an encrypted message exponentially. For instance, it would take about 22 years to break a 56-bit algorithm using the same resources.

The US restrictions on the export of encryption have been criticized by civil rights activists and the US software industry. They have also not been effective in keeping strong encryption technology out of the hands of parties adverse to the United States. Some of the world's best cryptographers live in countries other than the United States and many have been working for foreign commercial entities in the development of products that provide encryption that is substantially stronger than the products that US companies are permitted to export.

The initial response by the US government was to support the use of hardware incorporating what became known as the "Clipper Chip," which utilized a proprietary, supposedly more secure, encryption algorithm. This technology was combined with a proposal for a key escrow scheme, whereby a trusted third party would hold the backdoor keys in escrow with the government or law enforcement agencies having access to such keys in appropriate circumstances (i.e., by court order). The initial proposal was to utilize two government agencies as the escrow agents but this was later revised to allow two commercial entities to hold the backdoor keys. However, these proposals were strongly resisted due to a lack of trust in government authorities and concerns by the US computer industry as to whether it could successfully market such products internationally.

---

[7] The strength of an encryption process depends on the integrity of the encryption algorithm used (i.e., that it does not contain any "back doors" which could be used as opposed to a "brute force" attack) and the length of the encryption key (i.e., password) used to encrypt and decrypt the messages. The size of an encryption key is measured by the number of "bits" or the number of digits. The strength of the encryption increases exponentially as the key length is increased.

In recent years, the US government has proposed numerous variations of a key recovery scheme. The latest initiative would permit US companies to export encryption products which incorporate key lengths of up to 56-bit if such companies commit to the development of key recovery mechanisms into their products. The interest of the US government is to ensure that law enforcement agencies have the means of obtaining access to the encryption keys without notice to or the consent of the user (although presumably under court order). Canada would likely follow if an international consensus in favour of key escrow emerges.[8] However, a report by some of the most eminent cryptographic experts released May 21, 1997[9] has criticized even this latest initiative, labelling it as risky, costly and impractical.

There is growing support by industry groups for a relaxation of the US government's control over encryption technology. This has resulted in legislative initiatives such as the so-called "pro-code" Bill[10] and court actions attacking the constitutionality of US export restrictions on encryption products. One such case was *Bernstein v. United States Department of State,*[11] in which Bernstein claimed that the ACEA and ITAR were unconstitutional as violating his First and Fifth Amendment rights, and as being vague and overbroad. A United States District Court agreed and held that the government's licensing requirements for the export of encryption software was an

---

[8]    This is in contrast to the cold reception given to the Clipper initiatives which were rejected on the grounds of Canadian sovereignty (presumably because the US government had access to the keys).

[9]    <http://www.crypto.com/key_study>.

[10]   Senate Bill S.1726 (the "Pro-CODE" Bill) would specifically reject compulsory key escrow and permit the export of generally available software and hardware if a product with comparable security is available from a foreign source.

[11]   *Bernstein v. United States Department of State*, No. C95-CV-582 (N.D. Cal. Feb. 21/95). Daniel J. Bernstein, a graduate student, developed an encryption algorithm called *Snuffle* which he expressed both mathematically in an academic paper as well as in source code. The State Department denied Bernstein's request to export his algorithm. A State Department motion to dismiss the case on the grounds that the issues were not justiciable was denied and the Court found that the source code was held to be "speech" for the purposes of First Amendment analysis.

unconstitutional prior restraint on Bernstein's First Amendment rights of free speech.[12]

Some software vendors have taken a pragmatic approach. For example, IBM has used an innovative approach to obtain approval for the export of a 64-bit key length encryption scheme in its Lotus Notes product. It developed the product in such a way as to permit the US government to access a backdoor to 24 of the 64 bits, with the result that the government would then only need to decrypt 40 bits of the key. This allows the product to provide superior protection against commercial and potential foreign eavesdroppers while still providing an equivalent level of access by the US government as that provided by products with lower encryption levels.

Other software vendors have also grown impatient with contrived restrictions on the export of encryption products and have sought means to avoid such controls by partnering with foreign companies.[13] As long as the development and distribution of cryptographic code is performed outside the country that imposes export controls on such technology, such as the United States, and is carried out by non-citizens or nationals of that country, then in most cases such activities will not contravene domestic laws.[14] Any cryptographic code developed "off-shore" may then be imported into the domestic jurisdiction as well as being distributed internationally.

As mentioned above, Canada, like the US, also imposes export controls on certain goods, including encryption products. Most of such goods can be freely exported to Canada from the US subject to a bilateral agreement whereby Canada has agreed to restrict the further export of such US origin goods. However, unlike the US, Canada characterizes encryption technology as an information security product rather than as a munition.

---

[12] District Court decision filed August 25, 1997. However, the decision was very narrow in its application.

[13] For instance, Sun Microsystems purchased a minority stake in a Russian network software company, which was asked to develop encryption software for Sun which could then be exported to the world market.

[14] One caveat that must be observed is that the cryptographic code must be developed from scratch using resources available outside the domestic jurisdiction. Any transfer of technology from the domestic jurisdiction may constitute an unauthorized export.

Canada's system of export controls is administered by the Department of Foreign Affairs and International Trade (DFAIT). Exports from Canada are subject to the *Export and Import Permits Act* (the Act) and regulations adopted under the Act. Export permits are required if goods are: (a) destined for a country on the Area Control List (ACL) (regardless of the category of products being exported); (b) listed on the Export Control List (ECL); or (c) of US origin. Any nation that is subject to an embargo by the United Nations may require additional approvals over and above any export permit which may be required.

An Individual Export Permit (IEP) must be obtained in order to export any goods to any countries on the ACL unless an exemption to such requirement is granted under a particular General Export Permit (GEP). As well, an IEP is required for the export to any country of any goods that are listed on the ECL unless otherwise indicated in a particular ECL. Exporters must ensure that any conditions for the export of any goods set out in a General Export Permit are fulfilled and that the goods in question are covered by the GEP.

Unlike the US, Canada does not differentiate between low-grade and high-grade encryption. A product that incorporates any form of encryption would make the product subject to export controls and require an export permit (unless another exemption is applicable).

Also unlike the US, Canada provides an exemption for software that is made freely available to the public through widespread channels such as retail stores or is "in the public domain" (defined as "technology" or "software" which has been made available without restrictions upon its further dissemination).

General Software Note to Group 1 provides an exemption for "software" which is either:

- Generally available to the public by being:
    - Sold from stock at retail selling points, without restriction, by means of:
        - Over-the-counter transactions;
        - Mail order transactions; or

- Telephone call transactions; and

- Designed for installation by the user without further substantial support by the supplier; or

- "In the public domain."

If a product meets all the requirements set out in the above definition, then it appears that the product will not fall within the restrictions imposed in Group 1 of the ECL and no export permit would be required.

This exemption for publicly available software appears to have been exploited by at least one Canadian firm. Entrust Technologies Ltd., placed Entrust/Solo, a software program which provides data encryption, digital signature and data compression functionality, on its Web site.[15] The powerful encryption engine utilized by Entrust/Solo was developed in Canada, and allows Entrust to exploit the difference in regulations between the United States and Canada.

Entrust/Solo is subject to a shareware type licence agreement that restricts its use for commercial purposes to a 30-day evaluation period. However, the licence does not contain restrictions on "further dissemination."

Strong encryption products which can be exported to countries outside North America will be especially attractive to many multinational companies who can then standardize on a single product and utilize strong encryption for all inter-company communications, and not just those between branches located in North America.

Restrictions on export to countries on the ACL or under a United Nations embargo must still be observed, notwithstanding the availability of an exemption to the ECL for goods on the ECL or the fact that goods do not fall within the ECL. For instance, Entrust/Solo, which is freely available for downloading from Entrust Technologies Ltd.'s Web site, cannot be downloaded by users from Libya, Iran, Iraq, Cuba, Angola, Syria and North Korea. Requests from France and Singapore to download a copy of the software are also blocked

---

[15]    <http://www.entrust.com/>.  Signal 9 Solution, another Canadian firm located in "Silicon Valley North," also utilizes the publically available software exemption to market its virtual private network software.

because those countries have restrictions on the import of encryption technology.

Both Canada and the US provide a number of exemptions to permit the export of devices not capable of encrypting user-supplied data, devices used to descramble video or audio signals for a restricted consumer audience, and cryptographic equipment specially designed and limited for use in machines for banking or money transactions.[16]

US and Canadian restrictions on the export of encryption technology do not affect its internal use. It is therefore legal to use encryption technology within these jurisdictions and even to transmit an encrypted message internationally, as long as the encryption program itself is not transmitted.

The European Union has not as yet adopted a uniform set of rules governing the use or export of encryption technology. Some member states of the European Union, such as France, restrict the distribution, use or export of encryption without a government permit, while other countries are also considering such legislation.

A further issue relating to the use of encryption technology across the Internet is that because the Internet involves use of packet switching technology, a user typically has little control over which of many possible routes is followed when a message is sent to the destination. This means that an encrypted message may start and end its journey in countries that do not prohibit the use of encryption (even if the export of the technology is prohibited), but may be transmitted through a country which restricts the use of encryption and may therefore violate the law of the intermediate country.[17]

It should be noted that Canada's encryption policy is under review. In February 1998, the government released a discussion paper entitled "Setting a Cryptography Policy Framework for Electronic Commerce — Building Canada's Information, Economy and Society."[18] The discussion paper provides an introduction to cryptography, describes

---

[16]    For instance, see the Note to Item 1154 in group 1 of the ECL.

[17]    Even if the encryption technology itself does not pass through this intermediate country.

[18]    Task force on Electronic Commerce, Industry Canada, February 1998. See <http://strategis.ic.gc.ca/crypto>. For opposition, see <http://www.efc.ca/pages/crypto>.

Canada's current cryptography policy, sets out considerations for developing Canada's cryptography policy and lists policy options.

The Government of Canada recognizes that Canada's success in the 21st century depends increasingly on its ability to compete in the information economy and to support the growth of electronic commerce, which requires an environment where participants can feel secure.    An important enabler of electronic commerce is the availability of strong cryptographic tools.

Cryptography can be used to protect and safeguard confidential data stored or transmitted over public networks such as the Internet. Cryptography is also required for the implementation of digital signatures, which in turn can be used to authenticate participants, ensure that participants cannot repudiate their messages and protect the integrity of data.    However, the very elements that make cryptography attractive for protecting privacy can also thwart the information-gathering abilities of law-enforcement and security agencies.    These competing objectives, combined with recent developments in cryptography products and use, have prompted the Government of Canada to review its policy on cryptography.

Export permits have generally been easy to obtain in respect to cryptographic products that employ "weak" encryption.    Also, Canada's cryptographic policy has worked well in the past. However, the growing availability and use of products that incorporate strong cryptography is raising concern with law enforcement and national security agencies.    These entities are worried that the widespread use of strong encryption without some capability for lawful access will significantly impact their investigative capabilities.

The discussion paper acknowledges the important role that cryptography plays in supporting the information economy. Civil liberties and privacy rights are other considerations.  However, the discussion paper also highlights the significant obstacles that strong cryptography can present to the detection and investigation of criminal activities and security threats, as well as the inspection of computer records to monitor compliance with commercial, taxation, environmental and other legal and regulatory requirements.    The challenge is to develop a balanced policy which takes all of these considerations into account.

Policy options are reviewed in the three following areas: encryption of stored communications, encryption of real-time communications, and export controls for encryption products. In the case of stored data, one option is to continue with current practices and impose no new laws or licensing conditions. The discussion paper lists the disadvantages associated with this option and encourages an approach which incorporates the definition of minimum standards by the government regarding key recovery capabilities.[19]    Another option that is presented involves the implementation of legislation to mandate law enforcement access by prohibiting the use of encryption products without key recovery capabilities. The latter option would also require the government to prohibit the manufacture, import or use of non-key recovery products in Canada.

With respect to real-time communications, one option would be to maintain the status quo.    When served with a court order, telecommunications carriers would be obliged to assist in the decryption of encrypted communications travelling over their facilities, to the extent that they are capable.

A second approach would be for the federal government to impose requirements by legislation that all federally regulated communications carriers retain the ability to decrypt messages for law enforcement or national security agencies on receipt of a court order. However, a weakness in the latter approach is that some users could still employ encryption.

A third option would require prohibiting users who encrypt their own messages from using non-key recovery products. Carriers would be prohibited from transmitting encrypted messages unless such messages are encrypted by products that support key-reader technology or unless the carrier is provided with the encryption key prior to transmission.

Finally, the discussion paper reviews options available regarding export controls. The options would be to relax, maintain or extend the existing controls on the export of products that incorporate

---

[19]    Key recovery refers to various techniques that permit lawful access to encrypted data without the decryption key.

cryptography. Relaxing the current controls would support the growth of the Canadian cryptographic industry. This type of liberalization could be accomplished by recognizing the availability of similar-strength cryptography products in foreign markets, a common practice employed with other controlled products and by other Wassenaar signatures.

Another option would be to extend export controls to mass marketed software and public domain software. This could be done unilaterally or in co-operation with other Wassenaar partners. It could also be coupled with a relaxation of controls for products that support key recovery. However, unless such an approach was also adopted by all other cryptography-producing countries, Canadian manufacturers would be placed at a competitive disadvantage.

## 9.4  DIGITAL SIGNATURES

Those persons developing and implementing a wide variety of forms of electronic commerce are turning to digital signatures as providing reliable authentication and document integrity that, if properly implemented, can exceed that provided by traditional paper-based methods. In late 1996, the ABA Section of Science and Technology issued their Digital Signature Guidelines, a legal overview of cryptography, electronic signatures and authentication.[20]

Already, a number of jurisdictions in the US, including Utah and Florida, have passed legislation recognizing digital signatures as the equivalent of manual signatures. California recognizes digital signatures in communications with public entities.[21] In fact, most states have digital signature legislation pending or under consideration.[22]

A number of European states, including Germany, Denmark and Sweden, are at various stages in the process of enacting digital

---

[20] ABA Section on Business Law Ad Hoc Task Force on Electronic Contracting, "Memorandum" re: NCCUSL Drafting Committee on Electronic Contracting - Proposal on Scope of Model Act, dated December 10, 1996. See also, Freeling and Wiggins, "States Develop Rules for Using Digital Signatures," *National Law Journal*, October 20, 1997 <http://www.ljx.com/internet/1020digsig.html>.

[21] <http://www.ss.ca.gov/digsig/digsigfaq.html>.

[22] <http://www.mbc.com/ds_sum.html>.

signature legislation. The International Chamber of Commerce has produced a draft document entitled Uniform International Authentication and Certification Practices (UIACP) which sets out various authentication practices in general, including digital signatures. The United Nations Commission on International Trade Law has begun consideration of a model International Digital Signature Statute. A draft report is expected shortly although the project is expected to take up to two years to conclude.

Digital certificates may soon extend electronic IDs to include personal data. In March 1997, VeriSign Inc., the leading supplier of digital certificates, introduced a major enhancement to its certificates that make them a secure container for storing other types of data including demographic information such as age, gender, address, postal codes/ZIP codes or other personal data.

The new certificates can be used by Web site operators to identify more accurately who is visiting their Web site and to generate dynamically customized Web pages for each individual. The captured information can also be used to provide advertisers with more accurate demographic information about who is viewing their online advertisements.

## 9.5  TECHNICAL PROTECTION FOR WEB CONTENT

A number of vendors are developing technology that can be used to protect digital information on the Internet. One such technology used to protect digital pictures is PictureMarc from Digimarc Corp. PictureMarc works by inserting a digital watermark into an image without a noticeable effect on the image itself. The digital code is hidden within the random variation normally found in an image. According to Digimarc, the watermark remains intact even if the image is cropped, colour corrected or otherwise edited.

When a watermarked picture is opened with a compatible graphics program,[23] PictureMarc provides the viewer with information as to the author and copyright owner and information about licensing the image from its owners. Use of digital marks such as PictureMarc will

---

[23]  Watermark embedding and identification software is included in ninety percent of new image-editing software programs, such as Adobe Photoshop, Corel Draw and Micrografx.

make it substantially more difficult for infringers to argue that their use of unauthorized images was innocent and should make it easier for copyright owners to obtain statutory damages, and in some jurisdictions, attorney fees.

The benefits of utilizing PictureMarc are enhanced when it is combined with Digimarc's MarcSpider, a service that scans the Internet for images that contain the watermark.[24] Copyright owners can use the service to identify quickly and easily any unauthorized use of their works.

IBM has also developed technology solutions to protect digital information. IBM's technology can be used to seal electronic information in "cryptolope" containers, which can only be opened with a matching cryptographic key. Cryptolope containers can protect copyright material including text, audio, visual information, and other rights-protected digital data against unauthorized access and provide a mechanism for owners to be reimbursed for the use.

Certain computer programs also incorporate security devices that are designed to prevent illegal copying by preventing a single, licensed copy of a computer program from being installed and used on more than one computer at one time. A number of "cracker" tools are available to allow the circumvention of copy protection devices. Making such tools available on an Internet server, or possibly even providing links to other Internet sites providing such tools, can potentially be construed as contributory infringement.[25] (See Chapter 6 for more information on liability for links and use of frames.)

Concerns about unauthorized copies of multimedia content being placed on the Internet have prompted the creation of services that will search the Internet for copyrighted music and video files. MusicReport, a service offered by Intersect, uses crawler/spider technology to search the Web for audio and video, including Real Audio and the latest MPEG format, MP3.

---

[24] When MarcSpider visits a Web site and finds a watermarked image, it notes the time and Web address, or URL, where it found the image.

[25] *Adobe Systems, Incorporated, Claris Corporation, and Traveling Software, Inc. v. Tripod Inc. and Bo Peabody*, No. 96CV30189 in the United States District Court for the District of Massachusetts, October 7, 1996.

## 9.6  LEGAL PROTECTION FOR TECHNOLOGICAL DEVICES

Legal protection against tampering with devices intended to protect copyrighted works may soon be available. Article 11 of the WIPO Copyright Treaty adopted by the Diplomatic Conference in Geneva on December 20, 1996 requires "Contracting Parties" to provide adequate legal protection and effective legal remedies against circumvention of technological measures used by authors/creators or performers/producers to protect their work against infringement. Contracting Parties are also obligated to provide adequate and effective legal remedies against intentional interference with electronic rights management information or transmission of a work knowing that rights management information has been tampered with.

Even prior to consideration by WIPO, The Canadian Information Advisory Council on the Information Highway in its *Final Report of the Copyright Subcommittee,*[26] had recommended that the tampering or bypassing of encryption or safeguards of any kind for purposes of infringement should be a criminal offence under the (Canadian) *Copyright Act.*

In the United States, legal protection for technological protection measures implemented to protect copyright are a component of the *Digital Millennium Copyright Act of 1998.*[27] Civil and/or criminal remedies would be available against any person who:[28]

- circumvents a technological protection measure;

- manufactures, imports, offers to the public, provides or otherwise traffics in any technology, product, service, device, component or part that is:

  - primarily designed or produced for the purpose of circumventing a technological protection measure;

---

[26]    See Information Highway Advisory Council, *Copyright and the Information Highway: Final Report of the Copyright Subcommittee* (Ottawa: Information Highway Advisory Council Secretariat, 1995).

[27]    Bill 5.2037, passed by the Senate May 14, 1998.

[28]    Section 103 that would add a new Chapter 12 to Title 17 of the United States Code.

- has only limited commercially significant purposes or use other than to circumvent a technological protection measure; or

- is marketed for use in circumventing a technological protection measure;

• intentionally removes or alters copyright management information; or

• distributes or imports for distribution copyrighted material knowing that the copyright management information has been removed or altered.

# 10

# Jurisdiction: Territorial Application of Laws

## 10.1 INTRODUCTION

Any person carrying on Internet-related activities must consider whether such activities may be subject to the laws of jurisdictions other than the country in which that person resides or carries on business. This will be of particular concern if the person has assets in other jurisdictions. Recent decisions in the US have suggested that in some cases, electronic contact through the Internet with residents of a state may be a sufficient nexus to allow the courts of that state to assert jurisdiction over a non-resident.

In the past, jurisdiction was based on certain basic principles of international law. A basic tenet was that each state would have exclusive jurisdiction over activity taking place within its boundaries, but would not seek to apply its laws outside its territory. The courts of any state were reluctant to assume jurisdiction over a person unless that person was a resident of that state or his or her activity had a substantial connection to the state.

The global reach of the Internet raises difficult questions of jurisdiction because commercial activities and electronic contacts may cross traditional geographical or political boundaries. A person wishing to conduct business by means of a Web site may operate the site from a server located on its own premises or may use the Web hosting facilities of a local service provider. With equal ease, the person may arrange for a foreign service provider to operate its Web site or a mirror copy of its Web site. The decision will be made based on cost considerations or the desire to provide access to customers in the target markets.

Establishing a Web site on the Internet allows a person to reach users in any country who have Internet access. The Web site can be used to communicate a commercial message or solicitation, or may allow an interested user to place an order for a product or service. Intangible products such as software, sound recordings, photographs or information can also be delivered electronically through the Internet. Certain types of services such as gambling or adult-oriented video conferencing services can also be performed and delivered electronically.

A defamatory statement or a copy of a work that infringes another person's intellectual property that is made available in one jurisdiction may be accessible instantaneously in any part of the world. An activity which may be legally carried out in one jurisdiction may have an effect in another jurisdiction where such activity is prohibited.

The Internet is unlike other types of media which involve contacts that are one-to-one (such as mail) or one-to-many (such as publishing or broadcasting). The Internet, by contrast, supports many-to-many contacts and therefore enables numerous types of new interactions between participants. In many cases, different aspects of the transaction may affect entities located in different states.

The types of contacts established through the Internet can therefore transcend the laws of any one state. Internet activity that crosses political boundaries raises the question of which courts should have the authority to resolve a dispute or prosecute an offense, and which laws should be applied to govern the conduct in question. In many cases, more than one state may assert that a sufficient component of the transaction occurred in that state or otherwise affected its residents so as to permit the courts of each state to assume jurisdiction.

## 10.2  ASSUMPTION OF JURISDICTION IN CIVIL CASES

In the Province of Ontario, the first step for an Ontario court to assume jurisdiction is that a person must be served with process. Rule 17.02 of the Ontario Rules of Practice sets out the criteria for the service of process, including the following:

- The person has real or personal property in Ontario
- The contract relating to the transaction was made in Ontario
- The contract provided that it would be governed or interpreted in accordance with the laws of Ontario
- A breach of contract occurred in Ontario
- A tort was committed in Ontario
- Damage was sustained in Ontario; or
- The person was ordinarily resident in or carrying on business in Ontario.

Similar rules have been adopted in most other provinces in Canada. The assumption of jurisdiction by a Canadian court may also need to comply with constitutional limitations. A court in any province may assume jurisdiction provided that there is a "real and substantial connection" between the province and the cause of action.[1] In the case where a defendant is located outside Canada then the *Hague Convention on the Service Abroad of Judicial and Extrajudicial Documents in Civil or Commercial Matters* must also be considered.

US courts have assumed jurisdiction over persons for purposes of civil proceedings based on the following doctrines:

(1) The person is physically present in the state and is personally served with process within the borders of the state (territoriality);

(2) The person is domiciled in the forum state even if not physically present when served (for example, a person maintains a permanent home coupled with an intention to make that place his or her home);

---

[1] *De Savoye v. Morguard Inv. Ltd.*, [1993] 4 S.C.R. 289. See also *Hunt v. T&N plc.* [1993] 4 S.C.R. 289. See also Peter Hogg, *Constitutional Law of Canada* (3rd ed.) at 13.5(b), where he observes that the rule of substantial connection bears a striking resemblance to constitutional law which has been developed in the United States with respect to the limits of "long arm" jurisdiction, and that the due process test, elaborated in those cases, could serve as a test of extraterritoriality under the Constitution of Canada. However, other commentators have expressed the view that constitutional limitations on the exercise of extraterritorial jurisdiction by Canadian courts may be less stringent than those placed on US courts by their constitution.

(3) The person consents to jurisdiction, which consent may be either express (such as by agreement or appointment of an agent within the state to accept service of process) or implied (for example, in some states, a non-resident is deemed to have appointed the registrar of motor vehicles as his agent for service while driving in the state);

(4) The person commits an act that brings him or her within the forum state's long arm statute;[2] and

(5) The person waives jurisdiction by voluntarily appearing and defending a case without challenging the assumption of jurisdiction.

In most cases where a US court exercises personal jurisdiction over a non-resident defendant, it is on the grounds that the defendant's activities bring the person under the forum state's "long arm" statute.[3] This is typically the basis on which a court would seek to assert jurisdiction over a non-resident operator of a Web site.

Even if a defendant's conduct brings him within the forum state's long arm statute, the assertion of personal jurisdiction over the defendant by the forum state must not violate the due process requirements of the United States Constitution. Due process means that the non-resident defendant must have purposefully established 'minimum contact' with the forum state such that the maintenance of the suit would not offend "traditional notions of fair play and substantial justice."[4]

---

[2]   For instance, section 8.01-328.1(A)(4) of the *Virginia Code* permits personal jurisdiction to be exercised over a defendant who "regularly does or solicits business, or engages in any other persistent course of conduct, or derives substantial revenue from goods used or consumed or services rendered" in Virginia. Subsection (3) permits personal jurisdiction over a person who causes "tortious injury by an act or omission" in Virginia. In the case of the later section, courts have generally held that the subsection requires that the defendant be personally physically present in Virginia when causing the injury. However, courts have been moving away from that requirement.

[3]   Rather than continually updating their long arm statutes, some other states have simply enacted long arm statutes that authorize the assumption of jurisdiction to the extent permitted by the Constitution.

[4]   *Darby v. Campagnie Nationale Air France*, 769 F.Supp 1255, 1262 (S.D.N.Y. 1991), quoting *International Shoe Co. v. Washington*, 326 U.S. 310, 316, 66 S. Ct. 154, 158, 90 L.Ed. 95 (1945).

The minimum contact requirement can be satisfied by systematic or continuous activity within the state. The minimum contact requirement can also be satisfied if the non-resident performs or causes to perform certain acts within the state (i.e., by entering into a contract or committing a tortious act within the state, or by performing certain acts that have effects within the state). However, the cause of action must have arisen out of the contact with the state and the defendant must have purposely availed himself of the privileges or protections of the forum state[5] or must have engaged in an activity whereby he would reasonably have anticipated being haled into the court of the forum state.[6] The court will also take into account the interest of the forum state in adjudicating the dispute, the plaintiff's interest in obtaining swift and effective relief and the burden on the defendant in having to litigate in a foreign jurisdiction.

In many recent Internet-related disputes in the US, the defendants brought motions to dismiss the actions on the grounds that the courts lacked "personal jurisdiction." The motions were brought at an early stage of the litigation, prior to an evidentiary hearing or discovery. At that stage in the proceedings, the plaintiffs may defeat such motions merely by making a *prima facie* showing of jurisdiction. Since the plaintiffs are generally entitled to have their complaints heard and affidavits interpreted, any doubts as to jurisdiction for purposes of such motions are resolved in the light most favourable to them.

In *CompuServe v. Patterson,*[7] the United States Court of Appeals for the Sixth Circuit found that contacts that were almost entirely electronic in nature were sufficient to meet the minimum contacts requirement. In that case, a software developer from Texas subscribed to an online service provided by CompuServe, based in Ohio. The service permitted the developer to upload computer programs which could then be copied by other CompuServe subscribers. Any subscriber could review a list of available programs and select one for downloading upon payment of a fee. CompuServe kept a

---

[5]    *McGee v. Int'l Life Insur. Co.*, 355 U.S. 220 (1957).

[6]    *World-Wide Volkswagen v. Woodson*, 444 U.S. 286.(1980).

[7]    *CompuServe, Inc. v. Patterson*, 89 F.3d 1257, 1996 FED App. 0228P (6th Cir.), Docket No. C-2-94-91 (S.D. Ohio August 11, 1994).

percentage of the fee and remitted the balance to the software developer.

The court found that the software developer, Patterson, specifically targeted Ohio by entering into an agreement with CompuServe to sell his software through the CompuServe system.[8] Patterson advertised his software through the service and repeatedly transmitted his software to CompuServe. These facts lead the court to conclude that Patterson had "reached out" from Texas to Ohio and "originated and maintained" contacts with Ohio. However, the decision did not find that entering into a contract with a resident of a state would be sufficient by itself to establish the minimum contact required for the courts of that state to assume jurisdiction.

Not all forms of electronic contacts are likely to be sufficient to support the exercise of personal jurisdiction over a defendant. A defendant's actions in performing data processing activities in a state or transmitting e-mail directed specifically to residents of a particular state[9] may be sufficient for the state to assume jurisdiction. However,

---

[8]    Patterson had entered into a "Shareware Registration Agreement" ("SRA") with CompuServe. The SRA incorporated by reference two other documents, the CompuServe Service Agreement and the Rules of Operation, both of which were published on the CompuServe Information Service. Both the SRA and the CompuServe Service Agreement provided that they were made in Ohio and the CompuServe Service Agreement further provided that it was to be governed and construed in accordance with Ohio law. The Court noted that the SRA required a new shareware provider like Patterson to type "Agree" at various points in the document in recognition of his online agreement to the terms and conditions contained in the agreement. Thus Patterson's assent to the SRA was first manifested at his own computer in Texas and then transmitted to the CompuServe computer system in Ohio.

[9]    *EDIAS Software International, L.L.C. v. BASIS International Ltd.*, No. CIV 96-0932 PHX-PGR, 1996 WL 700063 (D. Arix., Nov. 21, 1996). In that case, the sending of defamatory statements by e-mail to certain customers, through a posting on the defendant's Web page and on a CompuServe forum, where the defendant knew that the messages may damage the plaintiff, was found to be sufficient to allow a court in the plaintiff's state to assume jurisdiction. See also *Playboy v. Chuckleberry*, S.D.N.Y. No. 79 Civ. 3525, 939 F. Supp. 1032 motion for reconsideration denied, 39 U.S.P.Q. 2d 1846 (S.D.N.Y. June 19, 1996). This case involved an Italian Web site that was found to have violated a 1981 US injunction against distributing certain material in the United States. Playboy had obtained an injunction prohibiting the use of the word "playmen" on the cover of a magazine published, distributed, imported or sold in the United States but was not able to prevent the use of such word on a magazine sold in Italy. In 1996, the defendant created a Web site located in Italy containing copies of the cover of its Playmen magazine. The issue before the court was whether the defendant violated the 1981 injunction by creating the

a defendant's action in obtaining access to a database stored on a server located in a state would not likely be sufficient for the state to assume jurisdiction over the defendant.[10]

It is also not clear whether posting information on a passive Web site is sufficient to support personal jurisdiction. In the *Bensusan* case,[11] the court had to consider whether the creation of a Web site on a server located outside New York, was an offer to sell a product or service in New York.[12] The court found that a New York resident who wished to obtain access to the Web site and utilize the information obtained at the site would have to take several affirmative steps. The mere fact that a person could obtain information about the allegedly infringing product did not mean that the defendant was advertising, promoting, selling or otherwise making an effort to target its product in New York.

In *Bensusan*, the court held that the creation of a Web site may have an impact nationwide, or even worldwide, but that act by itself is not an act purposefully directed toward the forum state.[13] The court held that advertising the defendant's club, including providing a phone number to call, on its Web site did not meet the "purposeful availment" requirement.

---

Web site. The court held that the defendant's solicitation of US customers from the Italian Web site, by asking them to send faxes to register and by sending passwords to them by e-mail, was sufficient to constitute "distribution" in the United States.

[10]  *Pre-Kap, Inc. v. System One Direct Access, Inc.*, 636 S.O.2d 1351 (Ct. App. Fla. 1994).

[11]  *Bensusan Restaurant Corp. v. King (Missouri Jazz Club)*, 96 Civ. 3992, 937 F. Supp. 295 (S.D.N.Y. 1996) affirmed by Second Circuit, 1997 WL 560048 (2d Cir. Sept. 10, 1997). Available at <http://www.leepfrog.com/E-Law/Cases/Bensusan_v_King.html>.

[12]  King, the owner and operator of a small jazz club called "The Blue Note" located in Columbia, Missouri set up a site on the World Wide Web to promote his club. The site contained general information about the club, a calendar of events and ticketing information. Bensusan, a New York corporation and the creator of a famous jazz club in New York City also known as the "The Blue Note" and owner of a federally registered trademark for that name, brought an action against King for trademark infringement, trademark dilution and unfair competition. King moved to dismiss the action for lack of personal jurisdiction pursuant to 12(b)(2) of the Federal Rules of Civil Procedure. The court concluded that even after construing all allegations in the light most favourable to the plaintiff, its allegations were insufficient to support a finding of assuming jurisdiction based on the long arm statute.

[13]  Relying on *Asahi Metal Indus. Co. v. Superior Court*, 480 US 102, 112, 107 S. Ct. 1026, 1032, 94 L.Ed. 2d 92 (1992).

A number of other US cases appear to support the reasoning in *Bensusan*. In *Cybersell Inc. v. Cybersell Inc.*[14] the US Court of Appeals for the Ninth Circuit held that maintaining a Web page with a local phone number was insufficient to establish personal jurisdiction in Arizona in circumstances where the defendant had done nothing to encourage residents of Arizona. Such activities, without "something more" to evidence the defendant's purposeful availment, were inadequate to establish personal jurisdiction. A similar result was reached in *Smith v. Hobby Lobby Stores Inc. v. Boto Co. Ltd.*[15]

US Courts have also refused to find personal jurisdiction where an Internet activity was directed at a national audience and not specifically to residents of a particular state. In *Hearst Corp. v. Goldberger*[16] the court analogized the defendant's Web site to an advertisement in a national magazine and found that there was not sufficient evidence to establish personal jurisdiction in New York State.

Advertising on a Web site, combined with other activities, can be sufficient to establish personal jurisdiction.

In *Zippo Manuf. Co. v. Zippo Dot Com, Inc.*,[17] the defendant's Web site allowed visitors to sign up for the defendant's news service. The court concluded that the fact that the defendant had 3,000 subscribers in Pennsylvania and had entered into agreements with Pennsylvania ISPs was sufficient to show that the defendant had purposefully availed itself of Pennsylvania's jurisdiction and had minimum contacts with the state to support personal jurisdiction.

In *Inset Systems, Inc. v. Instruction Set, Inc.*[18] a Connecticut

---

[14]    1997 WL 739021 (9th Cir.).

[15]    968 F. Supp. 1356 (W.D. Ark. 1997).

[16]    1997 WL 97097 (S.D. N.Y.).

[17]    952 F.Supp.1119, 1124 (W.D. Pa. 1997).

[18]    *Inset Systems, Inc. v. Instruction Set, Inc.*, 937 F.Supp. 161, 1996 US Dist. LEXIS 7160, (D. Conn., April 17 1996). Advertising on a Web site accessible to residents of a particular state has been found by some courts to be equivalent to directing a "continuous stream" of advertising into the forum state. The combination of this activity and making available an 800 number accessible from that state, strengthens the case for the court to assume jurisdiction even without proof that the site was actually seen by a resident of the state.

district court held that the operation of a Web site accessible to residents of the state combined with a toll-free number was sufficient to provide a basis for jurisdiction. The decision in *Inset* was followed in *Telco Communications v. An Apple A Day*,[19] which found that posting an advertisement or solicitation (or in that specific case, an allegedly defamatory press release) on a Web site was sufficient for the exercise of personal jurisdiction. Extensive exchange of e-mail may also be sufficient to establish personal jurisdiction.[20]

It should be noted that, in order for the operation of a Web site to provide a basis for the exercise of personal jurisdiction, the claims must arise out of the operation of the site. The creation of a Web site located outside the forum state, which is accessible to residents of the forum state, would not be sufficient to allow a court to assume jurisdiction where the claims in question were not related to the Web site.[21]

Another basis for the assumption of jurisdiction by US courts is where the effect of the defendant's conduct can be felt in that state. In a domain name dispute involving an alleged trademark dilution, a California court asserted jurisdiction over a non-resident defendant where the defendant knew that the plaintiff located in California would be affected by the defendant's conduct.[22] It might also be

---

Case available at <http://www.leepfrog.com/E-Law/Cases/Inset_v_Instruction.html>. See also *Heroes Inc. v. Heroes Foundation*, 958 F. Supp. 1 (D.D.C. 1996) where operation of a site that solicited e-mail and donations, that listed a toll-free number and used the placement of advertising in local papers were found to represent sufficient contacts to confer jurisdiction.

See also *Maritz, Inc. v. Cybergold, Inc.*, 40 U.S.P.Q. 2d 1729 (D. Miss. 1996) where a Missouri court assumed jurisdiction on the basis that 131 hits had come from the state of Missouri.

[19]   Civ. Act. No. 97-542-A (E.D. Virginia, September 24, 1997).

[20]   *Resuscitation Technologies Inc. v. Continental Health Care Corp.*, 1997 WL 148567 (S.D. Ind. 1997).

[21]   *McDonough v. Fallon McElligott, Inc.*, No. 95-4037, 1996 US Dist. LEXIS 15139, 40 U.S.P.Q.2D (BNA) 1826 (S.D. Cal. Aug. 5 1996).

[22]   *Panavision Int. v. Toeppen*, 938 F. Supp. 616 (C.D. Cal. 1996) (denying motion to dismiss), partial summary judgment granted, 945 F. Supp. 1296 (1996) (against defendant Toeppen), partial summary judgment granted, No. 96-3284 DDP (JRx), 41 U.S.P.Q. 2d 1310, 1996 WL 768036 (Nov. 27, 1996) (for defendant Network Solutions Inc.). On April 17, 1998, the 9th Circuit Court of Appeals upheld the lower court decisions that found Toeppen was attempting to extort money by trying to sell back domain names of other

appropriate for a US court to assert jurisdiction if the sender intentionally engaged in conduct calculated to cause injury, and the sender knew and intended that the effects of the conduct would be felt in the forum state.[23]

## 10.3  CRIMINAL AND REGULATORY OFFENCES

### (a)  Criminal Offences

The global reach of the Internet means that any criminal conduct carried out by use of the Internet is likely to involve more than one country. In a number of reported computer crime cases, the activities involved in the commission of the offence occurred in more than one country. Such cases raise the question of whether the courts of one country have jurisdiction to try an offence where some of the activity necessary to constitute the offence occurs in another country. This question must be resolved according to the principles of law in effect in the jurisdiction where the charges are laid.

The rules applicable to the assumption of jurisdiction may be different for criminal or regulatory offenses as compared to civil actions. In countries which share a heritage with English common law, criminal jurisdiction is generally based on activities occurring within the jurisdiction. Under this principle, the courts of one country do not have jurisdiction to try matters that relate to activities performed outside the jurisdiction. The rationale underlying the territorial principle is first, that a country has generally little direct concern for the actions of malefactors abroad; and second, that other states may legitimately take umbrage if a country attempts to regulate matters taking place wholly or substantially within their territory.[24]

A court following such a principle will assume jurisdiction to try a case only where the offence in question has been "committed" in that jurisdiction. There are several alternative interpretations as to when an act may be deemed to be committed in a particular jurisdiction. For example, it may be necessary to show that (a) the act

---

entities he had registered.

[23]  *Naxos Resources (U.S.A.) Ltd. v. Southam, Inc.*, No. CV 96-2314 WJR (S.D. Cal. Aug. 16, 1996).

[24]  *R. v. Libman* (1985), 21 C.C.C. (3d) 206 at 228, [1985] 2 S.C.R. 178, 62 N.R. 161, 12 O.A.C. 33 (*sub nom Libman v. R.*) 21 D.L.R. (4th) 174, [1985] 2 R.C.S. 178 (S.C.C.).

is carried out in totality in that jurisdiction; (b) the act is "commenced" in that jurisdiction (reflecting what is commonly referred to as the subjective territorial principle); (c) the act is completed in that jurisdiction, i.e., the last constituent element occurs in this country (reflecting what is referred to as the objective territorial principle); or (d) the act has an effect in that jurisdiction.[25]

International comity, however, does not prevent a particular country from exercising jurisdiction with respect to criminal acts in that country that have consequences abroad, nor does it give immunity to any person for conduct carried out abroad that has harmful consequences in that country. Further, the rules of international comity are not static and modern nations are no longer as sensitive about exclusive jurisdiction over crime as they may formerly have been: "In a shrinking world, we are all our brothers' keepers. In the criminal arena, this is underlined by the international co-operative schemes that have been developed among national law enforcement bodies."[26]

In Canada, a person may be convicted of a crime committed outside Canada as long as there is a "real and substantial link" between the offence and Canada.[27] This test can be satisfied as long as significant portions of an offence take place in Canada. This test would likely mean that where a criminal offence is committed through the offering of a Web site from outside Canada, there may be a sufficient connection to Canada where the preparatory work occurs in Canada.

On March 4, 1998, US authorities charged owners and managers of 6 off-shore gambling companies under US laws in respect to illegal use of interstate telephone. If the charges are pursued, the cases could set US law on fundamental online issues, such as jurisdiction and national sovereignty, as well as online gambling.

---

[25]    S. Williams and J. G. Castel, *Canadian Criminal Law: International and Transactional Aspects* (Toronto: Butterworths, 1981) at 29-30, 72-82.

[26]    *Libman, supra,* at 233.

[27]    *Libman, supra.*

## (b)  Consumer Protection

A company engaged in online commerce from one jurisdiction may also be subject to consumer protection legislation in other jurisdictions. In *State of Minnesota v. Granite Gate Resorts, Inc,*[28] the Minnesota Attorney General filed suit against Granite Gate Resorts, Inc. for consumer fraud. The defendant maintained an advertisement on its Web site for WagerNet, a service to be provided by a Belize company through a service to be located in Belize. Interested parties were invited to contact the defendant for more information and to sign up for an e-mail mailing list. The ad contained a statement that WagerNet would soon operate an electronic betting service. The ad warned users that they should consult their local authorities to determine the legality of placing bets by telephone with off-shore betting facilities before they registered with WagerNet.

The Minnesota Attorney General had previously posted a warning to ISPs and Internet users setting out its position on jurisdiction, particularly as it related to Internet gambling. The state Attorney General contended that the ad placed on the defendant's Web site falsely suggested that electronic betting was legal, and as such, represented false advertising, deceptive trade practices and other forms of consumer fraud in violation of Minnesota's consumer protection statute. Granite Gate maintained that it had never entered into any transaction or contract in Minnesota or collected any money from a citizen of Minnesota. The Attorney General took the position that making Web pages accessible in Minnesota constituted "doing business" in the State of Minnesota for purposes of jurisdiction. Consequently, any Web page that could cause "the mere likelihood of confusion" about anything "business-related" would be subject to civil liability in the State.

The Court held that since the ad and e-mail distribution list on the Web site would be continuously on the Internet and could reach national markets including Minnesota, the defendant had established sufficient contract to make it proper for Minnesota to assume jurisdiction.

---

[28]    No. C6-95-7227 (Minn. Dist. Ct., 2nd Dist., Dec. 11, 1996) (Available at <http://www.leepfrog.com/E-Law/Cases/Minn v. Granite Gate.html>.).

## (c)  Securities Regulation

The use of the Internet for the delivery of financial products and services requires securities regulators to review the types of activity which requires registration. In Canada, provincial securities statutes typically apply to any form of investment advice or solicitation to purchase securities.

Any offering of, or solicitation regarding, securities using the Internet will likely be subject to the same regulatory regime as may be applicable to offerings or solicitations made through other forms of communications.[29] Securities regulators in one jurisdiction may also seek to regulate foreign persons who send out electronic newsletters or other information to residents of that jurisdiction. The issue is whether the activities in question constitute either the solicitation of the public or an offering of securities, or the provision of investment advice, for which there must be compliance with the applicable securities legislation.

### (i)  Solicitations

The Securities and Exchange Commission (SEC) issued an Interpretation (Release 33-7516) to provide its views on how issuers, investment companies, broker-dealers, exchanges and investment advisors may use Internet Web sites to solicit off-shore securities transactions and clients without being registered with the SEC. According to the SEC, application of the registration provisions of US securities laws depends on whether the site offers solicitations or other commuinications targeted towards the United States.

Offerors that implement measures reasonably designed to prevent sales to US residents would not be considered to have targeted offers to the United States. What constitutes adequate measures will depend upon all the facts and circumstances of any particular situation, but the Web site should include a prominent notice that the offer is not directed to persons located in the United States. Regardless of the measures adopted, solicitations that appear, by their content, to be targeted at US residents will be viewed as made in the United States.

---

[29]  For a summary of the requirements in the US, see Raysman and Brown, "Securities Offerings Over the Internet," The *New York Law Journal*, April 10, 1997.

An example would be an offer which emphasizes the investor's ability to avoid US income taxes on the investments.

The SEC also indicated that it is considering whether to provide further guidance regarding use of the Internet in respect to securities transactions.

### (ii) Investment Advice

A growing number of electronic newsletters and Web sites related to investments are available on the Internet. Where the information provider and the recipients reside in the same jurisdiction, the provider of the newsletter would likely be required to be registered as an investment advisor. Registration would also be required where the provision of information would be construed as a solicitation to purchase securities.

It appears that the Ontario Securities Commission takes the position that it can regulate the provision of investment advice on the Internet.[30] The Ontario Securities Act requires advisors, defined as people in the business of giving investment advice, to be registered. However, certain exemptions, such as opinions provided in paid-circulation financial publications, are explicitly exempt.

In June 1997, the OSC ordered the closure of an online investment newsletter which gave advice on buying and selling of securities.[31] The newsletter, which was distributed without charge, was not covered by any of the applicable exemptions under the *Securities Act*.

The Securities and Investment Board in the UK has taken the position that the *Financial Services Act 1986* could apply to an entity located outside the UK that runs a Web site which includes an "investment advertisement." This is the case notwithstanding that the advertisement is published outside the UK. Two factors to be considered are whether the offer is directed, as a matter of fact, to

---

[30]    The retired Chairman of the Ontario Securities Commission, Edward Waitzer, suggested in a 1996 speech, that regulatory authorities should focus more on transactions rather than attempt to regulate the information that is posted from their own geographic area.

[31]    Federal Bureau of Investments page on Silicon Investor Inc.'s Web site. See <http://www.siliconinvestor.com>.

potential investors in the UK, and the degree to which technical steps are taken to restrict the material from being accessible by residents of the UK.

### (iii) Notices and Disclaimers

The use of notices and disclaimers may be especially important on a Web site providing investment-related information. The Securities Commission of British Columbia has taken the position that if a party communicating information on the Internet does not intend to direct the information to a resident of B.C., a disclaimer to that effect should be included at the beginning of the communication. A similar approach seems to be the preference of other securities administrators. The North American Securities Administrators Association Inc. has adopted a resolution encouraging states to exempt offers of securities made on the Internet if the offer indicates that the securities are not offered to residents in a particular state and the offer is not specifically directed to any person by or on behalf of the issuer of securities.

However, the inclusion of a disclaimer at the Web site to indicate that the contents are not directed to residents of a particular jurisdiction may not be sufficient in all cases. It may also be necessary to take the further step of using a registration process to prevent use of the site by persons located outside a particular jurisdiction.

### (d)  Cross-Border Provision of Financial Services

Entities operating in regulated industries, such as financial services, may find that some of the existing restrictions applicable to their operation may be overcome by the delivery of services through the Internet.

The advent of the Internet as the vehicle for delivery of financial services demonstrates the differences in the powers that may be exercised by Canadian financial institutions when they carry on business domestically, compared to the powers they may exercise when doing business in other jurisdictions. Outside Canada, Canadian financial institutions may carry on business, conduct their affairs and exercise their powers to the extent and in the manner permitted by the laws of the foreign jurisdiction. However, the differences in powers may require some accommodation as to the manner in which financial services are delivered by means of the Internet to both Canadians and non-Canadians to ensure legislative restrictions applicable to Canadians are respected.

At the same time, some of the existing restrictions may be overcome by the Internet delivery of financial goods and services. For example, the Internet raises the possibility that the constraints placed on Canadian deposit-taking institutions such as a bank, trust company or credit union with respect to the sale of insurance will become less relevant. Specifically, it is arguable that since an Internet Web site is not a "branch" of a deposit-taking institution, prohibitions against the promotion of an insurance company agent or broker affiliate of the deposit-taking institution or an insurance policy of such insurance company, agent or broker affiliate would not apply. These activities would clearly be prohibited if conducted through a branch.

While the Internet may offer opportunities for entering new markets, it may still be necessary to comply with the regulatory requirements of these jurisdictions. For instance, under Part XII of the *Bank Act*, no foreign financial institution may carry on financial services which are regulated in Canada without establishing a physical presence in Canada. In the case of a foreign insurance company, the options are to establish a branch of the foreign company or a Canadian insurance company subsidiary.

There is uncertainty as to the circumstances in which a foreign financial institution will be deemed to be carrying on financial services in Canada. In 1997, a major US commercial bank, Wells Fargo Bank, expressed an intention to offer commercial banking products to small and medium-sized Canadian companies over the Internet. Traditionally, a financial institution would not be deemed to be engaged in banking in Canada if most or all of the activities are performed outside of Canada. However, the proposed activities by Wells Fargo may make it subject to Canadian regulatory authority since the customer will be in Canada and the products or services will be delivered in Canada presumably by Wells Fargo or an agent. It is quite likely that such activities would be characterized as the undertaking of banking activities in Canada.

In summary, an entity operating in a regulated industry and desiring to offer products and services through the Internet may need to comply with the requirements of all jurisdictions in which such entities plan to offer their products and services.

### (e)  Obscenity: Whose laws, Whose Standards?

The growing use of the Internet and other forms of electronic communications is changing our traditional notion of community. In the US, the Supreme Court has adopted the "contemporary community" standard as one prong of a three-prong test to judge obscenity.[32]

The application of this standard may vary according to the jurisdiction where the dispute is heard. In *United States v. Thomas*[33] a California couple was prosecuted in Tennessee for violation of federal obscenity laws[34] in connection with their operation of an adult bulletin board system (BBS) out of their home.

A postal inspector in Tennessee, responsible for investigating the distribution of pornographic material by mail, signed up on the Thomas' BBS and ordered materials. Some of the material was sent by UPS to an address in Tennessee while other parts were transmitted using the telephone system through modems to Tennessee. The jury applied local Memphis community standards and found the material obscene. The court found it proper to apply the community standards of Tennessee even though such standards varied from those of the defendants' place of residence.[35]

The defendants and *amicus curiae* appearing on their behalf argued that the use of computer technology required a new definition

---

[32]    In *Miller v. California*, 93 S.Ct. 2607 (1973), the US Supreme Court set out a three-prong test for obscenity, of which the first prong involves an enquiry as to whether the "average person applying contemporary community standards would find the work taken as a whole appeals to the prurient interest."

[33]    1996 WL 30477 (6th Cir. Tenn.).

[34]    18 U.S.C. section 1462 (which prohibits the transport of obscene material via a common carrier) and 18 U.S.C. Section 1465 (which prohibits the transport of obscene material in interstate or foreign commerce).

[35]    In fact, the Thomas' BBS had been raided previously by the San Jose Police Department and that investigation found that the material was not sufficient to produce an indictment.

of community, i.e., one based on the broad-ranging connections among people in Cyberspace rather than the geographic locale of the federal judicial district of the criminal trial. However, this argument was not accepted in this case because access to the defendant's system was limited to pre-approved members and the applicants were subject to a screening process. Accordingly, the court did not find it necessary to adopt a new definition of "community." However, in a future case, it may be open to a court to re-define the applicable community for purposes of determining the standards to be applied.

It should also be noted that in the *Thomas* case, access was controlled and the operators knew the location of each subscriber. The court found that the defendants had implemented methods to limit access to pre-approved users. If the defendants did not wish to subject themselves to liability in jurisdictions with less tolerant standards for determining obscenity, they could have refused to give passwords to members in those jurisdictions, thus precluding the risk of liability.

In conclusion, operators of Web sites should recognize that where the legality of content placed on their Web sites is to be judged on the basis of community standards, the standards to be applied may be those of the locations where such content is accessed as well as the location of the Web server.

## 10.4 "DOING BUSINESS" REQUIREMENTS

The operation of an Internet Web site to transact business with residents of a foreign jurisdiction may result in a finding that the Web site operator is carrying on business within that foreign jurisdiction. In such event, the Web site operator may be subject to certain filing or licensing requirements and other obligations, which may include the obligation to collect taxes applicable to transactions conducted with residents of that foreign jurisdiction.

The type and level of activity sufficient to constitute the carrying on of business, and the legal consequences of being found to carry on business, will vary from one jurisdiction to another. For example, in Ontario, the *Extra-Provincial Corporations Act* requires a corporation incorporated outside Ontario to obtain a licence prior to carrying on business in Ontario.[36] Other provinces have similar legislation. An extra-provincial corporation which fails to obtain a licence, unless exempt, is guilty of an offence under the Act, and is not capable of maintaining an action or any proceedings in any court or tribunal in Ontario in respect of any contract made by it.

Subsection 1(2) of the Act provides that an extra-provincial corporation carries on business in Ontario if (i) it has a resident agent, representative, warehouse, office or place where it carries on business in Ontario, (ii) it holds an interest, other than by way of security, in real property situated in Ontario; or (iii) it otherwise carries on its business in Ontario. Under subsection 1(3), an extra-provincial corporation does not carry on business in Ontario by reason only that it takes orders for, or buys or sells, wares and merchandise or it offers or sells services of any type by use of travellers or through advertising or correspondence.

There has been limited judicial consideration regarding the definition of "carrying on business." The existence of an office in Ontario is one of the indicia of carrying on business in Ontario pursuant to paragraph 1(2)(a) of the Act. Another is the preparation of documents with an Ontario address on them. In one case, the court suggested that the Ontario legislature intended that most commercial transactions and activities with some nexus in Ontario should be governed under the Act.[37]

To obtain a licence, an extra-provincial corporation must file an application, disclose general corporate information about itself, provide evidence of its existence and corporate authorization to apply for the licence, file a name search report, appoint an agent in Ontario

---

[36]    A corporation incorporated federally under the CBCA must also file a Form 2 if operating in Ontario.

[37]    In *Success International Inc. v. Environmental Export International of Canada, Inc.*, 123 D.L.R. (4th) 147, 23 O.R. (3d) 137, 19 B.L.R. (2d) 111, 41 C.P.C. (3d) 244, 1995 CanRepOnt 25 (Ont. Gen. Div.) the Ontario Court of Justice (General Division) held that a New York corporation with its registered office in New York was carrying on business in Ontario and was required to obtain a license under the Act. Although the relationship between the New York corporation and its Canadian customer was based on a single contractual transaction, the magnitude and duration of the transaction, together with the activities associated with it, established that the New York corporation was carrying on business in Ontario.

for service of legal documents and pay the applicable filing fee. The onus is on the applicant to satisfy itself that its corporate name (or business name) is available for use in Ontario.

In addition, all corporations carrying on business in Ontario are required, under the *Corporations Information Act*, to file initial information notices and notices of change. The information required to be provided includes corporate name, place of business and names and addresses of directors and officers.

## 10.5  ENFORCING FOREIGN JUDGMENTS

Even if a court from outside a defendant's place of residence assumes jurisdiction to hear a dispute, there is still an issue of whether that court's judgment will be enforceable in the defendant's jurisdiction. A number of jurisdictions have enacted legislation for the recognition of foreign judgments. In other jurisdictions, the courts may seek a certain level of connection between the defendant and the foreign jurisdiction where the action is heard.

The laws of some countries provide that even if a consumer contract is governed by the laws of a foreign country, the consumer may still receive the protection of the laws of the country in which he or she is resident. This would likely mean that the domestic court in the jurisdiction where the consumer is located may refuse to enforce a judgement obtained in a foreign court if the consumer would have had a defence had the action been prosecuted in the domestic jurisdiction.

Courts may also refuse to enforce a foreign judgment if the foreign jurisdiction does not provide for the same protection of constitutional rights as may be recognized by a domestic court. For example, US courts have shown a reluctance to recognize British libel judgments, as repugnant to public policy, because British defamation laws lack First Amendment protection.[38]

---

[38]    *Matusevitch v. Telnikoff*, 877 F.Supp. 1 (D.D.C. 1995); *Bachchan v. India Abroad Publications Inc.*, 585 N.Y.S.2d 661 (N.Y. Sup. Ct. 1992).

The leading Canadian case on the enforceability of foreign judgments is *Morguard Investments Ltd. v. De Savoye*[39] where the Supreme Court of Canada held that a court should recognize and enforce a monetary judgment of another province if there was real and substantial connection between the damages suffered by the plaintiff and that other province. *Morguard* was followed by *United States of America v. Ivey*[40] where the Court held that the test of a "real and substantial connection," as stated by *Morguard,* is also applicable to the enforcement of non-Canadian judgments.

## 10.6  CONCLUSION

If electronic commerce on the Internet is to realize its full potential, the parties doing business must know what rules will be applied to their activities. The principles governing jurisdiction are still under development and in many cases will depend on the laws in force in the country in which the question is raised. In addition, there may be conflicting policy objectives. On the one hand, any rule that requires any entity engaged in commerce on the Internet to ascertain and comply with the laws of each country in which potential users of the product or service in question may be located would hamper the potential expansion of the Internet beyond the local market. On the other hand, users should not be expected to lose all rights of protection under the laws where they reside by acquiring products or services through the Internet, especially if they are being actively targeted by a particular business entity.

An operator of a Web site can take steps to minimize the potential of being subjected to jurisdiction in another province, state or country. These include:

(1) Making the Web site as passive as possible. The more interactive a Web site is, the more likely that its operator will be subject to the jurisdiction of a foreign court.

---

[39]  (1990), 76 D.L.R. (4th) 256 46 C.P.C. (2d) 1, 15 R.P.R. (2d) 1, 122 N.R. 81 [1991] 2 W.W.R. 217, 52 B.C.L.R. (2d) 160, [1990] 3 S.C.R. 1077, [1990] R.C.S. 1077 (S.C.C.).

[40]  [1995] 27 B.L.R. (2d) 221, 18 C.E.L.R. (N.S.) 157, 130 D.L.R. (4th) 674, 26 O.R. (3d) 533 (Ont. Gen. Div.) aff'd 30 O.R. (3d) 370, 27 B.L.R. (2d) 243, 21 C.E.L.R. (N.S.) 92, 139 D.L.R. (4th) 570, 93 O.A.C. 152 (Ont. C.A.) leave to appeal refused 33 O.R. (3d) XV, [1997] 2 S.C.R. x 104 O.A.C. 80 (note) (S.C.C.).

(2) Including a notice that access to the site is only intended for the residents of the operator's jurisdiction.

(3) Taking steps to prevent access to the Web site by residents of other jurisdictions. This could involve requiring visitors to fill out registration forms which asks them to identify their location and then using such information to restrict access to the site.

(4) Utilizing governing law/jurisdiction clauses in any contracts and online agreements and including a "terms of use" agreement that is applicable to the use of the site.

# 11

# Internet and E-Mail in the Workplace

## 11.1 EMPLOYER CONCERNS: IMPROPER USE OF RESOURCES, SEXUAL HARASSMENT AND EMPLOYER LIABILITY FOR EMPLOYEE'S ONLINE BEHAVIOUR

Most organizations with internal e-mail systems have installed Internet gateways to allow the exchange of e-mail between users on their internal network and other entities on the Internet. Many companies have also implemented secure firewalls to permit their employees full access to all of the resources of the Internet from their desktops. These developments provide opportunities for employees to add new value to their employers' business.

Employers are concerned that these facilities may be used for inappropriate purposes. These improper uses may include the transmission of confidential information or corporate trade secrets through an employer's e-mail system[1] or the use of the employer's Internet facilities for purposes of operating the employee's own business.

Employers have legitimate grounds for concern that they could be held liable for improper uses of e-mail or the Internet by their employees. In most cases, employee e-mail or Usenet postings carry the employer's name or trademark as part of the employee's e-mail

---

[1]    In one case, it was alleged that a former Borland executive had disclosed confidential corporate information using e-mail to the CEO of a competitor, Symantec, shortly before he left Borland to take a position with Symantec. The e-mail was contained in Wang's MCI Mail account which Borland had paid for. Borland claimed that its right to read the messages was based on a written corporate policy granting it a right to search company property for company information. The ability to protect confidential information is discussed in Chapter 5.

address. On this basis, defamatory statements or hate messages sent outside the company by employees may be attributed to the employer.

Defamatory or other harmful statements made within an organization can also result in liability or increased damages resulting from other actions. In a Nova Scotia case, an employer was found liable for aggravated damages of $40,000 when an employee was fired and management sent an e-mail within the company making negative comments concerning the employee.[2]

Employers also have an obligation to provide a work environment free of discrimination and harassment. Pornographic images downloaded by employees and displayed on their monitors can lead to a finding that the employer created a "hostile" work environment. They can also attract negative publicity. In December 1996, an employee working for Canada's Department of National Defence was arrested and charged with possessing and distributing child pornography. The images were being stored on a computer system belonging to the government.

The obligation to provide a work environment free of harassment or discrimination may also be violated by the internal circulation of inappropriate material by e-mail. In a New York case, the court allowed a former female employee of Microsoft to use sexually explicit e-mail messages as evidence in her harassment and discrimination case against the company.

A further concern is that much of the content accessible on the Internet is protected under copyright law or other intellectual property laws. The ease with which such content may be reproduced may result in an infringement of intellectual property rights, which in some cases may be based on a bona fide belief by employees that their conduct is for the benefit of their employer.

In addition to preventing inappropriate behaviour such as that set out above, employers may wish to monitor the use of e-mail and the Internet by their employees in order to keep track of employee

---

[2]    *Russell v. Nova Scotia Power Inc.* (1996), 22 C.C.E.L. (2d) 208, 150 N.S.R. (2d) 271, 436 A.P.R. 271, (N.S. S.C.). See also a case digest in *Information and Technology Law* 1:4 (May 1997).

productivity. In some industries, such as banking, insurance, telecommunications and travel, employee monitoring has been commonplace for some time. As many as 80% of employees in such industries may be subject to some level of telephone or computer-based monitoring. With the advent of the Web, many businesses now wish to ensure that company resources and company time are not wasted on personal "surfing" or other inappropriate activities.

The above-mentioned areas of potential liability are not new risks created by the Internet. The same risks may arise if an employee sends defamatory messages on an employer's letterhead or tapes up photographs from an adult magazine. Employees can also engage in many forms of unproductive behaviour in the workplace apart from their access to the Internet.[3] Such behaviour may be dealt with in many cases through general corporate policies and proper management. However, because the Internet and the use of corporate e-mail accelerate the potential harm that can be caused to employers, it is important for employers to review and update their policies and management procedures.

## 11.2  PRIVACY RIGHTS

Some employers have taken the position that their e-mail systems are owned by them and that such ownership rights extend to all information contained on their systems. Opponents of e-mail monitoring counter, by analogy, that the fact that the company owns its telephone system does not give to the employer the unrestricted rights to monitor employees' telephone communications.

Concerns have also been expressed that access by an employer to an employee's e-mail account for the purpose of monitoring abuses of the system can provide information about the employee's personal life. This information can then make its way to co-workers or even to future prospective employers. It may also be used for making decisions regarding the future career advancement of the employee based on illegal or otherwise inappropriate factors.

The interception of private communications, whether electronic or otherwise, may be prohibited by law. For instance, in Canada, the

---

[3]   For instance, consider the hours of productivity lost on personal phone calls.

*Criminal Code*[4] makes it an offence for any person to use a device to wilfully intercept a private communication.[5] Any wilful use or further disclosure of an unauthorized interception may also constitute a separate offence.[6] For the purposes of these provisions, "private communication" is defined to mean "any oral communication or any telecommunication made under circumstances in which it is reasonable for the originator thereof to expect that it will not be intercepted by any person other than the person intended by the originator thereof to receive it."

Certain exceptions[7] are available, such as where the implicit or explicit consent has been obtained of either the sender or recipient. Furthermore, not all types of communications are protected. Transmission logs captured by a computer or telecommunications system may be distinguished from the content of messages and may not constitute "communications." Logging Web sites visited by employees, a feature now routinely provided by most Internet firewall products, may therefore not come within the prohibition of the criminal legislation. Also, an employee's downloading of a Web page does not appear to fit within the above definition of a "private communication".

In the US, the *Electronic Communications Privacy Act*[8] (ECPA) prohibits the interception and disclosure of electronic communications. The ECPA permits the owner of a system to inspect or disclose e-mail as a necessary incident to the rendition of service or the protection of the rights or property of the provider of the service. This should permit an employer to inspect and disclose e-mail communications if the inspection is done in the normal course and is necessary for business purposes or to protect that employer's rights or property. However, it is not clear that this exception would permit systematic monitoring of messages that senders would expect to be kept private.

---

[4]    R.S.C. 1985, c.C-46.

[5]    Section 184(1).

[6]    Section 193.

[7]    Section 184(2).

[8]    18 U.S.C. s. 2701.

The ECPA also contains an exception where the consent of the originator or intended recipient is obtained. To take advantage of this exception, the employer must announce its monitoring policy prior to actual implementation. Employees who are made aware of the policy and who do not raise any objection may be considered to have given their implied consent to the monitoring.

Other statutes applicable to electronic eavesdropping or wiretapping may also prohibit an employer from listening in on telephone conversations in which an employee has a reasonable expectation of privacy. However, the applicability of such statutes to e-mail communications is not clear.

Some Canadian provinces have enacted legislation creating a statutory tort for one person to violate the privacy of another. Various federal and state statutes and state constitutions in the US contain provisions granting citizens explicit privacy rights.[9] Some jurisdictions may also recognize a number of common law torts relating to privacy.[10] One of the key factors that will determine whether an employee may succeed in an action for invasion of privacy is whether the person whose communications are monitored had a reasonable expectation of privacy.

## 11.3  INTERCEPTION OF E-MAIL

The topic of privacy in respect to e-mail was the subject of a paper issued by Ontario's Information and Privacy Commissioner. In "Privacy Protection Principles for Electronic Mail Systems,"[11] Tom Wright stressed the need to respect and protect the privacy of e-mail users and the importance of adopting an explicit corporate policy to address this issue. There has been some litigation, particularly in the US, as to whether an employer's interception of an employee's e-mail

---

[9]  For example, Article I, section 1 of California's state constitution provides an express right to privacy. Although this right has been held to protect residents of the state in both the public and private sector, the scope of protection has been limited by the decision of the California Supreme Court in *Hill v. NCAA*, 7 Cal. 4th 1 (1994). In that case, the court dealt with a claim regarding drug testing of athletes and ruled that a compelling state interest need not be shown to justify a privacy right infringement under Article I, section 1.

[10]  For example, the torts of unreasonable intrusion into a person's private affairs, public disclosure of private facts and placing someone in a false light.

[11]  February 1994. See <http//www.ipc.on.ca/>.

constitutes a violation of privacy, but the issue has not been clearly resolved. To date, US courts have generally sided with employers and have not provided as much protection to an employee's right of privacy for e-mail communication as they have provided for other activities.

By way of example of the protection given for other activities, US courts have found that a search of an employee's locker in a situation where the employee was allowed to use his own lock was a violation of that employee's right to privacy[12]. Another case found that a search of an employee's desk and file cabinet used only by that employee was a violation of that employee's right to privacy;[13] however, the court also stated that an employee's expectation of privacy could be modified by an office policy.

With e-mail related cases, however, courts have not been as sympathetic to employees' rights to privacy. In a California case, the court rejected a claim by an e-mail administrator who was fired by Epson for complaining that her e-mail had been read.[14] The court found that there was no invasion of privacy. This was notwithstanding that Epson had told its employees that their e-mail was confidential.

A similar lawsuit filed against Nissan Motor Company alleging tortious interception of employee e-mail messages was also unsuccessful.[15] In that case, the appeal court affirmed the trial court's decision that the employees did not have a reasonable expectation of privacy because they had signed a waiver acknowledging that it was "company policy that employees ... restrict

---

[12]   *K-Mart v. Trotti*, 667 S.W. 2d 632 (1984).

[13]   *O'Connor v. Ortega*, 480 US 709 (1987).

[14]   *Shoars v. Epson America, Inc.*; Shoars also filed a class-action suit on behalf of herself and other employees claiming invasion of privacy under California's constitution and a wiretapping statute, California Penal Code section 631, which provides for a private cause of action for illegal interception of private wire communications. The case was dismissed on the grounds that e-mail was not covered by California's wiretapping statute and that the right to privacy provided by the state's constitution covered personal but not business information. *Flanagan v. Epson America, Inc.*, No. BC007036 (Cal. Super. Ct. Jan. 4, 1991).

[15]   *Bourke v. Nissan Motor Corp.*, No. B068705 (Cal. App. 2d Dist., Div. 5, July 26, 1993).

their use of company-owned computer hardware and software to company business."

A US District Court in Pennsylvania held that an expectation of privacy did not arise even where an employer, Pillsbury, had repeatedly promised not to intercept e-mail on its system.[16] In that case, the employer had advised its employees that all e-mail communications would remain confidential and privileged and that e-mail communications could not be used against its employees as grounds for termination. An employee who was fired for sending what the company deemed to be inappropriate and unprofessional comments[17] to his supervisor using the e-mail system sued the company. The court dismissed the employee's claim before it even reached trial stating that it did not find a reasonable expectation of privacy in the communication notwithstanding the assurances by management. The court noted that because the intended recipient of the message was a person in management who could have initiated disciplinary action, including dismissal, a reasonable person would not consider the company's interception of the communication to be a substantial and highly offensive invasion of privacy in the circumstances.

Courts have increasingly been protecting employees' rights of privacy in the office. The recent e-mail related cases may simply be reflective of the law lagging behind implementation of new technology. There may also be a balance of an employee's right to privacy with an employer's need to utilize reasonable means to protect itself from the many forms of liability that may arise from employee use of e-mail. Courts may also be more receptive to recognizing and protecting an employee's privacy interest where an employer has recognized rights either explicitly, such as through statements in manuals or corporate policies, or implicitly through a course of conduct.

Accordingly, at present there is a risk that, in some circumstances, the use or disclosure of either the contents of messages sent by

---

[16]  *Smyth v. Pillsbury Company*, 914 F.Supp. 97 (E.D. Pa. 1996).

[17]  Michael Smyth, an employee of Pillsbury, had sent his manager e-mail that was critical of the company and had threatened to "kill the back stabbing bastards" and had referred to an upcoming holiday party as the "Jim Jones Koolaid affair."

employees or other information logged by the employer's computer system such as the identity of the sender and recipient may be found to constitute an unjustified invasion of privacy giving rise to civil damages even if such activity is not prohibited under criminal legislation. The risk of liability of an employer may be higher if messages are intercepted for purposes unrelated to the protection of an employer's reasonable business interests.

## 11.4  EMPLOYEE'S EXPECTATION OF PRIVACY

The question of whether an employer's monitoring activities may be found to constitute a violation of the criminal law or an employee's privacy rights will be determined according to whether the users of the system had a reasonable expectation that their messages would not be intercepted or accessed by any person other than the intended recipient. The use of passwords to gain access to the system and references to e-mail messages and mail boxes as being private are factors to be considered in determining the reasonable expectation of users.[18] Other factors to be considered are any organizational policies or other representations communicated to employees that the privacy of such messages will be protected.

This expectation of privacy may be negated if users are advised as to the circumstances in which a message sent through the system may be subject to interception. It is not in an employer's or employee's interest to leave the issue ambiguous. Each party's rights and expectations can be clarified through the use of a corporate policy and through the use of sign-on messages which are displayed whenever users log into the system.

It should be noted that even where an employee's expectation of privacy with respect to e-mail is negated by an employer, third parties communicating with that employee through Internet e-mail may still have a reasonable expectation that their communications will not be intercepted.

---

[18]  Many employees believe that e-mail messages constitute private messages. The use of user identification codes and passwords create an impression that the messages are private. Also, the similarity between electronic mail and regular mail, the latter being highly protected, as well as the necessity of a sender to specifically address e-mail to particular recipients, reinforces the belief that the electronic mail message will be private.

## 11.5  CORPORATE E-MAIL AND INTERNET USE POLICIES

To avoid lawsuits arising from improper employee use of e-mail or the Internet, or from employer monitoring of such usage, it would be advisable for a company to adopt an explicit written policy governing such activities. Such policies should state that the company owns the e-mail system, that the system is intended for business purposes and that the company may monitor messages from time to time. Many companies such as Intel, K-Mart and Sun Microsystems have adopted such written policies.

The corporate policy should set out the proper use of the employer's computer and telecommunications facilities and indicate the circumstances in which the employer reserves the right to monitor employee communications. Monitoring should be conducted pursuant to a specified procedure by designated personnel only. Employees should be made aware of the policy, the reasons for the policy, the purpose for which any information obtained through any interception by the employer will be used and the penalties for violations.

An employee's use of the employer's computer system after notification of the policy may constitute an implied consent. However, it is preferable to obtain an employee's explicit written acknowledgment to the terms of such a policy. Such an acknowledgment may be obtained as part of an agreement addressing matters such as the employee's obligation not to disclose confidential information and to assign to the employer intellectual property rights to new development made by the employee. To avoid questions of enforceability, it is advisable to obtain the acknowledgment as a condition of the commencement of employment or upon a promotion being made (to serve as the "consideration" for the acknowledgment).

The following is a summary of the matters that should be addressed as part of a corporate policy governing the Internet and e-mail:

### (a)  Scope of Policy

An initial consideration is what company resources are to be covered under the policy. It may be advisable for the policy to cover use of all company computing facilities and network services, including Internet access and e-mail facilities. An employer may also wish to have at least some parts of the policy cover the company's voice-mail systems.

### (b) Permitted Use of Company Resources

The policy should set out the permitted use of the company's computing resources. For instance, the policy should specify whether such use is restricted solely for company business or whether some level of personal use is acceptable. Since browsing and downloading of material from external networks, including the Internet, can be quite time-consuming, employers may wish to require their employees to limit their online time to business-related matters.[19] In order to maximize productivity, each employee agreement should be tailored to allow for specific types of online activities dependent on the employee's corporate function.

Even where some level of personal use is permitted, most companies prohibit the use of the company's computing facilities or Internet access for personal gain (such as operation of a personal business or searching for positions outside of the company).

### (c) Access to Inappropriate Content

The policy should prohibit the use of the company's computing facility, including the Internet access facility, to knowingly access or download, upload, store, transmit or distribute material that:

- is illegal or that advocates illegal acts;
- is profane, obscene, sexually explicit or pornographic;
- contains abusive, obscene or otherwise objectionable language or humour;
- advocates violence, hatred or discrimination[20] towards other people;

---

[19]    Such business-related matters may include use for research and educational purposes, and for communications within the company and with customers and suppliers.

[20]    Such discrimination may be on the basis of race, creed, colour, gender, religion, disability or sexual orientation.

- constitutes messages of sexual harassment or which contains any romantic overtones;
- would infringe copyright or other rights of any third party;[21]
- would result in a violation of federal, state, provincial or other applicable law;
- contains defamatory statements; or
- contains any religious or political messages.[22]

Such prohibitions on inappropriate content should minimize the risk of liability or public embarrassment for the company.[23]

## (d)  Discretion in E-Mail Messages

Employees should be made aware that although e-mail is often perceived as a less formal means of communication, it should be treated in the same manner as written documents. E-mail messages may be susceptible to discovery in a legal proceeding. Inappropriate comments can potentially expose the sender, recipient or the company to legal liability or may harm a particular party's reputation. For instance, employees should be advised that the e-mail facility may not be used to criticize either the company or any management, staff or customers of the company.

A message deleted from a particular employee's e-mail box is not necessarily deleted from the e-mail system. Other copies may continue to reside in the mailboxes of the sender, the original recipients or other recipients to whom the message may have been forwarded. Copies may also be kept as part of backups maintained by the system administrator.

---

[21]  For instance, reproducing and/or distributing copyrighted materials without appropriate authorization.

[22]  Employees should be told that a display or download of inappropriate content could create a hostile work environment for other personnel or could result in public embarrassment for the company.

[23]  The more specific the prohibition, the less likely a dispute will arise in respect to whether a breach has occurred.

### (e)  Security

Employees should be required to keep their password secure and not disclose the password to any other party. Management should educate employees as to what types of passwords should be avoided and what constitutes a safe password. In addition, management should encourage employees to memorize or conceal their passwords. Network software should be configured so that new passwords are required on a regular basis. Any employees expected to be absent for a lengthy period of time should have their access disabled to discourage unauthorized access. Employees should be made responsible for all activities carried out using their passwords.

Proper password control should be recognized as only one element of a more comprehensive policy relating to the security of e-mail systems. Other matters to be addressed include the need for employees to log out of their computers when they are not in use, an obligation to lock up any unattended office where the computer is used, and the need to take proper care of any portable computers used for business purposes.

Employees should agree that they will not attempt to circumvent any security or control measures implemented on company computing facilities. Employees should also be prohibited from using the company's computing facility to monitor, interfere with, tamper with, destroy or gain unauthorized access to work being performed by others.

Employees should agree that they will not attempt to conceal or to misrepresent the origin of any communication that they might initiate or forward to another person. Employees should be prohibited from impersonating another person or using another person's User ID to gain access to any computing facility, whether belonging to the company or to a third party.

Employees should also be made aware of the risk that software and data downloaded from external networks may contain viruses. Employees should be made aware of the various methods by which viruses may be introduced into a company's computer system, such as the following:

• infected downloaded files;

- e-mail attached files;

- malicious "macros" that can be stored in a document (such as a word processing document created with an application such as Microsoft Word).

The policy may require employees to follow proper virus immunization procedures for any downloaded files, particularly where the downloading is not performed automatically by the employer's computer system. Specifically employees should be required to scan all software as well as data and text files, including those received as e-mail attachments or obtained on floppy diskettes, using an anti-virus program provided by the company.

## (f) Confidentiality

Employees should be advised that many Internet Web sites can record the identity of visitors and their access of such Web sites can be traced back to the company.

Unless reliable encryption methods are used, any information communicated over the Internet may be accessed by unauthorized third parties. A corporation may wish to take the position that certain types of confidential information either must not be transmitted via the Internet or that the information must be encrypted. The policies and agreements in question must take into account any particular statutory, regulatory or other duties to which the users are subject.[24] In some cases, the consent of the other party should also be obtained before any confidential information relating to that other party is transmitted.

Employees should be asked to designate clearly any e-mail communications to in-house or external legal counsel which are intended to be treated as privileged (i.e., whenever the communications are for purposes of obtaining legal advice or assistance with respect to matters that may become litigious).

---

[24] For example, in most jurisdictions, lawyers have a duty to take reasonable steps to maintain the confidentiality of client information. A lawyer could be in breach of this duty if the Internet were used to transmit sensitive client information, particularly if the consent of the client was not obtained.

### (g)  Appropriate Use of Resources

Employees should be advised that their access to the company's computing facilities may not be used in a manner that would degrade system performance and that they will not knowingly run, install or transmit any malicious programs[25] into the company's computing facilities or to a third party computer facility through the Internet or otherwise.

Employees should be made responsible for managing the information kept on the system so as to make efficient use of storage space. The Internet can be used to obtain access to an enormous amount of material that can be downloaded by employees. If stored on shared servers, such material can displace space required for other business purposes. For this reason, it may be desirable to require employees to store any material downloaded from the Internet on their local hard disks, to impose limits on the amount of files that may be stored and to delete, in a timely manner, any files no longer required.

Consideration should also be given to limiting (at least during business hours) the downloading of certain types of documents or programs (e.g., programs which continually or periodically poll the contents of other sites) since such activities may reduce the bandwidth available for use by other employees.

For the same reason, it would be advisable to include a prohibition on the initiation or propagation of chain letters.

### (h)  Intellectual Property Rights

The policy should contain provisions relating to the use of materials which are protected by copyright. Employees should be made aware of the potential for copyright infringement arising from downloading information from the Internet and the use or modification of that information.

Employees should be advised that the installation or storage of illegal or pirated software on the company's computer systems will not be tolerated. The unauthorized copying or electronic transmission

---

[25]   This includes programs intended to damage a computer system, including programs known as computer viruses, Trojan Horses or worms.

of any software owned by or licensed to the company should be prohibited unless expressly authorized by an appropriate representative of the company.

Many software programs available through the Internet are distributed as shareware, which means that they are still protected under copyright. The use of such software may be restricted (i.e., for a short evaluation period or for non-commercial use only). New software programs may also create operational problems when downloaded to the company's computer systems. For this reason, some companies completely prohibit the downloading of any external programs for use on company-owned computer facilities.

### (i)  Document Retention

Companies should consider the costs of complying with orders for discovery[26] of e-mail messages, including backup or archival copies. It is recommended that a procedure be implemented to "electronically purge" all e-mail messages and backup copies periodically, unless the messages are specifically archived (e.g., when required to be maintained for any statutory or other purposes) or are relevant to any pending or threatened litigation. It may also be advisable to back up the e-mail system separately, apart from routine system backups, in order to provide greater control over how often backups are performed and the length of time they are retained.

The company may also have other data retention policies that may be applicable (e.g., policies requiring messages relating to management matters or contracts to be retained for a certain period of time).

### (j)  Other Prohibitions

Corporate policies should address employee involvement in Internet discussion facilities. Electronic chat-lines or discussion groups can be used by an employee to communicate with thousands of people. Although these resources may be used to the benefit of the company, their use can also lead to legal liability. As discussed

---

[26]  Discovery refers to a request for relevant documents made during litigation.

earlier, a corporation may be held vicariously liable for improper messages or obscene materials transmitted by its employees.

A corporate policy should stipulate the scope of authority of an employee to enter into contracts on behalf of the company. Agreements made between two companies carrying on business by electronic means should specify the employees who are authorized to enter into any transactions and their associated electronic addresses. Such companies should consider appropriate mechanisms, such as digital signature technology, to authenticate the origin and content of electronic messages. Employees should be advised not to represent themselves through e-mail as acting on behalf of company unless properly authorized to do so. When participating in "Usenet," "Listserv" mailing lists or other forms of discussion groups, management may also require its employees to incorporate a disclaimer in their personal e-mail and online messages, which would state that the opinions expressed are those of the employee and not of the corporation. A corporation may wish to require its employees to use personal-use addresses lacking any reference to the corporation's identity for the transmission of personal messages.

Employees should be prohibited from engaging in any activities that would interfere with any other person's use of the company's computing facilities, e-mail facilities or the Internet, that may violate the privacy of others, or that are likely to have similar adverse effects. Management should consider educating employees about inappropriate activities, such as transmission of bulk e-mail or sending the same message to a large number of Usenet newsgroups.

### (k)  Access to Employee Files and Messages

An employer may wish to state in its policy that, subject to certain exceptions, information stored in personal voice-mail, e-mail or computer directories ("user accounts") will be accessible only to the authorized user. However, the company should reserve the right to monitor and/or access user accounts in order to conduct its business in a secure and reasonable manner. The company should advise users that it reserves the right to authorize certain individuals who are specifically designated by the company,[27] to access such accounts in certain specific circumstances which may include the following:

- if the user is unavailable or absent[28] and the company determines in its discretion that it needs to access information contained in the user account for business purposes;

- if the user is suspected of any breach of the policy or other wrongdoing involving the user account, or has violated his or her employment agreement or any applicable law.

In setting out the circumstances in which a corporation reserves the right to monitor and review an employee's e-mail, a corporation may wish to make a distinction between personal messages and those that relate directly to the business of the company; while employees may have a reasonable expectation of privacy with respect to personal e-mail messages, this may not be the case with respect to business messages. The company should also state that, where required to protect the company's business interests or to comply with any legal obligations, the company reserves the right to disclose the contents of e-mail files to outside parties, such as law enforcement officials, without the consent of the employee and without giving prior notice to the employee.

The policy should advise employees that the company's computing facilities, including e-mail facilities, are the sole property of the company. The fact that employees may have been assigned confidential passwords in order to access company computing facilities should not be interpreted to mean that the e-mail system is for personal confidential communications, nor does it mean that any e-mail messages or any files stored on the company's computing facilities belongs to the employee.

It is also advisable to consider other supplementary actions to reduce employees' expectation of privacy in their e-mail messages.

---

[27]   Other employees should be prohibited from intentionally intercepting, eavesdropping, recording, reading, altering or receiving any other persons' e-mail messages without proper authorization.

[28]   A user may be unavailable or absent if on a leave of absence, on vacation or has been transferred from one department to another.

These may include providing an online reminder during login and providing periodic training sessions on the proper use of e-mail.

In developing policies governing the use of e-mail and external networks, a corporation must take into account the privacy interests of both the users of the systems and the persons who may be the subject of any electronic communications. On one hand, employees may have an expectation that their messages will not be monitored or intercepted by other persons within the organization, including system administrators, senior management or co-employees. On the other hand, persons working within a company have a reasonable expectation that other persons will not use any e-mail system or the Internet to transmit libellous or harassing messages.

If applicable, employees should be advised that a record may be maintained of specific Web sites accessed through the company's Internet facility and such activity logs may be reviewed from time to time for inappropriate behaviour.

Employees should be advised that those who are terminated or laid off or who leave their employment do not have the right to obtain copies of their e-mail messages, including personal e-mail, and will not be allowed to access the company's e-mail system.

### (l)  Discipline

Employees should be told that the company considers any violation of this policy to be a serious offense. Employees should be advised that failure to comply with the policy may result in disciplinary action, including, without limitation, any of the following:

• access privileges being restricted or revoked; and

• disciplinary action up to and including dismissal.

Employees should also be advised that some violations of the policy are also covered under existing legislation such as the *Criminal Code* and the *Copyright Act* or under other corporate policies such as the company's harassment and discrimination policy and that the company may elect to seek appropriate penalties under such legislation or other policies.

## (m)  Agreement with Policy

Employees should be asked to sign an acknowledgment that they have read and understood the policy and that they agree to abide by it. Ideally, such an acknowledgment should be signed at the time the employee is offered employment. If an acknowledgment is requested after an employee has been hired,[29] it may be prudent to state that such agreement is being made in consideration of the company providing the employee with access the Internet and in consideration of eligibility for future pay increases.

The policy should include an acknowledgment by the employees that their continued use of the company's computing facilities (and/or Internet facilities) shall constitute their agreement to be bound by any future revisions of the policy which may be communicated to them.

---

[29]  Employees should also be required to periodically sign an acknowledgment that they have read and understood the policy and are not in breach of it. This will provide an additional ground for discipline or dismissal in the event of violation (i.e., dishonesty).

# Index